Kane Basin

Ellesmere

Island

Lancaster Sound

VOYAGES OF THE ALBANS

Baffin

Basin

Greenland
(CRONX)

Baffin Island

Davis

Foxe Basin

Cape Dyer

Strait

NORTHERN FIORDS

SOUTHERN FIORDS

Cape F

Hudson Strait

Ungava

Hudson Bay

Ungava Bay

Cape Chidley

Payne Lake

Okak

Labrador Current

Labrador

Belle Isle

Newfoundland

Gulf Stream

Spitsbergen

Arctic Ocean

Greenland
Sea

SURPLUS PROPERTY
City of Albuquerque

Scoresby Sound

Strait

Husavik

...alik   Breidafjordur   Iceland
(TILLI)
Faxafloi   Hofn
Vestmannaeyjar?   Vatnajokull
...inger Current

Faeroe Islands

Shetland Islands

Orkney Islands

Hebrides

Scotland

North
Sea

Norway

Sweden

Denmark

Erris Head

Ireland   Irish
Sea

England

Belgium

North

Atlantic

St. George's Channel

Land's End
Isles of Scilly
uxsnant Channel Is.

English   Channel

Seine R.

ARMORICA

Loire R.

Rhone R.

Marseille

LIGURIA

Bay
of
Biscay

FARFARING
OF THE
MEN OF ALBA

Basque
Provinces

Oporto

Spain

Gibraltar

Corsica

Sardinia

Mediterranean Sea

the farfarers

FARLEY MOWAT

the farfarers

BEFORE THE NORSE

RIO GRANDE VALLEY
STEERFORTH PRESS
SOUTH ROYALTON VERMONT
LIBRARY SYSTEM

SV

Library of Congress Cataloging-in-Publication Data

Mowat, Farley
The farfarers : before the Norse / Farley Mowat — 1st pbk. ed.
Includes bibliographical references and index.
ISBN 1-883642-56-6 (alk. paper)
1. America—Discovery and exploration—Pre-Columbian. 2. America—Discovery
and exploration—Pre-Columbian Fiction. 3. Canada—Discovery and exploration—
British. 4. Canada—Discovery and exploration—British Fiction. 5. Alba (Kingdom)
Fiction. I. Title.
E103.M73 2000
970.01'1 — dc21   99-43310
                              CIP

PHOTO AND ILLUSTRATION CREDITS
Pages 19, 37, 142: Illustrations by Rob Tuckerman. Pages 44, 54, 121, 160, 162,
220, endpapers: Maps by Rob Tuckerman. Pages 2, 4, 6, 7 (top and bottom), 8,
165, 205: Photos by Thomas Lee. Courtesy of Robert E. Lee. Pages 201, 203:
Photos by Robert E. Lee. Courtesy of Robert E. Lee. Pages 11, 67, 248 (top and
bottom), 330: Photos by Farley Mowat. Pages 68, 83: Courtesy of the Shetland
Islands Tourist Board. Page 10: Copyright the British Museum. Page 290: Courtesy
of the Canadian Museum of Civilization (image number S89-1831).

For Vilhjalmur Stefansson,

Thomas Lee, and

Thomas Lethbridge,

who lighted me on my way

CONTENTS

F A R F A R E R S T I M E L I N E

B C

c. 5000   A warming climate following the retreat of glaciation brings the first human occupants to the Northern Islands of Shetland, Orkney and the Hebrides.

c. 4000   Having mastered the arts of making and sailing skin boats, the Northern Islanders become distant seafarers.

c. 3000   Similar megalithic structures, such as standing stones and henges, appear in Mediterranean and Northern Island cultures.

c. 2000   The climate continues to improve, allowing natives of arctic Canada to colonize northeastern Greenland.

1500-1200   Migrant Indo-European tribes, including forebears of the Celts, enter Europe from Asia.

c. 1000   A severe climatic deterioration forces high arctic dwellers south. Forebears of Beothuks and Tunit are living in Newfoundland.

c. 700   Inhabitants of Britain move from the Bronze Age to the Iron Age.

c. 500   Climatic conditions in Greenland become so severe that natives abandon it.

c. 330   Pytheas voyages from the Mediterranean to Britain, traveling as far north as Orkney and Thule (Iceland), which receive their first mention in British history.

400-300   The Belgae, a Celtic tribe, cross the channel and invade southern Alba (England).

c. 250   Celts occupy most of the lowland country of England and Ireland.

c. 150   The Celtic invasion of Alba is halted by indigenes at the line at Solway Firth-River Tweed. Alba continues to exist north of this line.

51-50   Picts and other Armoricans flee western Gaul and seek refuge in Alba (Scotland).

c. 40   Apparent outbreak of war between the Picts and their Alban hosts.

c. 1   Armoricans control the lowlands of Scotland north to the Great Glen. Albans retain the mainland and the islands to the north of the Glen.

A D

43   The Claudian invasion of Britain begins.

71   The Solway-River Tyne line has become the *de facto* frontier between Roman Britain and the "Barbarians to the north."

79   Agricola attacks northward into Pictland.

85   The Romans begin withdrawing from northern Scotland, after a naval visit to Orkney.

100-200   The Picts are continuously engaged with Roman Britain. Alba north of the Great Glen is relatively untroubled.

363   Theodosius takes a Roman naval expedition north, at least to Orkney and probably to Tilli (Iceland).

400-450	After raiding deep into Britain, the Picts come under sustained assault from Roman-Celts, Saxons, Angles and Irish.
500	The North Atlantic climate becomes sunnier and drier, encouraging distant navigation. The priest Brendan sails from Ireland to the Faeroes, probably to Iceland, and possibly to within sight of Greenland.
550-600	Pictland, beleagured on the south and west. The Northern Islands are raided by the Irish and Saxons. Picts and Albans join forces and the old kingdom of Alba in Scotland is reborn.
650-700	The Norse acquire their first truly seaworthy vessels and begin venturing westward. They reach Shetland and Orkney where trading soon changes to raiding.
711	Defeated in the south by Saxons and Angles and harrassed on the west by the Irish, Alba abandons the Northern Isles to the Vikings.
729	Oengus, King of Alba, tries to recover Shetland and Orkney, but his fleet is destroyed. The Norse overwhelm the islands and the inhabitants flee west to Tilli where crofts had been established previously.
850	The Norse control most of northern Britain and Ireland. Albans have settled along the coasts of Iceland and are visiting Greeland. Contemporary church documents refer to Christian establishments in Iceland and Greenland.
c. 850	A Viking named Naddod sails to Iceland, probably on a raiding venture.
c. 850-890	Further Viking visits to Iceland culminate in Norse occupation of the island.
900	By this time Alban walrus hunters appear to have rounded southern Greenland, gone north to the head of Baffin Bay, and reached Hudson Strait and Ungava Bay to the westward.
981-985	Outlawed from Iceland for three years, Erik the Red sails to Greenland. In 985 he leads a fleet there and colonizes the southern Greenland fiords.
985	Icelandic merchant mariner Bjarni Herjolfsson is storm-driven to the east coast of Newfoundland.
996	Leif Eriksson sails with Bjarni on a voyage to Newfoundland.
1004-1007	The Thorfinn Karsefni, Icelandic/Greenlandic expedition to Labrador and Greenland.
1025	Icelander Gudlief Gudlaugson lands in Newfoundland, where he encounters people possessing horses.
1059	A Saxon or Celtic priest travels from Greenland to Vinland (Newfoundland).
1112-1118	Bishop Eric Gnupsson makes a prolonged visit to the Vinland region.
1200-1300	The Norse settlement in south Greenland becomes virtually a theocracy, while the northern one drifts toward paganism.
c. 1285	Norse adventurers enter Hudson Strait.
1347	A Norse ship sails from Greenland to Labrador, thence to Iceland.
c. 1350	An expedition from south Greenland claims to have found the northern settlement abandoned to Skraelings (Thule-culture Inuit).
1380-1400	The period of the Zeno voyages to Labrador, Newfoundland and Nova Scotia.
1418	Southern Norse settlements in Greenland are attacked and seriously disrupted, evidently by people from the northern settlement.
c. 1450	The first Basque whalers may have reached the Gulf of St. Lawrence.
1497	John Cabot lands on southwestern Newfoundland.

ACKNOWLEDGEMENTS

I AM GRATEFUL TO MANY NORTHERN ARCHAEOLOGISTS, but especially to Drs. William Fitzhugh, Elmer Harp, Jane Sproull Thomson, William Taylor, Robert McGhee, Maxwell Moreau, Callum Thomson, and Peter Schledermann. They provided me with invaluable information, encouragement, and advice (not all of which was heeded).

Many others gave a helping hand, including Alistair Goodlad of Shetland, John Mowat of Orkney, Alexander Mowat of Caithness, Calum Ferguson of Lewis, Dr. Njordur Njardvik of Iceland, Joseba Zulaika of the Basque Provinces, and Canadians Matthew Swan, Leonard Muise, Dr. Ian Macdonald, Robert E. Lee, Robert Rutherford, and Ginevra Wells. My thanks also to my indefatigable assistant, Mary Elliott, and my wife, Claire, who graciously hosted Alban ghosts for three decades.

WHY AND
WHEREFORE

SOME FORTY YEARS AGO I BEGAN INVESTIGATING pre-Columbian European voyages to Canada. By 1965 I thought I had got it about right so I published *Westviking—The Ancient Norse in Greenland and North America*.[1]

I went on to pursue other interests, write other books; but during the time I worked on *Westviking*, a worm of unease had entered my subconscious. Beginning as a minute suspicion, it grew to a conviction that the Norse were not, after all, the first Europeans to cross the Western Ocean.

They had been preceded—of that I became certain—but by whom? Orthodox histories provided only the vaguest, most ephemeral hints as to a possible identity. At best, any putative forerunners appeared as insubstantial wraiths; at worst, as mere figments of the imagination.

I tried to exorcise them, but they refused to go away. The worm of doubt metamorphosed into an implacable presence that nagged until I capitulated and began what turned out to be a thirty-year quest for a people who had disappeared from recorded time.

During those three decades the wraiths never left me alone for long. They led as far afield as Asia Minor, northern Britain, Iceland, Greenland, the Canadian Arctic, Labrador, and, finally, to Newfoundland.

We may never know what these forgotten folk called themselves but since they appear to have been known to their contemporaries as Albans, this is the name I give them.

Insofar as these things can be determined, the origins, ancestry, and history of the Albans unfold in the ensuing pages. However, since they were illiterate (we do not even know what language they *spoke*), and got only peripheral mention in the records kept by others, immense lacunae exist.

Rather than let these voids remain empty I have filled some of them with vignettes which, I believe, come as close to the realities as one can reasonably expect. These are set in special type so as to be easily recognizable.

Inevitably I have had to engage in a good deal of supposition unconfirmed by archaeological or documentary evidence. If I have trespassed against the usages of professional historians, I have tried to do so in such a fashion as to mislead no one.

A footnote in Gibbon's *History of the Decline and Fall of the Roman Empire* can serve me as well as it did him: "I owe it to myself and to historic truth to declare that some circumstances in [what follows] are founded only on conjecture and analogy. The stubbornness of our language has sometimes forced me to deviate from the conditional into the indicative mood."

The plain fact is that my book makes no pretence at being history in the academic sense. It is the *story* of a vanished people: their successes, failures, and ultimate fate. I believe it to be a true story.

Because, in my view, footnotes tend to interfere with effective story telling, I have placed all elucidations, validations, and explanations at the end of the book, where they can be found by any who care to seek them out.

FARLEY MOWAT
River Bourgeois, Nova Scotia
1998

CHAPTER ONE

BEGINNINGS

I SPENT MOST OF THE SUMMER OF 1966 VISITING
native communities across the Canadian Arctic from the north tip of
Labrador to the Alaskan border. My purpose was twofold: to gather
material for a book, and to record interviews for the Canadian Broadcasting
Corporation's Northern Service.[1]

I travelled in a single-engined Otter float plane, a heavy-paunched
beast with the plodding pace of a plough horse and the voice of an outraged dragon. But she was reliable. She carried the pilot, an engineer,
and me into and out of any number of unlikely places. When the weather was too bad to fly, her cabin provided us with a dry floor upon which
to unroll our sleeping bags, and a place to dine, quite literally by can-
dlelight, on such delicacies as boiled caribou tongues and sun-dried
Arctic char.

My original plan had been to visit only Inuit and Indian communities, but on August 11 I made a departure from the schedule.

Several years earlier, while deep in research for *Westviking*, I learned
that William Taylor, an archaeologist employed by the National
Museum of Canada, had made a remarkable discovery on Pamiok Island
at the mouth of the Payne River, which drains into the west side of
Ungava Bay.[2] Local Inuit had led Taylor to what he described as: "a huge
rectangular structure measuring 85 feet long by 20 wide....The walls,
which were collapsed, were made of stone."

Taylor had time for only a hurried look at this imposing structure,
which was quite unlikely anything previously reported from the Arctic.

A puzzle to archaeologists, this stone foundation was discovered by Dr. Robert McGhee on the coast of Prince Albert Sound in the Canadian Arctic. See also plan of site on page 141.

Reasonably enough, neither he nor any other specialist cared to hazard an opinion as to its provenance until it had been properly excavated.

If, and when. By 1965 most of a decade had slipped away without the National Museum having evidenced any further interest in the Pamiok Island conundrum, the solution to which might, I hoped, shed light on Norse ventures to the Canadian Arctic. When I asked a friend at the museum the reason for the institution's lack of interest, he replied that certain quarters felt it could turn out to be archaeologically embarrassing, so had decided to leave it alone.

A short time before setting off on my 1966 Arctic journey I heard that Thomas Lee, an archaeologist from Quebec's Laval University, planned to conduct a dig at Pamiok that summer. Although *Westviking* had already been published, I decided, time and weather permitting, to visit Pamiok.

On August 10 we were at the Inuit village of Povungnituk on the east coast of Hudson Bay, about as close to Pamiok Island as we were likely to get. I decided to try for it on the morrow.

The eleventh broke overcast and threatening; nevertheless, an hour after dawn, the Otter was in the air labouring eastward across the 250-mile-wide waist of the Ungava Peninsula.

We were buffeted by a strong headwind that held us to what seemed not much better than a fast gallop. A monochromatic panorama of water, rock, and treeless tundra slowly unrolled beneath our wings. To counter the effect of the gale, the pilot flew so low that we several times sent herds of caribou streaming away from us as if we were a gigantic hawk and they a mob of mice.

From the midway point at Payne Lake we thundered down the valley of the Payne River at "deck level" until we came to a broad stretch about ten miles from its mouth. As driving rain and mist threatened to obscure everything, we made a hurried splashdown in front of a small Hudson's Bay Company trading post.

There was no hope of flying on to Pamiok in such foul weather, so I arranged with Zachareesi, a local Inuk, to take me the rest of the way in his outboard-powered canoe.

The tidal range on the west Ungava coast is of the order of thirty feet, and the tide was falling fast as we set out into a confusion of channels and islets. The post manager, a young fellow from Orkney, warned me of the necessity of getting clear of the estuary before we became marooned in a morass of mud and broken rocks from which there would be no escape until the rise of the next tide.

The murk became thicker as Zachareesi fishtailed his canoe through a swirling maelstrom of currents pouring past, and over, unseen rocks. He was "smelling his way" towards the northern headland of the estuary.

Suddenly he shouted and pointed to the left. Wavering in the gloom was a dim shape. The fog swirled away, revealing a stone tower nearly twice the height of a man. Smiling broadly, Zachareesi announced we had reached Tuvalik Point at the mouth of the river and were free of the tormented waters of the estuary.

We went ashore for a smoke. I examined the structure with great interest, and some affection, for it had served us well. It was constructed of flat stones carefully fitted together without mortar to form a cylinder nearly five feet in diameter. It had evidently once stood twelve or more feet high, but had lost a number of upper-level stones, which were scattered around the tower's base. Notably, the undersides of these fallen stones lacked the thick, crusty coating of age-old lichens which clothed the undisturbed surface of the tower.

I asked Zachareesi who had built this useful beacon and when. He grinned and waved his stubby pipe-stem to the north.

Zachareesi stands beside what is probably intended as a Christian cross, beside the Payne River in Ungava.

"Old-time people. Not Inuit anyhow."

The canoe was in imminent danger of being left high and dry by the receding waters, so we pushed off and in a little while reached Pamiok Island.

This barren mound of sea-wracked rock facing the swirling fogs of Ungava Bay could hardly have seemed less inviting. Seen through a scud of driving mist and rain, it appeared to be a singularly inhospitable place. But appearances were deceptive. Situated close to the mouth of a major river route to the interior caribou country, convenient to bird islands, walrus haul-outs, and excellent sealing grounds, it had been the chosen home of countless generations of human beings.

However, when our canoe nosed up on Pamiok's stony shore, we found the island inhabited by only two people: Thomas Lee and his teenage son, Robert. Their home was a squat tent, struggling to keep a grip on the ground in the teeth of a stiff easterly wind pelting in over the icy waters of the bay.

Lee waded out through the fringe of kelp to greet us. He was then

fifty-one years old and looked somewhat like a burly and grizzled barrenland bear graced with a round and ruddy face and a Roman nose.

He had no time to waste. I had barely introduced myself before he
was leading me off to tour the island. Late that night I recorded my
impressions.

*At least this Godforsaken place has no mosquitoes! Too wet, cold, and windy for the
little bastards. A corpse shroud of fog came rolling in as I stumbled after Lee across
a jumble of shattered rocks and sodden muskeg....*

*We came to a bunch of knee-high mounds of stones. "Tombs," he told me
cheerfully. "Look inside." I bent down by one, peered through a crevice, and saw a
jumble of what could be human bones, but no skull. "I collected the skull," said Lee.
"Perhaps it's Eskimo, but I doubt it. I've found five skulls altogether and at least
two are more European than Eskimoan. The others look in between."*

*Almost every little hollow or more-or-less-level bit of ground on the island
seems to have its stone tent ring, some of them twenty feet in diameter. There are
also numerous depressions Lee said were the remains of semi-subterranean winter
houses of ancient pre-Eskimo cultures.*

*Near the east end of the island we came to three cairns, cylindrical and about
six feet high. They don't look anything like the Eskimo inuksuak [stone men] I've
seen all over the Arctic. I made the point to Lee and he agreed: "Yes, too big. Too
regular. Too well made. Not Eskimoan at all. And look at the thickness of the lichen
growth on them. They're too old to belong to the historic period."*

*We trudged back along the south shore. The tide had fallen so far that the sea
was only distantly visible across a vast, glistening plain of jumbled rocks, boulders,
and mud. Lee pointed out a sort of broad pathway or ramp running seaward from
the high-tide line. Somebody had put in a hell of a lot of work clearing it of the
worst of its jagged rocks. Again Lee ruled out natives: "No Eskimo would go to that
much trouble to make a boat landing. They wouldn't need to for kayaks and canoes.
I think this must have been a haul-out for big boats."*

*By now I was rain-soaked below the waist and sweat-soaked above. Whatever
else he may be, Lee is a bloody dynamo. He trotted me into a bit of shelter behind a
ridge of frost-shattered rock to the site he was digging.*

*Not very impressive. A muddy rectangle about forty-five feet long by maybe
fifteen wide, with turf, moss, and stones stripped away to a depth of a few inches,
at which point the diggers had hit bedrock. I could just make out the remains of*

Diana Island at the junction of Hudson Strait and Ungava Bay is dominated by a trio of tower beacons. The largest is the one in the foreground.

some low stone walls. Lee waited about ten seconds for questions, then beat me to the punch.

"This is some sort of longhouse. Not the kind the Six Nations and other Indians built in the south, but its own kind. There are three like it on Pamiok—two this size and one much larger. The Eskimos say there're several more to the north. Nothing like them has ever before been described in Canadian archaeology.

"I've traced the outline of this one. See, it's somewhat boat-shaped, with slightly curved sides and rounded ends. The walls were of stone and turf and low—four feet at most. I've found little in the way of artefacts except a lot of Dorset-culture [pre-Eskimoan] litharge [scraps and flakes of flint], much of it on top of rotted turf from fallen walls. Dorsets seem to have camped here after this longhouse was abandoned."

These are two views of Tom Lee's speculative reconstruction of Longhouse No. 2, on Pamiok Island, near the mouth of the Payne River estuary in Ungava Bay.

Young Robert Lee had been busy making tea. He caught up to us and almost apologetically suggested his father and I might like to come to the tent for a warm-up.

"Not now," Tom replied brusquely. "Too much still to show this man. Let's look at the big house."

He led me up an easy slope and I almost stumbled over the ruin before I saw it. Boulders, tumbled every which way, blended so well with the mess of other rocks, it needed to be pointed out to me. Then I could make out the shape of what looked like

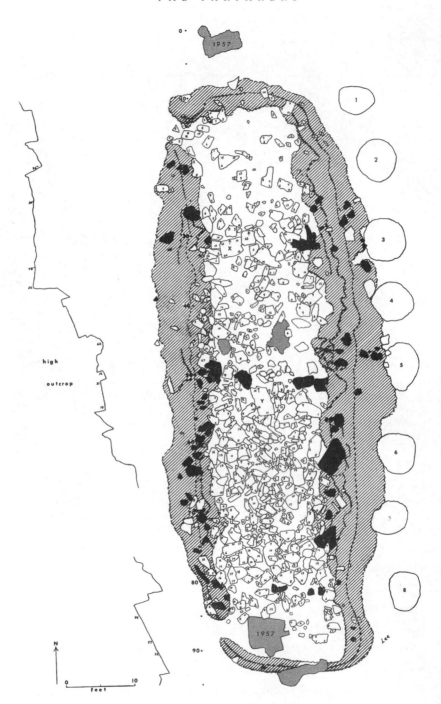

Pamiok Longhouse No. 2 in plan. Although the original walls had collapsed, stones shown in solid black are believed to be in their original position.

a tomb for Gargantua. It was at least eighty feet long, maybe twenty wide, and bloody massive!

In some places the walls still stood three feet high but were mostly broken down, with their boulders rolled into the central space. I say boulders because that's what a lot of them were. Lee guessed some weighed more than a thousand pounds. All were coated with a layer of lichens that must have taken hundreds of years to grow.

Looking across this enormous jumble, Lee summed up his thoughts: "Difficult to believe this was built by Eskimoan people. What earthly reason would they have had? Eskimos may have sometimes pitched their tents inside these longhouses, and Dorset- and Thule-culture [palaeo-Eskimos] probably did the same. But I doubt any of them built these longhouses."

"Then who did?"

He smiled quizzically. "Well, now, Mr. Mowat, I suppose that's for me to find and you to ask. At this stage a cautious professional wouldn't say. But I don't think you'll be surprised if I predict they'll turn out to be Europeans. Possibly Norse."

In the years ahead Tom and I became friends, exchanging findings and opinions. He supplied me with copies of his meticulously detailed archaeological reports. I gave him the results of my research into early Norse history. In 1967 he went back to Ungava and found an even larger longhouse on another island a few miles north of the Payne. He then returned to Pamiok and began an intensive investigation of the big house there. This dig required three seasons to complete and yielded remarkably little enlightenment in view of the enormous amount of time and energy Lee expended on it. Nothing emerged to satisfactorily explain its purpose or identify its builders. It remained an enigma comprising a number of mysteries.

One of these was how the Pamiok big house or, indeed, any of these Arctic longhouses, could have been roofed. Lee's excavations (together with those undertaken in later years by other archaeologists on similar sites) have failed to produce evidence of roof supports, whether of wood or of such possible substitutes as whale bones. Furthermore, the nearest timber suitable for roof construction at the time they were built was at least 120 miles to the south of Pamiok, and *1,500 miles* to the south of a group of similar longhouses found in the 1970s on the shores of Kane Basin in the high Arctic.

The roof question has bedevilled every archaeologist who has investigated it. Some have concluded the longhouses weren't "houses" at all and so need never have been roofed. But, if not houses, what were they? The orthodox opinion seems to be that they served some kind of ceremonial or religious purpose; but there is no evidence to buttress such a hypothesis and, as we shall see, the distribution of the sites makes such an explanation inherently improbable.

Tom Lee would have none of it. He suspected the structures were temporary shelters built by Norse voyagers visiting the region around A.D. 1000. Indeed, ground plans of Norse croft houses of that period in Iceland, the northern British Isles, and parts of Scandinavia resemble these Canadian Arctic longhouses. All are long and narrow, often with slightly curved side walls. Proportions and dimensions are generally comparable. There the resemblance ends. Norse (including Icelandic) longhouses were invariably *roofed*, with sod, turf, bark, or thatch *supported upon robust wooden frameworks* which have, almost without exception, left archaeologically identifiable traces.

A number of years were to pass following my visit to Pamiok Island before the Arctic longhouses began revealing their mysteries to me. They first did so on the far side of the Atlantic Ocean.

It rained almost incessantly during the first visit of my wife, Claire, and me to Shetland. This cluster of treeless, windswept rocks off the northern tip of mainland Scotland, which, together with its sister archipelago of Orkney, comprises Britain's Northern Isles, was living up to its reputation as a womb of bad weather.

We hardly cared. We had come to Shetland at the invitation of salmon farmer and antiquarian Alistair Goodlad, who had promised to immerse us in Shetland history until, as he inelegantly put it, "'tis coming out your orifices."

Under Alistair's guidance we sloshed our way to many ancient monuments, including five-thousand-year-old pit houses, recently excavated from under thick layers of peat; subterranean stone tombs of later mesolithic settlers; crumbled neolithic promontory forts; Bronze Age village sites; Iron Age broch towers; and the tumbled walls of Viking houses built a mere thousand years before our time.

Boat-roofed houses remain traditional with the Northern Islanders, as this modern home near Kirkwall, Orkney, testifies.

Shetland seemed to be a world of ruins, not all of them ancient. Croft house after croft house stood abandoned, slowly crumbling back into the land from which generations of pastoralists had raised them.

Alistair was savage about the empty crofts. "Modern times leave no room for the wee chap, be he fisherman or crofter. After five thousand years making a living on these islands his like has to get out of it now to make way for oil refineries and nuclear power stations. But that's the way of a world gone witless, wouldn't you say?"

We came across other curious things in the course of our wanderings. Along the eastern coasts of the islands of Yell and Unst stood several drystone beacon towers. Some were on headlands, but others were obscurely located near the bottoms of bays and inlets. They reminded me forcibly of those I had seen at, and near, Pamiok Island.

But what particularly captured my interest was a number of buildings roofed with overturned fishing vessels that had, presumably, outlived their seaworthiness. Some of the structures were lowly cattle byres and outbuildings; but others were, or had been, human habitations. One that we later saw on Orkney was fully modern, elegantly built of brick, and sporting two large picture windows staring out, wide-eyed, as it were, from beneath the beetling brow of a capsized wooden vessel that must have been sixty feet in length.

We learned from Alistair that it was an ancient island custom to convert ships that had served their time at sea to this final service. Many Shetlanders, he told us, had been "conceived, lived, and died under or in a boat."

On the final day of our visit he took us up on the hogback of Yell to show us Fetlar, a smaller island seemingly adrift in a wind-whipped sea to the eastward.

"'Tis a weird wee world of its own out there. Supposedly the place the Old Ones held out the longest. There's some believe they're out there still, coming and going in ghostly boats from places the like of which we only get to see in dreams...."

Shetland and Pamiok were but two steps along the tortuous path I would follow as I worked my way back in time. But telling the tale backwards as it actually unravelled is not the way the old story tellers would have done it. They always began at the beginning.

And so shall I.

PART ONE

THE
OLD
WORLD

CHAPTER TWO

FARFARER

The northern dawn breaks clear of fog and the tired young helmsman can just make out the loom of high land on the starboard bow. If this is Yell, he knows he has done his job and can be proud of himself, for it is no easy thing to hold a steady course when the stars are hidden and there is only the wind and the run of the seas to serve as guides.

A tousled, rough-bearded man emerges from the narrow confines of the cuddy in Farfarer's bows. Seizing the forestay, he hauls himself into the eyes of the little ship and hangs there precariously, scanning the lightening horizon. Squinting at the still-indistinct land mass to starboard, he grunts in pleased recognition. He glances up at the broad belly of the big square sail. It is taut and pulling strongly in the fresh westerly. His gaze shifts aft, to where his son stands in the stern sheets, legs astride for balance, one arm on the tiller, the other pointing questioningly landward.

"Aye, lad, 'tis Yell!" the skipper shouts while relieving himself into the green waters foaming under his vessel's forefoot. "Let her fall off a bit...there, that'll do. If the breeze holds we'll haul ashore on Fetlar tomorrow morn."

He swings inboard, bends down, and reaches into the cuddy, where the rest of his crew of kinsmen slumber on. His fingers find a sack of dried cod. He pulls out two chunks and, balancing beside the swaying gunwale, makes his way aft and gives one to his son. The two men tear at the sun-hardened fish, savouring its strong taste, washing it down with swigs of water from a seal-bladder flask.

"Fresh mutton and hot bere bread tomorrow," the skipper promises. "Aye, and then the long winter ahead for you to raise a little hell and make babies, if you can catch a girl. You've earned it...we've all earned it." He chews reflectively for a moment. "All the same, by next spring you'll be ready for the long beat westward, back to Tilli and the tuskers and the water bears. Well, I'll take her now. Go forward and get some sleep."

"Twenty times I've made this passage," the skipper thinks, as he takes the tiller. "Twenty springs since first I saw Tilli's big white skull on the horizon....Could hardly believe the place, though I'd heard enough about it. Ice mountains with their heads in the clouds...stinking fountains of boiling water spouting out of the bowels of the earth....And tuskers so thick it put my heart in my mouth the first time I rowed in amongst them."

He had made his first deep-water voyage soon after the birth of Christ. Barely thirteen, he had gone to sea, as was customary, in a vessel built, manned, and owned by his kinfolk.

Before that, at the age of ten, he had watched Farfarer being reborn on the shore of the sandy cove below the family steading on Fetlar, and could vividly remember how she had risen into being from the long keel timber of her previous incarnation.

She was fifty feet in length, with a beam of fifteen, her new ribs, gunwales, and thwarts shaped from oak and ash, and her stringers from pine battens, all fetched back to the treeless home islands by Fetlar trading men. It had taken fifteen full tusker hides each split in two, stitched together with sinew, to clothe the lightly built frame. The women had made the vessel's big, loose-footed square sail out of thinly scraped and oil-soaked leather.

Much of her was new; but her core was old, for her keel had been the backbone of several successive predecessors, all bearing the same name. Her mast and yard had served for almost a century since being found by the skipper's great-grandfather as driftwood washed ashore on Tilli. Nobody knew what kind of wood they were or from what unknown world they came, but the wood was tough as iron and resilient as whale baleen.

Now those same staunch spars were bringing the current Farfarer home again. The skipper eyed them fondly. His wife believed they were inhabited by spirits of great power. He smiled, thinking of his wife; she was getting on now, but her welcome home would be as warm as ever.

NO EXAMPLES OF FARFARER'S BREED HAVE SURVIVED for they were built of perishable materials that could not long endure unless cared for by devoted hands. Her origins are lost in time, but it may be possible to throw some light on them.

The first-footers who arrived upon the northern coasts not long after the withdrawal of the glacial ice still maintain a presence there. Local people refer to them as "strand lopers," which is to say, beach walkers. Winter storms are forever washing the sands away from beaches and dunes to reveal their ancient hearths and kitchen middens.

Fragments of charcoal and burned bits of clam shells have little to tell the casual passer-by; but if one is lucky enough to walk the shores of northern Scotland with someone as knowledgeable as Walter Mowat of John o'Groats, they speak in tongues.

Down on his knees just above the high-tide mark on the long beach of Dunnet Bay, Walter carefully sifted through a band of charcoal and calcined shells until he came upon a fragment of worked quartz. He held it out for my inspection.

"The last laddie to hold this wee bit of a stone knife would have been one of the strand lopers a good many thousand years ago." He paused, looking intently at the broken artefact. "It almost makes me feel I'm touching the old chap's hand myself."

The ancient people who once camped along those northern beaches can still reach out and touch the present. They are by no means so distant as our glittering world of science and technology would have us believe. The first-footers are with us yet. And they have much to tell.

Their earliest kitchen middens are chiefly composed of limpet, oyster, and clam shells; but later mounds include the bones of fishes, seabirds, and sea mammals. So we know that, although the strand lopers initially foraged mainly at the edge of the sea, there came a time when they ventured out upon the unquiet waters to catch fishes, seals, and porpoises, and to visit distant reefs and rocks after seabirds and their eggs. Eventually they became such practised boatmen they were able to reach, and in most cases settle, the most remote and storm-lashed offshore islands.

To accomplish all this, they had to invent or acquire seaworthy boats.

British archaeologist Thomas Lethbridge has suggested that the early strand lopers sheltered under domed tents made by stretching skins over a framework woven of Arctic birch or willow branches, for there were as yet no forests and few, if any, real trees in northern Scotland. The skins would have been sewn or laced together and smeared with animal fat for preservation and waterproofing. The resultant lightweight structure would have looked something like a big upside-down bowl—or a *coracle*, the round skin boat used by early southern Britons.

Lethbridge envisioned a sudden offshore squall flipping one of these onto its back and blowing it into the nearby sea—where it floated lightly as a gull. Or perhaps some early thinker and tinkerer, lying in his bed of skins and contemplating the curved roof of his home, came to the conclusion that the thing might be made to float. With a few modifications to give it better stability and greater strength, the house could become a boat. Furthermore, the transformation could be reversible. Carried ashore and turned over, a skin boat could as readily become a shelter.

Certain it is that almost every Stone Age people throughout the northern circumpolar region depended upon skin boats. The *kayak* is a well-known, if highly specialized, example. The less familiar *umiak*, or Inuit woman's boat, was more versatile and even more widely distributed. As late as the 1970s Alaskan Eskimos still made umiaks sheathed in walrus hides that could carry thirty or forty people across the stormy Bering Strait. When bad weather (or good hunting) brought such travellers ashore, they would turn their umiaks upside down to provide themselves with shelter. A big one upturned on a stone-and-turf foundation could provide comfortable housing for a large family, even in winter.

Skin-covered houses…into boats…into houses….[1]

By as early as the fifth millennium B.C., having mastered the art of making and using skin boats, the first-footers had become islanders wedded to the sea.

Although surrounded and protected by salt water, they were not stay-at-homes, ignorant of the outer world. Seagoing skills and sea-kindly vessels gave them the ability to come and go across broad reaches of ocean.

Many ancient peoples were of this stripe. South Sea Islanders routinely, and with marvellous insouciance, sailed frail outrigger canoes thousands of miles from land. Secure in *their* mastery of the seas, the Northern Islanders would not have hesitated to visit faraway places and distant folk.

By about six thousand years ago, climatic conditions in the Northern Islands of Britain—Orkney and Shetland—had much improved.

This cut-away drawing gives an impression of the construction and carrying capacity of a fifty-foot, skin-covered vessel of Alban type.

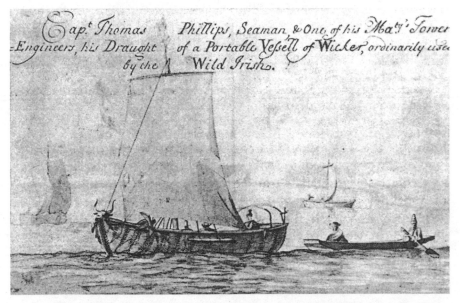

Cap.ᵗ Thomas Phillips, Seaman & One of his Ma.ᵗʸˢ Tower Engineers, his Draught of a Portable Vessell of Wicker, ordinarily used by the Wild Irish.

This Irish curragh, probably sheathed in ox hides, was drawn by an 18th century English sea captain. She would have been about 36′ in length.

Although still essentially treeless, the island landscape was no longer Arctic. Tundra was being replaced by grass and sedge, and arable soil was accumulating in protected places. Now the Northern Islanders imported cattle descended from the wild ox, together with coarse-haired sheep, and goats. As the climate continued to warm, they brought home certain hardy cereal grains such as barley, and bere, an ancestor of oats.

Although some considerable portion of their food was now coming from the land, the sea continued to nurture them and to command their allegiance. It beat at the very heart of their existence. It still does. To this day an Orkneyman is a crofter who usually also fishes, while a Shetlander is generally a fisherman who also crofts.

Standing on the thrusting beak of Duncansby Head at Scotland's northern tip during an easterly gale, I heard an echo of that ancient alliance between islanders and the sea from Alexander Mowat, Walter's father, who had spent most of his life fishing the wild waters of the Pentland Firth between Caithness and Orkney.

As we leaned against each other, steadying ourselves from the buffeting of spume-laden gusts howling in from the North Sea, Sandy pointed towards the indistinct shape of Stroma Island in the midst of the maelstrom. To my horror, I saw the mazed outline of a lobster boat tossing about like a demented thing in the terrible rip tides called the Boars.

She was evidently trying to gain the scant shelter of the pier at John o'Groats. The black bulk of her steersman, tiller clamped under his arm, seemed rooted to her like an extension of the stern post. The little double-ender bucked under him like a manic horse. It seemed certain she would not make it.

"God Almighty!" I shouted in Sandy's ear. "He'll go under! Hadn't we better call the Huna lifeboat? They might still get to him in time!"

Sandy's reply came in a roar of laughter louder than the storm.

"Nae, laddie! Robbie'd think us daft. He's an island man, ye ken. The sea shaped him and she'll no do him ony hurt. We'll hae a dram wi' him at the pub tonight, but dinna tell him you was for sending the lifeboat out!"

The sea shaped the Northern Islanders, and shaped the evolution of their vessels. Small craft, which sufficed for coastwise fishing and inter-island travel, lacked the carrying capacity or seaworthiness necessary for long-distance voyaging. That problem was solved by developing broad-beamed double-enders that could carry several tons of cargo while still riding the grey-beard seas of open ocean as lightly as birds. Perhaps the most extraordinary thing about these vessels, from our modern point of view, was that, large as they were, they continued to be sheathed with animal skins.

Even after trading voyages began to take the Islanders to forested coasts where ship-building timber was available, they continued to use skin coverings, not because of innate conservatism, but because this construction served them best.

Skin-sheathed vessels were lighter than wooden ones, were cheaper and easier to build, and could be more readily repaired. To this day the hull sheathing of a ship, whether it be wood, steel, or plastic, is referred to as her *skin*.

Although the skin might have to be renewed, the frame would last a long time, and timbers could endure for generations. The elasticity of the framing limited overall length to about eighty feet. However, that same flexibility bestowed exceptional seaworthiness since it permitted the hull to "work" in a seaway.

Paddles and oars, which sufficed for the propulsion of small craft in more-or-less-protected waters, proved inadequate for seagoing ships, so harnessing the wind became essential. The rig adopted by the Islanders (one still in use on big Irish *curraghs* into the eighteenth century) centred on a large square sail that could be set in such a way as to enable the vessel to go to weather as well as run before the wind. The efficiency of the square sail must not be underestimated. The finest wind ships ever built were the great square-riggers of the late nineteenth and early twentieth centuries, some of which regularly outran steam-driven vessels on the long haul between Britain and Australia.

We do not know how far afield the Islanders went, or how early, but by around 3000 B.C. they and certain Mediterranean peoples were sharing such characteristic cultural elements as henges, chambered tombs, and standing stones.

It used to be thought that this megalithic tradition originated in the Mediterranean, perhaps with the Mycenaeans; but now some suspect it may have *begun* in the north and spread southward.

Remnants of a sophisticated megalithic culture that reached its zenith between 3000 and 2700 B.C. are still very visible on the Islands. In western Orkney alone they include two great stone circles marked out by massive monoliths in the style of Stonehenge; a number of tall, independent, standing stones; and one of the most impressive megalithic structures extant, the monumental chambered tomb known as Maeshowe.

These and other structures show that the ancient Islanders were somehow able to achieve sufficient prosperity and leisure to indulge the human propensity for raising monuments on a grand scale. It is estimated that the construction of the Maeshowe complex alone required as much as a quarter of a million man-hours!

From very early times the Islanders were in contact with distant cultures, from whom they obtained bronze tools, better pottery than could be made from island clay, and exotic jewellery, including gold sun discs, black jet, green jadeite from the Alps, and amber.

Two questions arise: What could they possibly have produced that was valuable enough to be exchanged for goods like these? And how could they have afforded to expend so much labour on monument building?

The islands themselves held no terrestrial sources of wealth; no significant ore deposits; no precious stones. Moreover, what amounted to subsistence production on poor soils in a rigorous climate could have produced little if any wealth in the form of agricultural surplus.

What about the surrounding seas? These offered none of the fabulous valuables found in warmer waters, such as pearls, or murex snails, from which came the rich purple dye so valued in Mediterranean countries.

Yet there *was* wealth in plenty in those northern waters, and the aboriginal people of the Islands learned early how to harvest and make use of it.

C H A P T E R   T H R E E

T U S K E R S

It is five thousand years before our time. The sky over Orkney on this June day is streaked with tendrils of cirrus cloud. A puffy easterly breeze tells of dirty weather in the offing, though for the moment the sun burns brazen.

On Sanday Island a saffron-coloured beach several miles long hones its edge in the heavy roll of ocean. This glittering scimitar is discoloured here and there by rough-textured patches, several acres in extent. Each consists of hundreds of immense, cylindrical creatures crowded so close to one another as to be virtually a single entity. Most are sprawled lethargically on their backs, careless that their exposed bellies are beginning to glow an alarming shade of copper-pink.

Goggle-eyed faces, spiky whiskers, deep-wrinkled cheeks and jowls make them resemble a multitude of Colonel Blimps—except that each, no matter what age or sex, carries a down-curving pair of gleaming tusks. Those of the biggest bulls are as long and thick as a man's arm. They glitter in the harsh sunlight, imparting an aura of primal power to their ponderous owners.

Formidable as they may seem, there is nonetheless something endearing about these lumpen beings packing the long sweep of beach like so many middle-aged holiday makers. Perhaps this is because they seem so patently content with life. Not all are lolling on the sands. Just beyond the breakers small parties of cows lave their sunburnt hides while keeping alert eyes on calves sporting in the surf.

In the water these mighty creatures are transformed into sleek and sinuous masters of another element from which, were it not for the requirements of calving and the joys of sex and sunbathing, they would have no cause ever to depart. Water is their true medium, and has been since their ancestors rejected life on the land millions of years ago.

U P TO FOURTEEN FEET LONG, SUPERBLY MUSCLED, CLAD in a hide as tough as armour, adult walrus fear nothing in the ocean. Gregarious, and amiable except when roused in defence of kith and kin, they once lived in vast and far-flung tribes in all the northern oceans.

They have been known by many names. Eskimos called them *aivalik*; Russians called them *morse*; Scandinavians knew them as *hvalross*; English-speakers have called them *sea-cows* and *sea-horses*.

By whatever name, walrus have been a major source of wealth for human beings from dim antiquity.

One day in the museum of the Arctic and Antarctic Institute in Leningrad, a Siberian archaeologist handed me an intricately carved piece of yellowed bone. What did I think it was?

"Ivory?" I hazarded. "Elephant, or maybe mammoth?"

"Ivory, *da*. The hilt of a sword from an excavation in Astrakhan on the old trade route to Persia. But it is neither elephant nor mammoth. It is *morse*. You must know that for a very long time *morse* tusks were the main source of ivory in northern Asia and Europe. Sometimes they were worth more than their weight in gold."

He went on to tell me of a Muscovite prince captured by Tartars whose ransom was set at 114 pounds of gold—or an equal weight in walrus tusks. This was no isolated example. From very ancient times until as late as the seventeenth century, walrus ivory was one of civilization's most sought-after and highly valued luxuries. Compact and portable, the teeth in their natural "ingot" state served as currency or were carved into precious objects—some purely ornamental; some quasi-functional, as sword and dagger pommels; and some religious, including phallic symbols in fertility cults.

"The tooth of the *morse*," the archaeologist continued, "was white gold from time out of mind. There was nothing: no precious metals, gems, spices, no *valuta* more sought after.[1] How odd that such hideous monsters should have been the source of such wealth."

Wealth derived from walrus was not limited to ivory. The inch-thick leather made from the hides of old bulls would stop musket balls and offered as much resistance to cutting and thrusting weapons as did bronze. For tens of centuries it was the first choice of shield makers and their warrior customers.

Walrus ivory was chosen for the most costly and elaborate carvings such, as these chess pieces, part of a set from the Outer Hebrides.

The hide had other uses as well. Split into two or even three layers, it made a superb sheathing for ships' hulls. A narrow strap, cut spirally from a single hide, could yield a continuous thong as much as two hundred feet in length. When rolled into the "round," such a thong became rope as flexible and durable as that made from the best vegetable fibres, and it was a good deal stronger. In fact, walrus-hide rope remained the preferred cordage and rigging on some north European and Asian vessels until as late as the sixteenth century.

Although walrus are today restricted almost exclusively to Arctic waters, they were formerly found in Europe south to the Bay of Biscay and, in the western Atlantic, as far to the south as Cape Cod. However, as people became more numerous and more rapacious, and as walrus ivory steadily increased in value, the more southerly herds were exterminated, one by one.[2]

The afternoon was well advanced before the skipper turned the homeward-bound Farfarer *into the tidal bore pouring out of the narrow sound between Unst and Yell.*

Swirling waters shouldered her about in rough fashion as the crew stared hungrily at familiar shores. Thin coils of pungent peat smoke blew away from the roofs of stone-and-sod crofts scattered along green slopes. Here and there a tiny figure waved at the passing ship.

Then a crewman happened to look forward over the bows.

"Tusker!" he cried in astonishment.

All hands craned to see a beast which would hardly have merited a passing glance in Tilli. Here, it was a novelty. The men cheered and waved as the bull walrus thrust himself half out of the water to stare back at them. The skipper, at the helm, caught only a glimpse of a great domed head, bulbous eyes, and the gleam of ivory before the beast submerged. He laughed aloud at being welcomed back to home waters by a creature now so rare amongst the Islands that a decade had passed since the last one had been sighted.

According to the old people, the seas around the Northern Islands had once thronged with tuskers. In the spring they had hauled themselves out in thousands on every available beach. Having himself witnessed such spectacles on the strands of distant Tilli, the skipper did not doubt that they had once been commonplace amongst the home islands.

His sighting recalled folk memories of his people.

In the beginning men had mostly left the tuskers alone. Fishers in small boats had given them a wide berth for they could be mortally dangerous if interfered with. Occasionally some foolhardy soul might kill a calf that had strayed away from sunbathing multitudes on a beach. But such a deed was unnecessarily risky since there was no shortage of other food to be had from waters alive with seals and fishes. Moreover, these great creatures that spanned the void between land and sea bore a totemic relationship to human islanders and so were virtually sacrosanct.

People and walrus shared the Northern Islands and surrounding waters without conflict until, one nameless summer thousands of years ago, an Island crew made a venturesome voyage to the south.

The travellers hoped to obtain some of the hard yellow metal born of the union of tin and copper. In those times bronze was still so scarce in the north that few Islanders had even seen the substance, though all had heard of its superlative qualities.

The inhabitants of the first mainland coast the voyagers visited possessed only a little bronze, and none to spare. However, they spoke of other peoples still farther south supposedly rich in the metal. So the Islanders sailed on, coasting unfamiliar shores, until one day they came upon a settlement so large they were afraid to approach it.

Wattle-and-daub houses clustered in a meadow at the bottom of a sandy bay upon whose broad beach many wooden boats were drawn up. While the Islanders apprehensively rested on their oars, people streamed from the houses to the beach, shouting and gesticulating. Their tongue was unfamiliar, but they brandished no weapons and it seemed they were inviting the strangers to come ashore.

Doubtfully, the Islanders beached their big skin boat. They were received in friendly style and, to their delight, saw that many of the residents wore yellow metal knives and ornaments. Delight turned to disappointment when they found that the carefully worked flint tools, soapstone pots, skin bags filled with eiderdown and spun wool they had brought with them would not fetch so much as a finger's length of bronze.

Their hopes seemed blighted until the local headman pointed to a magnificent walrus tusk lashed to the prow of the Islanders' vessel—and proffered a bronze knife for it. After some hesitation, for the tusk was the vessel's talisman, the Islanders agreed. After the trade was made, the headman gave the strangers to understand that foreigners still farther to the south had an abundance of bronze which they exchanged for rare and beautiful things…and what could be rarer, or more beautiful, than the ivory brought by the Islanders?

On this occasion the travellers returned home nearly empty-handed, but bringing knowledge of a world where bronze could be had in exchange for walrus tusks.

Initially, the Islanders contented themselves with scouring their home shores and dunes for the tusks of long-dead animals. These they carried south to distant shores of the Irish Sea, where the ivory was exchanged for implements and ornaments. As the people's appetite for bronze increased, "found" ivory became scarce. Inevitably the day came when the Islanders turned upon the living bearers of their talisman— and that was the start of a killing which would see beaches throughout the northern world run red with blood for centuries to come.

No accounts survive to tell us how the Islanders conducted the slaughter, but we do know how latter-day walrus hunters prosecuted the gory business.

In 1603 an English ship belonging to the Muscovy Company chanced on tiny Bear Island in the Arctic Ocean between Spitzbergen and Norway. Jonas Poole, a member of her crew, kept an account of what ensued.

We saw a sandie Bay in which we came to anchor. We had not furled our Sayles but we saw many Morses swimming by our ship and heard withall so huge a noyse of roaring as if there had been a hundred Lions. It seemed very strange to see such a multitude of Monsters of the Sea lye like Hogges in heapes upon the beach.

To see them was one thing. To attack them quite another. These men knew next to nothing about walrus and were frightened of them.

In the end we shot at them, not knowing whether they could runne swiftly and seize upon us or no.

Smooth-bore guns proved largely ineffective against the tuskers' massive skulls and armoured hides.

Some, when they were wounded in the flesh, would but looke up and lye down again. And some would goe into the Sea with five or sixe shots in them, they are of such incredible strength. When all our ball shot was spent we would blow their eyes out with bird shot, and then come on the blind side of them and, with our Carpenter's axe, cleave their heads. But for all that we could doe we killed but fifteen.

Ivory, and the oil rendered from the fat of these fifteen, whetted the appetite of the Muscovy Company, which sent the ship direct to Bear Island the succeeding summer. Its crew had been briefed on how the job was done elsewhere.

The year before we slew with shot, not thinking that a Javelin could pierce their skinnes, which we now found contrary, if it be well handled; otherwise a man may thrust with all his force and not enter; or if he does he shall spoyle his Lance upon their bones; or they will strike with their forefeet and bend a Lance and break it.

Getting the feel of the job, Poole's crew killed about four hundred walrus and sailed home with eleven tuns of oil and several casks of tusks. When they returned to Bear Island the following year, they were professionals. On a typical day Jonas Poole, in charge of a gang of eleven men, would make his way along the water's edge of a walrus beach, dropping off a man every twenty yards or so, until he met the leader of a similar group coming the other way and so "enclosed the Morses that none of them would get into the Sea."

The line of hunters then turned inland, stabbing every walrus within reach in the throat or belly and causing such panic that the great beasts humped frantically away from their one hope of refuge, the sea. Once they had exhausted themselves, thrusting blades and swinging axes finished them off.

> Before six hours ended we had slayne about six or eight hundred
> Beasts.... For ten days we plied our business very hard and took in two
> and twenty tuns of the Oyle of the Morses and three hogsheads of their
> Teeth.

Within eight years of Poole's first visit to Bear Island, thirty to forty thousand walrus had been butchered, and so few remained as to be not worth hunting.

An even worse slaughter took place in New World waters, especially in the Gulf of St. Lawrence, where every year more than 100,000 sea cows hauled out on the beaches of the Magdalen Islands alone. In 1765 a Royal Navy officer reported on the slaughter taking place there.

> When a great number of Sea Cows are assembled on a beach they are fol-
> lowed by others coming out of the sea who, in order to get room, give
> those in front a push with their tusks. These last are pushed on by more
> following until the Sea Cows farthest from the water are driven so far
> inland that even the latest arrivals have room to rest.
>
> The *échouries*, as these beaches are called, being so full that the hunters
> can cut off three or four hundred, ten or twelve men prepare themselves
> with poles about 12 feet long. The attack is made at night and the principal
> thing to be observed is the wind, that must always blow from the animals
> to prevent the hunters being discovered.
>
> When they have approached to within three or four hundred yards of
> the échourie beach five men are detached with poles. These creep on

hands and knees until they are close to the flank of the herd. The reason for this is that if the Sea Cows had the least apprehension they would all turn and retire into the water. In which case, so far from being able to stop them, it would be great good fortune if the men saved themselves from being pressed to death or being drowned.

Being ready to attack, the first man gives the Cow in front of him a gentle strike with his pole upon the buttocks, imitating as much as possible the push they give each other. So he proceeds with the next Cow, making it advance up the beach while one of his companions secures him from harm from the Cows to seaward of him.

So they continue to the other side of the échourie, having by this process made a passage which they call the *cut*. All this time they have observed the utmost silence, but now they begin to halloo and make the greatest possible noise to frighten and alarm the Sea Cows. All the men now range themselves along the cut, driving and beating the Cows to prevent them falling backward to the sea. Those Cows that turn back from farthest inland are prevented from escaping by the men belabouring the seaward Cows toward them, and the collision of the two groups forms a bank of bodies twenty feet high and upwards.

The men keep exercising their poles until the beasts are quite fatigued and give up the attempt to escape, after which they are divided into parties of thirty to forty Cows that are driven to a place generally a mile inland from the échouries, where they are killed.

Up to 25,000 walrus were killed each year on the beaches of the Magdalen Islands during the 1700s. When, in 1798, another British naval officer was sent to evaluate the sea cow fishery there, he reported to his superiors, "I am extremely sorry to acquaint you that the Sea Cow fishery on these islands is totally annihilated."

Northern Islanders probably used similar hunting methods. Their kills may not have approached the wholesale butcheries achieved in modern times; nevertheless, every spring Orcadian, Shetland, and Hebridean beaches would have been soaked in blood, and every spring fewer tuskers reappeared to haul themselves ashore. Here, as would later be the case in the Gulf of St. Lawrence, tribes that had once numbered in the hundreds of thousands shrank to tens of thousands; to tens of hundreds; and, finally, to none at all.

So walrus numbers dwindled even as the human inhabitants of the islands were becoming ever more numerous—and more avid for imported goods, including gold and silver ornaments, gemstones, pottery, wood, iron, and amber. Demand for ivory increased inexorably. By the middle of the first millennium B.C. only a remnant population of walrus still survived in the Northern or Western Islands of Britain. Yet something more than a memory of them still remained. When, in the fourth century B.C., the Northern Islands first appear in recorded history, they bear the name *Orcadies*—Islands of the Orcas—a Greek word signifying monsters of the sea. There can be little doubt but that walrus were the sea monsters for whom the remote islands were named.3

Some two hundred miles northwest of, and almost equidistant from, the Outer Hebrides, Orkney, and Shetland, another archipelago thrusts itself out of the ocean depths. Once called Bird Islands, now the Faeroes, it consists of a jagged array of high-rearing mountains separated one from the other by fathomless troughs in whose narrow reaches fierce tidal currents churn.

Larger than either Orkney or Shetland, most of the Faeroe land mass is nearly vertical, offering small inducement to human settlement. However, millions of seabirds breed on the many cliffs and, in ancient times, the seas about abounded in whales, seals—and walrus.

Northern Islanders must have been aware of the existence of the Faeroes from very early on. In good weather, its three-thousand-foot peaks are visible from sixty miles to seaward, and tell-tale cumulus clouds that gather over them in summer can be seen from twice that distance. Even if no Island boatman had ever been blown far enough from home to actually see the Faeroes, people would still have known land lay that way because of the vast flocks of ducks, geese, swans, and other birds that headed north and west from Shetland each spring and returned from that direction every autumn.

The Faeroes could be reached from any of the other three archipelagos in two or three sailing days.4 We can be sure that, as walrus grew scarce in home waters, Islanders would have gone to the Faeroes in search of more.

Hunting them in the Faeroes would have been more difficult than in home waters. As a Faeroese fishing captain, who, in his youth, hunted walrus in Svalbard (Spitzbergen), explained to me:

"Ya, there was sure to have been *hvalross* on our islands one time. You would not much catch them on the beaches though, because not many beaches. You would hunt them like we did in Svalbard. Find a bunch of the boogers hauled out on rocks and come onto them in boat from seaward. With the sun behind so they don't soon see you. When you get close you shoot in head, but have to be good shooter because head is small target and hard like iron. We also fished with harpoons and good, strong lines. When *hvalross* is tired, you haul boat up to him and bash his head with axe or maul. Sometimes he come at boat, then you got to watch out! I see tusks come through three-inch oak keel and go through pine plank like butter. I don't want to do that kind of fishing in skin boat!"

The Islanders would not have much wanted to do it either. Although their harpoons and lances were tipped with quartz blades sharper than the sharpest steel, hunting walrus in the water would have remained a risky and relatively unproductive business.

Regardless of the difficulties involved, determined pursuit of walrus in the Faeroes led to a predictable result. The population eventually became so reduced as to be no longer worth the hunting.

It was going to be an early autumn. Already long skeins of swans and geese were sweeping out of the northwestern skies, some to spiral down to rest briefly on the Bird Islands, others to overfly them on their way south.

Two men of a crew from Fetlar stood together on the shore of Sandy Island, so called because it possessed one of the very few sand beaches in the Faeroes. They were watching and listening as seemingly endless flocks of whooper swans, greylag, and pink-footed geese swept overhead, filling the dawn with sonorous voices.

"One of these years," mused the younger of the two, "someone will take the Swan's Way and fare to the land those birds are coming from. So many of them! It must be a great land."

The older man stared westward across the wastes of ocean and nodded.

"Maybe so, though who's to say? No man has gone that far."

"No need before now," the younger one replied with some asperity. "Used to be

tuskers in plenty at home, and even here on the Bird Islands. Now they've mostly gone, and where else could they be but to the west? We ought to go after them."

The biting stench of burning seaweed drenched in seal oil assailed their nostrils. They turned and walked towards a gravelly shelf a hundred yards from the water, where their ship had been upturned upon a foundation composed of stones and sod to make a summer home. Several of their fellows were busy near it, stoking the smoky fire and preparing a morning meal.

They were in a surly mood. This season's hunt had been the worst in memory. During past springs as many as a dozen vessels had sailed to the Bird Islands and gone home again in autumn heavy with cargoes of oil, hides, and ivory. This year only two vessels had bothered to make the voyage, one from Shetland and one from the Outer Hebrides. Their crews had found only a scattering of walrus hauled out on the few suitable beaches. And these had mostly been young or female, with small tusks. Furthermore, they had been so wary as to be almost unapproachable. Between them the two crews had killed fewer than twenty animals on the beaches. At great risk they had speared a half-dozen more in the water but, all in all, the hunt had been a failure. The Hebridean crew had already sailed home in disgust.

That evening, over a meal of boiled seal meat, the young man who had spoken of faring farther west boldly broached the subject. The rest of the crew listened intently. One of the elders ventured the opinion that the land where the geese and swans nested might be dangerously distant.

"Men can go wherever lesser creatures can!" a younger man interjected contemptuously. "There's no more tuskers in these waters. They've gone somewhere, and where can it be but west? Ours is the best seaboat in the Islands! What's stopping us?"

The discussion went on far into the twilit night. Eventually it was agreed that, if the weather at dawn promised fair, a reconnaissance would be made to the northwestward one day's sail out of sight of the highest peak of the Bird Islands. If by then there were indications of new land ahead, they might go on. Or they could turn back.

Dawn brought clear skies and a steady sou'west breeze. After a hurried breakfast, the crew carefully levered their ship off the foundation, turned her right-side up, and half-carried, half-slid her to the beach. The cooking fire was still smoking as they launched and loaded her. With sail sheeted for a broad reach, she headed lightly into the northwest, a little curl of white foam flickering at her cutwater.

The good weather held and she bowled swiftly along, rising easily to the long swells. By the time the sun dipped below the horizon for a brief interlude before rising again, the highest peak of the Faeroes was barely visible astern.

Nothing was to be seen ahead except the emptiness of ocean. The skipper held his course, and there was no grumbling amongst the crew. No man wanted to be thought timorous.

When, three hours later, the sun rose again they had lost all sight of land. Still the weather held. If anything, it improved as the breeze swung into the south. Dawn brought flights of swans and geese streaming southeastward overhead as if to confirm that the ship was on the proper course.

Tension mounted as the day wore on. Faint wisps of high cloud appeared, warning of a change in weather. The waters were alive with whales—so many that the steersman sometimes had to alter course to avoid collisions. But there was no sign of land ahead.

The afternoon was growing old when the skipper made his decision. "Wind's going to go westerly this evening, and rise. Soon it'll be smack on the nose....We'll hold this course 'til sunset, then turn back."

Two hours before sunset they encountered a pod of big bull tuskers assembled as if to block the vessel's path. The great beasts reared their bodies partly out of the water and glared enigmatically.

Shortly thereafter the lookout let out a bellow:

"Land ahead! No, by the gods, it don't look like land! But something's there!"

Apprehensively, the men watched the "something" lift slowly above the horizon. Instead of a dark shape looming against a pallid sky, the massive presence gradually revealing itself was ghostly white.

There was fear in many hearts, yet no man showed his feelings. The skipper held the course with a steady hand. The breeze began to freshen and veer into the southwest as the ship snored through rising seas. The sun seemed to be sinking directly into the whiteness ahead, and the glitter became so intense men could no longer look directly at it.

Suddenly the skipper put the helm hard over to spill the wind out of the vessel's sail. As she lost way the crew crowded aft, their voices a babble of interrogation. The skipper yelled for silence, then:

"Now we decide! This wind will be a howler by morning. If we turn and run for it, we'll maybe find shelter amongst the Bird Islands. If we hold on towards that white place, only the gods know what awaits us. It's for all of you to say!"

It was a crucial moment. The young man who had originally suggested the westward venture swung up on the little afterdeck beside his skipper.

"You all saw the tuskers in the sea! That's our sign! There'll be many more ahead....I say...let's go on."

So it was that in the afterglow of sunset the ship from the Northern Islands closed cautiously with a new land. When dawn came clear the crew saw they had come to a country ringed by dark mountains from whose inner reaches swelled a white dome of overwhelming size. The shores of this weird world seemed to consist of endless stretches of black sand beaches along which they coasted for half a day, sheltered by the high land from what was becoming a full gale. The beaches were alive with tuskers, and so were the seas through which they sailed.

Near midday the lookout spotted a break in the beach line. Putting in towards it, they found a channel running into a broad lagoon. Once inside they dropped anchor in perfect shelter. Then they launched the ship's boat, and the skipper and five men rowed ashore to land upon the great mid-oceanic island of the north, which the Islanders would henceforth know as Tilli.

As for the vessel that had brought them there—she would become the first to bear the name Farfarer...a name destined to echo down the generations for more than a thousand years.

PYTHEAS

ALMOST ALL OUR FIRST-HAND KNOWLEDGE OF THE life and times of the ancient inhabitants of Britain stems from a remarkable voyage undertaken around 330 B.C. by a peripatetic Greek named Pytheas.

Pytheas first caught my attention in 1938 when, as a schoolboy in landlocked Saskatchewan, I was taken to a lecture given by Canadian Arctic explorer Vilhjalmur Stefansson. Stefansson extolled Pytheas as one of the great seafarers of all time, and thereafter I used to dream about accompanying the Greek venturer to a mysterious Arctic world more than two thousand years into the past.

Although Pytheas wrote a book about his journey, only fragments of it have been preserved, mostly in brief commentaries by later classical writers. During the nineteenth century it was fashionable in some, mainly Scandinavian, quarters to deride Pytheas and all his works as mythical creations. However, in the present century most historians have come to accept the reality of the man and his accomplishments. It is no less than his due.

What follows is my reconstruction of his epic voyage.

Six centuries before Christ was born, people from Phocaea, a small but prosperous Greek state in Asia Minor, sailed west almost the full length of the Mediterranean to found a settlement close to one of the mouths of the Rhône. They called it Massilia. Eventually it became Marseilles.

The Phocaeans were distinguished amongst their fellow Greeks for

Seafaring vessels of a bygone age.

Farfarer—50 feet

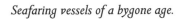

Viking Knorr—50 feet

Greek Holkas—50 feet

Armorican merchant
vessel—70 feet

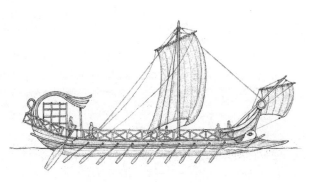

Roman galley—80 feet

their business flair. They were fierce competitors of the Phoenicians, Semites from Lebanon who, as early as 800 B.C., had sailed westward to found Carthage on the North African coast, from which they were afterwards able to control traffic through the Strait of Hercules (the Strait of Gibraltar) linking the Middle Sea to the Outer Ocean.

The Phocaeans founded Massilia to prevent the Carthaginians from controlling inland trade routes between the Mediterranean and lands to the north bordering on the Atlantic. Massilia's location allowed the Phocaeans to dominate the Seine, Loire, and Rhône river systems, and therefore the trade with far-distant regions on the western and northern verges of the known world.

By the time Massilia was established, goods had been moving between the barbarian northwest and Egypt, Crete, and Mycenae for at least two millennia. Faience beads, bronze tools and weapons, pottery, fine cloth, even wine travelled to Britain and to North Sea and Baltic ports in vessels coasting the shores of the Bay of Biscay, or in river craft ascending the Rhône then descending west-flowing rivers to the Atlantic coast. Returning traders brought back Irish gold, Baltic amber, British tin—and ivory.

As Carthage tightened her stranglehold on the Strait of Hercules, the trans-Gaul river routes grew in importance until, by 400 B.C., Massilia had become one of the foremost commercial centres in the Mediterranean world.

Grown rich, the city on the Rhône also became famous for its natural philosophers, amongst whom was Pytheas. An eminent mathematician, he was the first Greek to show that the tides were controlled by the moon and the first to devise an accurate method of determining relative latitudes.

I envisage him as a pleasantly rotund (upper-class Massiliots would have eaten well) fellow of middle height and years, dark-eyed, and decisive in his ways.

Pytheas seems to have had an insatiable curiosity. All his life he had watched exotic cargoes arriving in his home port and must have pondered the nature of the northern lands and peoples from which they came. Massilia's merchant-rulers would certainly have shared such an interest, if only for purely practical reasons. When Pytheas decided he must go and see the hyperborean world for himself, he was provided with a stout ship, a crew, and stores for an extended voyage.

But why a *ship* for a river journey?

It appears that, a few decades before the turn of the fourth century, the Carthaginians briefly eased their blockade of the Strait of Hercules, and Pytheas seized the opportunity to go north by sea.

His vessel would have been a *holkas*, the standard Greek merchant-man of the day, about seventy feet long with a twenty-foot beam, deep-bellied, bluff-bowed, and heavily built of oak and pine. Although she carried long sweeps with which she could be rowed (albeit slowly), her main driver was a big, loose-footed square sail that could give her four or five knots in a brisk, favouring breeze.

The voyage began on a spring day late in the fourth century B.C. As the *holkas* coasted southwest along the Mediterranean shores of Spain, her crew kept a wary lookout for Carthaginian war galleys. Luck was with the Massiliots. They slipped safely through the strait, probably at night, and by dawn were headed northwest into the open ocean on a course designed to give a wide berth to Gades (now Cadiz), the most northerly Carthaginian stronghold on the Atlantic coast.

One of Pytheas's few surviving observations for latitudes during the voyage corresponds closely to the position of modern Oporto. Continuing north, the *holkas* rounded Cape Finisterre, turned eastward, and coasted the Bay of Biscay to reach one of the trading posts estab-lished by Massiliots at river mouths along the Atlantic coast. Here the vessel lay at anchor for a day or two while Pytheas gathered information from his fellow countrymen about what lay ahead.

They told him that incursions by bellicose tribesmen from the northeast, whom the Greeks called Keltoi, were becoming more fre-quent and more disastrous for the inhabitants of the interior. However, the native coastal dwellers, known as Armoricans, were successfully holding their own. The Armoricans were noted as first-rate seamen, possessed of good ships, well-defended ports, and effective weaponry.

Pytheas continued northward. Near the western tip of France, he went ashore to take an observation on an island in Armorican territory called Uxisama, modern Ushant, for which Pytheas's given latitude is in error by less than thirty miles.

Uxisama was the traditional point of departure for traders bound across the hundred-mile width of the Channel to the great island known to Greeks and Phoenicians alike as Alba.[1] The *holkas's* master set his vessel on a due-north course and the ship left the continent astern.

After a day and a night at sea, the Massiliots raised the highlands of the Cornish peninsula. They put into harbour somewhere along the southern shore, perhaps at Mount's Bay near present-day Penzance, or a little farther east, in Falmouth Bay. Both were ports from which Cornish tin had been shipped to Mediterranean bronze makers through a millennium or more.

Pytheas went ashore and journeyed into the interior to visit some of the tin mines and satisfy his curiosity about the way of life of the local people, whom he called *autochthones*, which is to say, aboriginals.

Up to this point he had broken no new ground, but now unknown territory lay ahead to the north. The peoples living in Hyperborea (the land beyond the North Wind) had always brought their goods south to trade with Mediterranean merchants at the Oestrimnides, islands near the southwestern tip of Britain. The Roman poet Avienus, quoting fragments from a Carthaginian periplus (seaman's sailing directions) dating to the sixth century B.C., described this rendezvous as follows:

> To the Oestrimnides come many enterprising people who occupy themselves with commerce and who navigate the monster-filled ocean far and wide in small ships. They do not understand how to build wooden ships in the usual way. Believe it or not, they make their boats by sewing hides together and carry out deep-sea voyages in them. Two days farther north [from the Oestrimnides] lies the great island formerly called Holy Island [Ireland] where the Hierne people live adjacent to the island of Alba [mainland Britain].

It was to the Oestrimnides (now the Scilly Isles) that Pytheas sailed after his excursion ashore in Cornwall. Here he met native traders from Hyperborea who had come south in their big, hide-covered vessels. They welcomed him, for not only did the Greeks provide a market for northern goods such as walrus ivory, they were major suppliers of much-desired southern products, including wine.

Pytheas mingled with the men from the north at what was, in effect, a trade fair on the Scilly Isles. When he let it be known he would dearly love to visit their homelands, some of the northern Albans invited him to sail north in their company.

So one summer day a squadron of skin vessels made its way into the Irish Sea, with a Massiliot *holkas* in its midst.

A problem soon arose. Despite the best efforts of her crew, the *holkas* could not keep station. In any sort of breeze she fell astern of the swift skin vessels. The Albans politely shortened sail.

Pytheas's next surviving observation places him near the Isle of Man. Thereafter the ships passed out of the Irish Sea into the Minches. Here they began meeting fishermen and sea-hunters from islands whose name Pytheas recorded as Ebudae—the Ebud Islands. Today they are the Hebrides.

Now mostly forested lands lay astern, and the Massiliots found themselves entering a most unfamiliar world. Lifeless-looking peat bogs and heather moors rolled inland from rocky shores to barren peaks. However, if the land seemed desolate, the waters seethed with fishes, seals, and whales. Perhaps, somewhere in the North Minch, Pytheas was lucky enough to glimpse the ivory-tusked sea monster of which he had heard so much.

His next recorded observation was made in the latitude of Loch Broom, where the ships sheltered from a storm. Their arrival attracted people from all the nearby crofting and fishing communities. When the visitors sailed on again, they were accompanied by a flock of small local craft, whose crews were as fascinated by the *holkas* and her people as the Massiliots were by them.

Although very different in their dress, equipment, and many aspects of their way of life, the two peoples were not dissimilar in physical appearance. Both were rather slightly built, yet strong and supple. Both were dark-haired, dark-eyed, and olive-skinned. Both possessed lively and vivacious natures. In truth, it seemed to Pytheas that the Albans could have been distant cousins had it not been for their language, which was so alien that all communication with them had to be conducted through interpreters.

Now the vessels rounded Cape Wrath and sailed into the roiling waters of Pentland Firth. Mainland Alba lay to the south. To the north sprawled twin archipelagos to which Pytheas gave one name— Orcadies—Islands of the Orcas. According to Diodorus Siculus, a Greek writer of the first century B.C., Pytheas also identified the northeastern corner of mainland Britain (now Caithness) as the Orcadian Peninsula.[2]

One by one, the Alban ships began to haul away for their own home ports, which were now close at hand. With a diminishing escort, the *holkas* continued threading her way northward through straits and channels between the many islands.

The visitors were piloted past the towering cliffs of Hoy Island into Hoy Sound. On the croft-strewn lowlands surrounding the Loch of Stenness stood an assemblage of monumental structures which even the worldly Massiliots found impressive. Foremost was Maeshowe, a mighty mound raised over a corbelled vault whose size and workmanship are unsurpassed by any other megalithic structure of its kind. Within a mile or so of Maeshowe were ceremonial circles outlined by stone pillars, some being eighteen feet tall and weighing several tons. Although built two thousand years before Pytheas's time, the Ring of Brogdar, the near-by Ring of Bookan, and the Standing Stones of Stenness were still hallowed places when he visited the Orcadies.

As the *holkas* voyaged on amongst the islands, the Massiliots admired the varied and skilful ways the Islanders used the layered red sandstone that underlay much of their land. Trees and timber being virtually lacking, sandstone was made to serve instead. Not only did it provide the stuff from which almost all buildings were constructed, sandstone slabs were neatly formed into bureaus, cupboards, bed frames, benches, and tables. Drystone field walls, so well constructed they seemed to have been moulded, ran over the treeless slopes and moors in all directions. Harbour works, ship haul-outs, sheep folds—the list was endless—were all made of skilfully laid-up sandstone. Even the skin-covered boats and ships were ballasted with shaped tablets of red sandstone. So accomplished were the masons that they seldom needed mortar, of which they made what small amount *was* required by burning seashells to obtain slaked lime. The Northern Islanders were artisans in stone par excellence.

They had no towns, living instead in scattered crofts or in clan clusters of fewer than a dozen stone-walled, sod-thatched buildings. For the most part, their small and shaggy cattle, horses, sheep, and goats remained out of doors year round.

The chill winters and cool summers that then prevailed had caused sequential crop failures and consequent massive population shifts on the Continent, but had wrought few hardships on the Northern Islanders. If their free-ranging domestic animals were unable to feed them, they could turn to an ever-generous sea. Nor were they entirely dependent on what land and sea could provide directly. The cargoes of valuta they sent south each summer were as readily transmutable into grain and meal as into hard goods.

The Mediterranean visitors found these islands bleak, windswept, and chill, but noted that those who dwelt upon them not only lived in peace and freedom but, by the standards of the times, lived well.

One other aspect of island life that impressed the Massiliots, although not necessarily favourably, was that here were no castles, mansions, or great houses; no high and mighty lords; and, in fact, little visible difference between men. It was essentially an egalitarian society.

Cruising leisurely north, with frequent visits ashore, the crew of the *holkas* reached the northernmost tip of the twin archipelagos—an islet now called Muckle Flugga, which Pytheas correctly located at the Massiliot latitudinal equivalent of 60° 52'.

He had now reached a point much farther north than any previous Mediterranean traveller; yet he was not content. Although he was told that thousands of orcas—the creatures he most wished to observe—had once swarmed in these waters, they were now all but vanished. Only windrows of bleaching bones, half-hidden by beach grass, remained to speak of the cargoes of ivory that had once been harvested here.

Yet ivory *still* flowed south, *and* in quantity.

In response to Pytheas's inquiries, the Islanders told him of Tilli. It was a great land, they said, lying in the grey sweep of ocean five or six days' sail to the northwest.[3] Not only did it harbour multitudes of orcas, it was home to many other exotic creatures. These included narwhals, whose single tusks of spiralled ivory were even more valuable than walrus tusks; white water bears; white and smoky-blue foxes; majestic gyrfalcons; flightless auks the size of geese; and ducks and other waterfowl beyond counting.

Map of Iceland. Known as "Tilli" by the Albans, the island is northwest of what is now known as Britain.

Tilli was a rocky world, the Albans explained, partly covered by vast ice mountains and sometimes riven by thundering volcanoes. Each spring ships from the Northern Islands made their way to it. Some few even overwintered. When they sailed for home again they no longer skimmed the waves but wallowed, deep-laden with valuta destined for the trade fair at the Oestrimnides.

Pytheas was determined to see Tilli for himself. The Islanders concluded that time enough remained for a voyage there and back before autumnal gales would render such a venture perilous. However, they rejected any notion that the Massiliots attempt the voyage in the *holkas*. This, they said, barely concealing their disdain for the unwieldy wooden ship, would be madness. Instead, they offered to take Pytheas to Tilli in one of their own vessels.

They sailed first to the Bird Islands—now the Faeroes. Three days after leaving those stark pinnacles astern, a lookout picked up the loom of the ice mountains of Tilli. Closing with the land, they coasted the southern shore, and the Massiliots wondered at the majestic, glacier-covered mountains; the black cliffs and sands; and, most of all, at the legions of tuskers in the water and on the endless beaches.

Perhaps they landed on what are now called the Westman Islands in order that Pytheas might view a smoking crater at close range. Then the Albans steered their ship back to the mainland shore to show their guests the verdant sweep of meadowlands and birch woods in the south coast river valleys.

Pytheas reported in his now lost book that he went a day's sail *beyond* Tilli, and there encountered a "sluggish and congealed sea" that could be traversed neither on foot nor by boat. The Albans had piloted the insatiably curious Greek far enough north and west of Tilli to show him the disintegrating ice (called slob by those familiar with it) drifting south on the East Greenland Current. They may also have given him a glimpse of yet another and even vaster western land crowned by the stupendous Greenland icecap.

Putting back, the vessel rounded Tilli's northwestern promontory and sailed along the north shore, completing a circuit of the island before setting course for the Orcadies.

On his return to those islands, and to his *holkas*, Pytheas said his grateful farewells to his Alban hosts and guides, then sailed into the North Sea and so home to Massilia, having first made a venture into the Baltic to satisfy his curiosity about the origins of amber.

But we will not follow him; for now, as singers of the old songs used to say, he is out of the story.

ALBANS
AND CELTS

A LTHOUGH IN ANCIENT TIMES BRITAIN BORE THE
name of Alba, she was by no means alone in doing so. Tens of
scores of place names derived from *alb* were scattered all the
way from the Hindu Kush of Afghanistan to the Atlantic Ocean. A surprising number of these have endured into our times. I had no trouble
assembling a list of more than three hundred contemporary place
names containing an *alb* component, and many more are to be found in
Asia Minor and in northern Africa.

They are especially abundant from the Caspian Sea westward. The
most notable concentrations occur in mountain country such as the
Caucasus; the highlands of northwestern Iran and northeastern Turkey;
the Balkans; the Alpine (originally *Albin*) massif; the Apennines (*Alpes
Poeninae*); the Carpathians; France's Massif Centrale; the highlands of the
Iberian peninsula; the Cambrian massif in Wales; the English Pennines;
and the mountains of northern Scotland.

The name was prominent in classical times, when several full-
fledged countries bore some version of it. In addition to British Alba,
these included the land of the Albii in the Alborz massif of northeastern
Iran; Albania Superior and Albania Inferior in the Caucasus and
Armenia; Olbia on the northwestern shore of the Black Sea; Alba in
Romania; Elbistan in Turkey; the land of the Albicci in Liguria; Alba
Longa in Italy; Alba and Albicet in Spain; and, of course, the Albania,
which survives to this day in the Balkans.

The literal meaning and origin of *alb* remain obscure but, for reasons which will appear, I conclude it was closely associated with, if not the generic name of, the majority of the indigenes who inhabited Europe, Asia Minor, and probably also North Africa, until they were displaced from their lowland territories by largely Indo-European invasions. Thereafter it continued in use by those who survived in mountainous and other physically difficult regions where they were able to withstand the interlopers from the east.[1]

But who were these people who left their name all across Europe and beyond and who have now mostly vanished out of memory?

In those distant times when most of Europe was still blanketed by thick forests and inhabited by scattered bands of hunter-gatherers, some folk belonging to the mesolithic tradition had already begun domesticating wild animals.

Amongst them were people who had become adept at hunting sheep and goats in the original habitat of these creatures: mountain slopes and plateaus where forests would not grow but alpine pastures flourished.

It was a relatively easy step for them to evolve from hunting to herding. At least as early as ten thousand years ago, men had already begun following these sure-footed animals, not as hunters but as protectors. A symbiotic relationship developed whereby groups of people took it upon themselves to guard wild herds from attack by wolves, bears, and other predators. In exchange, the protectors took their pound of flesh.

In the spring these herdsmen-in-the-making followed retreating snowlines and ascending flocks to flower-fragrant meadows at high altitudes. During the winters they endured blizzards and subarctic conditions when necessary to fulfil their part of the bargain. Their relationship to wild sheep and goats would have been comparable to that of today's Sami with their reindeer herds.

In 1991 climbers in the high Alps between Italy and Austria came across the freeze-dried body of a man melting out of glacial ice. The discovery of this Ice Man, as he was inevitably dubbed, became a nine-day wonder.

It was, in fact, a five-thousand-year-old wonder that began on an autumnal day around 3000 B.C. when a mountain herdsman climbed to a sheltered little col overlooking the vast panorama of the Alps. It was an ideal place from which to keep an eye on his clan's sheep; watch for beasts of prey; and, if he was lucky, ambush a wary ibex, king of the wild goat tribe.

About thirty years old, standing five foot two in moccasin-like foot gear, he was lean, but strongly muscled; had long, wavy black hair, a curly beard, dark eyes and skin. He wore a knee-length deerskin jacket; deerskin leggings; and, over all, a long, thick cape woven of downward-pointing grass that would have been equally effective in shedding snow or rain. On his head was a conical bearskin hat.

He was outfitted for a prolonged stay. In a pouch at his waist he carried tinder and chunks of iron pyrites from which sparks could be struck. He had a fish net for taking trout from mountain streams; sinew and fine twine for snaring birds and small mammals; and birch-bark containers for milk—if he could catch a lactating ewe.

He also had a copper-bladed axe, a flint knife, and flint scrapers and drills. His chief weapon was a bow and a quiver full of arrows. The six-foot bow, of mountain yew, was not yet finished. Completing it would have been a task for the long hours when there was not much to do but watch the sheep.

The bow never was completed. One night the herdsman lay down with his cape spread over him—and did not rise again. What happened is unclear or, rather, how it happened is unclear. Perhaps an unseasonable blizzard burst over the high col that night and, before it ended, buried the herdsman to such a depth that he suffocated. Ice formed from that and succeeding snowfalls preserved his body through five millennia.

The life of mountain herdsmen was rigorously demanding. Most existing hillmen, of whom the Kurds and Iranian-Afghani are good examples, are tough, wiry, immensely enduring people of small-to-middle stature, with sharp features, black hair and eyes, and dark complexions. They are characterized by indomitable courage, fierce loyalties, and passionate allegiance to clan and country. They are almost certainly of Alban ancestry.

They have never submitted to outside authority. Lowlanders stigmatize them as intractable barbarians, wild hill dwellers snapping at the heels of civilization. Because they are natural people in a natural world, they do not take kindly to what we so fondly call civilization. However, their own systems of tight clan structures and deep-rooted connections with non-human animals have produced a culture that has sustained them through aeons that have seen the collapse and disappearance of one lowland civilization after another.

During the late autumn of 1966 I flew to Georgia in the USSR seeking a little warmth after spending six weeks travelling through a mostly frozen Siberia. I was welcomed in the capital city of Tiblisi by Givi Cheliz. A dark, slightly built, hawk-visaged man of my own age, Givi was an infantry survivor of the Great Patriotic War against the Nazis. He was also an authority on the ancient mountain races of this region, from one of which he was himself descended.

Givi had read some books of mine, about my own wartime experiences with the infantry in Italy, and about my travels in the Canadian North. Friendship was born between us and we nurtured it on new wines drawn from huge earthenware vats on local farms.

One day we set out into the Caucasus. With some hesitation Givi's old Volga carried us to the village of Belokany on the slopes of Mount Dyultydag. The peak, towering to thirteen thousand feet, was clothed in tatters of storm cloud through which we caught glimpses of distant snowfields. The sun was setting and the whole of this world of titans was cloaked in purple and gold. We sat on an outcrop overlooking a dark and fathomless valley, and sipped wine from a leather flask while Givi told me stories about the mountain people. Stories such as this one.

During the summer of 1942, when the German armies were at the northwestern gates of the Caucasus, Givi was detailed to lead a patrol to investigate rumours that a gang of deserters had taken refuge in the labyrinth of colossal gulches surrounding Mount Elbrus (Givi pronounced it *Alb*rus) which, at 18,500 feet, is the highest mountain in Europe.

It took several days for the patrol to penetrate into the interior, scrabbling up water courses, goat tracks, and scree slopes to get there. One evening they smelled the unmistakeable aroma of fires fuelled with goat dung. Following their noses, they came to a cleft in the mountains, at the bottom of which some small stone houses clustered. They descended with weapons at the ready—and found, not a gang of desperados, but five families of mountain people.

"They were Albkhazastani," Givi explained; "among the oldest folk in the Caucasus. They didn't speak Georgian *or* Russian, only their own tongue. Because I have Albkhazastan blood I also have a little of the language. So I found out they knew almost nothing about the most terrible war in history, except there was 'trouble' to the north.

"So I told them about the millions of German soldiers, tanks, and planes coming towards them right at that moment. They were not impressed. They cooked a splendid meal for us, roasting two whole sheep on big iron spits. All they wanted to talk about was sheep and goats.

"We spent the night, and when we left in the morning one old fellow walked a little way with us. He pointed north and assured me, 'Nothing to worry about, my lad. If the folk you speak of come this way, we and the mountains will turn them back. We've always done that to those who bring us evil.'

"*Da!*" Givi concluded, taking a sip from the flask. "And they always will!"

By the time the agricultural revolution began turning lowland forest hunter-gatherers into farmers, highland people had been pastoralists for scores of generations. They had developed other talents as well. Perhaps because good herdsmen are so acutely attuned to the weather or, it may be, because they can bear physical adversity so well, they have always made good seamen. For whatever reasons, the Albans produced a number of seafaring offshoots. Amongst these were the Basques, Aquitainians, and Armoricans of northwestern Spain and the Bay of Biscay. Also to be included were the Alpuani of the southwestern Italian Alps and Liguria who sailed to and settled the islands of Corsica, Sardinia, and Elba (Alba). Still another maritime-oriented tribe spread from Scotland to all the northern and western islands of that Alba which eventually came to be known as Britain.

Albans were living in their ancient ways when, about 1500 B.C., an outpouring of migrant tribes burst into Europe from the east and southeast. These were the Indo-Europeans, the stock from which the majority of modern Europeans are descended.

By about 1200 B.C. most native lowlanders as far west as the Alps had been overrun and swamped. The invaders shattered the physical fabric of indigenous lowland societies, and smothered cultural identities, replacing native languages with their own. Before many centuries had passed, Indo-European tongues were almost the only ones to be heard in lowland Europe.

This was not so in mountain country or on many remote and rugged islands. Here some natives retained their language—and their freedom. There were notable exceptions. One was a tribe living on what are still called *Colli Albani* (Alban Hills), an isolated volcanic spur of the western Apennines. Surrounded by Indo-European invaders, these people eventually capitulated. The survivors were herded to the site of a new city being built by their captors and put to work as slaves. The city was Rome. The river flowing through it from the blue reaches of the Apennines had once been the Albula, home to a prophetic water nymph named Albunea. Now it became the Tiber, and the pastoral people who had long lived in the highlands at its headwaters vanished into the shadows. They were amongst the unlucky ones.

Others were more fortunate. In the seventh century B.C. Britain was still home to a Bronze Age society just entering the Iron Age, a society principally composed of lowland farmers and highland pastoralists, together with some tin and flint miners, coastal and island fishermen, and seafarers. Evidently they were a pacific folk for there is little evidence to indicate that warfare or serious internecine strife played much of a role in their lives. Although we do not certainly know what *they* called their island home, Carthaginian and Greek visitors knew it as Alba.

While British Albans went on about their age-old business, a new fury of Indo-Europeans swept into the western marches of Europe. Fairhaired, pale-skinned, and often blue-eyed, these were the people of Aryan lineage whom the Greeks called *Keltoi*.

The Keltoi were greatly feared—and with good reason. Ruled by a warrior caste, they were slavers and sometimes head hunters. They raised livestock (or their slaves did) but, in the main, Keltoi men, and some of their women too, lived by, and for, war. They exulted in it and were experts with the weaponry of their time, especially the war chariot. Nurtured on the Druidic religion, which promised a heroic and eternal afterlife to those who died in battle, the Keltoi, or Celts as we currently spell the name, were supremely effective human predators.

By as early as 600 B.C. Celtic war bands were nearing Europe's western shores. They had experienced little difficulty in overrunning and subduing the native lowlanders of the interior but, near the coast, they met implacable resistance. Although one of their tribes, the Belgae, did succeed in breaking through to the sea, the indigenes south of the mouth of the Seine (whom the Greeks and Romans would call Armoricans) were able to hold their own.

These seafaring people withdrew into fortified enclaves on coastal headlands and islands, or in flooded estuaries. Possessors of big, powerful vessels, they were able to defend their sea-girt bastions from invaders who were essentially landsmen born and bred.

In defending themselves, the Armoricans were also protecting British Alba. But the Belgae, who had occupied the Low Countries to the north of the Seine, could see Alba across the narrow Strait of Dover. They began raiding the coast on the other side of the Channel, doubtless in captured vessels crewed by local men. By the fourth century B.C., they had a foothold in southeastern England.

First occupying capes and islands, the invaders eventually established deep bridgeheads from which they thrust boldly inland. Their weaponry was superlative. In addition to the fearsome Celtic war chariot, the Belgae were armed with iron swords, daggers, and iron-tipped spears, against which the defending Albans could generally pit only bronze, stone, and wood.

Prisoners taken by the Celts who were not massacred were frequently enslaved. Scottish historian Ian Grimble, quoting classical sources, writes that the Celts would barter a slave for a jar of wine, or even for a drink, as though slaves were too readily taken to be of much value. Grimble also notes that iron slave chains used for fastening victims together in batches have been excavated from a number of Celtic sites in Britain.[2]

No agreement exists as to the scope, nature, and timing of the Celtic invasion and occupation of Britain. What follows is my own reconstruction.

Where the terrain favoured their weapons and tactics, the Celts drove irresistibly forward. Only those natives who lived in, or who fled to, dense swamps, thick forests, or the highlands avoided being overwhelmed.

The Belgae seem to have made their primary bridgeheads along the coasts of what are now Sussex, Kent, and Essex. But by the mid-third century B.C., they, together with other Celtic invaders, had occupied most of lowland Alba south of Morecambe Bay on the west coast and Tynemouth on the east.

Lowland Alba, be it noted. The highlands of Wales, Cumbria, and the Pennines, together with most of the rugged Cornish peninsula, remained bastions of resistance. The *autochthones* of the Welsh, Pennine, and Cumbrian highlands were *never* entirely subdued, although, at a much later time when the Celts themselves became refugees from new invaders, Celts and their language inundated the high country.

Cornwall, which seems still to have been free of Celts at the time of Pytheas's visit, may have held out until as late as the first century B.C. It was probably able to do so not just because of its difficult terrain, but because its people were supported by related Armorican tribes of Brittany, whose naval prowess the Celts were never able to match.

Ireland did not escape. By the end of the third or fourth century B.C. the Celts, having subdued the lowlands of central Britain, reached the shores of St. George's Channel. Soon they began crossing over to raid the Irish coast. Land-taking followed, and in due course most of Ireland was occupied.

Northward advance of the Celts in England was slowed by the nature of the country. Britain's interior grows more mountainous as the waist of the great island constricts. Celtic advances by land beyond the Morecambe Bay–Tynemouth line had to be made along ever-narrowing coastal corridors squeezed between highlands and the sea. And the highlands were held by Albans.

The Cumbrian Mountains crowd so close to the western ocean that northbound invaders would have been at constant risk of being attacked on their landward flank and driven into the sea. Some few seaborne Celtic raiders seem eventually to have bypassed the Cumbrian massif to establish a tenuous foothold on the shores of Solway Firth, but that appears to have been their high-water mark.

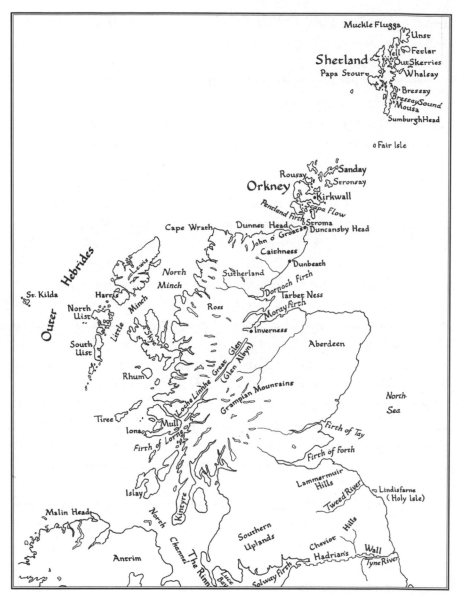

Map of Scotland.

    The eastern invasion route north from Tynemouth was somewhat less formidable, at least in its southern reaches. Here the coastal plain was generally broad enough to have permitted war chariots to manoeuvre. However, highlands always loomed threateningly close, and these were held by men able and willing to make an enemy advance difficult and costly.

By about the middle of the second century B.C., the Celtic invasion had dragged to a halt somewhat to the south of the line of the Cheviot Hills, between Solway Firth on the Atlantic and the mouth of the River Tweed on the North Sea.

Much of British Alba was now no longer Alban. The Celtic influx had submerged most of Pytheas's *autochthones*, excepting those who were ensconced in highland refuges. *And* except for those north of the Cheviot line.

Alba still survived in good order in the north. The mainland population of Scotland remained essentially what it had been for millennia: pastoral hillmen in the central and western regions and plainsmen in the east, but stockmen all, with flocks of long-legged sheep and herds of shaggy cattle as their principal terrestrial source of sustenance.

Life in the Northern and Western Islands also continued to unfold as of old. Although the climate had by then become too cool and wet to nurture many crops, the surrounding waters still thronged with fishes, seals, and whales. In season, flightless great auks abounded on offshore skerries, and bird cliffs were crowded with nesting murres, gannets, gulls, and fulmars. In spring and fall migrant ducks, geese, and swans filled freshwater lochs.

The Islanders continued voyaging to Tilli. Orkney traders carried valuta south to the Scillies and brought back foreign goods. Returning southern voyagers may sometimes have been accompanied by Armorican vessels from the Channel coast of France. The presence of the formidable Armorican ships would surely have been welcomed by the Islanders as additional defence against Celtic buccaneers in the Irish Sea.

By the first century B.C. the situation in Britain seems to have become more or less stabilized. But a new disruption was threatening from across the Channel. The same people who had dispossessed the tribes of the Alban Hills were moving west.

Rome's legions were on the march.

CHAPTER SIX

ARMORICA

O NE DECEMBER NIGHT IN 1942 I FOUND MYSELF
in charge of a platoon of weary infantrymen taking part in a
battle exercise near Oban in western Scotland. Laden like
beasts, we had scrambled for six hours through morasses of saturated
bog, up and down ankle-turning scree slopes, in and out of icy streams
and tarns, always under a deluge of frigid rain mingled with gusts of sleet.

Shortly after midnight we scaled a ridge which might, or might not,
have been our intended objective. I was by no means sure. One thing *was*
certain: we had gone about as far as we could go. So we "went to ground,"
and I reported back by radio that we had reached the objective.

"Just where the hell are you? You've been gone long enough!" The
static-distorted voice was that of my company commander.

"Two sections sited forward on the ridge, sir," I replied evasively.
"Platoon headquarters established in a—" I peered at a damp map in my
flashlight's dim glow "—in a Pict house under the crest."

The earphones crackled. "God Almighty, Mowat! I hope to hell you
got permission before you moved in! I've had enough goddamn trouble
already with civilian claims for damages. Bleeding Scots don't seem to
know there's a war on!"

"Not to worry, sir. There'll be no complaints from this lot."

I could be reasonably sure of that. The *Pict House* marked on my disintegrating map was no more than a depression in a sea of boulders—
one that had not been occupied by anyone or anything except stray
sheep since time immemorial.

What my company commander did not know was that Pict Houses are peppered all across the ordinance survey maps of Scotland. The name clings to hundreds of otherwise unidentifiable ruins, mounds, or depressions which were thought to have had a human origin. Or maybe, in the case of the Little People of Scotland, a non-human one.

For countless generations the name has been synonymous with the mysterious—not just amongst ordinary Scots, but amongst scholars too. An actual Pictish presence in Scotland during the first millennium A.D. is confirmed by Roman and other sources; yet almost nothing seems to have been certainly established about the origins of a people who neither spoke nor wrote any known language and whose intricately carved, but inscrutable, symbol stones, found all across Scotland, confound historians to this day.

Who *were* the Picts? Where did they come from? Questions seemingly without answers.

My December-night brush with Picts remained buried in the back of my mind for several decades. However, after I began seeking the identity of the shadowy figures who had preceded the Norse across the North Atlantic, the Picts emerged from memory. It seemed possible that they might hold part of the answer to my quest.

The maritime districts of west-central Gaul, especially Normandy, Brittany, and Poitou, constituted the Armorica of classical times. In the second century B.C., these regions, which included the highlands of Colline de Normandie and the Breton peninsula, were home to more than a dozen tribes sharing ancestry with the Aquitainians and Basques to the southward, and with British Albans across the Channel. Their ancient cultural connections are memorialized by an astounding array of megalithic constructs, including the remains of ten thousand standing stones at Carnac on the south coast of Brittany; a fantastic assemblage of dolmens, burial chambers, and tumuli in Galicia in the western Pyrénées; the titanic ruins of Stonehenge; and the massive stone structures of western Main Island in Orkney.

The Armoricans of classical times were prosperous traders and skilled navigators whose shipping dominated the Bay of Biscay, the English Channel, and portions of the North Sea. They carried cargo between the Mediterranean and northwestern Europe in big seaworthy ships. These vessels, combined with virtually impregnable island fortresses, made the Armoricans almost invincible. Almost. They had been successfully repelling the Celts for generations, if not centuries, when, in 57 B.C., Julius Caesar arrived on the scene intent on conquering western Europe and Gaul in particular.

Initially the Armoricans welcomed the Romans as allies against a common, Celtic enemy. When Publius Crassus, one of Caesar's generals, marched the 7th Legion into their territories on a pretended reconnaissance mission, they received the Romans in friendly fashion. Even when Crassus demanded hostages for good behaviour, the Armoricans acquiesced.

While Crassus was thus infiltrating Armorican territory, Caesar's legions were busy elsewhere with sword and spear, smashing the Belgae north of the Seine and driving Germano-Celtic tribes out of northeastern Gaul. By the end of 57, Caesar had crushed most of the Celtic tribes in central and southeastern France.

Crassus had not been idle. Applying the principle of divide and conquer, he had maintained friendly relations with the Armoricans *north* of the Loire (especially with the powerful Veneti tribe), while he dealt with those south of the Loire, including the large and wealthy state of the Picts (*Pictones* in Caesar's *Commentaries*). History does not tell us how he accomplished his purpose, only that he succeeded in "pacifying" the Pictones. Later events suggest he did this by seizing their ports and shipping while the Picts were treating him and his troops as allies.

This left the Armoricans north of the Loire still to be dealt with. Having seen what had happened to their kinsfolk to the south, they were not about to fall victims to the same ploy. So Crassus devised a different gambit.

During the winter of 57–56 he sent military missions to the northern Armorican states, demanding tribute. The Armoricans were outraged. This was no way to treat allies! Not only did they refuse but, as Crassus had doubtless anticipated, they seized the Roman emissaries, vowing to hold them until their own hostages were released.

Caesar now had what he considered to be a legitimate excuse for attacking the Armoricans.

To this end, he constructed a fleet of warships on the Loire, then, having instructed Crassus to keep the Pictones quiet, and to prevent the Aquitainians from sending help to their northern neighbours, he led his army into Brittany.

The campaign went badly. The Romans had great difficulty dealing with Armorican coastal redoubts. If and when they did threaten to capture one, the defenders simply embarked their people, possessions, and supplies, and sailed off to another stronghold.

Caesar had no choice but to try his luck at sea. The vessels that had been built for him on the Loire were mostly galleys: light and low, equipped with rams and grappling hooks, and powered by oars. Most Armorican vessels, on the other hand, were merchant ships. They are described in the *Commentaries* as being of great size, oak built, strong and high as citadels, fastened with iron nails as thick as a man's thumb, and equipped with dressed leather sails that could withstand the worst Atlantic gales. They were fit to go almost anywhere, and indeed made regular voyages to Britain, south to Spain, and north into the Baltic.

Given open water and a breeze of wind, they had little to fear from Roman galleys. But Caesar surprised the Armorican fleet harboured in the shoal-strewn and confined waters of Morbihan Bay in Veneti territory. To make matters worse, what little wind there was dropped out, leaving the Armorican ships becalmed and unable to manoeuvre. In this state they were mobbed by scores of galleys, and boarded. Although the battle lasted eight hours, it ended with the capture of most of the Armorican fleet. "By this victory," the *Commentaries* tell us, "the war with the Veneti and the whole of the sea coast was finished."

Not *quite* finished. To drive the lesson home, Caesar had the entire Veneti senate murdered. Captured Armorican sailors and soldiers were slaughtered out of hand, except for the young and comely, who were sold into slavery.

Caesar had now effectively completed his conquest of Gaul and had imposed upon it the *pax Romana*...but not all his victims were ready to resign themselves to defeat and servitude.

In 52 B.C. a Celt named Vercingetorix, chief of the Arverni tribe, raised what soon became a country-wide rebellion. Having learned the hard way that they could not trust the Romans, the Armoricans now chose to throw in their lot with their one-time Celtic enemies in a war of liberation against Rome.

The rebels had a number of initial successes; then they began to lose. Vercingetorix was captured and sent to Rome in chains. Thereafter, Caesar's legions destroyed the Celtic forces piecemeal.

By 51, little resistance remained, except in the country of the Picts, where most of the Armorican land force had concentrated. Although their cause was as good as lost, they chose not to surrender—perhaps because they were all too well aware of the fate awaiting them if they did. As the Romans closed in from all sides, they fought on. Then, late in the summer of 51, the legions surprised what remained of the Armorican army as it was attempting to withdraw across the Loire into the high country of Brittany. According to the *Commentaries*, the Romans "slew as long as their horses had strength to pursue and their hands to strike. So more than twelve thousand armed men and men who had thrown down their arms were slain."

Gaul was now become a savaged and a ravaged land, having endured massive bloodshed, enormous physical devastation, and the dislocation of many of its peoples. Rome had conquered, in the name of civilization, and Caesar was free to enjoy his triumphs.

As for the Armoricans, they were free to choose between being slaughtered, sold into foreign slavery, or reduced to servitude to retired legionnaires and immigrants from Roman client states. It was Rome's intention, and the Armoricans' fate, that they should disappear.

Recorded history is almost devoid of any further mention of them. They appear to have vanished from the face of the earth. But, as we need frequently to remind ourselves, history is generally written by the victors and, as such, can be exceedingly misleading, when it does not deliberately lie. In the case of the Armoricans, I believe the truth is that they survived—in part at least. What follows is my reconstruction of the missing pages of their story.

Late in the summer and on into autumn of the ill-fated year 51 B.C., scores and perhaps hundreds of vessels of all sizes put out from the great sweep of coast lying between the Seine and the Garonne. They were filled to the gunwales with livestock, material possessions, and people turning to the sea in order to avoid destruction upon the land.

The Armoricans still retained control of the offshore islands. These included the Channel Islands (Jersey, Guernsey, Alderney, and Sark); Ushant, off the tip of the Breton peninsula; and others along the shores of the Bay of Biscay. Unfortunately, none was large enough, or sufficiently beyond Roman reach, to serve as a long-term sanctuary.

Nevertheless, the islands could, and did, afford temporary refuge. Their harbours were soon jammed with shipping; their meadows overrun with cattle; their houses and sheds bulging with people; and their hillsides patched with tent villages. They had become staging places for an exodus to distant shores.

But *what* distant shores could offer a new home? To the south, the Roman legions ruled. The lands to the north and east of Roman-occupied Gaul belonged to bellicose Celtic and Germanic tribes who were no friends to the Armoricans.

The refugees' best hope for sanctuary lay across the English Channel.

In earlier times they might have emigrated to southern Britain and settled amongst a related people with whom they had visited and traded for centuries. But by now most of Britain south of the Cheviot Hills, together with all or most of Ireland, was in Celtic hands. And the short-lived marriage of convenience between Celts and Armoricans had ended with the completion of Caesar's conquest of Gaul.

Furthermore, a massive new Celtic exodus led by a particularly fearsome Belgic tribe, the Atrebates, was streaming across narrow Dover Strait into southern England, itself trying to escape extermination at the hands of the Romans. The arrival of the Atrebates in Britain touched off fierce clashes with earlier Celtic invaders. Any Armoricans foolhardy enough to have sought refuge in southern Britain at this time would have been scorched between raging fires.

There remained one place still out of reach either of Rome or of the Celts, where Armoricans might hope to receive, if not a warm welcome, at least a non-hostile reception. This was the surviving bastion of old Alba in the north. Its inhabitants were of the same ancient physical and linguistic stock as the Armoricans. And not only did they share many cultural traits; they also shared a common enemy, the Celts.

So north Alba became the destination of the exiled Armoricans. To reach it they faced a long voyage in heavily laden ships sailing along

mostly hostile coasts. Good sailing weather was of paramount importance; and the best came in summer. There was also the need to arrive in
the new land with time in hand to settle in before the onset of the northern winter. Since the summer of 51 was already nearly spent, the departure
of the refugees from the islands was postponed until the following year.

The intervening months were spent refitting ships and stocking
them with food for people and fodder for cattle. During the autumn of
51, scout vessels reconnoitred Britain's coasts for places where landings
might safely be made and supplies of food and water renewed. Swift
ships bearing leading men of the several Armorican tribes were dispatched to apprise the northern Albans of what was happening and to
negotiate a friendly reception.

The exodus began late in the spring of 50. Not all the refugees
departed from the same ports or followed the same courses. Most of
those fleeing from the south, including the Picts, took their departures
from Ushant. In squadrons of varying size, sailing as weather and the
state of preparedness allowed, they steered across the mouth of the
Channel to the Scilly Islands, which had for close to a thousand years
been the principal rendezvous for men from Mediterranean, west
Iberian, and Biscayan ports trading with the British Isles.

This contingent intended to go west around England, sailing through
St. George's Channel into the Irish Sea, thence to the west coast of southern Scotland via the North Channel. Once in the North Channel the
ships could anticipate friendly, or at least neutral, shores to starboard.
However, the coast of Ireland was firmly in Celtic hands—as one flotilla
of Pictish ships discovered for itself.

> The Britons [Celts]…who, carried over into Britain, it is reported, from
> Armorica, possessed themselves of the southern parts. When [sometime
> after] they had made themselves masters of the greatest part of the island
> beginning in the south, Picts from Scythia [the Scillies], as is reported,
> putting to sea in a few large ships, were driven by wind beyond the shores
> of Britain, and arrived on the northeast coast of Ireland, where, finding the
> nation of the Scots [Irish Celts], they begged to be allowed to settle amongst
> them, but could not succeed in obtaining their request.[1] The Scots
> answered that the island could not contain them both, but "we can give

you good advice what to do: we know there is another island, not far from ours, to the east, which we often see at a distance when the days are clear. If you go there you will obtain a settlement."...The Picts accordingly, sailing over into Britain, began to inhabit the northern part of that island.

So wrote the Venerable Bede. There are ambiguities in his account, which is hardly surprising considering that he lived and wrote several centuries after the event. What surely *is* surprising is that such a clear and unequivocal description of a major event in British history, and one, moreover, recorded by an authority of Bede's stature, should have been consistently ignored or belittled by most professional historians. Possibly because it was at odds with the orthodox view of history, scholars have generally chosen to relegate it to the realm of mythology, thereby transforming the sole surviving account of the arrival of the Armoricans in northern Britain into nothing more than a piece of Irish embroidery. The Venerable Bede knew better, and so did the Picts from Gaul who became the Picts of Scotland.[2]

Fugitives from northern Armorica (the coastal tribes between Brittany and the mouth of the Seine, including the Curiosolites, Redones, and Unelli) assembled at the Channel Islands, which had always been Armorican strongholds.

These people then sailed "east around," keeping the British coast to port. Although this route was slightly longer, it offered a major advantage in that it led directly to the extensive and fertile coastal plains between the Firth of Forth and Moray Firth.

The eastbound contingent also consisted of a number of squadrons, each composed of a small enough number of vessels to be able to keep contact in bad weather. Sailing both by day and by night, and maintaining a good offing, they entered the North Sea. Even then they avoided closing with the land, for the great seaward bulge of Norfolk and Suffolk offered little shelter and, moreover, was firmly in Celtic hands.

Eventually they made their way to the Farne Islands some twenty miles south of the mouth of the Tweed. This may have been their final rendezvous before bringing the long voyage to an end.

The decision as to how to deal with the would-be Armorican immigrants posed a considerable dilemma to the northern Albans, who were faced with something of a Hobson's choice. If they refused permission to land, they could expect to be invaded by several thousand desperate refugees. But how were they to absorb such a flood of new people in a land whose resources were already strained by influxes of Albans from the southern parts of Britain that had earlier been overrun by the Celts?

I suspect that the northern Albans attempted to make a virtue out of necessity. The Armoricans had a well-found fleet. If they could be settled on what currently amounted to border lands between Albans and Celts, they might serve Alba's interests on land as well as at sea.

These border regions were in jeopardy. Pressure from the influx of Celtic refugees into southern Britain was now being felt along the frontiers of Alba. Probing Celts were already turning the fertile sweep of the Merse plain in the green valley of the Tweed into a no man's land. Raiders were even probing northward into the guardian hills between the Tweed and the heartland Forth country. Realizing that the Tweed valley was in danger of being lost, I think the Albans "gave" it to the immigrant Armoricans to have and to hold…if they were able.

A similar situation obtained in the west. There the Celts controlling the south shore of Solway Firth were warring for the flat and fertile lands at its head and along its northern shore. Armoricans settled there could serve to keep the Celts at bay.

The number of immigrants involved remains unknown. The *Commentaries* tell us the Armoricans contributed 30,000 men (of whom a quarter were Pictones) to Vercingetorix's rebellion. This suggests an Armorican population of at least 150,000. Taking into consideration losses suffered at Roman hands, and assuming that not all survivors were able or willing to flee the country, it may be that only a few thousand émigrés reached northern Alba.

Nevertheless, the Armoricans (with the Picts foremost amongst them) would henceforward play a major role in the history of the land that eventually came to be known as Scotland.

CHAPTER SEVEN

WAR IN
THE NORTH

BEING ESSENTIALLY PASTORALISTS, AND SPENDING the greater part of their time with their flocks and herds, Albans would have had small tolerance for urbanites. But Armorican society had been essentially urban. And if these one-time town dwellers ran true to form, they would have regarded their hayseed hosts with condescension, if not contempt. Inevitable friction between people of two such disparate ways of life could alone have led to serious conflict.

Nor was it likely to have been long before the Armoricans, whether cast in the role of frontier guards or simply because they felt penned up in inadequate pockets of Alban land, began looking covetously northward, especially towards the spacious plains east of the Grampian mountain massif. For their part, the Albans would have found themselves in a situation comparable to that of the fabled Arab who allowed a camel to put its head inside his tent.[1]

By as early as 40 B.C., tensions between the two peoples may have already erupted into open hostilities.

Doubtless the Armoricans had the initial advantage, for they had long been used to living at arms and were skilled fighters. Northern Albans seem to have been militarily unpractised prior to the appearance of Celtic invaders on their borders not so many generations before the arrival of the fugitive Armoricans. The Celtic threat had been contained, not so much because of any military prowess possessed by the Albans as because the Celtic thrust ran out of steam. Nevertheless, the Albans proved to be talented innovators in the art of defensive warfare.

Stalemated along Alba's southern borders, the only significant threat the Celts continued to pose was from sea-borne raids of the hit-and-run variety, chiefly undertaken in pursuit of vengeance, slaves, and loot. A dozen Celts in an open boat, or perhaps two or three boatloads acting in concert, might come skulking along the coast, seeking to surprise an isolated Alban croft; capture or kill the inhabitants; slaughter the livestock; rob the houses of anything worthwhile; then set the thatch aflame and row away before the neighbours could rally.

People living along such threatened coasts responded by building ring- or D-shaped little strongholds (now called duns, Gaelic for forts), of unmortared stone. These structures, raised by the descendants of megalithic master masons, were so well made that the cost of reducing them would generally have been more than their contents were worth.

Few duns have been found along the east coast, where Celtic seaborne raiders seem never to have been much of a problem. However, Albans in the west erected numbers of such small "homestead" forts. As time passed and raiders grew more determined, the defenders became increasingly inventive, producing so-called galleried duns, which are thought by some to have been ancestral to one of the most remarkable and effective defensive structures of antiquity—the broch.[2]

One June day my wife and I visited the Broch of Carloway on the northwestern coast of the Isle of Lewis. A gale blowing out of the Western Ocean had cleared the skies, leaving them as harshly blue as the eye of a Celtic god. They glared down on burnished seas that raged against the Outer Hebrides, roared out their fury, and fell away in a smother of foam from the feet of a bald ridge topped by a round stone tower.

Although partly ruined, the tower still stood to a height of forty feet, almost as high as it was round. It still looked as steadfast as it must have seemed to the men who reared it on its granite ridge some two thousand years before our time.

We climbed to it up a slippery pathway through a swirling mob of sheep, seemingly the only other living beings about. In the canyoned little cove below us, a cluster of Hebridean blackhouses, their thatched roofs rotted away and low stone walls overgrown with green turf, testified that people, too, had once lived under the protection of this tower.

We had to bend low to enter the sole portal, which was capped with

Claire Mowat beside the ruins of the Broch of Carloway, which still stands guard on the west coast of the Isle of Lewis in the Hebrides.

a lintel stone that must have weighed a ton. A tunnel-like entrance passage, layered deep with sheep dung, pierced the ten-foot-thick ring foundation supporting the broch's double walls, opening into a central chamber about twenty feet in diameter, tapering upward like the barrel of a gigantic cannon.

An even smaller interior doorway gave access to a dark and narrow intramural space up which a stone stairway had once spiralled to the top of the tower. The surviving stone treads were slimy with moss, but I scrambled up until a jackdaw, disturbed from her nest, flapped black wings in my face, and a stone dislodged by my passage fell with a warning clatter into the darkness under foot.

Before descending, I peered through a crevice in the outer wall and found I could see right across the wide mouth of Loch Roag, and beyond to a maze of islands through which the boats of raiders from the south would have had to thread their way.

When I regained the floor of the central chamber, Claire drew my attention to a rotted timber protruding from a black heap of stones. I knew that any wood which might have been used in the broch's original

An aerial view of the Mousa broch in Scotland—perhaps the best preserved broch extant.

construction would long since have turned to dust, so later that day when I encountered a local historian I asked him about this anomaly. He told me we had been looking at the remains of a roof made of pole rafters covered with thatch.

"'Twas a hoosie inside the broch, ye see, built by a crofter for his family. Puir folk, they were. Driven off their wee holding in my own grandfather's time to make room for the laird's sheep. Their croft was pulled down around their haids by the laird's men, so they fled to yon auld pile o'stanes for shelter."

He paused and looked past me into the darkened western sky.

"They wouldna' hae been the first, ye ken. Though maybe the last."

Brochs bear a superficial resemblance to the cooling towers of nuclear power stations, but were entirely constructed of drystone masonry. No mortar at all was used, yet they could sustain themselves to heights of fifty feet. No windows pierced the outer of a broch's double walls. Entrance could be gained only through one small portal at or near ground level. This could be stopped up with a massive wooden door and was further protected by internal guard cells set into the walls of the entrance passage.

Flaming arrows could not fire a broch, and its walls were too high to be topped by scaling ladders. Until the advent of war engines capable of flinging heavy or explosive projectiles, brochs were virtually impregnable to direct assault.

They could, of course, be laid under siege. But the people crowding the multi-tiered wooden galleries circling the inner walls had either a well or a cistern to provide water, together with quantities of dried or preserved food for man and beast. Starving them out would have required more time than most raiders could have afforded.

Some scholars contend the broch was the end product of a long and gradual evolution; but there seems to be a mysterious gap between the most advanced dun and the earliest broch, giving the impression that the latter sprang onto the northern stage full blown in all its elegant intricacy. A friend tells me he has seen hollow-walled towers of very similar construction in the mountainous interior of Corsica—which was itself an Alban stronghold until relatively modern times.

The earliest British brochs may have been reared on the Rinns of Galloway, an almost-island peninsula to the west of Solway Firth. The Rinns parallels the northeast coast of Ireland for nearly thirty miles and is only a little more than twenty miles distant.

It is a green and pleasant land favoured by humankind since the mesolithic era. In Alban times, its fat cattle and sheep must have been much coveted by Irish Celts who, in good weather, could (as Bede has told us) have seen it across the North Channel. I suspect the Scotti and their neighbours made a practice of raiding the Rinns—until brochs sprouted up on the peninsula, effectively spoiling the raiders' fun.

It does not require much imagination to envisage disgruntled Celts on the Antrim coast of Ireland directing the Pictish refugees of the Venerable Bede's account to the Rinns across the water—in hopes of killing two birds with one stone, or at least of seeing them kill one another.

Three ruined brochs still stand on the Rinns, sited so as to protect the rich farmlands along the shores of Luce Bay. All three are so similar in design and construction as to almost certainly have been the work of one directing mind. Was this the place the broch was born?

Very few of the five hundred known brochs are south of the mighty rift called the Great More, the Great Glen, or, as some old maps testify, Glen

Albyn, that divides northern Scotland into two almost separate regions.

In fact, only five brochs have been found in western Scotland south of Glen Albyn, and eight to the south and east of it. Three of the latter stand in south-facing valleys of the Lammermuir–Moorfoot mountains separating the Tweed valley from the lowlands of the Forth. Two others stand near the foot of the Forth itself, and two more north of and inland from the Firth of Tay. All are of the same early type as the Rinns brochs, and some show evidence of hasty construction.

This eastern group seems to have been sited in an attempt to block invasion from the south, but this is a role the broch was not designed to play. The garrison of a blocking fort should be able to sally out to disrupt the progress of an invading force; yet brochs had no sally ports, just a single narrow door through which only one man at a time could emerge to engage the enemy. Furthermore, these early brochs had no outer defence works, which are an absolute necessity if a blocking fort is to do its job.

Although the Albans may have built this handful of southern brochs to discourage Celtic raids through the hill passes, they might also have been intended to stem a breakout to the north from the Tweed valley by Armorican "guests." If this was the case, it would have been wasted effort, since the Armoricans seem to have made their move by sea instead of by land.

Here is how I see the conflict unfolding.

In the east the newcomers used their ships to execute a right hook around the Lammermuir–Moorfoot barrier in order to seize bridgeheads northward along the eastern seaboard. Successful landings near North Berwick and on the Fife peninsula gave them control of the Firth of Forth. Bypassing the two brochs which were all that still stood in their way, they pressed westward across Scotland's narrow waist to link up with compatriots advancing from the Atlantic side.

Those Armoricans who had settled on the north shore of Solway Firth outflanked the Rinns brochs by sea to land along the shores of the Firth of Clyde and seize the lowlands between Ayr and Ardrossan. They then thrust up the Firth Valley to meet their compatriots from the east.

Thereafter the two groups joined forces to make further landings on the east coast, leapfrogging northward until they were in possession of all the eastern lowlands up to Moray Firth. They do not seem to have made much of an attempt to seize land in the west north of the Clyde, probably because this rough country was of little agricultural worth.

The Albans were unable to prevent the occupation of much of their country. Forced to abandon the lowlands, some fled north by boat or on foot. Some retreated into the hills south of the Clyde–Forth valley or withdrew into the rugged Grampian massif to the north of it, where they maintained a hillman's way of life of the sort many beleaguered Alban people elsewhere had been forced to adopt in the past.

By the end of the first century B.C., the situation had become more or less stabilized. Armoricans held most of the arable land south of Glen Albyn. Free Alba had shrunk to that part of Scotland north of the Glen, including the several archipelagos.

For some time the Armoricans did not push beyond the Glen, both because the country north of that great rift was extremely rugged, and because they had land enough to meet their current needs. The day would come when they would go north again; but when they did, they would encounter an almost impregnable Alban defence.

Seizing the Alban lowlands had been one thing. Living on them proved to be something else.

Aided by their brethren north of the Glen, Albans who had retreated into the interior of the southern and central regions waged guerrilla war on their former guests, subjecting Armoricans in the lowlands to punishing raids.

Unable to pacify the interior, the Armoricans attempted to contain it by sealing off its exits with a ring of forts, each large enough to shelter nearby settlers while serving as a base from which the garrison could sally out to repel raids.

The Armoricans built scores of such forts, virtually encircling the southern and central mountain massifs and, in the north, forming a defensive line against incursions from beyond Glen Albyn. Most were variants of a type traditional in central and western Europe. Stone-faced walls were back-filled with earth, rocks, and rubble—the whole being stabilized by transverse timber baulks.

Known to archaeologists as "timber-laced forts," these structures were relatively easy to build, but had a serious weakness. When their massive wooden tie-beams dried, they became extremely flammable. If an assailant was able to start a blaze against an outer wall (or inside, by means of fire arrows), the bracing timbers would be likely to ignite, whereupon the entire structure was able to become a raging pyre. The resultant conflagrations generated such intense heat that stone facings and fill sometimes melted, producing characteristically fused heaps of rubble now known as "vitrified forts." It is surely significant that a high proportion of Scotland's timber-laced forts have been "vitrified."[3]

Alban highlanders harassing Armoricans in their lowland holdings were doubtless reinforced by men from free Alba filtering across the Glen Albyn frontier into the heart of the Grampians. The frontier zone extended roughly from the Isle of Mull, northeast along the Great Glen to the vicinity of Glen Urquhart, where it swung north to follow the edge of the high ground to reach the sea at Dornoch Firth.

Despite their forts, few Armorican settlements could have felt secure. The threatening presence of highland reivers so shadowed the lowlands as to become an integral part of the traditions of Scotland.

Unable to root the hillmen out of their lairs, the Armoricans retaliated against free Alba. Because the mountainous interior north of Glen Albyn was virtually impenetrable—it is still called *Rough Bounds*—they attacked the Glen's seaward ends.

In the west, with the help of their navy, they managed to force a corridor from the Sound of Arisaig up Loch Eil to Glen Albyn. In the east they took Black Isle and a large part of the Tarbat Peninsula. The abundance of vitrified forts throughout these regions testifies to the fierceness of the struggle.

But, try as they might, the Armoricans were unable to make any further gains of consequence, because by now the Albans had learned how to use their best weapon to best effect.

Some unsung genius had hit upon the idea of erecting several brochs close enough together to be mutually supporting. Individual brochs could keep in communication through line-of-sight signals, including smoke by day and fire by night. Now they were also provided with outworks from which sorties could be launched. If one broch was dangerously beleaguered, men from the others could mount a counter-attack against the enemy's rear or create a diversion by threatening to cut his line of retreat, a particularly potent ploy against seaborne raiders since it threatened their boats.

By shortly after the turn of the millennium, a stone forest of brochs had sprung up along free Alba's endangered coasts and in some strategic inland regions. These proved so effective against enemy incursions that Alba lost no more territory.

The small island of Tiree in the southern reaches of the Hebridean Sea provides a good example of the new defence.[4] Largely covered by pasture land, Tiree was, and remains, one of the most agriculturally desirable islands in Scottish waters, a nearly irresistible target for raiders and would-be land takers. Its defenders reared *eight* broch towers within sight of one another. Under their protection, Tiree seems never to have fallen into the hands of either Armoricans or Celts, although, as we shall see, the Irish made at least one strenuous attempt against it.

All over free Alba, and especially in Caithness, Orkney, Shetland, and the Hebrides, the brochs repelled attempts to seize the lands they guarded. They formed a palisade of dragon's teeth.

If the Albans' enemies were unable to establish permanent footholds north of the Great Glen, seaborne raiders could nevertheless still thrust and harry. This they did along the mainland coast from Dornoch Firth to Pentland Firth and occasionally as far north as Shetland. They also struck inland up the major river valleys of Sutherland and Caithness. But although they undoubtedly took a toll of people, livestock, and crops, they were not able to dispossess Albans of their land. Emerging from the safety of their towers after a raid, the crofters rebuilt what had been destroyed and carried on with their lives.

Armoricans mostly raided in northeastern Alba, while Irish Celts did the same in the west. Old Irish annals give us a glimpse of one such raid led by the semi-legendary Labraid Loinseach:

> He smote eight towers in Tiree...and eight strongholds of the men of Skye....He ventured upon many of the islands of Orkney.

Notably, this celebration of Gaelic valour does not claim that the mighty Loinseach *captured* any of the brochs he "smote." Excavation of a broch at Gurness in Orkney starkly reveals the price attackers such as he were forced to pay. Ian Grimble tells us, in *Highland Man*, how excavation of the garbage dump of the Gurness broch revealed

a grisly reminder of the past, a pair of severed hands flung into the midden before anyone had even removed the five rings from their fingers. These belonged to the superb Celtic tradition of continental metalwork of an earlier age, and one may picture their wearer, perhaps tall, blond haired and bedecked with gold toque and armbands, done to death on one of his raiding expeditions by the broch builders.

CHAPTER EIGHT

PICTLANDIA

AS THE FIRST CENTURY A.D. UNFOLDED, ALBANS continued to wage guerrilla war from the highlands. Free Alba north of the Great Glen remained unsubdued. In the west, the Irish were becoming ever more aggressive and more covetous of the rich lowlands of Galloway and Argyll. British Celts had taken advantage of the conflict to press north—towards Solway Firth on the west coast and, on the east, to the approaches to the Tweed valley.

Worse was to come.

In A.D. 43 the Claudian invasion of Britain began. Within thirty years Roman legions were slashing their way into the territory of the Celtic Brigantes who controlled the country on both sides of the Pennines. By 71 the Solway–Tyne line had become a de facto frontier between the new Roman province of Britain and the "barbarians of the north."

Our knowledge of what was happening in the north around this time comes mainly from the writings of Publius Cornelius Tacitus, a protégé of the powerful Roman Gnaeus Julius Agricola. Tacitus tells us:

> Agricola was consul and I but a youngster when he betrothed me to his daughter, a maiden of noble promise even then. When his consulate ended he married me to her then immediately departed to become governor of Britain.

Tacitus repaid Agricola by faithfully, if not impartially, recording his patron's achievements.

In the late summer of 78, Agricola crossed the Channel to find his new province in turmoil. The new governor marched north, bloodily rapping the knuckles of various rebellious Celtic tribes en route. By the autumn of 79 he had re-established Roman control up to the Solway–Tyne line.

The record is not clear what happened next. Many historians have made their own reconstructions. What follows is a synthesis of these, viewed in the light of my own investigations.

If he was to hold the salient he had established, Agricola had to neutralize the hilly, densely wooded, and almost impenetrable Strathclyde border country. Early in the summer of 80, he set out to do this by means of a double encirclement, one arm of which would sweep north and east to, and beyond, Solway Firth, while the other swept north along the eastern coastal plain, then west to meet its fellow.

The earlier Celtic thrust along the eastern corridor had failed because Celtic supply and communication lines had been at the mercy of Alban raiders driving down from the mountainous left flank. Agricola had an answer to that. He deployed a fleet of naval and transport vessels to render his marching troops largely independent of land communications. As the vanguard troops of the Roman army in the east fought their way north from a base near the mouth of the Tyne, they built a string of heavily garrisoned forts, supported and supplied from seaward.

The east-coast thrust ended for the season at an unidentified place called Taus, which may have been the lagoon lying behind Holy Island, or Lindisfarne, as it is now called. In the west the Romans reached Solway Firth in the vicinity of Carlisle.

The campaign of the following year was mainly waged against a people the Romans at first called Caledonians. Tacitus seems to have thought they were yet another British (Celtic) tribe, but later Romans called them Picts.[1]

If Agricola failed to realize who these people were, they were in no doubt as to who *he* was. Not much more than a century earlier, his ancestors had driven theirs out of Gaul. One can imagine the hatred and the fury with which the Armoricans would have viewed the approach of these not-so-ancient enemies.

Tacitus gives no details of the early stages of the ensuing conflict. He tells us only that in the summer of 81 Agricola occupied the narrow isthmus between the Firth of Forth and the Firth of Clyde.

> The estuaries of Clota [the Clyde] and Bodotria [the Forth] carry the tides of two opposite seas so far back into the country that they are separated by only a narrow strip of land. This strip Agricola began to defend with a line of forts and, as the country to the south was now in our hands, the enemy was pushed [north] into what might be considered almost another island.

The claim that "the south was now in our hands" was premature. Much of the western border country south of the Clyde remained in Pictish hands.

Agricola returned to the attack in the spring of 82—but instead of striking northward across the isthmus, his troops had to cross back over the Clyde somewhere near its mouth and fight their way south and west to complete the encirclement of southern Scotland. This took most of the summer, during which Agricola seems to have been briefly tempted by a new prospect to the westward.

> He stationed troops in that part of the country looking toward Ireland, anticipating a fresh conquest....I have heard him say that with a single legion and a few auxiliaries he could take and occupy Ireland, and that this would have a salutary effect on all Britain since Roman arms would then be everywhere, and all freedom banished.[2]

Much as Agricola may have lusted after conquest in Ireland, the need to crush the barbarians in northern Scotland remained paramount. "He dreaded a general mobilization of these frontier tribes," Tacitus tells us. And with good reason. During the winter of 82–83, "the tribes of Caledonia flew to arms and advanced to attack our forts [in the isthmus, where the Roman army was wintering] a challenge which filled us with alarm."

Agricola responded by seizing the initiative. Early in the spring of 83 he launched another combined operation with the twin objectives of isolating the Fife peninsula (thereby safeguarding his right flank), then crossing the Tay River to put his troops in position to break out into the broad, northeastern coastal plain.

The Picts seem to have been caught off balance and at first things went well for the Romans. "The enemy, as we learned from prisoners, was confounded...."

However, the Picts were not so confounded that they could not counter-attack. During the late hours of a summer night, a Pictish battle group swept down upon the walled and ditched camp of the 9th Legion somewhere in the green valley of Strath Earn.

> Surprising and cutting down the sentries, who were asleep or panic-stricken, the enemy broke into the camp. The battle was raging fiercely before Agricola could marshal his best soldiers to attack the assailants in the rear....There followed a furious conflict within the narrow passages at the gates until the enemy was routed....But they, thinking themselves cheated not so much by our valour as by our general's skill, lost nothing of their arrogance and, removing their wives and children to a place of safety, assembled to ratify with sacred rites the confederacy of all their states against us.

Tacitus, who never portrayed his father-in-law except in the best of lights, is ambiguous about the results of this imbroglio. According to him, it buoyed Roman morale and depressed that of the barbarians. In truth, it was a serious setback for Agricola, bringing his advance to an end for that season and forcing him into defensive positions for another winter.

In the summer of the following year he again struck out to the north-east, determined to bring the long campaign to a conclusion.

> Having sent a fleet ahead of him to cause widespread alarm by its ravages, he advanced as far as the Grampian Mountains....The enemy, in no way cowed by the results of the last engagement, had made up their minds either to be avenged, or enslaved, and had assembled their entire fighting strength—more than 30,000 armed men.

Chief amongst the leaders was a man the Romans called Calgacus, who, according to Tacitus, treated his troops to the following resounding indictment of Rome and, indeed, of all empires in all time ...including our own.

The terrible Romans from whose oppression escape is vainly sought through obedience and submission [are] robbers of the world. Having by universal plundering exhausted the land, they even rob the sea. If their enemy be rich, they are rapacious. If poor, they lust for dominion over him. Neither east nor west has been able to satisfy them. They justify robbery, slaughter, and plunder with the lying name of Empire. They make a desolation, then call it peace.

The place where the Pictish forces made their stand was probably in the rolling country between the Howe of Mearns and Stonehaven, beyond which the coastal corridor opens onto the broad and vulnerable plains of Buchan.

The battle of Mons Graupius, as Tacitus calls it, was certainly fought in open country since neither Picts nor Romans were hill fighters. Perhaps it was watched from the heights of the Mounth by Alban highlanders hoping to see the Armoricans cut to pieces.

The Armoricans fought well, but their levies could not withstand Agricola's tightly disciplined and superbly trained swordsmen and cavalry and, after a long and terrible struggle, they broke.

Then indeed the open plain presented an awful and hideous spectacle. Our men pursued and captured prisoners, but slaughtered them when other prisoners came their way.... The enemy fled in whole battalions, though some rushed to the front and gave themselves up to death. Everywhere weapons, corpses, and mangled limbs lay scattered, and the earth reeked with blood.... Night and weariness of bloodshed put an end to the pursuit.

The Picts are supposed to have lost ten thousand men, a figure which is doubtless exaggerated. Yet, although the victory earned Agricola a triumph, it was by no means conclusive. The Roman army got no farther north that year, nor ever would thereafter.

The Picts, as history would come to call all the Armoricans of Scotland, had been bloodied but not crushed. They now proceeded to make things so difficult for Agricola that he had to withdraw to the land of the Boresti tribe (perhaps the region around Perth), where his army again had to winter in a fortified camp in hostile territory.

The hard truth was that the great general had bitten off considerably more than he could chew. The Picts gave themselves over to waging total war with such ferocity that, within a decade, they forced the Romans to abandon all the ground the legions had captured north of the Cheviots. Before the end of the century they were attacking Roman frontier posts along the Solway–Tyne line, where Hadrian's Wall would be built in a less-than-successful attempt to shut them out of England.

In the event, the Picts fought on until, centuries later, the last legion sailed away from Britain. The greatest military power of the times had failed to crush them.

Northern Alba had not been neutral during this new war in the north. Not long after Claudius invaded Britain, a delegation sailed south from Orkney, which then seems to have been a centre of free Alba. It came to offer submission to, and alliance with, Rome.

Such an alliance promised well for both parties. Alba stood to gain formidable support against both Celts and Picts, and Rome to gain an ally well positioned to assist in the subjugation of northern Britain. Seafaring Albans would be able to rely on the Roman navy for protection, Rome being anxious to ensure there was no interruption in the flow of northern valuta, which was much in demand amongst the Empire's elite.

Nothing more is recorded about this alliance, but we can guess that Alba contributed information, guides, pilots, and perhaps bases for Roman ships. If nothing else, Alban highlanders behind the Armorican lines would have been invaluable as an intelligence source. Tacitus makes no mention of Alban military assistance, but then he seldom gives credit to Rome's allies.

What he *does* tell us is that, after Mons Graupius, Agricola sent part of his naval force to complete the circumnavigation of Britain.

Round these coasts of remotest ocean the fleet sailed, for the first time establishing that Britain is an island, and at the same time discovering and conquering what are called the Orkades [which included Shetland].

The fleet is also reported to have glimpsed Thule (Tilli) on the distant horizon.

Tacitus's use of the phrase "discovering and conquering" reflects his commitment to glorifying Agricola's achievements; but finds of Roman coins of the period in Shetland and Orkney point to a peaceable Roman visit to a client state.

T.C. Lethbridge was of this opinion. As he wrote in *Herdsmen and Hermits*:

It is hard to believe that, provided as it was with an efficient naval force, the Roman high command could not have organized the destruction of the brochs and most of their inhabitants.[3] It clearly did not attempt to do so. If it had, it is scarcely credible that the destruction of the towers would have escaped mention in Tacitus's account of Agricola's exploits. The answer surely is that the broch people were hostile to the murus-Gallicus tribes [builders of the timber-laced forts] and were either bought off by the Romans or actively assisted them.

Although Rome failed to subdue the Picts, she succeeded wonderfully well in diverting their attentions away from free Alba. Henceforth the Picts directed their military energies southward against Rome and Rome's British-Celtic allies. The long vendetta between Albans and the exiles from Armorica began to atrophy. Although enmity between the two continued for many years, in the future it was expressed mostly in minor raids and acts of piracy.

By the end of the first century A.D., the famous brochs were no longer vital to Alban survival. Nevertheless, those in the northwest continued to serve a useful purpose. Pictish raids diminished, but the Irish increased the intensity of theirs. Overall, these forays may have amounted to little more than nuisances, but severe and bloody ones they must have been to those communities which had to endure them. Having a broch at hand in which to take refuge when Irish rovers hove in sight would have long remained a source of comfort to many Alban coastal and island dwellers.

CHAPTER NINE

FETLAR

On a brisk September day early in the second century of the Christian era, a vessel bearing the venerable Farfarer name thrust her bluff bows around Sheep Head and entered home waters.

The broad reach of Tresta Bay on the south coast of Shetland's Fetlar island now lay open to her. As she turned into it, her weather-stained sail was spotted by two boys out on the headland searching for strayed sheep. Shrieking with excitement, they raced for a cluster of low, sod-covered houses crouched at the foot of Tresta's inner cove.

The ship had been gone for a year and a half. Gone to Tilli, that mystical island far out in the Western Ocean. During her absence women, children, and the clan's old folk had worked an increasingly parsimonious land. Through centuries of chill, wet weather, peat had been thickening on the island's hills, remorselessly smothering fields and pastures. Wiry sheep and the munificence of the surrounding seas contrived to make human life possible, but it was the far-faring men, and the valuta they brought home, who made it not just possible, but good.

The forty-odd people of Farfarer's clan lived in five houses set in a curve across the mouth of a small valley whose stream debouched into the home cove over a stretch of sandy beach.

The houses were low because their earth and flagstone floors were sunk two feet deep into sand and silt. Their turf walls, ballasted with stone and rubble, were thick enough to contain cells that served as bed and storage chambers. This cellular construction also had the advantage of reducing the roof span so it could be bridged by very short rafters—a matter of moment in a land bereft of trees.

The roofs were cambered, thatched with bracken, and covered with turves laid

Shetland's Mousa Broch has stood for as long as eighteen centuries.

shingle fashion. They could deflect even the almost horizontally driven rains of
winter. Grass grew so lushly over all that the structures could have been mistaken
for natural mounds, save for blue wisps of peat smoke wafting upward from their
rounded peaks.

A stone-walled hearth under the smoke hole was at the centre of each house,
giving warmth and light. The latter was supplemented by soapstone saucer lamps
fuelled with pungent sea mammal or seabird oil. Furniture consisted of benches and
"dressers" made of flat sandstone slabs and driftwood. Spare clothing and
household and fishing gear hung from roof and walls.

The houses waiting just beyond the beach promised a snug and cosy welcome to
Farfarer's crew, after an absence of eighteen months, during which they had mostly
lived under their vessel's hull upturned on Tilli's beaches.

As the vessel neared the shore her sail came down with a run. Black dogs, which
seemed as much at home in the water as on the land, were the first to plunge into
the surf to welcome the homecomers. They were followed by a laughing, shouting
mob of people wading out waist deep to seize the lines flung to them.

Her cargo included enough coils of walrus-hide rope to provide standing and
running rigging for many ships. There were whole hides with which to sheath, or re-

sheath, boats and vessels. Out of her hold came dozens of sealskin sacks filled with fetid seal tar for caulking ships' seams. Other sacks were stuffed with eiderdown. There were bales of white fox furs, and the creamy pelts of four water bears, fit to adorn the houses of lordly folk in far-off lands.

Most important of all were several wooden casks bulging with tusks, each cask so heavy that two men were needed to carry it. Here was ivory to trade for sufficient grain, honey, even raisins, to last the clan a year or more. And with plenty left over for southern pottery, flaxen cloth, wood, copper, iron, and other goods, not forgetting finery for the women.

As soon as the hold was empty, crewmen leapt into the surf to grab at screaming girls and women, or to wrestle with young kinsmen, until the skipper shouted with mock ferocity:

"Haul her up, you feckless clods! Up on the beach with her now! And be bloody careful! Tear her skin and I'll rip the hide right off your backs!"

But he was grinning, for he knew Farfarer could not have been in more caring hands.

For two weeks everyone celebrated. People entertained, and were entertained, not only in their own clan homes but in other settlements around the island. Then, one sunny day made auspicious by a sportive nor'west wind, Farfarer slid back into her own element. Re-laden with most of the cargo she had brought from Tilli, she was now crowded with people of both sexes and all ages. In holiday mood, they set out to the southward, bound for Orkney's Main Island, which had been the social, trade, and religious centre of the twin archipelagos since time immemorial.

Since this was the tag end of the year and a time for taking life easy, the voyage was leisurely. By day Farfarer coursed along with a white bone of foam in her teeth, but at night she ran her bows up on some convenient beach, or anchored off one of the scores of little coastal settlements on the scattered islands along the way. Her people were welcomed wherever they landed, for the Islanders were all of one blood.

On the third day Farfarer fell in with an island ship returning from a voyage to the land of the Northmen where her people had traded walrus rope and seal tar for timber. The two vessels put into harbour together that night, and there was a great exchange of seafaring gossip.

None of the Fetlar men had ever made the crossing to Norway. Although this could be accomplished in two or three days, weather permitting, the nature of the reception at the other end was always in doubt. The Northmen had a name for being quick with sword and battleaxe, and their contempt for strangers could be deadly. The crew of the visiting vessel had played safe by anchoring at the mouth of a fiord. Northmen had come off to them in slim, lap-strake, wooden boats, built more like canoes than ships.

"They towed rafts of timbers out to us, but called us worms when we would not go ashore. And they mocked our vessel, threatening to skin her like a fat cow if we did not give them double what their wood was worth. It's as well they stick to their own coasts. I would not like to see them come to ours...."

The third night Farfarer rested her head on the beach at Sandwick under the protective loom of the Broch of Mousa. Her people were welcomed by the Sandwick folk and surfeited with mutton. Many stories were told and songs sung around the smoky peat fires. The visitors listened, not for the first time, to the gory tale of a Pictish raid on Mousa that had taken place fifty years earlier. Four boatloads of Picts had tried to rush the broch and, when repulsed, had laid siege to it. But they neglected to keep a proper watch on their boats.

"One black night our Sandwick men rowed across the Sound with muffled oars. Quiet as otters they landed, seized the pirates' boats, and, when the Picts came roaring down to the beach, met them with arrows and sling stones. Then our folk, penned up in the tower, stormed out and took them in the rear with spears and axes...."

On the fifth day Farfarer steered into open ocean past the great cliff and swirling tide rip at the southern end of Shetland. At dusk the lookout raised Fair Isle, midway between Shetland and Orkney. Here the ship was storm-bound by a howling nor'easter for two days. Her people ate and slept in the snug houses of the small island's one clan; old friends, who also sent men to Tilli every year.

A day's sail south from Fair Isle brought Farfarer to the coast of Sanday, a low, verdant island fringed by miles of saffron-coloured beaches. This was a legendary place where, in ancient times, legions of walrus had been used to coming ashore to sun themselves on the broad sands. Storms still uncovered their bones from the shore dunes, or rolled them up from the sea bottom.

The Fetlar people visited relatives at Sty Bay, where they were shown a giant tusk washed ashore by the nor'easter only two days earlier. Time-yellowed and sand-polished, it was more than a yard long. Visitors and residents alike took its resurrection as a good omen for the future.

Departing from Sanday on a sou'westerly course, the vessel made her leisurely *way amongst the low, fertile, well-peopled Orkneys. Almost always a broch, sometimes several, were in view. Although now growing unkempt from long neglect, the towers remained a comforting presence.*

In due course Farfarer *arrived at Wide Bay, which knifes into the north side of Main Island. Not only was Main the largest in the Orkney group, but it had always been the most prosperous. It was here that the Old Ones had built their most massive stone circles; raised the highest standing stones; and constructed the magnificent monument of Maeshowe.*

Through countless generations the greatest part of all northern valuta, whether originating in Shetland, the Faeroes, or Tilli, had been brought into Wide Bay, to be carried over a narrow isthmus to a cove in Scapa Sound where Orkney ships trading south to Scilly awaited it. The narrow isthmus between the two harbours had early become, and remained, the site of a great annual trade fair which took place at summer's end.

Far-faring valuta seekers, crofter-fishermen, and Orkney southfarers foregathered at the isthmus. Those belonging to Main generally came on foot or riding small, shaggy ponies; most others arrived in skin-covered boats ranging in size from four-oared skiffs to ocean-going ships. Although a few clans maintained permanent sod-walled shelters at the isthmus, the majority camped under their own overturned vessels set on sod-and-stone foundations just above the high-water mark. Seen from a distance, these resembled elongated tortoise shells bleached to the colour of old bone.

On the day Farfarer *nosed up on the beach in Wide Bay, a pair of big Orkney merchantmen, not long arrived from Scilly, lay at anchor in Scapa Bay. Their cargoes were being unloaded and ferried ashore to be displayed in booths set up upon the isthmus separating the two bodies of water.*

While Farfarer*'s skipper and the clan elders saw to the exchange of goods, the rest of her people made the most of the opportunities for visiting, feasting, love making, story telling, singing, drinking, and, on occasion when beer had flowed too freely, fighting.*

The fair was about far more than trade. It was the principal forum for an exchange of news about other islanders and about the world beyond. The days hardly seemed long enough for all that had to be seen and done—said and heard.

The boys from Fetlar were especially curious about the Orkney merchantmen. Although built to the same double-ended design as Farfarer*, the southfaring vessels were larger, broader, and able to carry huge cargoes. They also carried large* crews—not so much to handle the ships as for protection. The waters between Little Minch in the Sea of the Hebrides and Solway Firth were infested with swift Pictish vessels. An Orkney merchantman could hope to survive attack only if she had a large crew well skilled in the use of the bow, the sling, and the long pikes designed to repel boarders.

"Your northfarers may have to contend with wild winds, mountainous waves, terrible sea beasts, even floating ice," an Orkney crewman told the group of Fetlar lads. "Aye, but we have to face human beasts worse than all those put together. The Picts, for one. They are said to be kin to us, but you would not know it if they boarded you and fed you to the fishes. The people on the Irish coast are not so handy at sea, but they're even more bloody minded. If they catch you they think nothing of ripping your belly open and making rope of your guts."

Everyone was keenly interested in a report that the Romans, whose warships patrolled British waters south of Solway Firth, were contemplating basing a squadron in Alban territory on the island of Mull. An Orkney skipper who had been convoyed south from Solway by a Roman galley brought this welcome news.

There were other cheering tidings from the south. Newly arrived Roman legions and Celtic auxiliaries were driving the Picts back to the Clyde–Forth line where, it was said, a new wall would be built to pen them in. What with one thing and another, it seemed the Picts would have little time or energy to spare for harassing Alba.

Northfarers had their own stories to tell, and Farfarer's skipper held everyone's attention with his description of a voyage made late that summer to the waters northwest of Tilli.

It had been an exceptionally warm summer and the river of pack ice which normally separated Tilli from the seldom seen, but always felt, presence of Crona, the great land to the westward, had thinned remarkably.[1]

As the skipper told it, "We had a bumper cargo, and some of the summer left before it would be time to lay course for home. I'd never seen the western waters so clear of ice. So I asked the lads if they'd like to take a look at Crona—a better look than what we'd ever had, even from the top of Tilli's mountains."

Farfarer sailed west for a day and a mostly sunlit night. On the morning of the second day, when pack ice finally stopped her, she was in full view of a giant's land. It was fringed, the skipper told his listeners, with peaks higher than any he had ever seen or heard about. And above these rose the most enormous mass of ice in all the world.

Farfarer's crew had been lucky. The window through which they viewed this majestic and mysterious land soon closed again as a spell of renewed cold and stormy weather descended on the north, and pack ice re-established its dominion over the Cronian Sea.

Farfarer's return home from the trade fair to Fetlar was quickly made. When all the newly acquired goods had been taken ashore, the ship was hauled well out of reach of the highest storm tide and overturned to become her own boathouse. Lashed down with walrus-hide ropes against the tug and thrust of nor'east gales, she crouched like a broody hen over the gear stored under her well-tarred "roof."

The clanspeople prepared themselves for winter. Peat that had been cut and dried on hillside bogs during the summer was brought down and stacked against house walls, where it provided added protection against the wind until it was needed on the hearths within. Bundles of sun-and-wind-dried fish and mutton were stacked in stone shelters, protected from the rain but open to the antiseptic sweep of wind. Storerooms built into the house walls were packed with sacks of imported grain and bladders redolent with the heavy odour of rendered sea-mammal oil and sheep tallow.

As the first great winter storms came blasting across the wide sweep of sea between Fetlar and Norway, the island grew comatose. Half-wild sheep retreated from the wind-and-sea-lashed coasts to seek shelter in inland valleys. In the smoky comfort of dim-lit houses men and women busied themselves with their crafts, while children played, asked questions, and listened to endless tales.

At night, when the peat had burned to white ash and the lamps had been doused, people dreamed of spring days to come. Farfarer's skipper dreamed mostly of Tilli...but sometimes of the vast and icy land called Crona.

CHAPTER TEN

ALBA REBORN

ET, COOL, AND STORMY WEATHER SEEMS TO HAVE dominated the northeastern Atlantic throughout most of the third century, making life more difficult for Alban crofters and farfarers alike. But at least they lived more or less in peace.

The Picts were too fiercely engaged with the Romans to have much time and energy to spare for Alba. British Celts were no longer a threat, for they were now more or less subordinate to Rome. The Irish posed a danger to Orkney southfarers sailing too near their shores, but Rome, anxious to prevent interruptions in the flow of northern valuta and to protect the coasts of her British province, had made herself mistress of the surrounding seas and so put a crimp in both Irish and Pictish nautical activities.

Around the end of the third century this state of affairs began to suffer a sea change. Stalemated on land by a combination of Roman legions and Celtic auxiliaries protected by forts and walls, the Picts moved to regain the initiative at sea. Anciently a seafaring people, they turned their talents to designing a small warship which was so effective that the Romans eventually paid them the compliment of copying it.

The Romans called this vessel a *picta*. It had a slim, wooden hull and was propelled by ten pairs of oars but could be sailed as well. Hull, sail, and rowers were camouflaged in blues and greens to match the colours of the sea. Low in the water, almost invisible at a distance, and extremely swift, swarms of these deadly little craft were able to strike from ambush and overwhelm larger, slower Roman ships, sometimes before the crews of these could even stand to arms. Perhaps the Picts were belatedly benefiting from the bloody lesson taught to their ancestors by Caesar's fleet at the battle of Morbihan Bay in their old homeland of Armorica.

Although the success of the *picta* was not the only factor involved, Rome's command of British waters was eroding. By early in the fourth century she had all but lost control of the seaways. Pictish squadrons were raiding as far south as the Bristol Channel and probably as far north as Tilli. Celts from Ireland, using both Alban-style skin-covered craft and wooden boats, were again descending on outlying Alban communities in the Hebridean Sea, and on Romano-British Celts on the western coasts of mainland Britain.

Other predators now moved in to exploit the decline of Roman power. Saxon freebooters appeared in southeastern Britain and were soon harassing the eastern coast. It may not have been long before some reached Alba and the Northern Islands. At least one broch has yielded evidence of re-occupancy in the fourth century. The people who sought refuge within its walls may have felt themselves threatened by Pictish, Irish, *or* Saxon marauders. Certainly something unpleasant was afoot in northern Britain, it seems.

In or about 363 a much-respected Roman general named Theodosius led a naval expedition north. Most of what little we know about it is contained in the rather florid verse of Claudius Claudianus, a classical poet who lived at the end of the fourth century. Claudianus wrote with chauvinistic smugness:

> It is to Rome's rule of peace we owe it that the world is our home, that we can live where we please, and that to visit Thule [Tilli] and explore its once dreaded wilderness is but a sport.

More to the point he also tells us that

> Theodosius's adventurous oars broke the surface of the northern seas.... He brought under subjection the coasts of Britain and laid waste in the north.... What avail against him the eternal snows, the frozen air, the uncharted seas? The Orcades ran red with Saxon slaughter; Thule was

warm with the blood of Picts; ice-bound Hibernia wept for the heaps of slain Scots....

Most scholars choose to ignore this, the only surviving account of Theodosius's expedition, or to impugn its worth. Because no corroboratory proof of a Saxon presence in Orkney in the fourth century has so far been found, some conclude that Claudianus invented the story. As for Picts in Thule—well, where's the proof? It *is*, however, generally (if reluctantly) admitted that the reference to Scots, as the northern Irish were called, seems historically valid.

Regardless of academic demurs, it cannot be reasonably doubted that Theodosius did lead a naval force north. He may have done so as part of a general attempt to regain control of the seas surrounding Britain; but we will not be far wrong if we conclude he was also motivated by urgent pleas for assistance from Alban allies.

I envisage him sailing up the east coast, engaging any Saxon, Frankish, or Pictish vessels he might meet. He may very well have encountered a nest of Saxons in Orkney waters, attacked and sunk the ships, and slaughtered the crews. He could then have responded to appeals from his Alban allies and sailed on to Tilli, there to surprise and scatter Pictish raiders preying on the valuta trade.

I see Theodosius, having done his duty by Rome's client, then turning south through western waters, engaging Pictish ships whenever he could, and going ashore in Ireland on occasion to make reprisals on the Dalriad Scotti and other Celtic tribes.

Claudianus's somewhat mellifluous style (he was a *poet*, after all) may irritate scholastic sensibilities, but that is no reason to reject his story.

During the late 1940s a remarkable discovery was made in Iceland. In his book *Gengið á rekja*, Icelandic historian Kristian Eldjarn describes the recovery of three ancient coins from old habitation sites at the head of Hamarsfjördur on the east coast of Iceland. All are Roman Antoniniani, minted between A.D. 270 and 305. A fourth Antoniniani belonging to the same age has since been found at another east-coast site.

Eldjarn does not believe, as some have suggested, that these coins were old loot brought to Iceland in the ninth century by his Viking ancestors. He suspects that a Roman ship caught in a gale in north

British waters was blown so far off course as to reach Thule, where she was wrecked.

I submit that it is at least equally likely the coins were payment for fresh meat or other country produce supplied to Theodosius's crews by Albans living on the east coast of the island. The apparent time discrepancy poses no problem. It often took several generations for coins minted in Rome to make their ways to the fringes of the Empire.

Whatever salutary effects Theodosius's expedition may have had on the "barbarians of the north," as the Romans continued to call the Picts, were short-lived. A few years later, after destroying a Roman fleet, Pictish vessels were attacking watchtowers and coastguard stations as far south as the English Channel. By 367 their land forces were battering Hadrian's Wall and, by century's end, had burst through it, overwhelming the Roman garrisons and storming southward.

The rapid decline of Rome's power in Britain resulted in an epidemic of bloody upheavals. Irish raiders took to attacking the west coast of Britain where and when they pleased. Increasing numbers of Saxons and Franks came marauding along Britain's southern and eastern shores. In the latter part of the fourth century all these assailants seem to have come together in a loose alliance with the Picts to overrun much of England, burning, looting, and slaving.

Those were perilous times in the north too. Although the Picts were no longer making concerted attacks against the rump of Alba, individual Pictish (and Irish) chieftains raided the Alban islands, if only for fun and glory and to keep their battle skills honed.

Irish annals proudly record that King Niall of the Nine Hostages ravaged the Hebrides between 420 and 430; and he was not likely to have been the first Irishman to have gone harrying in that quarter. Niall and his contemporaries were famous marauders. After a splendidly sanguinary career, he himself is supposed to have perished while raiding *i Alpi*. Scholars have translated this as "in the Alps"—which would be a very long way from home, even for an Irish rover. The phrase almost certainly means "in Alba."

Picts and Irish were not the only marauders. A cryptic entry in Nennius's ninth-century *History of the Britons* notes that around 443 the Orcadies were "wasted by Hengist." It is also known that around this time a Jute chieftain of this name was hired by the British king Vortigern to defend his territory against raiders, some of whom seem to have been Picts. Hengist may have struck a pre-emptive blow in the north. It would have made no odds to him whether his victims were Picts or Albans, even if he had known the difference. On this occasion Orkney seems to have run red with Alban, rather than Saxon, blood.

Traumatic events were becoming commonplace on both the Northern Islands and the adjacent mainland. Although Alba apparently lost no territory, people would have found it devilishly hard to carry on crofting, herding, and fishing while forever having to scan the horizon for the first glimpse of an alien hull bearing black fate their way. Once again the brochs seem to have become the people's shield.

Valuta gatherers and traders must have had their difficulties too. Although most Pictish and Gaelic pirates were perhaps reluctant to essay the long voyage to Tilli, they would have been ever ready and eager to assault Orkneymen carrying valuta south or fetching back southern goods.

I believe that, as vessel losses mounted, some of the trading skippers abandoned the waters between Ireland and Britain, choosing instead to cross from Shetland to Norway there to exchange valuta for goods brought north along trade routes running through France and Germany to Denmark and beyond.

This would have been a rough business. At best Northmen were unreliable trading partners, all too apt to simply seize what they wanted, whether it be goods, human beings, or ships. Trading with Norway would have been a species of Hobson's choice.

Further more, the Northmen were quick studies. I am convinced that exposure to, and experience with, ocean-going Alban ships and sea-farers was probably an important, perhaps even critical determining factor in the Norse transition from coastal to deep-water sailors; a transition which began around the end of the sixth century and ultimately resulted in their becoming the most destructive maritime marauders of all time.

The North Atlantic climate seems to have been undergoing dramatic improvement during this period. Decade by decade the weather became drier, warmer, and sunnier. This brought new heart to crofters on their sodden fields, and to fishermen looking for fewer storm-bound days.

In Tilli the Arctic pack retreated so far to the northward that it could no longer be seen from the island. With it went most of the white bears, which had been used to drifting south on the ice and coming ashore to give birth to their cubs.

Other sea mammals were also affected. Narwhals, whose spiralled ivory tusks were amongst the most sought-after products of the north, withdrew from Tilli's warming waters. And the enormous herds of ice seals—harps and hoods—that had once darkened the pack off north-western Tilli were no longer to be found.

To make matters worse, Tilli's walrus—originally so plentiful—were suffering the effects of centuries of slaughter. Their numbers had dwindled from generation to generation until far-sighted men could foresee the day when they would all be gone from Tilli's beaches.

Life in and around that island was in a state of flux. Birch forests were reaching for the pale skies while a tide of grasses and flowering plants submerged the lower slopes of the lava hills. Each spring saw ever vaster flocks of ducks, geese, and swans sweeping up from the southeast to take possession of breeding grounds newly unlocked from the glacial ice fields of the interior.

Not all the migrant birds remained in Tilli. Many flocks rested only briefly there before continuing west.

Their departures would have been closely observed. Although Tilli was becoming ever more attractive to crofters, it was fast losing its appeal to valuta seekers, who now looked westward after the high-flying flocks. A possible new hunting ground beckoned in that direction even as the river of Arctic pack ice which had long interposed an almost impenetrable barrier between Tilli and Crona dissolved.

Nature was in flux; and so were human affairs. Throughout the latter part of the fifth century, the old *pax Romana* in the British Isles collapsed into a morass of general wars, uprisings, and miscellaneous blood-letting. Not even zealots of the Christian religion, which was then spreading into the north, could find peace, except by retreating to almost inaccessible rock pinnacles around Britain's coasts, where they could mortify the flesh in their own fashion. Elsewhere the flesh of farmers, villagers, fishermen, sailors, artisans, and all sorts of folk was being mortified by bands of marauders introducing the rule of chaos.

In the aftermath of Rome's collapse even Pictland, which had so fiercely and for so long kept Rome at bay, was hard beset. By the middle of the fifth century the Picts were being assailed on all sides. Dalriad Scotti from Ireland seized the peninsula of Kintyre, together with the islands of Islay, Jura, and Arran, and threatened further inroads. Things were no better in the south. There, in 429, shortly after leading the terrible "barbarian" raids into England, the Picts sustained a crushing defeat from a Romano-British (which is to say, Celtic) confederacy. This disaster resulted in two British kingdoms, Strathclyde and Manau Gododdin, being carved out of Pictland's border country. Worse was to follow when Manau Gododdin was itself swallowed by the Angles, new and exceedingly warlike invaders from across the Channel. Nor was Alba idle. Taking advantage of the general harassment of an old enemy, Albans seem to have reoccupied the Pictish salients north of Glen Albyn.

By the end of the sixth century, Pictland had been squeezed into that portion of Scotland between the Clyde–Forth isthmus and Glen Albyn, minus a wedge of western mainland and islands held by the Scotti.

The Irish were not content with warring against the Picts. They also attacked Alba. Irish annals record that, in 568, Corall of Dalriada joined forces with another Irish king in a concerted attack on the Western Isles, probably including most of the Hebrides. Then, in 578 or 580, the Dalriad king, Aedan mac Gabrain, "led an expedition to Orkney." For every such recorded incident a number of others undoubtedly took place. Once again Alban islanders sought the protection of their old defenders. During the sixth century many a broch was repaired and ringed with makeshift shanties and cattle yards, the whole being surrounded by ditches and earthen ramparts.

Irish belligerence may have been the catalyst for the extraordinary and mysterious *rapprochement* that took place between Albans and Picts at about this time. We know little of how it came about. The only written reference to the event comes from a life of Saint Columba, the *Vita Sancti Columbae*, written by the priest Adomnan late in the seventh century.

In 565 Columba, then abbot of a powerful Irish clerical community on the island of Iona, visited Brudei, king of the "Northern Picts," at his capital near the northeastern end of Glen Albyn.[1] Columba's motive in risking this long journey into the heart of a country that ought to have been decidedly hostile to any Celt is not clearly stated, but he was probably impelled by zeal to disseminate the Irish version of Christianity before a British version, then seeping northward, could contaminate Brudei's people.

Brudei professed an interest in Columba's brand of Christianity, though his father-in-law was all in favour of throwing the Celtic rascal out. While at Brudei's court, Columba met a "subordinate" king from Orkney with whom he arranged safe passage for some of his missionaries to go amongst the Northern Islands.

Unable to understand the alien language of Brudei's people, the Celts conversed with them through interpreters. These reported that Brudei mac Maelchon (as the visitors styled him in Gaelic) was monarch of *both* the northern and the southern portions of what foreigners had formerly called Pictland *but which had now reverted to its ancient name—Alba*. The wheel had come full circle.

Although we cannot know just how this remarkable accommodation between Albans and Picts, who had been antagonists for six centuries, came about, we can make an informed guess.

The Picts were being assailed in the south and west by three powerful forces, and were also at enmity with Alba in the north. They were in desperate need of an alliance with at least one of their antagonists. And Albans and Picts were of similar racial, linguistic, and cultural stock, while Celts and Angles were foreigners in every sense. For their part, the Albans must have fully appreciated that Celts were again the common enemy and, in addition, they may already have seen the foreshadow of a new menace to themselves emerging in the distant northeast.

I conclude that the situation in Scotland had become so alarming as to persuade Albans and Picts—the Northern and the Southern Picts of foreign writers of the period—to bury their ancient differences and make common cause. This is certainly what they did. *Under the aegis of an Alban king.*

Sometime around the middle of the sixth century all of what is now called Scotland lying north of the Clyde–Forth isthmus (with the exception of that portion held by the Scotti) again became one country. The peoples of this kingdom called it Alba and themselves Albans, and were so called by Irish, Britons, and Northumbrians on their borders. They would continue to be called Albans even after the kingdom was finally engrossed by the Scotti more than two and a half centuries later.

And Alba in Scotland is not forgotten even yet.

CHAPTER ELEVEN

SONS OF DEATH

Fair Isle lies half a day's sail south of Shetland and an equal distance north of Orkney. A small and isolated island rough in its northern part, it is more hospitable in the south. At the beginning of the seventh century, it was home to forty or fifty people whose scatter of crofts centred on South Harbour. Although much of their sustenance came from the sea, they raised sheep and kine and took birds and eggs from the cliffs. They were superb mariners who had no difficulty finding berths on farfaring vessels, whether bound northwest for Tilli or south to Scilly.

One fine summer day two middle-aged Islanders were fishing from their skin boat a mile or two offshore when they saw a vessel bearing down from the north. They took it to be an Islander at first, though something seemed odd about the cut of its big, brown sail. When it drew closer, they saw by its shape and the fact it was wooden-planked that it must be one of the Northmen ships that had recently begun appearing in western waters with billets of crude iron and baulks of timber to trade.

Traders were to be welcomed. As the ship drew abeam, the fishermen hailed her in friendly fashion, bringing many big, fair-haired men crowding to her rail, shouting in a strange tongue. Neither side could understand the other, but the Islanders indicated by gestures they would be glad to pilot the vessel into their harbour. Grinning acceptance, the strangers beckoned the fishermen aboard.

Three days later a Fair Isle lad was found on a Fetlar beach, half-drowned, with an oozing wound in his back. He had a grim tale to tell.

"The Northmen anchored their vessel in South Harbour," he said, "then some rowed to land in the ship's boat and we greeted them on the beach. They seemed friendly enough and gave presents of iron nails to our men and handfuls of meal to the women. We took them to our homes, fed them, and made them welcome, but they would not sleep ashore. They were strapping big men and some of our older folk did not like their looks, thinking it as well they did not choose to sleep under our roofs.

"Before they rowed off to their ship, they asked to see what we had to trade. It was not much. Most of the goods our farfarers had brought back from Tilli had already been shipped off aboard a southfaring vessel. The Northmen seemed little interested in our bags of wool and seabird feathers and bales of dried fish, but let us understand they would nevertheless come ashore in the morning to trade.

"By the time the sun was well risen, most of the folk were gathered at the beach, for this was a visit the like of which had never happened before. The Northmen rowed their six-oared boat back and forth until they had landed their whole crew. These numbered twenty-three in all. Most wore two-handed swords at their sides. Some carried spears, and others axes. This made us uneasy for we had no such weapons. But they brought ashore some sacks of grain and other goods, so we forgot our fears and began to trade.

"Suddenly one of them blew on a ram's horn. It was such a blast we all turned and stared. At that moment trading ended and slaughter began. Before we knew what evil was upon us they had butchered most of our able-bodied men, sending the hot blood frothing across the cobbles into the sea. The shrieks of the dying were frightful, yet not as frightful as the yells of these men as they thrust and hacked and howled amongst us like merciless beasts.

"I was speared in the back when I tried to flee. Most of those still living were rounded up without resistance for they could hardly understand what was happening. Laughing and singing now, the Northmen drove us into a circle using the flats of their dripping swords and the butts of their bloody spears. Then, one by one, they pulled the older folk out of the circle. They slit the bellies of some so their guts fell out on the sand. Some they clove from shoulder to belt with mighty swings of their swords. They tore children away from women and tossed some of the babies to one another, from spear point to spear point.

"Then they began raping. My sister, of fifteen summers, bit one of them and he flung her from him onto her back, thrust his spear between her legs and leaned on it, cursing, until her screaming ended.

"Afterwards they sacked our houses then set the thatch alight, and fires roared like winter gales until all was consumed. They slaughtered as many cows and sheep as they could catch. It did not seem to matter to them what they killed, be it beasts or men.

"They tied the hands of us survivors, women, youths, and maids, and herded us into the boat and took us to their ship. Some were chained by the neck but there was not enough chain for all, so the rest were fastened with hide rope. We lay under the sun all that day without water, while the Northmen hunted the island, chasing those who had escaped the killings. That night they feasted on our cattle beasts roasted on great fires fuelled with our boats and anything else that would burn.

"Next day the ship set sail heading north and east. In the evening, off Funzie Head the helmsman altered course to the eastward and I knew we were bound for a foreign land. Darkness fell and there was much confusion as the Northmen fought with one another over our women. I wet the bonds on my wrists in bilge water and they slackened until I was able to slip them off and free my neck from its yoke. I crawled to the side and dropped overboard without being noticed. I did not think to see the dawn again, but it seemed better to drown than to stay in the hands of those sons of death."

M UCH EFFORT HAS BEEN EXPENDED ATTEMPTING TO cleanse the reputation of the Northmen, or Vikings as they are more usually known. The currently correct image is of rough-hewn, stout-hearted fishermen-farmers, who came west to the British Isles as homesteaders. It *is* admitted that there were piratical types among them whose deeds do not bear close scrutiny, but we are enjoined not to condemn the whole because of the few. Rather, we are encouraged to admire the Vikings for their pioneering spirit, their derring-do, their feats of seamanship, and their democratic ways.

This is not how they were viewed by those they came amongst.

A contemporary account of a Viking visit to the island of Lindisfarne off the Northumberland coast in 793 catches the feeling of the times.

The pagans from northern regions came with a force of ships to Britain like stinging hornets and spread on all sides like fearful wolves, robbed, tore, and slaughtered not only beasts of burden, sheep, and oxen, but even priests and deacons, and companies of monks and nuns.

And they came to the church at Lindisfarne, laid everything waste with grievous plundering, trampled the holy places with polluted steps, dug up the altars and seized all the treasures of the holy church. They killed some of the brothers, took some away with them in fetters, many they drove out, naked and loaded with insults, some they drowned in the sea.

Being himself a man of holy orders, the author of this account may have been somewhat prejudiced; but the terror and horror instilled by the Vikings was almost universal. A prayer offered in virtually every Christian church of the times included this plea: "From the Northmen and sudden death, Lord God deliver us."

"Sons of Death" was one of the epithets bestowed upon the Vikings. "Odin's Wolves" was another, although this does an injustice to wolves. Countless Northmen eventually *did* settle in Britain, but they devastated the land with fire and sword before setting their hands to the plough.

The British historian F. T. Wainwright has described them thus:

> The Vikings were primarily warriors and pirates, adventuring boldly on
> the open seas, looting, killing, feuding and harrying, blood-stained and
> blood-thirsty, wild heathen men from wild heathen lands. There were also
> settlers seeking new homes, and traders seeking to exchange fish and furs
> for wheat, wine and honey, but even those who travelled with peaceable
> intentions were never averse to gaining their ends by violence.[1]

Just who *were* these fearsome folk?

They came of the same stock as the Teutonic tribes that overran most of Europe and contributed so largely to the destruction of the Roman Empire. Their ancestors were the war bands of *Aesir* (Eastmen) who invaded Denmark first, then crossed into southern Sweden where they became known as the *Svear*, or *Suines* (eventually Swedes). The first to arrive in the Scandinavian peninsula seized most of the useable land in the south and east, leaving latecomers to make the best they could of what remained, including the mountainous and fiord-riven westward bulge of south-central Norway.

It is a misconception that Scandinavians have always been great sea-farers—born with salt water in their veins. The Aesir had no maritime tradition. They were inland-dwelling landlubbers until they reached the shores of the North Atlantic. Several centuries had to pass thereafter before they became familiar with the sea.

Although the remains of a number of Scandinavian craft built prior to A.D. 600 have been found, none was truly seaworthy. They were narrow, lightweight wooden shells with dangerously little freeboard, suitable only for coastal or inland waters. They were propelled almost exclusively by oars. Sails must have been rudimentary since the boats lacked effective keels, and sails would therefore have been of little practical value. Even the largest Scandinavian vessels—the aptly named longships, some of which were more than a hundred feet overall and formidable fighting craft—were fatally susceptible to swamping or breaking up if they dared to go deep-sea.

By the latter part of the sixth century, the narrow strips of arable land fringing Norway's coastal fiords and running inland along the steep river valleys were becoming severely overcrowded. People of a naturally bellicose nature were increasingly using warriors' weapons either to defend their own slivers of land or to engross those of their neighbours. Blood flowed. Feuds flared. And men found themselves forced to turn more and more to the sea for their daily bread.

Early in the seventh century, Northmen seem to have quite suddenly became seafarers rather than coast crawlers. I believe they accomplished this rapid transition by copying others who had long been master mariners.

The relative abundance of timber from trees native to Scandinavia, found in Shetland and Orkney archaeological sites of the Middle Ages, shows that Northern Islanders were in the habit of visiting the Scandinavian coast. It should therefore be no surprise that their vessels would become models for what would soon come sailing out of Norwegian fiords.

About the turn of the century, a new type of Scandinavian vessel, called *havskip* in Norwegian, later *knorr*, appeared in the Western Ocean. Shorter, broader, and deeper than previous Norse vessels, the double-ended *havskip* had much greater freeboard and, of utmost importance, a long keel to give her "a hold on the water" when under sail. Like Alban vessels, she was square-rigged and in such a fashion as to be able to point relatively close to the wind. She did not have to rely on oars as her predecessors had done. Apart from the limitations imposed by an all-wooden construction, she was probably as good a seaboat as her Northern Island equivalent, which she closely resembled in form and function.

The fiord dwellers who sailed these vessels soon became proficient in a new element and it is not unreasonable to suppose they learned the trade in good part from Alban mariners. They may even have used Alban pilots and sailing masters (willing or unwilling) when first they began to dare the Western Ocean.

Doubtless the first Northmen to reach Shetland came in peace, bringing cargoes of iron, meal, and wood. They may have made port in the excellent harbour of Bressay Sound, then as now the main entrepôt for the northern archipelago. The tales they would have had to tell, and the profits to show, on their return to Norway would have whetted the appetites of other men.

Not all of these would have been content to sail west as traders. Commerce was not every Northman's preferred vocation. Many were happier exercising ancestral talents as buccaneers.

Marauding tended to be much more profitable than trading. A raider had no need to invest capital in trade goods; nor did he have to content himself with whatever the other fellow might choose to offer in exchange. A third and even more cogent reason for preferring raiding to trading was that few things acquired by way of trade could surpass in value a commodity best acquired by force.

So much has been made of the Vikings' undoubted appetite for precious metals, gems, and the like that we tend to assume lust for such things was the primary motivation for their pillage of Europe. The truth is that such goods were only icing on the cake. What the Vikings sought, first and foremost, was human booty. As John Marsden puts it in *The Fury of the Northmen*,

> trading in amber, furs and walrus ivory was a prominent feature of
> Scandinavian expansion . . . but their predominant mercantile activity was
> slave trading.[2]

Scandinavians became so engrossed in this lucrative business that they did not even hesitate to enslave their own kind. Circa 1070 Adam of Bremen described how Sjaellanders of Denmark bought a licence from their king to plunder foreigners but used it instead as a permit to enslave other Danes.

> And as soon as one catches another, he mercilessly sells him into slavery, either to one of his fellows or to a barbarian.

Aesir society was anciently built on slavery and remained heavily dependent on it. As late as 1096 a census of Iceland listed only 4,560 free men in a population of at least six or seven times that number. Prosperous Norse households were seldom served by fewer than a dozen slaves.

Slaves not only powered the Scandinavian domestic scene, they were the backbone of foreign trade. The great Swedish trading centre of Birka was far famed for slave markets patronized by buyers from as far afield as Arabia. The *Annals of Ulster* for 871 preserve this revealing snippet dealing with the return of a Viking chieftain to Ireland after a raid on mainland Alba:

> [He] came again to Ath-Cliath [Dublin] from Alba with two hundred ships; and a great spoil of people, English, Britons and Picts, were brought by them into Ireland in captivity.

The commercial ascendency of Dublin under Viking masters was largely due to its importance as a slave market. By the latter part of the ninth century Dublin had become the hub of a Scandinavian slave trade stretching from Iceland to the Near East. Slaves from the British Isles commanded premium prices on the Continent, and the Swedes in particular imported large numbers for their eastern customers.

The Northmen may have kept their rapacious tendencies somewhat in check during early days in Shetland, if only because they were few in number. However, it could not have been very long before the Islanders began to feel the first effects of what would come to be known throughout the Western world as the Fury of the Northmen.

Isolated as it was, Fair Isle was likely to have been one of the first to experience that fury, unleashed by men of a sort the Northern Islanders had not previously encountered. The fierce militancy of the Picts and the casual ferocity of the Gaels would pale in comparison with the behaviour of the Vikings.

Their homicidal predilections, honed through the centuries, had hitherto mostly been exercised on their own neighbours; on cousins in other Scandinavian countries; or on luckless Balts and Finns. Now the Northmen were debouching into virgin territory where, in addition to the usual delights of rape and rapine, these followers of Thor and Odin could enjoy savaging the followers of White Christ, as Christians were contemptuously styled.

The manner and timing of Christianity's arrival in the Northern Isles remain obscure. When, in 565, Columba visited Brudei mac Maelchon, the Alban king was pagan. But it could not have been long thereafter, and it may have been earlier, that a proselytizing priest by the name of Ninian, operating from a mission called Candida Casa on the shore of Solway Firth, began making his influence felt in the north.

Janet Glover, in *The Story of Scotland*, envisages Ninian's missionaries slogging over the passes in the Grampians and down the Great Glen to Sutherland and Caithness before crossing over to Orkney. It is at least certain that Christianity was firmly rooted in the archipelagos before the end of the sixth century.

Although there is no knowing exactly when Norse raiding became a serious menace in the Northern Islands, there *is* clear evidence of a malevolent presence there before the end of the seventh century. Around that time a number of brochs were repaired and some people were abandoning outlying crofts to cluster close to the nearest tower. Religious communities were digging ditches and building ramparts behind which (so they must earnestly have prayed) they would be safe from the devils assailing the land.

There was trouble on the mainland coasts of Alba as well. In 681 somebody attacked Dunbeath on the east coast of Caithness; and Dunnottar, fifteen miles south of what is now Aberdeen. Nothing else is said about these two events, but a laconic entry in the annals of the following year mentions that the then king of Alba, Brudei mac Bile, led an expedition to the twin archipelagos constituting what was still called Orkney "which resulted in much devastation."

Who was fighting whom? Scholars have generally assumed these two incidents indicate a revolt by Northern Islanders against Brudei, but it hardly seems likely that, living under the menacing shadow if not the bloody presence of the Viking scourge, the Islanders would have chosen such a time to turn upon mainland compatriots who were their only possible source of support.

I conclude Vikings had seized some of the outlying islands and, using them as advanced bases, had begun to attack communities on the mainland. Such a development would have sent a clear and urgent signal to Brudei: he must either drive the Northmen back across the Norwegian Sea, or be prepared before long to have them plundering all of Alba's coasts.

Brudei mac Bile would have been the right man for such a challenge. He had earlier demonstrated his military skill in successful campaigns against the Scotti in the west; and would do so again in 685 by leading his forces south to rout the Angles of Northumbria at the battle of Nechtansmere. As paramount lord of the reconstituted Kingdom of Alba, he would have had the Pictish fleet at his disposal. In the event, I believe he inflicted "much devastation" on Northmen based in the archipelagos, perhaps even driving them out.

Brudei mac Bile seems to have succeeded in holding all Alba's enemies at bay for almost a decade thereafter. His death in 693 was a catastrophe for the kingdom. During the next three decades incompetent leaders and wars of succession brought chaos to the country.

Barely a year after Brudei's death, raiders, who are specifically identified as coming from Orkney, again struck the mainland coasts. No other details are given, but only a powerful Alban naval force could have prevented Viking fleets from returning to the islands and striking southward. Unfortunately, mustering and maintaining a sufficient defensive fleet seems to have been too tall an order for Brudei's immediate successors.

During the first quarter of the new century internecine strife gravely weakened the kingdom of Alba. In 711 its army was almost destroyed in a battle with the Northumbrians. Dalriadic invaders from Ireland began making new incursions in the west.

Beset from within and without, Alba abandoned the Northern and Western Islands to the Sons of Death.

FURY OF THE NORTHMEN

W RITTEN HISTORY HAS ALMOST NOTHING TO TELL us about what transpired in the Northern Isles in the seventh and eighth centuries. And that is remarkable, because something of paramount importance took place during that time.

Well into the sixth century the islands were vigorously inhabited by an indigenous people who had been there for millennia. A hundred years later they had been supplanted by Norwegians.

Some scholars contend that Norwegian immigrants came drifting into a vacuum created when the islands' indigenes abandoned their ancestral homes of their own volition and emigrated to mainland Britain. According to Norwegian historian A.W. Brøgger, Norwegian "settlers" came to an empty wilderness which was practically crying out for the ministrations of sturdy Nordic husbandmen. The islands were, he tells us, "a veritable museum of abandoned brochs, farmhouses and outbuildings."[1]

Maybe so; but I conclude the change in the occupants of the Northern Isles was effected somewhat differently.

By the early part of the seventh century, Norse fiordmen had become sufficiently versed in nautical skills to venture deep-sea. Shetland was the nearest overseas land and, as such, would have been an early destination.

Here is how I see events unfolding.

As already noted, the first *knorr* to find her way west probably came as a peaceable merchantman, laden with wood, iron, honey, meal, and trinkets from Baltic and Danish markets. Her crew would have been welcomed, as traders usually were. They, in turn, would have been on their best behaviour since they were few and far from home. Perhaps it appeared to the Islanders that the evil reputation fiordmen had acquired by their rough dealings with Alban vessels on their own coasts was exaggerated.

It may have seemed so at first. However, as the number of *knorrin* frequenting Shetland waters increased, the behaviour of their crews changed. Although continuing to trade when it suited them, some fiordmen took to pillaging outlying crofts. This led to fierce and bloody little conflicts. The time soon came when the sight of an approaching *knorr* was likely to send men running for their weapons.

Some Norsemen may have been content to continue making their livings as traders, but in the west these were a diminishing minority. Most found it more rewarding, and far more enjoyable, to combine their new-found maritime skills with their ancient passions for battle and brigandage. They were, after all, followers of Thor.

Although the thin-skinned vessels of the Shetlanders could outsail and outmanoeuvre the heavier, wooden *knorrin*, they could not outfight them. In consequence, the *knorrin* came to dominate the waterways surrounding the islands. But they could not spend all their time at sea. Their crews had to go ashore from time to time for food, water, and fuel; to effect repairs; and for shelter during spells of foul weather—all too frequent in the Northern Isles. However, raiders foolhardy enough to seek refuge on an *inhabited* Shetland shore would have been likely to meet a furiously hostile reception. In consequence, they established robbers' roosts and pirate lairs on remote and unoccupied offshore rocks and islets.

As their numbers swelled they began to seize larger, more salubrious, even inhabited, islands such as the Out Skerries and Foula and, eventually, Papa Stour and Whalsay. From these they were eventually able to exert a stranglehold on the entire archipelago.

By the mid-seventh century scores of *knorrin* were crossing to Shetland and the third stage of the Norse triad of trading–raiding–invading had begun.

To seize land on hostile shores, the Norse employed a tactic called *nesam*—ness taking, of which F.T. Wainwright gives the following description in his *Northern Isles*. The invaders

> landed on the sandy peninsulas and promptly threw up banks and ditches for their protection. Traces of such banks and ditches may be seen today; these cut across the narrow necks of peninsulas, and are obviously fortifications, apparently temporary fortifications, and they were clearly thrown up by people who, secure at sea, feared only attacks from the land....The evidence is sufficient to carry the conclusion that the first Scandinavian settlers [to the Northern Isles]...came with swords in their hands and were ready to fight for what they wanted.

By early in the eighth century, Vikings controlled the Shetland archipelago, but probably occupied only the best ports and havens. The land about, with its bleak, peat-grown hills and miserly little pockets of arable soil, was not yet attractive to Norse crofters. In fact, it was not until late in the eighth century, after all the good land in Orkney had been occupied, that Norse farmers came to Shetland in any numbers.

Early Norse settlers in Shetland were primarily Vikings, for whom the archipelago served as a forward base for raiding to the southward. In addition to giving resident Vikings the jump on competitors living in Norway, it was a good place in which to recoup after a long raiding voyage and from which to transship loot and slaves to Norway-bound vessels.

Shetland itself could never have been a significant source of wealth. Its holy places must soon have been picked bare and the few native men of property robbed blind. Local steadings were mostly hard-scrabble crofts able to support only a scattering of sheep and cattle. Valuta goods from Tilli would have been worth a Viking's while, but once the Norse had established a permanent presence in Shetland, farfarers would hardly have been fool enough to continue bringing cargoes there.

Shetland indigenes were too few to provide any considerable supply of slaves for sale abroad. And perhaps they were more valuable as local serfs producing country food, repairing damaged ships, or serving as pilots to southern lands. Certainly the island names of *Fetlar, Unst,* and *Yell* are not Norse, nor do they belong to any other known language. They appear to be indigenous and their endurance in the overwhelming sea of Norse nomenclature that swept over Shetland and Orkney suggests the survival of some aboriginals.

Existing Shetland traditions speak of a people called *Finns* who inhabited Fetlar and northwest Unst for some time after the Norse occupied Shetland. This name is identical with the one by which the Norse knew the aboriginals of northern Scandinavia. It was also the name given by Shetlanders (of Norse lineage) to a scattering of Inuit who, in kayaks, materialized amongst the Northern Isles during the eighteenth century. Presumably these unfortunates had been captured by European whalers working the Greenland grounds, and either escaped or were released when the ships neared British waters. In any event, Shetlanders used the same name for these small-statured, dark-skinned strangers that their ancestors had given to the people who preceded the Norse in Shetland.

Vikings may have spared some of Shetland's aboriginals but not all would have been so favoured. In 1958 excavators of a ruined chapel of pre-Norse origin on St. Ninian's Isle uncovered a wooden box buried under a stone floor. Amongst other things, the box contained several silver bowls, a communion spoon, and a number of brooches, all tentatively dated to the seventh century. This treasure had presumably been hidden in fear of a raid. The failure of its owners to reclaim it can best be explained by their having been killed or carried off into slavery.

Shetland may not have possessed much loot worthy of a Viking, but Orkney was a different matter. The first Norse traders who ventured to that mainly low-lying, fertile, and well-peopled archipelago would have brought back mouth-watering accounts of a marvellously green land richly endowed with herds of fat cattle and inhabited by people whose massive monuments spoke eloquently of affluence. The traders would also have noted many temples to White Christ, and associated religious communities that, in those times before celibacy became the priestly rule, thronged with men, women, and children.

Orkney's manifold temptations would have been irresistible. However, when Viking raiders drove south beyond Fair Isle, the Orcadians were forewarned and ready. They had repaired many of the old brochs; probably set up coastal watches; concentrated men and vessels; and were generally prepared for trouble. Doubtless they had also sent messengers to mainland Britain to warn the king of what was happening, and perhaps to ask for war galleys that could engage the *knorrin*.

With or without help, Orkney resisted. An island legend tells of a Viking raid met and repulsed by a phalanx of local spearmen. The story may be apocryphal but a twelfth-century Latin compendium called *Historia Norwegiae* carries the ring of truth. Distorted as it may be by its Norwegian author's contempt for Viking victims, it nonetheless provides our only glimpse of the Islanders as the Norse doom fell upon them. What follows is the essence of the text, which is reproduced in full in the notes, together with my comments.[2]

> Originally it was the "Peti" and the "Papae" who inhabited these [Northern] islands. The first of these people, I mean the Peti, were scarcely taller than pygmies. Morning and evening they busied themselves to an amazing degree with the building and fitting out of their towns. But at midday, thoroughly drained of all their strength, they lay low in their little underground houses under the pressure of their fears....
>
> But in the days of Harold the Hairy...some pirates [Vikings] kin to the very powerful pirate Rognvald advanced with a large fleet across the Solundic Sea. They threw these people out of their long-standing habitations and utterly destroyed them; they then made the islands subject to themselves.

The Islanders had no "towns," but did have brochs. This is a description of a people being harassed to exhaustion while trying to fortify themselves against an imminent and pervasive menace.

The note concludes with the brutally definitive statement: *"the islanders were utterly destroyed."*

By 681 Vikings were already thrusting beyond Orkney to raid the Alban mainland. Although, as we have seen, King Brudei did take his forces across the Pentland Firth in a venture that "resulted in much devastation," the relief was short-lived. After Brudei's death in 693, and the subsequent internal disruption in the kingdom of Alba, the way was open for the Northmen to return. This they quickly did, literally with a vengeance. Orkney was laid completely at their mercy...and they had little mercy to bestow.

Internal turmoil persisted in Alba through the first twenty years of the eighth century. It was finally quelled by a man whose name the keepers of the Irish annals rendered in Gaelic as Oengus mac Fergus. His antecedents are unknown but he was clearly a hard-driving military leader and ruthless politician.

He set out to save the kingdom.

First he initiated a rebellion against the then king, Nechtan, in an unsuccessful attempt to force that vacillating monarch to rally Alba against its several enemies. The first rebellion failed, but by 729 Oengus had established control over what remained of the kingdom. He spent the next thirty-odd years battling for its survival and, in the process, became one of the very few individual Albans to leave a mark on the historical record.

Oengus's first step seems to have been an ill-fated attempt to regain control of the Northern Islands. There is a tantalizingly brief entry in the Irish annals to the effect that in 729 a "Pictish" fleet of 150 vessels was lost off Ross Cuisini.

Ross Cuisini is Irish for Cape of the Picts, which would make it one of the prominent headlands facing west. A good candidate might be Cape Wrath (Cape Ross?) at the northwestern tip of Scotland.

I conclude that this formidable naval force, about which nothing else is known, was assembled in northern Alban waters for an attack on the Vikings in the archipelagos. Then disaster struck. Perhaps the fleet was shattered in battle, but it could have been destroyed by one of the fearsome storms for which the Pentland Firth is notorious. Whatever the cause of the calamity, the consequences were devastating.

Archibald Lewis writes in *The Northern Seas*:[3]

In the land of the Picts that naval power, so noticeable in the seventh century, disappears by the eighth. The complete decadence of maritime life is a most mysterious affair.... We hear nothing more of the Pictish fleet which had been active off the coasts of Scotland and about Orkney.... Now it was the mariners from Western Norway who began probing south, doing so with little opposition.

The loss of the fleet removed the last real hope of stemming a tide that would eventually overwhelm Ireland and much of Britain. It also signalled the absolute demise of Alba in the Northern Isles. Thereafter the islands would become, and remain, a Norse fiefdom for five hundred years.

The Norse seizure of the southern of the twin archipelagos was probably substantially different from what had happened in Shetland. Orkney was not nibbled to death but submerged by masses of men and ships pouring down on it from the north. Although preceded by raiders, the bulk of the incomers were bent on land taking and, in the absence of any effective naval defence, they swamped the islands.

By the middle of the eighth century, few if any of Orkney's original inhabitants could have survived on the home islands as free men. Even their once impregnable brochs could not have protected them. When one of these, the Broch of Burgar, was excavated, it yielded a pathetic cache of women's possessions of the Norse invasion period, including brooches and combs hidden, but never recovered, by their dispossessed owners.

Oengus was never again able to assemble the resources for an effective strike against his nemesis in the north. During the remainder of his reign, which lasted until 761, he was desperately engaged in land battles against Scotti in the west and Britons in the south. In 741 he smashed an invading Irish army, but the Scotti came again in 750 and defeated him. Although he had early victories against the Britons, they, too, counterattacked and, in 756, shattered the Alban forces.

With the loss of the fleet at Ross Cuisini, Alba north of the Great Glen no longer had the means to defend herself. The coastal regions of Caithness, Sutherland, and Ross were overrun by the Sons of Death, as were most of the inner islands in the Hebridean Sea. In their turn, the outer islands of Lewis, Harris, Uist, and Barra fell.

Before the century ended, Vikings were rampaging almost unchallenged through the west. The raid on "God's Church" at Lindisfarne took place in 793. Irish annals for the following year lament "the devastation of all the islands of Britain by the heathens."

By 798 Ireland herself was coming under sustained attack and the

Annals of Ulster reported "great devastations between Erin and Alba." Northmen were also ranging far to the south. In 789, according to the *Anglo-Saxon Chronicle,*

> King Beorhtric [of Wessex] took Eadburgh, King Offa's daughter, to wife. And in those days first came three ships. And then his reeve rode thereto and would compel them to the King's will, for he knew not what they were, and there they slew him. These were the first ships of Danish men that sought the land of the English race.

Later recensions of the *Chronicle* identify Dorchester as the site of the landing, and the raiders as Norse from Horthaland.

In 802, according to the *Annals of Ulster,* the famous monastery of Columba on the island of Iona, which had already been raided several times, was burned by the pagans. And by 836 the Northmen had made Dublin one of their main bases in the west.

The shrunken kingdom of Alba made its last stand in 838 at

> a battle by the Heathens against the men of Fortrui [Picts of south-central Scotland] and in it fell Eoganan, son of Oengus, and Bran, son of Oengus.... Many men of the Fortrui had fallen, almost without number.

The *Chronicles of Huntingdon* tells us that Alba never recovered.

> When the Danish [Norwegian] pirates, with the greatest slaughter had destroyed the Picts [at Fortrui] who defended their land, Kenneth [mac Alpin, King of Dalriada] passed into and turned his arms against the remaining territory of the Picts and after slaying many drove the rest to flight. And so he was the first of the Scotti to obtain the monarchy of the whole of Albania.

If Kenneth and his Scotti were not actually in league with the Sons of Death they must have had an understanding with them. How else can one explain that Dalriada, which by then encompassed most of western Scotland south of Glen Albyn, miraculously escaped the devastation visited upon all the neighbouring regions?

Independent evidence strongly suggests such an unholy alliance between Irish and Norse. The Icelandic *Landnámabók* tells us that

> Harald the Fairhaired subdued unto his power all the Hebrides but, when he returned to Norway, Vikings took themselves into those islands as well as Scots and Irish and harried and plundered wide about.

The *Annals of Innisfallen* for 798 recorded "the Hebrides and Ulster plundered by the Lochlachan," who almost certainly were Dalriada Scotti.[4] Then, too, there is the report of Olaf's return to Dublin after raiding western Alba. He brought two hundred ships to harbour laden with "a great spoil of people, English, Britons, and Picts." No Scotti, be it noted.

As the ninth century drew on, there was hardly a place on Britain's coasts, and precious few inland, secure from the fury of the Northmen.

One haven alone remained...far out in the northwestern reaches of Ocean.

PART TWO

WORLDS TO THE WEST

CHAPTER THIRTEEN

TILLI

Farfarer was reaching to the westward. A brisk breeze filled her sail. The high peaks of the Bird Islands had sunk into the sea astern, and the green sweep of the Western Ocean stretched to the horizon on every hand.

Eddies of fulmars and shearwaters swirled overhead. Gannets plunged into the sea like a rain of javelins. Great auks rafted in the vessel's path in such dense formations the helmsman had to resist the impulse to alter course.

He did alter course to avoid the vast bulk of somnolent whales when the ship found herself amidst such a concourse of them that their spoutings misted the horizon.[1]

Almost always, even during storms, *Farfarer* was accompanied by throngs of dolphins and porpoises who seemed to view her as a large but disadvantaged member of their own kind needing encouragement, if not entertainment.

Life was even more profuse beneath the surface. An unbaited hook dangled over the side would be seized by a fish frequently too large for one man to haul aboard. Hundred-pound cod and five-hundred-pound halibut were a confounded nuisance to fishermen equipped only with light hand gear.

Such was the world of waters through which this *Farfarer's* cutwater sliced. She may have been the tenth, or the twentieth, vessel to bear the name, yet in essence she was little different from her ancestors.

On this autumnal day in the seventh century A.D. she was returning to her new home port of Swan Fiord on Tilli's eastern seaboard after voyaging to Orkney to exchange valuta for southern goods. Tilli was still below the horizon but there could be no doubt where the mid-ocean island to which *Farfarer's* clan had emigrated from Fetlar a generation earlier lay. Seemingly endless skeins of ducks, geese, and swans were streaming southeastward from it along an invisible path known to generations of Northern Islanders as the Swan's Way.

The breeze held steady, and in due course a lookout spotted the luminous reflection of Whiteskull in the sky just where it ought to be, a point or so to starboard. Before the gleaming brow of the great glacier hove clear of the horizon, Farfarer encountered a cluster of Tilli's ancient residents. Hoary great heads with gleaming eyes, spiked whiskers, and scimitar-shaped tusks peered at the vessel. Two green hands from Orkney, making their first passage out, were awed by this meeting with the legendary orcas whose lives had been intimately intertwined with those of the Islanders since time out of memory.

Farfarer closed with the land near the promontory, called Horn, on the southeastern coast. Dusk was falling as, with her skipper's hand on the tiller, she bore up through a narrow entrance into the broad lagoon of Easthaven-under-Horn, Tilli's unofficial capital.

It had long been standard practice for westbound vessels to make their landfalls at Horn and for those bound east to take their departures from it. Within Easthaven's capacious lagoon, vessels could lie safely at anchor in any kind of weather, or be hauled high and dry on sandy beaches if needs must.

Easthaven was the rendezvous for all who came this way. Through generations, valuta seekers had paused here to exchange news and to refresh themselves with the produce of crofters, some of whose forebears had settled along the east coast as early as the fourth century. Transients and residents alike worshipped at a chapel presided over by a priest from Ninian's mission who lived with his wife and children on a croft adjacent to the chapel.

Farfarer came to anchor and her crew went ashore to stretch their legs amongst turf-and-stone booths built close to the beach. A tantalizing odour of roasting meat drifted from outdoor cooking fires. People from several ships wandered from hut to hut exchanging gossip and renewing friendships.

On this particular night, two topics dominated the talk.

One was the dwindling number of tuskers on Tilli's beaches and in the great island's fringing waters. Walrus had been slowly growing scarcer for generations; now they were so diminished, and so wary, as to be scarcely able to sustain the ivory trade.

"They're going out, and no mistake," grumbled an older man. "P'rhaps they've grown tired of Tilli and all gone west to Crona or beyond. What think ye, Skipper?"

The question was addressed to Farfarer's master, a vigorous, rough-bearded man of middle age. He took his time replying.

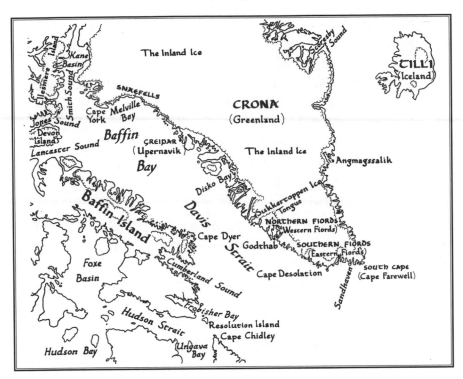

Map of Greenland and Iceland.

"Indeed, there's some orca to be found on Crona's eastern shores," he said cautiously. "As for the western coast...well, nobody's yet sailed along it more than four or five days beyond South Cape. No telling how far north it runs. A man might not be too surprised to find lots of ivory in that direction if he sailed far enough."

The other topic engrossing men's thoughts related to the home islands. Farfarer's crewmen had brought dire news.

Less than a week before departing Orkney, they had heard of a grim happening. Tiny Ninian's Isle had been assaulted; the church and most other buildings sacked and destroyed; men, old folk, and young children slaughtered; and girls and women carried away.

"The bloody Northmen!" raged a valuta seeker from Bressay who had been a year away from home. "They say they come to trade in peace—then act like devils! Each year there's more of them among the Islands...and more trouble. It's hard for a man to fare away and leave his folk at home with that lot ranging round."

"You should do what we've done, then," said one of Farfarer's men. "Shift out here, neck and heel. You can see for yourself, there's good land. And we're closer to *the Crona grounds. Yes, and 'tis a damned sight safer for them as has to stay put and mind the home fires!"*

Less than two decades had passed since Farfarer's clan had abandoned their age-old home on Fetlar for the shores of the east-coast lagoon called Swan Fiord, half a day's sail north of Horn. Although older folk still yearned for the familiar hills, the move had made things much easier for the valuta men, who could now reach their hunting grounds in half the former time.

The man from Bressay nodded thoughtfully as he chewed away at a steaming joint of seal. Tilli was looking better and better to a lot of Northern Islanders.

ICELAND IS A VAST PLUTONIC DOME BURSTING OUT OF THE North Atlantic roughly midway between Scotland and Greenland. It is larger than Ireland (about the size of Newfoundland or the state of Kentucky), and its northern coast touches the Arctic Circle but, because it is almost completely embraced by arms of the Gulf Stream it is blessed with a moderate oceanic climate.

That this has not always been the case is evidenced by four large and a dozen small glaciers which dominate its interior. Vatnajökull, the Whiteskull of the Albans, is almost a hundred miles long, fifty wide, and nearly a mile thick—a monstrous remnant of the last Ice Age.

Yet Iceland is also a land of boiling lava. New volcanoes continue to arise. In 1963 an undersea eruption not far from the Westman Islands threw up an entirely new island now called Surtsey. Ten years later the largest settlement on the Westmans was so threatened by another eruption it had to be evacuated.

These events do not compare with the catastrophe of 1783 when the Laki fissure south of Vatnajökull opened to spew out the greatest lava flow recorded anywhere on earth in modern times. Falls of ash and lava together with poisonous gases killed so many sheep and cattle island-wide that a fifth of the human population subsequently died of famine.

The glowing coals in Iceland's belly continue to give notice of their presence through innumerable hot springs and geysers.

The interior of this land of ice and fire largely consists of uninhabitable lava deserts, but there are green lowlands along most of the coasts and in some inland regions, where farmers and pastoralists have successfully struck root during favourable climatic periods. At all times the shores have boasted a plethora of marine life upon which hunters could depend for a living.

Although Northern Islanders had been familiar with Tilli since before the days of Pytheas, they may not have been the first to set foot upon it.

That iconoclastic British archaeologist Tom Lethbridge believed men may have walked Tilli's beaches in much earlier times. Indeed, North Americans could have reached Iceland via Greenland without much difficulty during a climatic optimum that occurred between c. 1800 and c. 1500 B.C. This warm spell saw a massive reduction in ice cover over the Arctic Ocean, in consequence of which very little pack flowed south between Iceland and Greenland. And during this period, when the ice barrier between the two great islands had virtually ceased to exist, men were travelling along the east Greenland coast.

From as early as 2000 B.C. northeastern Greenland had been home to tundra dwellers who lived chiefly on musk ox and caribou. They were good hunters—too good for their own good—and towards the latter part of the warm period had virtually exterminated musk ox in the high north. As is described in chapter 16, they then moved south along both eastern and western coasts, looking for new sources of provender.

Those who committed themselves to the east coast would have found no musk ox and precious few land mammals of any species south of Scoresby Sound. But the bright glitter of Iceland's glaciers, the vivid mirages characteristic of the high Arctic, the flight of waterfowl, and distant volcanic smoke by day or flames by night must have made them aware of the existence of a new land not far distant to the east. In truth, the highlands of Iceland and Greenland are visible to the naked eye of anyone who cares to scale the heights on either side of the intervening strait.

Crossing that strait would have offered no great challenge to people with boats good enough to navigate the rugged east Greenland coast. The shortest distance is only 175 miles, and the mountains backing the opposing shores are so high that a vessel making the passage in clear weather need never be long out of sight of land.

Either by accident or intent, these people may well have become the first of our species to visit Iceland. It probably would have disappointed them. Although blessed with an abundance of waterfowl and sea animals, it harboured *no* land mammals except Arctic foxes and white bears. Hunters from the west would have found no caribou (or reindeer, which are essentially the same thing), and no musk ox. People *can* eat foxes, and bears too if the bears don't first become the eaters; but neither species can be considered a sustaining food for any significant number of human beings.

If Iceland's first-footers did come from Greenland, they evidently did not remain long, and they left little evidence of their stay. *No* evidence, according to most Icelandic historians. But proof of an early and transient human presence in Iceland would necessarily be scanty. Volcanic eruptions have buried even many modern human habitation sites. Only extraordinarily good luck would have preserved the scanty detritus left by a small number of neolithic visitors.

Nevertheless, such a discovery may have been made. According to Kevin Smith of the Buffalo Museum of Science, a quartz core from which micro blades had been struck has recently been excavated in western Iceland. It is similar to cores left by people of the palaeo-Arctic tradition that, in the North American Arctic, date back at least three thousand years.

The earliest human beings *of record* to visit Iceland were the men who guided Pytheas there around 330 B.C., though they are not likely to have been the first of their kind to cross the wide waters separating Iceland from the Northern Islands.

What would Tilli have been like when the first Europeans came upon it?

If they arrived in spring they would have found every sea cliff whitened by nesting oceanic birds. Most of the larger islands and all of the inland reaches, excepting only sheer mountain slopes, barren lava fields, and equally barren glaciers, harboured legions of swans, geese, and ducks come to breed in one of the planet's greatest waterfowl havens.

The enormous bird population would have attracted flying predators, chief amongst these being sea eagles, golden eagles, peregrine falcons, and gyrfalcons—all of which were highly valued by falconers, the latter two being literally worth their weight in gold to royal practitioners of the sport in Europe and the East.

This avian world also has sustained great numbers of Arctic foxes, both white and blue, whose pelts were highly valued in European markets as exotic rarities.

The white or water bear was equally at home, whether in the sea or when it came ashore to fish in salmon rivers or to den and raise its young. Initially it must have been at least as abundant in Iceland as in southeastern Labrador, where, as late as the mid-eighteenth century, thirty or forty white bears were sometimes to be found fishing the lower reaches of a single salmon stream.[2] They were not called "polar" bears in those times. It was not until the nineteenth century that the remnants of the species, which by then survived mostly in high latitudes, acquired that name.

The sagas testify that water bears still occurred in Iceland in Norse times and that as late as the 1400s a white bear pelt was still worth a fortune in Continental markets, while a live cub was considered a gift fit for a king.

The land produced riches, but the sea surpassed it. Bowhead, black right, grey, humpback, fin, sei, and Bryde's whales abounded.[3] Although valuta seekers seem not to have hunted the great whales extensively, they probably collected baleen from strandings. And they actively hunted the narwhal, whose spiralled ivory tusk surpassed in value all other Arctic products, with the possible exception of gyrfalcons.

Ring, grey, and harbour seals thronged coastal waters, their rendered oil being an important source of the tar used in great quantities for sealing the seams of wooden ships and waterproofing skin-covered ones.

The variety of living creatures that could be converted into riches must have amazed the first European visitors to Tilli. But foremost were the walrus. We will never know how many tuskers encrusted Tilli's beaches, but can estimate (by analogy with the size of the herds encountered by latter-day exploiters in the Gulf of St. Lawrence and on Sable Island) that they must have numbered in the hundreds of thousands.[4]

So much ivory! So much leather! So much fat to be rendered into oil! Valuta-hunting ventures must have been undertaken almost as soon as Albans discovered Tilli.

Valuta voyages were never casual affairs haphazardly undertaken by a handful of adventurers in any old vessel. Each farfaring ship was painstakingly built and fitted for her task and crewed by the most skilful hunter-sailormen, accompanied by wives and sisters, sons and daughters, all of equal competence.

A vessel's outfit included everything necessary to keep the ship in good repair, but very little food. Valuta seekers took most of their livelihood from land and sea. Self-sufficiency was the order of the day on voyages that could last a year or more.

Hunters arriving in early summer would land on Tilli's southern coast, whose almost endless beaches, protected lagoons, and rich offshore shellfish pastures provided ideal seasonal grounds for enormous numbers of walrus. Each crew worked a stretch of beach belonging by tradition to its clan. Each vessel was unladen, hauled far enough up to be safely out of reach of storm tides, and overturned to serve as a shelter for her people.[5]

The walrus-killing season lasted until the fierce storms of autumn began to ravage the open coast and roaring breakers rendered the beaches unusable to walrus and hunters alike.

Both now made their separate ways to wintering grounds along the fiord-riven northern and especially western coasts. During the winter, walrus spent most of their time at sea, hauling out occasionally on reefs, rocky ledges, and wave-swept islets. Here they were seldom molested. Nobody relished hunting them from skin boats, preferring instead to make market kills at the mass haul-outs on summer beaches.

Faxaflói and Breidafjördur were particularly favoured Alban winter bases because they harboured an abundance of seals, which, in turn, attracted white bears. Bear hunting and fox trapping were major occupations during the dark, cold winter months.

Seals were also taken, especially in January, when grey seals whelped on offshore reefs. With the coming of spring some people busied themselves collecting eiderdown. Others departed on small-boat expeditions to slaughter flightless great auks on their island rookeries for fat and feathers. The younger and most agile men set off inland in search of gyrfalcon and peregrine eyries on high-country cliffs. People remaining at the camp caught and dried salmon, which flooded the streams in such numbers they could be forked ashore.

Salmon fishing could become exceedingly exciting when human fishers found themselves challenged by competing water bears. At such times the islanders' black dogs more than earned their keep by distracting the white giants.

As spring turned to summer, vessels were repaired and their skin coverings tarred preparatory to launching. Once again houses were transformed into ships. Some set sail for home in the Northern Isles. Others returned to Tilli's south coast for one more slaughter on the beaches before their final departure late in the second summer.

From very early times, individual Albans of the lone-wolf variety elected to live on the island permanently, in much the same fashion that white trappers have chosen in modern times to live isolated in the Canadian Arctic.

The exploitation of Tilli's riches had its ups and downs. Periods of deteriorating weather magnified the natural hazards of farfaring but the weather never became bad enough to prevent some determined valuta seekers from sailing to and from Tilli.

Valuta from Tilli (and beyond) sustained the Northern Islanders. But, as the eighth century A.D. approached, the land of fire and ice was destined to play an even more vital role in their survival.

CHAPTER FOURTEEN

SANCTUARY

FAVOURABLE WEATHER BEGINNING EARLY IN THE Christian era seems to have persuaded a few hardy crofters to join a scattering of loners sustaining themselves on Tilli as hunter-gatherers. A subsequent long cool spell around A.D. 300 might have discouraged settlement, although Roman coins of the period found in the Eastfiords, backed by the account of Theodosius's expedition to Thule in 363, suggest that eastern Iceland, at least, was then inhabited.

There were good reasons why settlement should have begun along the eastern coast. This was where Tilli lay closest to Britain; the Eastfiords abounded in good harbours; the east-coast climate (warmed by tendrils of the Gulf Stream) was especially favourable; and the countryside afforded a mixture of wooded and arable lands.

During the fifth century, the North Atlantic climate entered a long period of improvement. Fewer storms raged; mean temperatures rose; and there was less rain and snow. Enticed by Tilli's good pastoral prospects, and made increasingly uneasy by political and military uncertainties boiling up in the wake of Rome's departure from Britain, more and more Northern Islanders seem to have made the journey west.

Circa 550 a British priest named Brendan, accompanied by fourteen fellow clerics, set sail from Ireland in a *curragh*—a wicker-framed vessel built on the same principle as Alban boats but covered with cow, instead of walrus, hides. After diverse adventures, the voyagers reached the Faeroes, where they wintered with a resident religious community.

The following spring they sailed west to a nearby land that must have been Tilli.[1]

Here they visited another religious settlement that may have been on the off-lying island the Norse called Papey, presumably because they had found Christians in prior possession of it.

In the accounts of Brendan's voyage it is called Isle of St. Albe. Brendan and his companions were welcomed by a white-haired abbot and entertained by clerics who said their foundation had been established eighty years earlier by a priest named Albe whom they now honoured as their patriarch.

Irish church history tells us that St. Albe and St. Patrick were contemporaries. Albe reputedly spent his final years in Ireland, but there is no evidence he was Celtic. It seems fair to assume he was an Alban.

Historians generally admit there may have been a few Europeans in Iceland at the coming of the Norse, but write them off as of little consequence, assuming they amounted to no more than a small scattering of Christian hermits seeking isolation from mankind and devoting themselves to abjuring the profane and mortifying the flesh.[2]

The people Brendan met do not fit this image. We are told they ate white bread, which was the height of luxury in those times, and drank from crystal goblets. Rather than ascetic anchorites, they are portrayed as a high-living lot whose prosperity must needs have been maintained by a well-to-do parish.

Residents of Tilli in those days *ought* to have been relatively prosperous. Good land in quantity was available for the taking. The soil was far more generous than that of the constricted holdings on the home islands. Virgin ground and favourable weather would have produced bumper crops. Valuta goods were to be had in abundance. Of a certainty, resident clergy should have been well provided for.

On fine evenings people gather in the dooryards of their crofts; men to slouch about and yarn while mending tools and implements; younger women to season the air with the aromas of mutton, fish, or seabirds boiling in pots suspended from tripods over open fires. Older women knit and sew by the long light of the sinking sun. Youngsters bother their elders, and play with ever-attendant dogs.

If the weather turns foul, people withdraw into the long, low, single room of each turf-built house. They eat by the flicker of saucer-lamps, then listen to stories, or sing old songs until it is time to clear away the benches and lie down to sleep (some to make love) on, and under, piles of fleeces.

During daytime the houses belong to the women who, when they are not cooking or dealing with children, make butter and cheese, card wool, and weave homespun. They have much to do, but time remains for pleasuring themselves with talk and the practice of decorative skills.

The men's main summer task is to lay up a sufficient supply of hay. The half-wild sheep can look after themselves year round, as can the hairy little horses; but if cattle are to continue to give milk and to survive the winter, they must be stabled and provided with hay.

Harvesting wild grasses over rough and uneven ground with hand sickles is exceedingly laborious. If it becomes too tedious one can always go fishing. Nets are set in the runs between islands and at river mouths. On any day when it is not pouring rain or blowing a living gale, boys will be out jigging fish from little skin-covered boats not much larger than bathtubs. When the salmon run is on, all available hands spread out along the stream banks, spearing and gaffing the fat fish as they work upstream against the current.

Summer and winter, the men spend as much time as they can spare from the crofts, hunting and trapping foxes, seals, and other creatures whose produce will be added to the valuta brought home by the clan's farfarers. Men and youths also kill great numbers of waterfowl and seabirds and fill many sealskin sacks with swan, duck, and goose eggs preserved in oil.

On Sundays and feast days, the crofters assemble at their local chapels or, if they are near enough, at one of the large clerical establishments, there to worship God and to share the news of their small world. For the most part the news is good, and life is well worth living.

By early in the sixth century, Tilli had notably changed its spots. What had once been a valuta hunting ground par excellence had become home to a growing population of small holders, herdsmen, and fishermen whose crofts clustered along the habitable portions of the eastern and southern coasts.

However, as the numbers of people increased, those of wild creatures diminished. The tusker tribes were much reduced and the survivors had altered their ancient ways. Now they eschewed the great sand beaches, hauling out instead in small and wary companies on offshore reefs where they could be neither surprised nor driven

SANCTUARY

inland. This was especially hard lines for valuta men because a mounting vogue on the Continent for ivory religious carvings and decorations was making white gold more sought after than ever.

Valuta hunters were also having trouble finding bears and gyrfalcons. Bears were in short supply partly because of hunting but mainly because the polar pack, which was their summer seal-hunting ground, no longer came close to Tilli. Falcons were growing scarce because so many crofters were robbing fledglings from the nests.

As Tilli's animal resources began to fail, valuta men did as their ancestors had done in the past. They fared farther westward, searching for new grounds.

Climatic conditions for farfaring had never been better. By the mid-sixth century, the river of Arctic pack flowing south between Tilli and Greenland had become no more than a minor seasonal obstruction which, in some years, vanished entirely.

In the past, venturesome probes (to say nothing of involuntary voyages due to stress of weather) had been made to the land the Albans knew as Crona. There was now little to prevent valuta hunters from sailing there almost at will.

Cape Brewster stands about halfway along the east Greenland coast. The thousand-mile stretch of southeast-trending shoreline separating it from Cape Farewell is mostly fronted by a wall of glacial ice thousands of feet thick which, in many places, crowds almost to the sea. This is such an inhospitable shore, with such limited animal resources that, with the exception of a small region around Angmagssalik, it has repulsed even the efforts of the Inuit to maintain a foothold upon it.

However, for six hundred miles to the *northward* of Cape Brewster Greenland's east coast is of an entirely different nature. Here is a glacier-free land of mountains, moraines, and tundra-carpeted valleys as large as Iceland itself. The coast is deeply indented by convoluted fiords, one of which, Scoresby Sound, runs into the land for almost two hundred miles before encountering the inland ice.

These northeastern fiords and the country surrounding them have long been rich in animal life. Even as late as the early years of the twentieth century, more than 150 cabins belonging to Norwegian and Danish trappers dotted the shores of the fiord complexes. The wealth these men obtained from fox, bear, musk ox, ermine, and wolf pelts, together with seal skins and fat, walrus ivory, and narwhal horns, was so great that Norway attempted to annex the entire region, and was prevented from doing so only by the intervention of the League of Nations acting on Denmark's behalf.

Valuta seekers would have found here all the sources of wealth Tilli had once afforded, together with a number Tilli had never known, such as caribou, wolf, ermine, Arctic hares, and, especially, musk ox, whose woolly pelts came to be valued almost equally with those of white bears.

I conclude that, before the sixth century ended, most valuta men were working Greenland's northeastern grounds. Those with homes in the Northern Isles probably overwintered in Crona, for it was a long journey between the two places.

Sooner or later the distance between home and hunting ground would have persuaded valuta clans to emigrate to Tilli. Nor would it have been long before Orkney merchant skippers began sailing direct to Tilli to collect valuta for the southern trade, as well as to peddle southern goods to the island's growing population.

By the seventh century, most valuta clans had probably made the westward move. Thereafter their farfarers could sail to eastern Crona early in the spring and, if it suited them, return to their new crofts in Tilli in the autumn of that same year.

The foregoing reconstruction of the settlement of Iceland flies in the teeth of orthodox histories of the island, which maintain that, with the possible exception of a few clerical hermits, it was *terra incognita* until the arrival of Norse settlers late in the ninth century.

Belief in this view can be maintained only by rejecting weighty evidence to the contrary—evidence such as that which I have outlined in the note.[3] There are also the findings of Dr. Margrét Hermanns-Audardóttir.[4]

Between 1972 and 1978, this Swedish archaeologist and her team began investigating the remains of a fourteenth-century Norse steading on Heimaey, one of the Westman group of islands lying off the south coast of Iceland. However, the excavation revealed that under the visible remains lay a sequence of *at least ten* earlier structures. The site was clearly much older than had been assumed. The archaeologists took carbon-14 samples and the resultant dates were an astonishment to all parties and a source of embarrassment to some.

Dates obtained from carbon-14 tests, confirmed by stratigraphy and pollen analysis, showed that the first structure on the site must have come into existence *about 250 years before the Norse occupation of Iceland.*

Worse was to follow. Hermanns-Audardóttir's carbon-14 chronology revealed that the method previously relied upon by Icelandic historians to date human habitations (a method which had placed all previously examined sites within the period of Norse occupancy) was evidently based on a false premise. Dates had been assigned according to the presence or absence in wall and roof debris of layers of volcanic ash from eruptions, the most important of which were supposed to have taken place around 872–74. Hermanns-Audardóttir's data showed that the critical ash deposits, especially the so-called *landnam* and *Katla* layers, had actually been deposited at least a hundred years earlier. The corollary was that a considerable number of habitations, which had been confidently assigned to the Norse land-taking period, must have been occupied well before the Norse came to Iceland's shores.

But that was impossible! Icelandic history is adamantly predicated on the premise that the Norse did not reach the island until the latter half of the ninth century and that, when they did arrive, they found the country uninhabited except, perhaps, for a handful of anchorites seeking solitude at the end of the world.

On a spring day near the end of the seventh century, Farfarer sailed from her home port of Swan Fiord in eastern Tilli bound for the valuta grounds in Crona. She had one call to make en route. Two elderly people and a young couple recently arrived at Easthaven from the small Shetland island of Hasco had booked passage to Heimaey aboard her.

Most of Hasco's people had already abandoned their hard-scrabble crofts to seek a new life in Tilli. The first-footers among them had chosen Heimaey rather than the mainland coast because it seemed better suited to island ways, even though its sulphurous volcanic vent made an unnerving neighbour. Heimaey had not much usable land to offer, but what there was was fertile, and the island's snug little harbour provided one of the few secure refuges along Tilli's southern shore.

The first settler from Hasco built his sod-walled house, raftered with mainland birch and covered with turf, near a freshwater spring not far from the harbour. Since then, several houses had joined his around this spring, their small home fields making a verdant patchwork against the lava slopes beyond. A clutter of skin boats drawn up on the harbour shore testified to the little community's ongoing reliance on the sea. A few cattle ranged the lower pastures, while sheep and goats roamed the high places. Small patches of barley brightened the green of the home fields, and succulent angelica, the wild celery of the north transplanted from Hasco, grew thick in the swamp below the spring.

As Farfarer came abeam of Bear Islet (where a white bear had been killed some years earlier), she overhauled one of the settlers' boats laden to the gunwales with the enormous, grey-green eggs of the great auk. Farfarer took the boat in tow while its crew scrambled aboard to pilot the ship into Heimaey harbour.

Heimaey's settlers had only good things to tell the new arrivals. The previous winter had been so mild there had been no need to stable their cows. In the autumn they had harvested grain enough to supply porridge for a year, with enough left over to brew a little ale for the Yuletide celebrations.

More and more vessels were coming their way, they said. Some, like Farfarer, carried valuta men between Crona and crofts in Tilli's eastern fiords. A few belonged to Orkney merchant traders. The previous summer a trading vessel all the way from Ireland had appeared, laden with, among other things, a variety of bronze dress ornaments with which to tempt male and female settlers alike.

Much of the traffic consisted of westbound vessels bringing land-seeking immigrants together with their cattle, goods, and chattels. New crofts were being carved out of bogs, meadows, and birch copses along much of the southwest coast. Far from feeling they were at the end of the world, the Heimaey folk felt themselves to be quite at the centre of things.

Their buoyant mood was somewhat shadowed when they heard from Farfarer's passengers of increasingly bloody atrocities being committed by Northmen in the homeland. Nevertheless, one of the younger crofters could see a bright side even to this.

"All the more reason for folk with yeast in their guts to come west. When was there ever a time someone or other wasn't marauding about the home isles? Here in Tilli we've nothing worse to fear than a water bear amongst the sheep. We sleep easy, and eat well. There's room enough hereabouts for all the men, women, and children in the Northern Isles to join us, have they the sense to do it."

"Aye," agreed one of Farfarer's crew, "and if Tilli should ever get too crowded,

Crona's not so far away. Its south fiords might be no such bad places to live, so I've heard. Maybe when I'm too old to sling me sleeping robes in the cuddy of a boat I'll build a croft out there myself and settle down."

Immigration into Tilli increased markedly during the latter part of the seventh century. The climate had by then become so temperate that even more northerly parts of the island were probably able to attract crofters. A potent stimulus was the dire shadow of the Norse that was inexorably overspreading Shetland and Orkney.

When, early in the eighth century, Northmen began seizing land in the Northern Isles, waves of Shetlanders, Orkneymen, and even Hebrideans fled west. Before that rush subsided, Tilli's southwestern district was largely settled.

Homesteaders arriving during the first half of the eighth century found a good choice of land, and a climate so benign they could grow barley and wheat and raise pigs and domestic fowl as well as cattle and sheep.

A short-lived climatic deterioration that seems to have reached its nadir around the turn of the eighth century made things more difficult for latecomers; even so, a spell of mediocre weather was a small price to pay for being able to live in peace.

Even after the Norse completed their occupation of Britain's northern and western islands, refugees probably continued to reach Tilli from mainland Scotland and from Ireland. Old enmities between Celts and Albans would have been submerged by the current catastrophe. Both peoples were Christian (though following different rituals) and both were being savaged by Norse pagans.

The first half of the ninth century may have seen the heyday of Alba in Tilli, with little groups of croft houses clustered near the coasts wherever the quality of the land was good enough to sustain men and beasts. Settlement may even have spread into some interior valleys, such as Lagarfljót in the east.

Far from suffering adversity as a result of having been driven from their old homelands, settlers in Tilli would have found themselves generally better off, with crofts producing as much as, or more than, those abandoned to the Norse.

People involved in the valuta trade must also have been doing very well. As we shall see, farfarers seem to have rounded Cape Farewell before the end of the seventh century, and by early in the eighth were working new grounds as far north as Upernavik. Ice conditions would not have presented as formidable a problem then as they do now. In fact, by the middle of the eighth century the climate had become so warm that portions of the Arctic Ocean may actually have been ice-free in summer and the flow of pack ice southward into Baffin Bay so reduced as to pose no great difficulties even for seafarers in skin boats.[5]

By the ninth century, crofters and valuta seekers in Tilli would have been enjoying a prosperity hard to equal in mainland Europe. It was inevitable that Vikings would get wind of it.

CHAPTER FIFTEEN

ARCTIC
ELDORADO

Every spring for twenty years Farfarer *had sailed out of Swan Fiord bound for the northeastern grounds of Crona. Twenty times she had returned to her home port deep-laden with meat, hides, fat, ivory, furs, and seal tar.*

She and her crews had served the clan well; but in recent years cargoes had diminished. This was, in part, due to the fact that valuta seekers had by then been hunting the northeastern grounds for over a century, but also to an influx of hunters from Tilli anxious to supplement the income from their home crofts. Competition was becoming stiff, and some of the most valuable prey animals were growing scarce.

There had been much talk about this at Swan Fiord during the previous winter. Farfarer's *current skipper, a whipcord lean man in his early thirties, had been particularly outspoken.*

"Too many hunters!" he bluntly told his fellow clansmen gathered around the hearth in the headman's house. "And too few beasts. Musk ox nearly finished. Narwhals and walrus getting so leery you can hardly get nigh to them. And falcons! Those bloody crofters sail across for a month in summer and snatch every bloody fledgling! The grounds is overworked! We'd best find new ones soon."

"Where would we look, then?" someone asked.

"Ah, well, you all know the odd ship has rounded Crona's South Cape? They say they found good land down there, though not much of the kind of stuff we want. But supposing...supposing the western coast runs as far north as the east coast does. Wouldn't there likely be grounds up there in the nor'west as good as ever there was in the nor'east? I says we has to go and see!"

And so it was that next spring Farfarer *bore away from Swan Fiord on a voyage which would lend new lustre to her name.*

For a time she held close enough to Tilli's southern shore for her crew to relish the vibrance of budding birch forests and recently settled pasture lands on the river plains, but on the third day this pleasant scene was replaced by the dour lava coast of the Smoke Peninsula jutting out from the southwestern corner of the island. The sun was hanging on the horizon when the venturers took their departure from Cape Smoky—and from Tilli.

The weather remained moderate and, two days after losing sight of land astern, the lookouts raised the white glare of Crona's icecap. This time, instead of bearing to the north as she had always done before, Farfarer *turned south. She was soon closing with a coast whose appearance was so inhospitable that her crew was not tempted to try a landing. Keeping a safe offing, they continued southward for three days to Crona's southern extremity.*

Rounding South Cape, Farfarer *sailed into a friendlier world. The Inland Ice was now only dimly visible in the blue distance. A vast country riven with sinuous fiords revealed itself between ice and sea. If not so green as Tilli, Crona's southwestern shore seemed a veritable paradise by comparison with her eastern one.*

One full day's sail to the northward from South Cape took Farfarer *into a great bight full of islands and fiords. Here, the vegetation was sometimes almost lush, and birds and mammals, including caribou, abounded. However, here were no musk ox, few bears, and not many white foxes. And, although the surrounding waters were filled with fishes and many kinds of whales and porpoises, they harboured neither narwhals nor tuskers.*

Southwestern Crona was a place to attract a crofter, but not a valuta seeker. After a day ashore spent hunting caribou, the crew returned aboard, impatient to be on. Farfarer *took up her quest but, to everyone's disappointment, the coast trended westward for a day and a night. On the morning of the second day, the crew's hopes quickened as they rounded a massive headland to find the land again trending north.*

Now they coasted a shoreline of spectacular headlands thrusting seaward between a succession of deep fiords. Since at this season it never really got dark they were able to sail by day and by night so long as the weather favoured.

As time passed they began encountering occasional tuskers, and noted with delight that the numbers of these increased with the increase in northing. Three weeks' sail beyond South Cape they bore eastward into a bight of such immensity it required almost a month to explore. Long before that month was out, the men from Swan Fiord knew they had found what they sought—here were new grounds whose promise exceeded their most sanguine hopes.

THE VAST INLET ON GREENLAND'S WESTERN COAST embracing Disko Bay and Vaigat Strait, together with Umanak and Karrats fiords supports a marine fauna of stunning diversity and abundance. The surrounding ice-free lands are almost equally hospitable to birds and mammals. When, in later centuries, first Norse, then Inuit reached this region, it proved to be one of their most productive hunting grounds.[1]

Here is how I see the human story of this region unfolding during the eighth and ninth centuries.

The first valuta seekers found the new grounds so rewarding that, within a decade, most of Tilli's professional hunters had joined in its exploitation. Nevertheless, it was not nearly as extensive as the northeastern grounds, so it was not long before latecomers (or especially keen hunters) began pushing still farther north.

Beyond the Svartenhuk peninsula they met the Inland Ice pressing right to the edge of the sea with only a fringe of islands fronting its glacial cliffs. Still father north even the islands ended, leaving nothing but a glittering white wall curving west around the bottom of Melville Bay.

This coast was, and remains, the birthing place for the greater part of the icebergs that infest North Atlantic waters. During the warm summers of the eighth century, titanic blocks of ice came tumbling into Melville Bay, virtually filling it with bergs. But there would have been little or no summer pack ice about in those times, so if a vessel stayed well off the coast, and if her people gave the floating islands a safe berth, they would have had little to fear.

Before long some venturesome crew crossed the bay of bergs to find that the head of Baffin Bay and the adjacent reaches of southern Kane Basin nurtured an almost unimaginably abundant population of valuta animals, especially walrus. It was also able to provide a rich source of metal in the form of fragments of a huge nickel-iron meteorite that long ago had struck and shattered on Cape York's icecap.[2]

What ensued thereafter was somewhat comparable to a latter-day gold rush. Every seaworthy valuta vessel and competent crew that could be mustered sailed to the far northwest.

Although the rush turned out to be relatively short-lived, it may have engaged several hundred people and a score of vessels—no insignificant numbers for the place and times.

The remoteness of the new discovery posed a problem. Since the over-the-bottom distance between Iceland and Kane Basin at the entrance of the high Arctic was of the order of three thousand miles, a round-trip voyage could take most of three months. Overwintering was essential for successful exploitation of these high Arctic grounds.

As many explorers would discover the hard and sometimes fatal way, surviving the harshly inimical Arctic winter is no easy matter. Food and shelter are the prime requisites. Food can be found by those who know where and how to look, but finding shelter may be something else.

Aboriginal Arctic dwellers solved that problem with the snow house. Valuta seekers found their solution in boat-roofed houses, a construction which had been traditional with them for centuries past. Their own vessels, upturned on foundation walls built of stones and tightly chinked with moss or sod, could protect them from the most extreme winter weather.

During the relatively short time the high Arctic white gold rush lasted, it drew valuta men far into the eastern and central parts of the Canadian Arctic. Most built their camps and overwintered in the vicinity of the Arctic phenomena known as *polynyas*.

These are bodies of salt water that either do not freeze at all, or freeze later in the fall and open earlier in spring than adjacent waters. They are mainly kept open by currents, both vertical and horizontal, though wind also plays a part. They range in size from a few acres to several hundred square miles. Wherever they are found, polynyas provide breathing and gathering places for sea mammals which would otherwise be forced to abandon the region during part or all of the winter season.

It is no accident that the largest assemblage of boat-roofed house foundations in the high north is concentrated around polynyas. Most are in the Smith Sound region, the remainder being adjacent to polynyas as far south and west as Devon, Little Cornwallis, Bathurst, and Somerset islands.

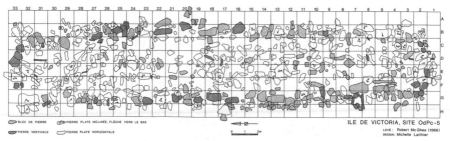

Two 50-foot vessels of 15-foot beam would have sufficed to form a roof over the foundation at Prince Patrick Sound, Victoria Island, shown here in plan.

One striking exception exists near the mouth of the Kuuk River on the west coast of Victoria Island. Slightly over one hundred feet long, this low walled structure discovered by Dr. Robert McGhee, head of the scientific section of the Archaeological Survey of Canada, stands alone on a desolate stretch of stony beach. Of the right dimensions to have supported two vessels overturned end to end, it may have been built by farfarers seeking an unclaimed polynya or forced far to the west by adverse ice conditions. On the other hand, McGhee has pointed out that the Kuuk River leads to a glacial deposit of native copper known to have been exploited by the Inuit, which could have been a source of copper for valuta seekers too.

Probably because of its isolation, the Kuuk River example is the best preserved of the forty-five boat-roofed foundations so far described or excavated. Most of the others have been quarried by natives for stones with which to build tent circles, meat caches, and shelters. Thule-culture people, impelled by a powerful animosity towards the original builders, may even have deliberately destroyed some of the foundations by systematically tumbling their walls. However, more than enough remain to provide a good idea of what the structures must once have looked like, of how they were built, and of how they functioned.

Although varying from about thirty to a hundred feet, the majority are of the order of fifty feet in length. Except for those few designed to support two, or even three, ships set end to end, they have an average length-to-width ratio of 3.5 to 1, roughly the same as that of north European working ships from circa A.D. 1000.

Walls were built only high enough to accommodate the curving shee

An Alban vessel upturned on a stone foundation to provide a home for her crew might have looked like this.

of the covering vessel and to provide internal headroom. Few seem to have been even as much as four feet in height.

Since there is little soil or sod in the high Arctic, foundations were constructed entirely of stones (sometimes very large ones) chinked with moss and lichens. In the subarctic they were generally built of sods ballasted with stones. Turf and sods reinforced with wood provided building materials south of timber line—a combination that time has reduced to almost invisible mounds.

Most were sited close to the high-tide and storm line. In several instances, rocks fouling a landing beach seem to have been cleared away to protect fragile vessels from damage when they were hauled ashore.

Once emptied of gear, ballast, and supplies, a fifty-foot skin boat would have been light enough to be manhandled to a mating with a prepared foundation. Larger vessels may have been moved on rollers, then overturned and eased into position using their own spars as levers.

There seems to have been only one (necessarily low) door, located in a side wall. There were no window openings, but well-oiled sea mammal skins are remarkably translucent. During the long winter night, the houses would have been lighted and, in the high Arctic, perhaps heated (Inuit style) by lamps fuelled with sea-mammal oil. Farther south, where wood was available for fuel, smoke could have presented something of a problem. But it would have been no trick to cut a smoke-flap in the "roof," an aperture that could have been easily patched before the vessel again took to the water.

Heating the entire interior of a large boat-roofed house would have been difficult. However, heatable cubicles could have been fashioned using animal skins (preferably caribou) for ceilings and curtain walls. This is a system I have myself used to good effect in the barrenlands of Keewatin.

Boat-roofed houses would have provided spacious, comfortable accommodations for the times when they were being built and used. They would also have ensured the best possible protection, from weather and from hungry animals, for the vessels themselves during the long winter months.

Valuta men took whatever of worth came their way, but concentrated on what was most rewarding. Walrus tusks and narwhal horns topped the list. Both animals gathered in polynyas, where they could be relatively easily harpooned.

High Arctic valuta stations were essentially factories, producing not only ivory, but walrus hides and the substance called seal tar.

Although bituminous (fossil-derived) tar did not become widely available in northern Europe until relatively recent times, large quantities derived from animals or plants were consumed in ship construction and maintenance. Some of this were produced from the gum of conifers, but most was made by evaporating sea mammal oil into a gummy substance generically known as seal tar.

Whether sheathed in wood or hides, ships required a lot of tar. Skin boats (especially the seams thereof) had to be liberally and frequently coated to waterproof and preserve them. Wooden vessels had to be caulked with fibrous materials soaked in tar. Pitch, as the substance was sometimes called, was also used to coat masts and spars and, heated with other substances, to make cutch, a preservative for sails. Deck seams were "payed" with pitch, as were cordage splices. And wooden ships sailing in even moderately warm waters often had their entire bottoms coated with tar as a protection against the teredo worm.

Vegetative pitch was always in relatively short supply, and was of indifferent quality because it tended to crystallize and shatter when it hardened. Pitch derived from sea mammals was much preferred, with walrus tar ranking highest because of its singular qualities of elasticity and endurance.

We do not know the exact process employed by valuta men in making seal tar, but we have a partial description of how thirteenth-century Greenland Norse made it and, of particular interest, where they procured the raw materials.

A medieval Norse history tells us:

> There at Greipar at the extreme end of Greenland they procured the largest quantities of seal-tar.... The melted blubber was stored in skin bags and hung in barred sheds until it hardened, and later on was prepared as it should be.

Greipar has been identified with the Upernavik district, the most northerly region the Greenland Norse hunters are known to have hunted. We are not told much about the process they employed in making seal tar, but an experience of my own may throw some light upon that.

In the autumn of 1947 I was travelling along the western shores of Hudson Bay in an old canoe whose canvas covering had become so frayed and torn that my partner and I had to spend almost as much time bailing as paddling. One day we saw a wisp of smoke near the mouth of a river. We put in and found a trapper living in a wooden hut whose roof had been water- and weather-proofed with a layer of black tar. I thought this might be just the stuff we needed to make the old canoe seaworthy.

We explained our plight and were given a pail of what looked like asphalt but stank like dead whale. The trapper, originally from Labrador, explained that this was blubber-tar he had made from the fat of walrus killed for winter dog feed at Marble Island a short way up the coast.

After we had gently warmed the stuff to a syrupy consistency on our benefactor's tin stove, we applied a coating to the canoe. It soon cooled into a rubbery substance which kept the canoe from leaking for the remainder of our journey. My gratitude was great; but so was my curiosity about this remarkable substance. That night our host explained how he prepared it.

First the blubber had to be diced into small pieces, then slowly heated "until the ile runs out o' the gristle." He stressed that the pot must not be allowed to boil or "'twill be ruined, certainly." When all the oil was floating free, the gristle was strained out. The pot was then pushed to the back of the stove and allowed to simmer until the contents became "thick as treacle." Stored in an outhouse over a period of several months, it would eventually "cure" into a black substance too thick to spoon, though not quite thick enough to cut with a knife, in which form it would keep indefinitely.

I carefully noted all this in my journal, together with our host's final remarks: "Yiss, bye, I sloshes dat stuff on me boots, me house, me canoes, and me old Peterhead boat. And nary a drap o' water'll get into ary one of they!"

I can testify to the effectiveness of seal tar, and also to its redolence, which can be breathtaking and would make it a difficult product to market in our fastidious era.

What I believe to be the largest walrus "factory" in the high Arctic is on the Knud Peninsula in southwestern Kane Basin. Here, in 1977, Canadian archaeologist Peter Schledermann found the first of several large and mysterious structures he called "longhouses." For the next several summer seasons he carried out extensive excavations at this site.

As has been the case with most archaeologists I have encountered, Peter has gone out of his way to help me in my own investigations, even though some of my interpretations challenge his. He insists, in his soft-spoken way, that his own conclusions are tentative, and therefore open to adjustment as new information emerges. One could wish that all historians, past and present, were of the same persuasion.[3]

The Knud Peninsula site is dominated by one of the most fruitful polynyas in the eastern Arctic. Each spring Schledermann watched walrus by the hundreds congregate in its relatively narrow compass. Seals and small whales also made good use of it as a staging place on their annual migrations.

The site is especially notable for the several stone-built enclosures that Schledermann calls longhouses and that I identify as boat-roofed house foundations. There are enough of these of the right dimensions to have served as single or multiple foundations for six or seven upturned vessels.

Around them are ranged long lines of curious small stone constructs which Schledermann has christened hearth rows. Each unit in such a row typically consists of a small square or oblong fireplace to which a stone-built platform is attached. At least fifteen such hearth rows, containing in total more than 140 units, snake their ways about the Knud Peninsula site.

Schledermann (and most other Arctic archaeologists) hypothesizes that the large foundations were ceremonial structures built by the people known to science as Dorset-culture palaeo-Eskimos. (For reasons which follow in the next chapter, I refer to these people as Tunit.) Schledermann thinks that the hearth rows, some of whose fire boxes still contain residues of sea mammal fat, may have served as communal cooking hearths for Tunit during mass assemblages.

There are difficulties with this explanation. Tunit were spread very thin on the ground, with a population density of no more than a few families to several thousand square miles. It is not easy to imagine how they could ever have mustered sufficient numbers to account for the size and abundance of the "ceremonial" structures and hearth rows at the Knud Peninsula, or at any of the other related sites. Furthermore, there is no evidence at any of these places of anything like the number of actual habitations (tent rings, pit dwellings, and the like) which would have been required by so many people. Schledermann suggests they might have been communally housed within the ceremonial structures; but there is no credible explanation of how, in the treeless Arctic, such large buildings could have been roofed.

Distribution makes it seem equally improbable that the longhouses should have belonged to the Tunit culture. All but three of the forty-five now known are in the eastern Arctic (east of Boothia Peninsula) and two of these are on the border between east and west. Yet a large Tunit population lived west of that arbitrary boundary. If longhouses *were* Tunit ceremonial structures, why were they not erected in comparable numbers in the west? Why, for that matter, have none been found in Newfoundland, which was home to a large Tunit community for more than a thousand years? It is surely also significant that longhouses in the eastern Arctic are massively concentrated in just two districts: Kane Basin–Smith Sound, and the northwest coast of Ungava Bay.

If the Tunit did not build the longhouses, could these indigenes have been responsible for the hearth rows? I submit that these, too, were constructed by valuta men—that they were, in fact, tryworks for the production of seal tar.

The heart of the tryworks employed by whalers of recent and relatively recent times was an enormous metal cauldron heated by a furnace. Valuta people possessed few metal vessels of any kind, and certainly none of sufficient size for large-scale processing of sea mammal oil.

I conclude that, in lieu of large pots, they used batteries of small, nonmetallic units, each consisting of a stone platform fitted with side pieces designed to support a skin "pail" filled with chopped blubber. Stones were heated in an attached fireplace. When the stones became hot enough, they were tonged into the blubber-filled pail. When they cooled, they were tonged back into the fire. This process was repeated until the blubber was reduced to oil, whereupon it was ladled, or poured off, the gristly bits being recovered and used to fuel the next rendering. Essentially this would have been no more than the application of a cooking process common to many peoples who did not have fireproof pots at their disposal.

Although the output from each such unit would have been small, one person could have simultaneously operated half a dozen or more hearths, and batteries of them could have approximated the output of latter-day metal trypots.

Carbon-14 dates obtained by Schledermann from charred willow, bones, and fat found in six hearth-row fire pits range from about A.D. 700 to 900. The average of the corrected age is close to A.D. 800, suggesting that the hearth rows were last used within a few decades one way or the other of this date.

I envision eighth-century valuta ships riding the northbound current up the west shore of Greenland to Smith Sound and Kane Basin, and some pressing on even farther to the westward. Departing Tilli in mid-spring, they would arrive on station with time in hand for a productive late-summer and autumnal hunt. Before the long darkness descended, the hunters hauled out their ships and overturned them on prepared foundations. Then they settled in for the long winter.

Winter was no idle time. Foxes, wolves, and bears could be trapped, and caribou, musk oxen, and Arctic hares hunted when weather and moonlight permitted. Boredom would have been warded off by the presence of white bears attracted to the carcasses of dead sea beasts floating or frozen in the nearby polynyas, or to the stocks of meat, tar, and other edibles laid up by human hands. As long as walrus were available in the polynyas, the stinking hearth rows glowed and smoked.

By the end of the ensuing summer—or perhaps the summer after that—it would be time to set sail for Tilli. Then vessels were repaired, tarred, launched, and laden; and one fine morning the long voyage home would begin.

CHAPTER SIXTEEN

TUNIT

Winter was drawing to an end; and none too soon. We were hungry. Keeping twenty mouths filled through the long night is never an easy task. Sometimes it is impossible. Then the Snow Walker comes—first for the youngest children; then for the elders; and, finally, if food is still not to be found, for the hunters and the women of child-bearing age.

This year it did not happen. The meat caches had been well filled the previous autumn, so we still had strength enough to trek across the heavy fiord ice to our traditional spring camp beside a polynya. We were guided to it by plumes of sea smoke rising from misty waters wherein heaved massive tuskers and sea unicorns.

Poles from the travois upon which dogs had hauled the gear from our winter camp were erected to serve as teepee supports. Women and children scurried about gathering handfuls of shrubbery for fuel, while we men hastened to the edge of the polynya to conceal ourselves behind upthrust blocks of pressure ice, harpoons at the ready.

As the days slipped by, the brief hours of daylight gradually lengthened. Blubber fires smoked blackly in a few of the ancient hearth pits that ran in rows across the campsite. Skin pots containing walrus meat bubbled as hot stones were dropped into them. Succulent smells wafted in the brisk air; and the bellies of dogs and people were filled to repletion. There was time to play and sing, and in the evenings to loaf about carving little images in ivory while listening to the old ones tell tales of other times.

Tales such as this one:

On a summer in the days of our forefathers, the People camped on an island from whose peak one could see the gleam of ice over that vast land that lies far to the eastward of us. The People had come to this place to gather seabirds' eggs.

Every day an endless procession of great whales swam northward past the bird island. One evening in the early autumn the People saw, coming across the strait towards them, a whale with an enormous wing sprouting from its back. They watched in wonderment until, as it came closer, they could see it was really a whale-sized boat. Closer still, they saw figures moving about in it.

As this giant boat made for the sandy cove on the shore of which stood the tents, the People grew fearful for they did not know whether the newcomers were spirits or living folk. Women retreated to the high ground and children hid among the rocks, but the men stood shoulder to shoulder on the beach.

The boat dropped its sail and came to an anchor a short way off shore. A crowd of dark-bearded strangers stared intently at our people and we stared back as intently. Then one of our men stepped forward and laid his harpoon on the ground. At that, the men in the boat held their arms high to show they held no weapons. Someone shouted friendly sounds and soon all were shouting, and our dogs were going crazy. Not long thereafter the strangers paddled ashore.

Then we could see they were men, like us, though hairier and with big noses, and dressed in strange clothing. But men—not spirits. Their words were a mystery to us, and ours to them. But they knew how to laugh, so it was not long before everyone understood there was nothing to fear from one another.

There were ten men and four women in that big boat, and they stayed with our people all the rest of that year and on into the beginning of the following summer. Some of us learned their tongue, and they ours. They told us they came from so far to the south and east it took them from the beginning of spring to the end of summer to make the journey, even in their swift-sailing boat. So we called them Far Ones; and they were the first strangers ever to come amongst us.

They had no wish to remain in our land—only to stay long enough to gather walrus tusks and other things they valued, most of which had little worth to us. We did not begrudge them what they wanted. They were peaceable folk.

When winter came, we helped them bring their big boat ashore and overturn it on stone walls they built for the purpose. Nowadays children play amongst the old walls that once helped shelter the Far Ones. Their houses were truly big; but draftier and colder than the tents or snow houses we live in.

The Far Ones came every year thereafter—sometimes as many as a dozen boatloads. We shared the country and our lives with them. It is certain that some of us carry their blood in our veins. I must be one such, for dreams come to me of places I have never been. It may be I am seeing the Far Ones' homelands.

They came amongst us for the space of three lifetimes; then one summer they failed to return. That was long ago. Now lichens cover the fallen stones of their great houses and the fireplaces where they boiled good oil until it was no longer fit to eat.

Aieee ... they have been gone a long while ... but we still keep watch to the southeast. Some day the Far Ones may come again.

THE HIGH ARCTIC WORLD TO THE WEST DIFFERED fundamentally from Crona in one important respect. It was already inhabited when valuta men arrived there.

Until a few years ago historians believed only Eskimos had ever lived in the far north. This view was not shared by the Eskimos themselves. They have always insisted that when their forebears arrived in the central and eastern Arctic they found it occupied by a strange race of people whom they called *Tunit.*

According to the Eskimos (Inuit, those in the eastern Arctic wish to be called), Tunit were big and strong.[1] Nevertheless, they were unable to defend their land. They are contemptuously depicted in Inuit stories as people who preferred to leave rather than fight.

This account of them given to Knud Rasmussen by an Igloolik man is typical.

> The Tunit were strong people, and yet were driven from their place by others [Inuit] who were more numerous ... but so greatly did they love their country that, when they were leaving Uglit, there was a man who, out of desperate love for his place, struck the rocks with his harpoon and made the stones fly like bits of ice.

The pacific nature of the Tunit is emphasized in many Inuit folk tales. There are no accounts of Tunit attacking Inuit, whereas Inuit attacked Tunit with or without provocation. Inuit legends tell us that their ancestors eventually drove the Tunit "away."

By the time modern Europeans arrived on the scene, Tunit existed only in Inuit memory. Even that tenuous vestige of them was then dispatched to limbo by ethnologists who proclaimed them to be no more than fabulous creations of Inuit mythology.

In recent years it has been established that the Tunit were, in fact, flesh-and-blood people, bearers of what is technically known as the Late Dorset culture; and that (as the Inuit have always insisted) Tunit occupied much of eastern and central Arctic and subarctic North America until displaced by ancestors of the Eskimo only a few hundred years ago.[2]

Nomadic hunters first entered the high Arctic regions of North America before 2000 B.C., in a climate much warmer than now. Whether they came from the east or west is not absolutely certain. It is generally assumed they came from the west, entering northern Canada along the strip of tundra lying between the Brooks Range and the Beaufort Sea.

They were primarily terrestrial hunters whose chief prey was caribou. However, before travelling very far eastward of the Mackenzie River they encountered another large mammal which proved to be equally rewarding. This was the musk ox.

Musk ox tend to be sedentary creatures. When threatened, they often crowd together in outward-facing herds, keeping potential predators at bay with their sharp horns. This static defence is effective against wolves or bears but makes the creatures vulnerable to human hunters able to wound and kill from a distance.

Whether or not the immigrants had previous knowledge of musk ox (*somebody* hunted the species to extinction in Siberia), they recognized a good thing when they saw it. They hunted the shaggy beasts so diligently as to effectively eliminate them from many regions. The hunters then pulled up stakes and moved on westward into the ever-widening wedge of tundra Vilhjalmur Stefansson would come to call the arctic prairie, for this was prime musk ox country.

Eating their way methodically eastward, the musk ox hunters reached the shores of Ellesmere Island by as early as 2000 B.C. From there it was only a short further step to Greenland.

In those relatively balmy times, tundra prairie dotted with musk ox stretched right around the north Greenland coast from Kane Basin to

Scoresby Sound. Within a few centuries, the forebears of the Tunit had reached the northeast shores of Greenland.

They had now hunted their way right across the top of North America and, although few in number, had decimated musk ox populations everywhere they went, forcing them to return to an earlier reliance on caribou.

But caribou were scarce in northern Greenland. To make matters worse, the climate began to worsen catastrophically. By c. 1800 B.C. the people in the far north of Greenland were freezing, and the larder was fast emptying. They had no choice but to move south. Some eventually found their way right around the southern coasts of the island continent, shifting from land hunting to sea hunting as they went. Instead of musk ox and caribou, seal became their staff of life.

By about 1000 B.C. the Arctic was undergoing what some climatologists call the Little Ice Age. Glaciers swelled in size and oozed closer to the coasts. Pack ice thickened and flowed southward so heavily as to effectively barricade most of Greenland's shores. Descendants of the musk ox hunters living on the North American continent proper withdrew farther and farther south, some as far as Newfoundland. There could be no similar retreat for those in Greenland. Only empty ocean lay south of Cape Farewell.

By around 500 B.C. conditions in Greenland seem to have become so extreme that human life could no longer endure there. Nor could it survive in any of the high, and most of the central, islands of the Canadian Arctic archipelago.

Not until the fifth or sixth centuries A.D. did a warming climate allow the descendants of the ancient musk ox people (hereinafter called Tunit) to return to the far north. By then the whole of Greenland and most of the high Arctic islands had been devoid of humankind for at least a thousand years.

A few Late Dorset sites have been found in Greenland's Thule district, but it does not appear that the Tunit recolonized Greenland to any notable extent. However, they did vigorously reoccupy much of the Canadian Arctic, while continuing to maintain themselves as far south as Newfoundland; in Ungava; on the shores of the Canadian Sea (Hudson Bay, James Bay, and Foxe Basin); and on the tundra plains of the

Arctic mainland. Here, they prospered until the invading Thule, ancestors of the Inuit, reduced them to a shadow people.

Archaeological investigations, especially those carried out by Elmer
Harp, Moreau Maxwell, Peter Schledermann, Callum Thomson, James
Tuck, and Robert McGhee, have restored substance to the Tunit shadows.

We now know that they dressed in tailored clothing made of caribou
and sea-mammal skins but, instead of Eskimo-style pullover hoods, their
parkas were fitted with three-sided fur collars.

Although there is no certain evidence for the use of dog sleds, we
know the Tunit had dogs. Perhaps these carried side packs or pulled
small *travois* as the dogs of the Caribou Eskimos were still doing in
Keewatin when I travelled among them in the late 1940s.

Tunit probably devised snow houses that became the prototypes of
those used by modern Inuit. They may also have invented the kayak.
Certainly they must have possessed first-rate boats.

They were amongst the most accomplished stone knappers of all
time. Their complex tool kits, made of flint, chert, and suchlike materials, were executed with such economy that the miniaturized results are
known to archaeologists as microliths.

These are most of the few things we do know about them. We do
not know what they looked like. Some think they may have been
Eskimoan in appearance; others that they resembled North American
Indians. Some of the carved representations they have left us seem
vaguely European.

We do not know what they believed. Their language remains totally
unknown. As we shall see, contemporary descriptions of them are rare,
and many of those that do exist have not been recognized for what they
are. We do not know how they dealt with death or even what they did
with their dead. Although a great many of their sites have now been
excavated, few Tunit skeletal remains (some of them dubious) have
been found.

We *do*, however, know one indisputable fact about them. They were
gifted artists. Carvings are amongst the most numerous artefacts recovered from their habitation sites. Generally small, superbly conceived and
executed in bone and ivory, most are images of animals, but not a few
have human elements or represent human beings.

Were these exquisite little carvings amulets? Did they have religious significance? Did they owe their existence simply to artistic exuberance and the joy of living? Were some of them portrayals of real people? As early as 1951, Henry Collins, one of the most experienced of the early post-war archaeologists to work in the eastern Arctic, noted that "Dorset bone carvings" seemed to portray two different kinds of human faces: one of them broad, with oblique eyes and a short, wide nose; the other long and narrow, with a long nose.[3]

Valuta men must have encountered Tunit almost as soon as they reached the high Arctic grounds. How did the two people react to one another? Neither seem to have been bellicose by nature and both were living essentially the same sort of lives, factors that would have favoured mutual accommodation. Albans could have had no conceivable interest in antagonizing, or trying to displace, the Tunit. On the contrary, it would have been greatly to their advantage to establish and maintain good relations with the indigenes, not only to guarantee their own security, but also because the Tunit possessed a vast store of local knowledge that would have been invaluable to the newcomers.

Good relationships work both ways. Tunit could have benefited from Alban skills and technical knowledge, as these pertained to boat building and sailing, for example.

There was also the matter of trade. Usable metals, specifically copper and iron, were extremely scarce in early Tunit times. Valuta seekers probably possessed no surplus either, but would surely have been able to spare *some* iron and copper as trade goods. A paucity of metals of provable European provenance in Tunit sites does not, as some archaeologists have suggested, prove that they were never present. Tunit owners of metal knife blades, hunting points, and other objects would have treasured and guarded them through the generations until they literally wasted away from use. And one can imagine the intensity of the search that would have followed if, by evil chance, a metal implement was misplaced or lost. And if its owners were unable to find it, what are the odds of it ever being found by an archaeologist? Especially since, as we know to have been the case, Tunit sites were thoroughly scavenged for metal by their Thule and Inuit successors.[4]

Although no living Tunit or Alban remains to testify as to how well (or otherwise) the two people got along, there are no indications of conflict, and there *is* convincing evidence that they coexisted. Every Arctic site occupied for any length of time by valuta seekers is strewn with a litter of Tunit debris. Carbon-14 and other dating techniques applied to this material have established that at least some of the sites occupied by valuta men must have been occupied simultaneously by Tunit.

I consider it a foregone conclusion that extensive mingling took place between Tunit and Albans. It can be supposed that, as was the case in historic times when many immigrant Europeans took Indian and Inuit wives, Alban valuta men did the same with Tunit women.

Tom Lee wrote to me in 1971, expressing his opinion on the matter.

There were a number of Dorsets around at that time and the longhouses drew them like magnets. If the Dorsets had been hostile, the longhouse builders would surely have been killed or driven out. I think we can take it that these Europeans got along with the natives at least as well as Europeans throughout the Arctic did in later times. They may have done better because of being much closer in cultural affinities and in their way of life.

CHAPTER SEVENTEEN

THE WESTERN GROUNDS

August in the high Arctic was well advanced before the ship named Farfarer took her departure from the clan station at Kane Basin. Heavily laden with seal tar, walrus hides, kegs of ivory, white bear skins, and the woolly hides of musk ox, she was homeward bound after an absence of more than a year.

Her people were impatient for they had a long way to go to Swan Fiord. The vessel slipped quickly down the west Greenland coast and when Disko Island hove in sight her skipper elected to forgo the sheltered inside passage. To shorten the distance he held along the bold outer shore of the island. He did this even though aware that the current spell of fine weather could not last much longer. Home was beckoning irresistibly.

Farfarer was not halfway along Disko's forbidding western cliffs when mares' tales began switching in the high dome of blue overhead, a sure harbinger of bad weather. The breeze, which had been light and from the nor'west, began to strengthen and swing into the nor'east. The mares' tails faded and an ominous darkness began to spread across the sky. The steersman's grip on the tiller tightened. He was an old hand. He could read the signs.

So could the skipper. A polar nor'easter was brewing. "Haul her to port," he ordered. "Hold her up, man! We'll run for shelter south of the island before the devil's wind really begins to blow!"

As the vessel's head came around, the crew sheeted-in the great sail. Farfarer heeled hard to starboard, the wind-lop slopping over her lee gunwale. Then, before anyone could slack the main sheet, a ferocious gust blasted over Disko's cliffs and dealt the vessel such a blow-me-down that she rolled her lee rail under. Two men with drawn knives sprang to cut the sheet. Before they could do so, Farfarer acted to save herself from overturning. With a gunshot crack, her mast went over the side, taking sail, rigging, and yard with it.

By the time her crew dragged the tangled mass of gear back aboard, the nor'easter was full upon them, whipping the rising surface of the sea to foam and driving the dismasted ship willy-nilly southwestward into Baffin Bay.

Soaked to the skin, men huddled in whatever shelter they could find...when they were not bailing. The skipper kept the helm. Crouched over the tiller, he suppressed the urge to glance over his shoulder at the great greybeards rolling up astern. Any one of them was big enough to engulf his ship.

The nor'easter howled for three days, during which Farfarer ran helplessly before it. On the fourth day the wind gradually dropped out.

As the massive sea began to flatten, a maze of glacier-crowned mountains could be glimpsed through the storm scud to starboard. The cloud blew away, the sun broke through, and Farfarer's people beheld towering glaciers as majestic as any in Crona. Breaking out the sweeps, they began rowing towards this unknown land in search of a sheltered cove where Farfarer could lie while her storm damage was being repaired. As they closed with the coast, they were observed with stolid indifference by a horde of tuskers.

They beached Farfarer upon a strip of gravel between two protecting headlands. While the women prepared the first decent meal in a week, men hurried to repair the mast by fishing the broken parts together with strips of soaked rawhide. As the wet hide dried, it shrank until it became almost as hard as iron. The join was waterproofed with seal tar.

Re-rigged, the ship was soon ready to resume her voyage. There was no question as to which direction she should steer. Crona must lie due east; and, as it turned out, the great island was much closer than anticipated. Half a day's sail after sinking the mountains of the new land astern, the lookout raised the distant glitter of the Sukkertoppen Ice Cap.

Farfarer had regained the known world. The remainder of her voyage home to Swan Fiord was routine—or as near to it as any voyage in high latitudes could ever be.

W

HETHER OR NOT THE FIRST SIGHTING WAS MADE
this way, discovery of Baffin Island would have been
inevitable within a short time of the arrival of European
voyagers on the west Greenland coast. Although Davis Strait is some 230
miles broad, the mountain and glacial massifs on the opposing coasts
are so high (more than eight thousand feet on the Sukkertoppen Ice
Cap, and seven thousand feet on the opposing Cape Dyer peninsula)
that in clear weather the "loom" effects are sometimes intervisible. In
any case, a vessel crossing between them need only be out of sight of
land for half a day.

The discovery seems not to have had much initial impact upon
valuta seekers. A new world to the west was an unknown quantity, while
the high Arctic had by now become a reasonably familiar and exceedingly rewarding place. The far north would continue to preoccupy valuta men for another half century.

Then they abandoned it rather suddenly.

Several factors seem to have determined their abrupt departure. One
might have been a dramatic, if short-term, deterioration in the climate
which began late in the eighth century and temporarily restored the seasonal dominance of the polar pack.[1]

Certainly another was the appearance on European markets of a new
product—a distillate made from fir, pine, and larch stumps and roots.
Stockholm tar, as this substance came to be known, began to replace seal
tar in many marine usages. In consequence, the latter declined in value
until, by the ninth century, it was hardly worth transporting all the way
from the high Arctic to European markets.

Another reason for the abandonment of the far north might have
been the realization that an equally productive walrus ground existed
on the west coast of Baffin Bay.

Walrus were, in fact, so abundant at the Cumberland Peninsula, the
part of Baffin Island closest to Greenland, that, near the end of the nineteenth century, a Scots whaling station there was still killing more than
four thousand tuskers annually as a *by-product* of its whaling activities.
Even as late as the 1920s, Canadian officials could report that the "largest
terrestrial walrus haul-out in the eastern Arctic" was in this district.

And, in addition to being rich in walrus, the Baffin coast was a thou-

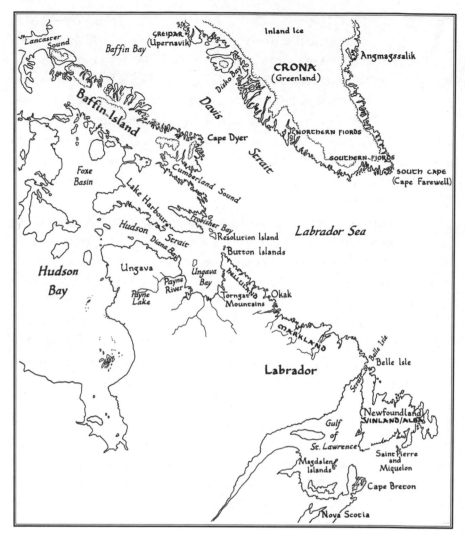

Map of the Canadian Arctic.

sand miles closer to Tilli and to market than were the high Arctic hunting grounds.

Around 800 a shift from the high Arctic to the new lands and waters in the west seems to have begun. Before the end of the ninth century, enthusiastic valuta seekers had probably explored most of the vast region that would eventually become their western hunting grounds.

As always, valuta men were primarily interested in tuskers. These were to be found in abundance along the Baffin coast from Cumberland

Sound south to Hudson Strait, in that strait itself, and in its adjacent waters. Large tribes of walrus also lived in Foxe Basin and among the islands in the northern portion of Hudson Bay. All these regions would eventually be hunted, but the one that most engaged valuta seekers seems to have been northwestern Ungava Bay.

Of the forty-five boat-roofed house foundations so far identified in the Canadian Arctic and subarctic, fifteen are on or adjacent to the western shores of Ungava Bay.

The foundations are not, however, the only spectacular ruins in the Ungava region. Associated with them are some forty remarkable stone pillars.

Stone cairns abound throughout the Arctic. The vast majority are the work of Eskimoan people and are called *inukshuk*, which is to say, *semblances of men*. Inukshuk are generally asymmetrical, under five feet tall, and built of a few large rocks balanced one on top of another. Primarily intended to mark travel routes across snow-covered landscapes, they serve a secondary purpose in imparting a sense of human presence to an otherwise desolate winter world.

A second category of cairns includes those built by explorers, navigators, surveyors, and people afflicted with the Kilroy-was-here syndrome. These markers come in many shapes and sizes but are generally rather broadly conical piles of stones. They betray their comparatively recent origins by the sparseness of the lichen growth upon them.

The cairns or, more properly, beacons with which we are here concerned come in two forms. One is a stela in the style of the neolithic *menhir*, or standing stone, found throughout northwestern Europe and especially numerous and conspicuous in Britain's northern and western islands. Although stelae are generally rare in the Canadian Arctic, several stand in the western grounds.

The second type is the tower beacon. This is a symmetrical, usually cylindrical (though sometimes slightly conical), structure whose outer courses are made of stones so carefully selected, laid, and butted without the use of mortar, as to be a credit to a master mason of any time and place. In most cases, the inner core is of rubble stone. The beacons stand from seven to fourteen feet high (unless they have been truncated by van-

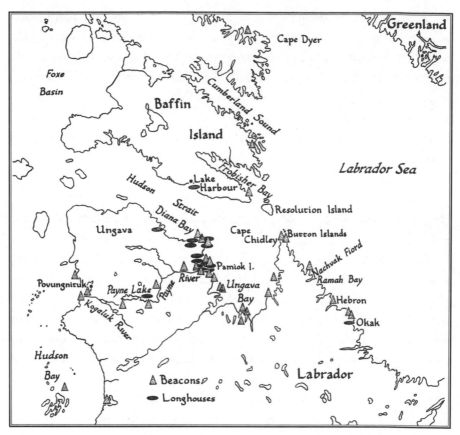

Map of beacons and longhouse ruins. The beacons were apparently built to identify Alban settlements. The longhouse ruins are the remains of boat-roofed house foundations.

dals) and range from four to six feet in diameter. Massive and almost inde-
structible except at human hands, they dominate their surroundings.

Tower beacons of this type are also found on Britain's Northern and
Western Isles, Iceland, western Greenland, the eastern Canadian high
Arctic, the Atlantic coast of Labrador, and Newfoundland. They may
stand alone but are frequently found in pairs, or even trios. An unknown
number have been destroyed by curio seekers hoping to find messages
or objects contained within. I know of three such demolished since 1960.
Apparently nothing of interest was found in these, but then, I am convinced that the tower beacons did not *contain* messages. They *were* the
message, speaking authoritatively to and for the people who built them.

One of the most spectacular groups of those still surviving stands on the crest of Ivik Island, a few miles south of Payne River. I have only seen the site from the air, but in 1968 Tom Lee visited it and wrote the following account. It begins as he and Zachareesi were approaching Payne Bay by canoe from the south.

As we crossed Brochant Bay we decided to stop at Ivik Island....As we landed it was apparent that there were three stone constructions, closely grouped, about a mile inland....On the long climb to the beacons, for such they are, the curving brow of the hill hid them from view. Breaking over onto the top we were confronted with a most impressive sight of the largest beacon thus far known in the Ungava Bay region, together with two smaller features. They were spaced only a few yards apart, but not in line.

The largest of the beacons is about 13 feet high and is further remarkable for its shape, which is surely purposeful. As with other beacons observed at several points up the coast...it is circular and rises from the base as a cylinder...but at a height of 3 feet where the diameter is about 5 feet, it begins to expand achieving a diameter of about 6 feet at 6 feet up. It then tapers to about 4 feet rising again as a cylinder and is crowned with a single large stone....Black lichens cover parts of the outer surface, but do not fill spaces between the stones.

The next highest beacon in the group is about 8 feet high...about 3 feet in diameter tapering to 2 feet at the top....The lowest beacon, only 4'8" high, may have been left unfinished. Although about 10 large stones have tumbled from it...its diameter is about 4 1/2 feet.[2]

Over the years I myself encountered a number of these remarkable structures in the Canadian Arctic, on the Labrador coast—and 2,500 miles to the eastward, where Alistair Goodlad told me, "All over Shetland are these big beacons. Fishermen still use them as shore marks to keep track of where they've set their gear, but Lord knows when they were built, or by whom, or for what."

The Ivik pillars are but one constituent in a string of towers running right the way around the coast of Ungava Bay. Another string extends west from Payne Bay following the Payne and Kogaluk rivers through the interior of the Ungava peninsula to emerge on the coast of Hudson

Bay. A southern chain extends down the Labrador and Newfoundland coasts. Tower beacons have also been found in Kane Basin, Jones Sound, and elsewhere in the high Arctic grounds once hunted by valuta men.

We may never know all the purposes served by the stelae and tower beacons. Some *may* have been raised as navigational aids. Most apparently convey some such message as *We are here* or *This is so-and-so's place*, or *Look for us to the north/south/east/west of this/these pillars*. One thing *is* certain. They were *not* erected simply to pass the time.

Who built them? Modern Inuit deny that they or their ancestors had anything to do with these monumental structures. One can discern no purpose they might have served in Dorset, Thule, or Inuit cultures. In any case, they (and the boat-roofed house foundations) are almost never found in the western half of territories occupied by any of these peoples. They belong to the eastern Arctic and to North Atlantic shores.

As their hoary lichen growths attest, the pillars are much too ancient to have been erected in historic times. I am confident they were built by the same people who constructed the boat-roofed house foundations, with which many of the tower beacons and stelae are closely associated.

According to Jimmy Ford, a long-time Hudson's Bay Company trader on Ungava Bay, the local Inuit believed the beacons were built by "white strangers who came to Ungava in boats a long, long time before we did."

Presumably valuta men first worked the western grounds from their homes in Tilli and, because the two places were so far apart, overwintered in the west. The distribution of boat-roofed foundations in the new grounds forms a pattern similar to one in the high Arctic, where ten foundations are concentrated within fifty miles of Cape Herschel on Smith Sound (the remaining seven being widely dispersed to the south and west). In the western grounds we find fifteen foundations concentrated along the eighty-mile stretch of coast between Payne and Diana bays, the rest being scattered to the south and west, except for one on the nearby north shore of Hudson Strait.

Both the high Arctic and the western grounds had their core areas within which most valuta seekers concentrated their efforts, leaving a few mavericks to establish themselves in more distant outposts. The

The tallest of the group of three lichen-encrusted tower beacons on Ivik Island, near the mouth of the Payne River.

heart of the high Arctic grounds was the southern part of Kane Basin, especially Buchanan Bay. The heart of the western grounds was Ungava Bay, and especially Diana Bay.

The ninth century was a time of expansion and prosperity in the west. As it drew towards its close, people in Tilli, Crona, and the western grounds alike were living peaceable and productive lives...unaware that a nemesis was again beginning to menace them from the east.

CHAPTER EIGHTEEN

WESTVIKING

ALTHOUGH THE LAST DECADES OF THE EIGHTH CENTURY saw the Vikings well launched upon the devastation of Britain proper, Tilli was still a safe haven attracting a steady flow of refugees. These may have included Islanders from as far south as Islay, together with some few mainlanders from Scotland and even Ireland. All fugitives from the Sons of Death, whether Celts or Albans, would surely have been welcomed in Tilli.

Some came west in their own wood-sheathed or skin-covered vessels. Others came as passengers in merchant ships trading between Tilli and the British Isles.

The existence of this maritime commerce is confirmed even in Norse sources. In the prologue to *Landnámabók*, which was written early in the twelfth century, probably by Ari Thorgilsson, Iceland's first historian, we are told:

> In that Book on the reckoning of time which the Venerable Bede drew up, mention is made of the Island called Tili, which in books is said to be six days' sailing north from Britain. There, he said, day came not in winter, nor night in summer when day is at its longest.... But Bede the Priest died 735 years after the Incarnation of our Lord, according to what is written, and more than one hundred years before Iceland was peopled by the Northmen. But before Iceland was peopled from Norway there were in it the people the Northmen called Papar; they were Christian people and it is held they must have come over seas from the west...and it is stated in

English books that in those times voyaging took place between the two countries [Britain and Iceland].

Bede himself tells us in his *De Temporum Ratione* that he had his information about Tilli "from certain men of our own age who arrive from these countries"...information from which he understood that travellers had circumnavigated the island.

Confirmation of sailings between Tilli and Britain is also found in *De Mensura Orbis Terrae*, a book written about 820 by a cleric named Dicuil.

Thirty years ago some clerics who had sojourned on that island [Thule] from the Calends of February to the Calends of August, told me that not only in the summer solstice but in the days around it the setting sun does not hide itself...so that there is no darkness for even a little while, and a man can do whatever he wishes, even pick lice from his robe, just as if the sun was shining....They are mistaken who have written that the sea surrounding Thule is frozen...since, sailing during the time when naturally it is coldest, they landed there and dwelt there ... but they did find a frozen sea one day's sail toward the north.

Settlers arriving in Tilli in the ninth century would not have found things as easy as in the eighth for they would have had to deal with the same inclement weather, which presumably contributed to the Alban abandonment of the high Arctic grounds. During the first part of the century, they endured low temperatures and heavy precipitation. However, similar conditions then prevailed all across northwestern Europe so, though a crofter's life in Tilli might have been difficult, the island continued to offer better prospects than European lands which were being overrun by Northmen.

Although the Norse probably knew a certain amount about what was happening in Tilli, during most of the ninth century they were preoccupied with rich and easy pickings from plundering the British Isles and the Continent.

By 807 they held a bridgehead in western Ireland and by 836 had turned Dublin into a major slave-trading base. During the early decades of the ninth century they seized most of Caithness, together with much of Scotland's west coast to and beyond the Isle of Man. In 839 they slaughtered the pick of Alba's mainland forces in a battle which so weakened the ancient kingdom that within thirty years it fell to the Dalriad Scotti. By mid-century the only opposition the Norse faced in northern Britain was from guerrilla bands, and from the Danes, who were now intruding on Norse turf with spectacularly bloody consequences to both parties, as well as to the unfortunate indigenes.

Big armies and big fleets became the order of the day as the Scandinavians descended on mainland Britain and the western coasts of Europe. The days when any entrepreneur could go a-Viking on his own account were ending. Danish and Norwegian sea-kings who now dominated the business evidenced a fatal antipathy towards independent operators. Furthermore, most outlying British settlements had already been pillaged, and the land occupied by Norse settlers who took a dim view of themselves being raided, even if by their own compatriots. By mid-century such outlaws' outlaws were being driven to the periphery of the Norse-dominated world, forced to lair in forbidding and inhospitable retreats. The brooding cluster of stone pinnacles constituting the Faeroe Islands undoubtedly became just such a robbers' roost.

Up to this time there is little contemporary documentation of what was happening, but from here onward much that illuminates the Norse story is to be found in accounts committed to parchment and preserved by Icelandic clerics, mostly in the eleventh and twelfth centuries.[1]

What follows is mainly derived from *Landnámabók* and *Íslendingabók*.

NADDOD

Some time around 850 a Viking's Viking by the name of Naddod made his way to the Faeroes. *Landnámabók* describes him in succinct but forthright terms: "Concerning Naddod, brother in law of Olvir Barnarkal. He was a notorious Viking. He settled in the Faeroe Islands because he was unwelcome elsewhere."

Olvir Barnarkal was himself a notorious Viking, although apparently somewhat lacking in true berserker fervour since, as *Landnámabók* tells us, "he would not allow children to be tossed on spear points as was then a custom of the Vikings."

This pastime required a group of warriors armed with spears to form a circle around one of their number who would then toss a baby into the air. The object was to catch the infant on the tip of one's spear and toss it across the circle to be impaled on the spear of another player. The infants were the offspring of captured women who, if they survived mass rape, could be sold into slavery unencumbered by babes at the breast.

No such amusements were available on the Faeroes and, after a time, Naddod's crew wearied of howling winds, swirling fogs, towering peaks, seabird stew, and the prickly company of their berserker comrades. There was nothing for it but to set out on a Viking voyage.

The question before Naddod was: where could he ply his trade without too great a risk of getting a split skull or an arrow in the gut? He seems to have been the first Viking to have decided to have a go at Tilli.

What did he expect to gain? Tilli boasted no richly furnished castles or merchants' premises, though it must have possessed some churchly treasures. It *did* produce wealth in the form of Arctic valuta, but Vikings could seldom have hoped to lay hands directly upon such loot because, while Alban ships could not outfight Norse *knorrin*, they could usually outrun them.

Tilli did, however, offer one major enticement. The island was home to many strong and healthy *Vestmenn*—Westmen—as the Norse called the natives of northern Britain, Ireland, and the Islands. And Westmen commanded premium prices in Continental slave markets.

Tilli would hardly have been an easy mark. As a result of their horrendous experiences with the Norse in Britain, the western island's inhabitants must assuredly have been ready and willing to make things very hot for any Viking who might come their way. A Northman falling into their hands could have expected his own plot of land: six feet by two feet . . . if indeed his corpse was not left out in the sun and rain for sea eagles and ravens to consume.

Nevertheless, one spring day Naddod sailed for Tilli with his band of twenty or thirty desperados—"Happy Warriors," as Icelandic novelist Halldór Laxness sardonically calls them.

They probably made a straightforward passage west to the traditional landfall of Horn in southeastern Tilli. But thereafter, instead of setting a course along the southeastern coast of the island, Naddod sailed north along the east coast until he reached Reydarfjördur, as it is still called.

Landnámabók reports that Naddod and his men then climbed "to the top of a high mountain from which they looked about, far and wide, searching for smoke or any indication of the land being inhabited, but could see nothing of the kind."

Naddod's failure to find people at Reydarfjördur is taken by many historians as proof the island was then unoccupied. However, in view of Naddod's subsequent behaviour, and of the Vikings who followed him, I conclude that, far from trying to *find* an inhabited place, Naddod was deliberately seeking an empty corner in a settled landscape.

Because a *knorr* was not large enough to serve for any length of time as a floating base, Vikings intending to work a foreign coast needed a bolt-hole ashore where ship and crew could take refuge in time of need. This was standard practice and a veteran such as Naddod would surely have adhered to it.

He may have landed on the bold headland of Reydarfjell and, after cautious reconnaissance revealed no settlements nearby, established his raiding base on one of the three small, eminently defensible (but pastorally uninviting) islands of Andey, Skrudur, or Seley, not far off the mouth of the fiord.

We are not told what Naddod and his braves did during the rest of the summer, but we can be certain they did not spend their time sightseeing. I envisage the *knorr* making surreptitious sorties culminating in swift raids on Alban steadings lying deep inside the fiord valleys. And equally swift withdrawals before the local people could rally for counter-attack.

Having seized a few slaves, cattle, and whatever other loot was available, Naddod's men would hasten back to their lair and wait for the turmoil following upon the raid to subside.

With a sufficiency of stolen beef and mutton to fill their stomachs, and a stock of Alban captives with whom to sport, the waiting could have been pleasant enough, by Viking standards.

Landnámabók simply records that "they went afterwards, in the autumn, to the Faeroe Islands, and as they sailed away [from Tilli] much snow fell and so they called that country Snaeland. They praised it very much."

Their praise of Snowland was clearly not for its climate; presumably it was for the rewards to be reaped there by enterprising Vikings.

Although Tilli's residents have left us no account of their reaction to Naddod's visit, it would necessarily have cast a pall of foreboding over them.

We can be certain that protective measures would have been taken. People in outlying steadings might have withdrawn to more defensible places. Perhaps watch and signal stations were built on prominent heights and headlands, hunting weapons modified for use against human beings, and weapons of warfare forged. The Albans in Tilli would not have been inclined to yield easily to this new assault by the marauders who had driven them out of their ancient homelands.

GARDAR

The next Norseman of record to reach Tilli was a Viking named Gardar Svavarson. He set out from the Hebrides "under the direction of his mother, who was a seer." I think we can safely assume that either he or his mother had sniffed wealth in the west wind in consequence of the voyage of Naddod or some other Viking.

Gardar, who clearly knew where he was going and how to get there, made the standard landfall near Horn, where "there was a haven." There is no suggestion that he attempted to enter this port. We are told that he "sailed around the land and so came to know it was an island."

Although *Landnámabók* again fails to disclose what the Viking and his men were really up to, this was clearly no pleasure cruise, voyage of exploration, or simple hunting expedition. It seems obvious that these men were pirates seeking loot.

Gardar may have had a more difficult time than Naddod, for the inhabitants of Tilli would by now have been on guard. My guess is that Gardar's vessel stirred such turmoil in her wake that her people *had* to keep on the move. They sailed along the south coast, then up the west coast to the inhospitable and probably then unoccupied northwestern fiords, rounded Dranga Peninsula, and headed east along the northern coast, which is deeply indented by enormous fiord-like bays.

Although the mountainous headlands separating these bays are swept bleak and barren by the lash of the north wind, the fiords' inner recesses are so well sheltered by the same mountain massifs as to nurture some of the best pastoral land in Iceland. It is hardly to be doubted that Alban crofters would have found their way to these northern "oases." In fact, a lake lying in the fertile valley of Reykjadalar, only about twelve miles south of Skjálfandi Bay, still bears the name Vestmannsvatna—Westmen's Lake—as evidence of a one-time Westman presence there.

Yet, so *Landnámabók* assures us, Gardar eschewed all such places in favour of a bleak, natural fortress called Húsavík on the outer shore of Skjálfandi Bay. A nineteenth-century traveller's description of Húsavík, then a hard-scrabble little fishing village, gives a vivid impression of what the place was like.

> The settlement lies at the height of more than 100 feet above the level of the sea, on the brow of perpendicular precipices. The harbour is reckoned one of the most dangerous in Iceland on account of rocks in the entrance and exposure to north and northwest winds.

Why would Gardar have chosen to winter at such a place when scores of well-protected, commodious, and comfortable havens beckoned from the inner reaches of the several great northern fiords? I believe the answer is simple enough: he did not *dare* seek shelter in the better havens because these were already occupied by people who would have taken his hide had he fallen into their hands.

Gardar wintered, perforce, at Húsavík not because he admired the wild and spectacular scenery there but, it seems, because the fortress ridge behind its dangerously exposed harbour offered protection against other human beings whom he had good reason to fear. What else but an acute concern for their lives could have persuaded Gardar's Vikings to voluntarily winter in such a place?

At winter's end, Gardar departed from Húsavík, perhaps raiding along Tilli's northeastern and eastern coasts before sailing to Norway, where "he highly praised the land" and presumably disposed of a profitable cargo.

Landnámabók adds:

> In the spring when he [Gardar] was ready to sail away [from Skjálfandi], a
> man named Nattfari drifted off in a boat in which also was a thrall and a
> bondwoman.

Who was Nattfari? The name is not Norse, nor is it Celtic. He may well have been an Alban slave. What seems to have happened is that three slaves (another recension of *Landnámabók* specifically refers to Nattfari's companions as "a man slave and woman slave") made their escape in the ship's longboat. Lacking another boat with which to pursue them, Gardar was forced to let them go. Nattfari's name is still preserved in a cove on the southwestern shore of the bay, called Nattfaravik—Nattfari's Harbour.

F L Ó K I

Assuredly, word of Gardar's exploits travelled swiftly in Viking circles. One of his contemporaries soon seems to have concluded that the land in the west might be a better place to live than the narrow, overcrowded Norwegian fiord country.

> Flóki, son of Vilgerd, was the name of a renowned Viking. He went to seek
> Gardar's Island....He went first to Shetland and lay there in Flóki's Bight,
> where his daughter Geirhild drowned in Geirhild's Water. Accompanying
> Flóki was a yeoman [a freeman] named Thoralf and another called Herjolf.
> A man named Faxi, from the Hebrides, was also in the ship.
>   From Shetland Flóki sailed to the Faeroes and from there put out to
> sea. He took three ravens with him. When he freed the first one it flew
> away aft, over the stern. The second flew up into the air then returned to
> the ship again. But the third flew straight away over the bow, in which
> direction they found land.
>   They hove in from the east at Horn, then coasted the land by the

south. As they sailed west around Reykjanes, the bay [of Faxaflói] opened out to them so they could see Snaefellsjökull, and Faxi remarked, "This must be a great land we have found for here are mighty rivers."

Flóki and his men sailed across Breidafjördur and landed in what is now called Vatnsfjördur on Bardastrandur.

This bay so abounded with fish, and they caught so many, that they gave no heed to gathering hay, with the result that all their livestock perished during the winter.

The following spring was rather cold; then Flóki went up to the top of a high mountain and discovered to the north, beyond the mountain, a fiord full of drift ice; therefore they called the land Iceland and so it has been ever since.

Flóki and his men wanted to go away from there that summer but by the time they were ready only a short time remained before the beginning of winter. The ruins of their houses are still to be seen east of Branslaek, together with the shed that covered their ship, and their firestead.

They could not beat around Reykjanes, and the ship's boat broke away with Herjolf aboard it. He made land at the place now called Herjolf's Haven. Flóki spent that winter at Borgarfjördur, and there they found Herjolf again.

They sailed to Norway the summer after and, when men asked them about the land, Flóki spoke ill of it, but Herjolf reported both the good and the bad, and Thoralf said that butter dripped from every blade of grass, for which reason he was called Thoralf Butter.

Flóki seems to have been a belated Norwegian emigrant to the west. By circa 865, when he brought his family and retainers to the Northern Isles, the best land would have been engrossed by earlier arrivals. Nevertheless, he seems to have tried to hallow ground, as the Norse saying went. Either because of the hostility of earlier settlers (he was, after all, a "renowned" Viking) or because his daughter drowned here, Flóki soured on the place and determined to venture yet farther westward.

The *Landnámabók* account of the three ravens suggests Flóki did not know how to find his way to Tilli, but this pretty little tale is probably no more than a saga man's embellishment. Flóki sailed to Horn along a by now well-known course and, having arrived there, steered south around the coast. Rounding Reykjanes, Tilli's southwestern cape, he then sailed all the way north to the bleak and formidable Dranga Peninsula. Having now coasted past the best and most hospitable of Tilli's lands, he chose to plant himself in Vatnsfjördur, a gash in the mountains of a region as inhospitable as almost any on the Icelandic coast.

To my knowledge no historian has ever explained why Flóki should have made such a peculiar choice. I believe he settled where he did because the better parts of Tilli *were already occupied* by people ready and able to fend off intruders.

The land Flóki hallowed was (and remains) marginal to pastoralists. We are told the would-be settlers became so entranced by the excellent fishing they neglected to gather enough hay to carry the cattle through the coming winter. In truth, the region was so botanically impoverished that enough hay probably was not to be found; so the cattle either starved to death or were eaten. This could hardly have been the place that sparked Thoralf's admiring comment that the grass in Iceland dripped butter!

When the return of spring brought no notable improvement, Flóki wisely ruled against trying to survive a second winter at Vatnsfjördur.

Landnámabók's account of what followed is somewhat vague. Flóki may have given up the idea of homesteading but, having no mind to return to Norway empty-handed, have hoped to recoup his losses by raiding Alban settlements in the south.

He was prevented from rounding Reykjanes, probably by a heavy gale, and lost his ship's boat. The vessel was blown back into Faxaflói, where Flóki wintered. I suspect he holed up on one of the small islands off the mouth of Borgarfjördur, where he would have had a better chance of defending himself against the hostility of the mainland inhabitants.

Flóki's venture seems to have been a failure on all counts. The following spring he sailed home to Norway, where he "spoke ill" of the new land in the west.

No Norseman seems to have tried to emulate Flóki's abortive settlement attempt for some time thereafter. But raiders continued to plague Tilli's coasts.

CHAPTER NINETEEN

LAND TAKING

One September day near the middle of the ninth century, Farfarer took what would be her final departure from Swan Fiord. Her forehold was piled so high with building timber that the steersman could scarcely see over the bows. The afterhold was packed with animals—cows, ponies, sheep, even a pen of lean little pigs. The ship's small working crew watched, hard-eyed, as the ship drew away from the snug harbour that had been the clan home for several generations.

Farfarer was outward bound on her fourth voyage of this eventful summer. On the first she had ferried most of the clan's able-bodied men to Crona, there to begin constructing new homes at Sandhaven in one of the southwestern fiords. Women, children, old folk, dogs, stock, and farm and household gear had followed on succeeding trips.

As the vessel came abeam of Horn on this last voyage, her skipper altered course to enter Easthaven's lagoon. It was his task to let the people of the port know that, henceforth, the Swan Fiord clan was to be looked for in new lands to the west.

The people of Easthaven had news of their own to impart. Only a week earlier two of the dreaded knorrin had appeared off the harbour mouth. Although they had not attempted to enter, spear-waving Northmen had shouted oaths and lurid descriptions of what they would do to any Westman they laid hands on. At dawn a day later the marauders had attacked some crofts a short way west. They had been beaten off, but at a cost of six good men of the defending force killed or wounded.

"The devils are starting to buzz around Tilli like carrion flies!" a villager warned Farfarer's skipper. "It could turn out here the way it did in the home islands in our grandfathers' time."

"Ah, your guts is changing to water," a young fellow derided him. "We can

outsail those bastards and *outfight 'em. Last summer the lads on Heimaey caught a boatload coming ashore in the night. Aye, and fed 'em to the crabs! We'll do as much!"*

Farfarer's *skipper was uncomfortable. Although his clan was moving to Crona mainly to be nearer the western grounds, some Easthaven folk suspected valuta clans of abandoning Tilli out of concern for their own skins. There was enough truth in the suspicion to discomfit the skipper. Having done what he had come ashore to do, he slipped away to his waiting vessel. Although it was already late in the day,* Farfarer *was soon standing out to sea on a course that would keep her in sight of Tilli's mountains and glaciers, but well away from a coast where killers hunted human prey.*

Valuta clans were the first Albans to leave Tilli for new homes in the west. It was true that they did so partly because of the increasing vulnerability of their home crofts, which were of necessity deprived of most men of fighting age for months or even years at a time, but an equally cogent reason was that merchantmen from Britain were growing reluctant to visit Tilli for fear of Viking pirates. Not a few had already begun bypassing the island altogether to do business with valuta men in the safety of Crona's fiords.

For those with eyes to see, the handwriting was already on the wall.

IF VALUTA CLANS WERE MOVING WESTWARD, SO WERE the Northmen. During the last part of the ninth century, more and more Vikings sailed west to try their luck on Tilli's coasts.

What follows is the story of two of their number, taken from *Landnámabók*. I have shortened the introductory portion of it.

Two friends, Bjornolf and Hroald, fled from the Telemark district of Norway after having slaughtered some men. They settled in Fjalir [in southern Norway]. Bjornolf's son fathered Ingólf and Helga. Hroald's son fathered Leif. Ingólf and Leif were raised as foster brothers. When they were of an age, they went on a Viking voyage with Earl Atli's three sons, Hastein, Herstein, and Holmstein.

These young men all got along so well that they agreed to make another expedition together the next summer.

That winter the foster brothers held a feast for the Earl's sons, during which Holmstein announced he would marry Ingólf's sister, Helga, and no other. Nobody paid much attention except Leif, who wanted Helga for himself. So a rivalry began between Leif and Holmstein.

When spring came, the foster brothers again prepared to go a-Viking with Earl Atli's sons but when they arrived at the rendezvous were attacked by Holmstein and his brothers. The battle was a draw until Holmstein was killed and Herstein and Hastein were forced to flee. Leif and Ingólf then sailed away on a Viking voyage of their own.

The following winter Herstein launched another attack against Leif and Ingólf but they, having been warned, were ready. A great battle ensued in which Herstein was killed.

Both sides now mustered their kinsfolk. Peace was finally arranged on condition that the foster brothers hand over their lands to the Atlis in recompense for the killings.

Now the foster brothers fitted out a large vessel and set out on a voyage to the land Floki of the Ravens had visited. They came to the eastern part of that country, which they found more rewarding to the southward than to the northward. They spent a winter there, then returned to Norway.

Next year Ingólf undertook a second voyage to Iceland, but Leif chose to go a-Viking to Ireland. There he found a big underground house and went into it. It was very dark, but he saw light gleaming from a sword and killed the man holding the sword, and took it, together with much treasure, and was thereafter called Hjorleif—Leif of the Sword. He harried Ireland far and wide and took much booty. He also captured ten slaves, including Dufthak, Geirrod, Skjaldbjorn, Halldor, and Drafdrit.

Then Hjorleif returned home to Helga, whom he had married. The winter after that, Ingólf made a great sacrifice and consulted oracles to learn his destiny. Hjorleif refused to have any part in this for he put no faith in sacrificing to the gods. The oracle predicted that Ingólf would make his home in Iceland.

Thereafter the foster brothers prepared their vessels for an Icelandic voyage. Hjorleif took along his Irish booty and Ingólf took the wealth they owned in common. When all was ready they put to sea. The two ships stayed together until Iceland was sighted, then they separated. Ingólf cast his high-seat posts overboard, vowing he would settle at whatever place they drifted ashore.[1]

Ingólf landed at the place now called Ingólfshöfdi, but Hjorleif sailed on westward along the coast.

Hjorleif and his people spent the winter near Minnthak Beach. In the spring he was of a mind to plant some grain and, although he had an ox, he nevertheless made the slaves drag the plough. While they were doing this, Dufthak conspired with his fellow slaves to kill the ox, to say a bear had done it, and then, when Hjorleif and the other freemen had dispersed into the woods seeking the bear, to set upon them separately and kill them one by one.

The slaves succeeded in murdering Hjorleif and his companions. Then they loaded the ship's longboat with all the chattels it would hold, together with the women, and fled from that place which is now called Hjorleifshöfdi. They steered for some islands they saw out to sea to the southwestward, and took up their abode there.

Ingólf had sent two of his slaves, Vifill and Karli, westward from Ingólf-shöfdi to look for his high-seat posts. When they came to Hjorleifshöfdi they found the dead men and hurried back to tell Ingólf the tidings.

Now Ingólf sailed west to Hjorleifshöfdi and, when he saw his foster brother's corpse, exclaimed, "Small things led to the undoing of this brave, true man; but so it goes with those who will not sacrifice."

Ingólf buried Hjorleif and his companions and took charge of their ship and chattels.

Then he climbed a headland and seeing some islands to the southwest concluded that the slaves might have gone there in the longboat.

He found Hjorleif's slaves on the islands at a place called Isthmus, eating a meal. Though the slaves scattered in terror, Ingólf slew them all. The place Dufthak was killed is now called Dufthak's Scar. Most of the slaves threw themselves off the cliffs and these islands have since been called Vestmannaeyjar [Westman Islands]. Taking the widows of his murdered countrymen with him, Ingólf went back to Hjorleifshöfdi, where he and his people passed a second winter.

After their first raiding voyage to Tilli, during which they had reconnoitred the island's coasts, the foster brothers came to a temporary parting of the ways. Raids on Tilli would have been less risky than attacks on British or Continental targets, but also less rewarding. When the next

Viking spring came round, Leif opted to try his luck in Ireland, while Ingólf chose to have another go at Tilli.

Leif, or Hjorleif, as he came to be called, seems to have made the right decision, for he returned considerably richer in loot and slaves.

At this juncture something traumatic happened at home in Norway. Perhaps the old quarrel with the Atli clan flared up, or the foster brothers became embroiled in a new feud involving "manslaughters" and were banished from Norway just as, in later times, Erik the Red would be banished from Iceland.

Whatever the extremity may have been, Ingólf asked the gods for advice and an oracle told him his future lay in Iceland. Thereupon the brothers departed their homeland, taking portable wealth, slaves, and family with them.

For unknown reasons (perhaps another difference of opinion between two stiff-necked warriors) the brothers went ashore at widely separated points in Tilli. Most significantly, neither selected a good, or even marginal, settlement site. Instead, both chose places along the southeast coast, most of which was an almost uninhabitable desert of lava and outwash plains. Although inhospitable to human settlement, it was well suited to marauding Vikings looking for safe places to lair.

Ingólf wintered at Ingólfshöfdi (as it is still called), a wind- and sea-swept pimple of rock and sand only a few acres in extent, lying under the brooding bulk of the glacier-capped Oroefa volcano sixty miles west from Horn. Tenuously linked to the mainland by a seven-mile sand and gravel bar criss-crossed by tidal gulleys, it is now frequented only by seals and seabirds. It can be reached from the landward side at low tide, but only after fording scores of fresh- and salt-water rivulets running through extensive quicksands and quagmires. Screaming multitudes of skuas pursue those with the hardihood to intrude upon these sodden wastelands.

Hjorleif rejected this, his foster brother's choice, in favour of a volcanic rock embedded in the sterile coastal plain below the mighty Myrdalur Glacier seventy miles west of Ingólfshöfdi. This triangular outcrop was almost surrounded by a morass of black, quaking sand and protected on three sides by steep cliffs.[2]

Ingólfshöfdi was almost inaccessible from the land. Hjorleifshöfdi

was hardly more accessible. Ingólfshöfdi offered no sustenance for a settler; Hjorleifshöfdi, precious little. However, both were so difficult to
reach, either by land or sea, that men roosting on them could have felt
reasonably secure no matter how much enmity their presence in Tilli
might have aroused.

Vikings were not masochists. It is inconceivable that they would voluntarily have chosen such desolate sites as these, had they been *able* to
winter in one of the well-sheltered havens lying to the east or to the
westward.

Historians have generally accepted *Landnámabók's* thesis that the
Westman Islands[3] derived their name from Ingólf's slaughter there of the
slaves who killed Hjorleif. However, as we have seen in chapter 14, the
Vestmannaeyjar had been inhabited by people the Norse deemed
Westmen, since the mid-seventh century. I conclude it was from these
people that the little archipelago took its name, that its Westman inhabitants received Hjorleif's fleeing slaves, and that the vengeful Ingólf raided
Heimaey, the chief and the only habitable island in the group, and slaughtered some or all of its inhabitants, together with the fugitive slaves.

Such a raid would have invited retaliation from any surviving
islanders and from the residents of the adjacent coast of Tilli proper. I
believe the likelihood of such retaliation is why Ingólf retreated to the
cold comfort of Hjorleifshöfdi, there to put in his second winter in
comparative safety.

Insofar as homesteading was concerned, Ingólf's second summer on
Tilli's coasts proved as unrewarding as the first. Although any amount of
good land existed, it clearly was not his for the taking.

Up to this point, the existing version of *Landnámabók* presents a relatively comprehensive account of events. But the remainder of Ingólf's
story is severely truncated, confused as to time and place, and consists
mainly of what seem to be snippets that have somehow survived a dis-
solution of the narrative matrix in which they were originally embedded. In what follows I have attempted to arrange these bits and pieces in
meaningful order. All the information preserved in *Landnámabók* is
included, together with what little is contained in the single paragraph
Íslendingabók devotes to Ingólf. Nothing has been added.

❧ ❧ ❧

The following summer Ingólf cruised the coast to the westward. He built a house at Skálafell and passed the third winter there. Then said Karli, "To an evil end did we pass by goodly countrysides that we should take up our abode on this outlying headland."

In those seasons Vifill and Karli found the high-seat pillars on Orns Knoll beneath the heidi [lava barrens]. In the following spring Ingólf went down over the heidi and took up his abode where the high-seat pillars had come ashore. He dwelt south of Reykjavik. His high-seat pillars are still there, in the Eldhouse [fire house].

Afterwards Ingólf seized land between Olfus River and Hvalfjördur, west of Brynjudaisá River, and all between that and the Axe River, and all the headlands to the southward. Ingólfsfjall west of Olfus River is where he seized land for himself. Some say he was buried there.

Ingólf gave Vifill his freedom and he settled at Vifillstofts and from him is named the mountain called Vifillfel. There he abode for a long time and was an upright man. Karli ran away with a bondswoman. Ingólf saw smoke against Olfus Water, and found Karli there.

Ingólf was the most renowned of all the Icelandic settlers for he came here to an uninhabited land and was the first to set up an abode upon it, and the others who settled there afterwards did so induced by his example.

We can imagine Ingólf's mounting frustration as, in his third season, he cruised northwest beyond the Westman Islands to Olfus Water—the estuary of the Olfus River. Behind this coast lay some of the most fertile land in Tilli, but its inhabitants were not about to let him settle any part of it.

Instead of returning to I Ijorleifshöfdi at the approach of the third winter, this time Ingólf pressed westward along the Reykjanes peninsula. This largely desert tongue of volcanic rock juts thirty miles out into the Atlantic, a waste of relatively recent lava barrens. Modern visitors to Iceland landing at Keflavik airport must drive the length of the peninsula in order to reach the capital. They are generally appalled by its almost lunar sterility. Indeed, it would be hard to find a more inhospitable and forbidding place. Only outlaws with every man's hands against them would have chosen to linger in its desolation.

The exact spot where Ingólf wintered is uncertain but the references to Skálafell and Reykjavik provide clues. There is a field of bubbling hot springs at the extreme southwestern tip of the peninsula, from whose steaming emanations (particularly visible in cold weather) the feature derives its name: Reykjanes—Smoking Headland. Most historians have assumed that the *existing* Reykjavik, capital city of the island, is the one referred to in the Ingólf narrative. The original Reykjavik was more likely to have been one of several harbours at the head of the Reykjanes peninsula.

The springs themselves are only a hundred yards from a prominent hill which is still called Skálafell—House Hill—perhaps in recognition of the fact that it was here Ingólf built his *skála*.

The best indication of where the party wintered is to be found in the caustic comment of the slave, Karli: "To an evil end did we pass by goodly countrysides that we should take up our abode on this outlying headland."

During this third winter Karli and Vifill are said to have found the high-seat posts Ingólf had thrown overboard on first sighting Iceland. A major lacuna then occurs in the *Landnámabók* account. "Afterwards," we are told, Ingólf seized what amounted to most of southwestern Iceland.

After what?

It is nowhere stated in the surviving sources (nor admitted by latter-day historians) that the Norse encountered any resistance in settling Iceland, yet everything points to such a conclusion. How else are we to account for the Norse failure to plant their initial settlements in the south and east of the island unless they were prevented from doing so? *Landnámabók* is emphatic in stating that these were, in fact, the *last* regions to be settled, although they were closest to Europe; had plenty of good land; thriving birch forests; a multitude of safe and convenient harbours; and had nearly limitless resources of wildfowl, fish, and flesh. Here, surely, was where the first incomers from Europe *would* have settled. *Indeed, this is where the earliest immigrants did make their homes.* Only...they were not Norse.

I think it self-evident that Ingólf and those who had preceded him were *unable* to make a lodgement in the east and the southeast because these districts were firmly in the possession of a population that had no intention of relinquishing them. The same was undoubtedly true of most of the rest of habitable Iceland.

The several years Ingólf spent coasting the island would have made it clear that he could never establish himself there through his own unaided efforts. This being the case, I believe he did what other Norse "pioneers" had earlier done in Shetland and Orkney, and what Erik Rauda would later do in Greenland.

I believe Ingólf sailed back to Norway, there to assemble a fleet manned by land-hungry adventurers whom he then led in an invasion of Iceland.

He would have had little difficulty raising such a force. Apart from the Norsemen's natural appetite for loot and land, there was the fact that King Harald Fairhair was then engaged in particularly brutal fashion in forcibly unifying Norway. Many independently minded warriors preferred to emigrate rather than submit to Harald's mercies. The names of a number of such are to be found in the pages of *Landnámabók* (the emphasis is mine):

Thord went to Iceland and, *under Ingólf's direction*, took land between Ulfars River and Leiruvag.

Hall went to Iceland and, *with Ingólf's direction*, took land from Leiruvag to Mogils River.

Helgi Bjola went to Iceland from the Hebrides and was with Ingólf the first winter [of settlement] and settled *under his direction* the whole of Kjarlarnes between Mogils River and Myrdalur River.

Orlyg settled land *by direction of Helgi* [see above] between Mogils River and Osvifs Brook....

Brief as these notes are, they indicate that a far-reaching and massive occupation of western Iceland took place under Ingólf's aegis. Ingólf probably launched his invasion in the almost uninhabitable, and so perhaps undefended, lava landscape around present-day Reykjavik. Having consolidated a bridgehead there, his forces struck northward to the Hvitá valley and eastward into the Olfus valley. Ingólf himself eventually seized land in Olfus, land where he reputedly lies buried below Ingólfsfjall, the mountain that bears his name.

The success of Ingólf's invasion would have paved the way for further incursions in the west; then in the southwest; and finally, as Alban resistance crumbled, in the southeast and east. It is certain that, by the time of Ingólf's death, c. 900, Norsemen had occupied most of habitable Tilli.

If there should be any lingering doubts as to what actually took place, this ingenuous statement from *Íslendingabók* should help dispel them.

At that time [the time of the land taking] *Iceland was wooded between mountains and seashore. Then Christian men, whom the Norse called papar, were here; but afterwards they went away, because they did not wish to live here together with heathen men.*

CHAPTER TWENTY

CRONA

THE MAJORITY OF VALUTA CLANS SEEM TO HAVE emigrated to Crona before Viking raids on Tilli became a major threat. Some of the more prescient crofters probably followed suit; however, it took Ingólf's invasion to trigger a mass exodus.

History does not answer the question of what happened to the Christians "who did not wish to live together with heathen men," nor tell us where they might have gone. Not that they had any great range of choice. To have attempted an eastward flight to their old homelands would have meant flying into the dragon's mouth. No reliable sanctuary was then to be found in the British Isles, and there was precious little assurance of safety in the western reaches of continental Europe.

The most sensible course for fugitive *papar* would have been to head westward to Crona and, if necessary, beyond. I have no doubt but that this is what most of them did.

Those who owned large vessels doubtless loaded them to the gunwales with stock and chattels and sailed direct for southwestern Crona. Those possessing only small craft would have crossed from western Iceland to the nearest point on the east Greenland shore before coasting south. Some overloaded or storm-tossed vessels may have foundered in passage, but the fate of their crews and passengers would hardly have been less dire than that of any of their fellows who attempted to survive the new regime in Tilli.

Either because they had no boats, or because they possessed a particularly strong faith in the efficacy of the Lord's protection, some people evidently *did* remain in Tilli, although taking the precaution of withdrawing into regions which would have been of little or no interest to the first waves of Norse invaders.

One such refuge was the gnarled maze of mountains and icy fiords of the northwestern peninsula. This desolate and now largely depopulated region boasts a singularly high concentration of place names derived from cross or church (such as *Krossi, Krossfjall, Kirkjuhammar, Kirkjugólf*) which seem to predate the Christianization of Iceland. The implication is that the northwest may still have been inhabited by papar, at least until latter-day Norse land takers such as Erik Rauda's father descended upon it.[1]

Other fugitives may have withdrawn into the interior, to the isolated southern valley of the Skaftá River, and to the shores of Lagarfljót, deep inland from the eastern fiords.

However, wherever they went, those who failed to flee the island would sooner or later have found themselves enmeshed by the Norse doom. Writing fifty years ago in *Herdsmen and Hermits*, Tom Lethbridge asked:

> Is it beyond the bounds of probability that some people, not monks but perhaps genuine farmers, were living in Iceland at the time of the [Norse] Settlement? Who, for instance, were the cave dwellers [mentioned in *Landnámabók*]? "Torfi slew the men of Kropp, twelve of them together. He also promoted the slaughter of the Holmesmen [Islanders], and he was at Hellisfitar, with Olugi the Black and Sturla the Godi, when eighteen cave dwellers were slain there."
>
> The silence of the *Landnámabók* [as to the identity of these victims] may just cover a feeling of shame because the chronicler's Viking ancestors had murdered the lot. The passage quoted above reads very much like an account of the early Tasmanian farmers' actions against the Aborigines.
>
> Those were rough days in Norse Iceland, when your neighbours might burn your house over your head at night because of some rude remark you made when you were drunk at a feast. And it was much better not to have any scruffy looking men living around in earth houses or on islands. Why, they might steal your lambs, or anything.

Norse land-takers in Iceland were certainly a rough lot. The book of settlement, *Landnámabók*, chronicles twelve pitched battles between

Norsemen; five bloody ambushes; seven "burnings-in" (when whole households went up in smoke and flame); thirty-six murders (always called manslaughters); and twenty-four feuds and duels causing loss of life. I tallied 260 violent deaths *of* Norsemen at the *hands* of Norsemen in a span of less than thirty years. Apart from the references cited by Lethbridge, there is, however, almost no mention of how lesser breeds were treated.

Fugitives who took refuge in the northwest amongst the crags and fiords surrounding the Dranga glacier may have survived the longest; but, in the end they too would have been overwhelmed as Norse latecomers penetrated into even the most peripheral places. Death or slavery would have been their lot.[2]

Rounding Crona's South Cape, fugitive Albans entered a region that seemed to beg for settlement. Beginning just north of Cape Farewell, a fretwork of islands and headlands stretched for 160 miles to the northwest. Behind this protective screen lay some two dozen fiords and major waterways. Although the land between and around these channels was mostly rough and rolling, it was surprisingly well vegetated. The wall of Inland Ice stood far enough to the north and east so that its frigid presence was only indirectly felt. All in all, this new country ought to have looked almost as good to Alban incomers as the one they had left behind.

Good crofting land would not, however, have been the primary concern of the valuta clans. The sixty-mile stretch of shore between Cape Farewell and Lund Island (Kaneq, it is now called), with its coves and inlets close to the open sea, would have been more to their liking. The disadvantages of living in such relatively exposed places were offset by the fact that these were the first ports of call for merchant vessels from Europe. They were also free of the ice cover which sealed off the inner fiords for long months of every year.

Crofters fleeing Tilli were of a different mould. They would have sailed past the exposed southerly fiords into the inner reaches of those farther north. Here grasses grew in some abundance. Birch and willow thickets provided fuel. Herds of caribou drifted like smoke across the plains and valleys. Untold numbers of geese nested near a multitude of ponds. Char and grayling filled creeks and rivers at spawning time.

Seals, and salt-water fishes, especially cod, were abundant in the fiords. Lowland pockets of alluvial soil enriched by the life and death of a myriad of generations of Arctic plants awaited cultivation.

Five or six days farther up the coast to the northwest lay a second set of waterways surrounded by ice-free lands. These northern fiords were not as hospitable as those in the south, but were more extensive. They were also handier to the northern hunting grounds, a distinct advantage to Alban crofters accustomed to obtaining part of their livelihood from hunting and trapping. Some refugees may also have been attracted to the northern fiord district because it was farther away from the killers who had driven them out of Tilli.

The Norse cast long shadows. Many settlers in the Southfiords sited their steadings so that the buildings could not be seen from the main waterways. Others chose places with commanding views affording ample warning of the approach of strangers. Not only were many crofts defensively sited, some were constructed like miniature fortresses.

Late in the summer of 1982 Claire and I were guests aboard a Canadian ice breaker bringing an official party to Greenland to help commemorate the one thousandth anniversary of Erik Rauda's arrival there.

I watched from the bridge as C.G.S. *Pierre Radisson* worked her way up Tunugdliarfik, longest of the Southfiords. It was still so choked with bergs and drift ice that even our modern ice breaker made slow progress. I had ample time to reflect on how the first European immigrants to this titans' land might have felt about their future prospects.

Fifty miles in from the bleak outer coast the fiord divided. We took the left-hand fork, which led into a hidden world fringed by a rolling ribbon of meadows surrounded by lowering mountains.

Although the long passage up the fiord had been almost devoid of visible life, here at its head was a plethora of living things. Still waters reflected the double images of motionless bergs amongst which bobbed dozens of seals and a school of porpoises overflown by arabesques of gulls. However, it was on land that life manifested itself most prominently.

A dozen or so brightly painted wooden houses were scattered along the western shore. A flotilla of small boats lay hauled out on the beach in front of them. People of all ages were wandering about dressed in holiday splendour. The grassy slopes behind the houses were dotted with sheep; and here and there a pony raised its head to glance incuriously at the red-painted apparition which had just dropped anchor in the reach.

We went ashore to join in celebrations hosted by the local folk. Although most had Danish names they considered themselves to be of the same stock as Canada's Inuit. They were not much impressed by the official fooferaw in honour of Erik the Red, but were very hospitable nonetheless.

Late that afternoon I asked a squat young man called Hans to show me the site of Erik Rauda's home. Hans obligingly led the way across a squelching bog to what had been a beach in primordial times but now lay high and dry half a mile inland.

Brattahlid, as Erik called his steading, stood on this raised beach commanding an unobstructed view of the entrance to the inner reaches of the fiord. No ship, no boat, nothing above water could have approached without being seen by someone here. But at the time of our visit the only residents were three dyspeptic-looking sheep and a pair of snow buntings.

Not much remained visible of the homestead. After some five centuries of human habitation, Brattahlid had lain abandoned for another five, during which its stone-and-turf walls and sod roofs had subsided into shapeless mounds. These had been excavated in the 1930s by Danish archaeologists. The sod had now grown back, but the spades had revealed that, over the centuries of Norse occupancy, a number of rooms had been added to and around an original single-roomed structure.

It was this structure that especially interested me. Referred to in the archaeological literature as "the earliest house known from Greenland," its walls enclosed a space about fifty feet long by fifteen wide—closely corresponding in size and shape to the structures in the Canadian Arctic I identify as boat-roofed houses. However, the turf-and-stone-built walls of this building were as much as twelve feet thick—much thicker than would have been necessary either for roof support or insulation. I suspect these massive walls were designed as much to defend the inhabitants against aggression as to provide shelter from the weather.

The impression that the house was intended to double as a bastion capable of withstanding siege is reinforced by the presence *within* the walls of a stone channel bringing water from a concealed external spring. Excavation of three other very early Greenlandic houses has revealed similar built-in water supplies, together with exceptionally thick walls. Notably, such features have not been reported from houses of indisputably Norse origin in either Greenland or Iceland.

I conclude that the original house on the Brattahlid site was probably built by Alban refugees from the Norse invasion of Tilli.

It is a well-established historical principle that successive inhabitants tend to plant their homes where others have built before them. I believe Erik Rauda either occupied a house already in existence on this site, or built upon its ruins.[3]

It is worth adding that, of all the artefacts found in the oldest levels of these "earliest" Greenland houses, *few, if any, are unequivocally Norse.* Most are everyday objects common to ordinary folk of those times throughout northern Europe.

Albans taking refuge in Crona would have had legitimate reason to fear they were still at risk. The distance separating the Southfiords from western Iceland was no greater than that separating Iceland from Norway. What the Wolves of Odin had done before they could be expected to do again.

However, fears that raiders would soon begin ravaging Crona were premature. For several decades after their seizure of Tilli, the Norse were so preoccupied with quarrelling about ownership of land, and about their relative status that, if they gave any thought to the departed Christians, it was probably along the lines of good riddance to bad rubbish.

Here is how I conceive of events unfolding during this period.

For half a century the Alban settlements in Crona prospered in peace. More than enough land was available in the two fiord districts to meet the needs of a considerable and growing population. By c. 900 the climate had become considerably warmer than today, and it continued to improve. Year by year Alban flocks in Crona grew larger and roamed farther afield. Children grew up and went homesteading on their own until there was hardly a grassy valley which did not harbour at least one croft.

Hunting and fishing remained integral to the crofting life and, at least in the early years, southern Crona offered a great diversity and abundance of animal resources. These were supplemented by summer hunting expeditions to Disko Bay and its surrounding region.

Despite the increased distance from Europe, Cronian Alba was neither materially nor culturally deprived. European merchants had begun sailing direct to Crona well before Tilli fell to the Norse. And why not? Sailors of those times faced no greater hazards going deep-sea than in coasting voyages, beset by rocks, reefs, lee shores and, all too often, pirates.

Most of the vessels employed in the trade seem to have been British, although some Alban vessels, perhaps descendants of Orkney ships that had gone south-faring in the long ago, may have voyaged east from Crona. British merchantmen came mostly from Bristol and other west-coast ports, generally taking their departures from Malin Head in Ireland. Their course was designed to carry them close enough to Iceland to see the loom of distant mountains while remaining far enough offshore to avoid being detected and intercepted by Norse pirates.

The distance to be travelled was about 1,800 miles, around eighteen sailing days under ideal conditions—which seldom occurred. An outbound vessel that reached Crona in three weeks would have done well. Homeward bound, with the prevailing westerlies astern, she could have expected to make a faster passage. Mariners did not yet have the compass, but could and did find their intended ports by sailing "down" lines of known latitude. Voyages to places as far afield as Crona were well within the capabilities of ships and sailors of the times; and the rewards for bringing a cargo of Arctic valuta back to a European port would have been worth the risks entailed.[4]

Inbound cargoes consisted mostly of staples such as meal, whole grains, honey (the only sweetener then widely available), and billets of smelted iron. A relatively small quantity of manufactured goods was probably imported, mainly iron tools, copper utensils, and a little pottery.

Cultural connections with the "old country" remained unbroken. Merchant ships not only brought out cargo but passengers as well, including clerics, for the church was an integral part of Alban life, as it had been since the sixth century.

The church had good reasons, both spiritual and mundane, for maintaining connections with Tilli and, after Tilli's abandonment to the

Norse, with Crona. Valuta goods, ivory in particular, received as tithes provided north European bishoprics with a significant portion of their wealth, and contributed not a little to filling the coffers in Rome as well.

Documentary evidence testifies to continuous connections between the church in Greenland and in Europe from at least as early as 834. These records establish beyond reasonable doubt that Greenland must have been part of the North Atlantic Christian community *150 years before Erik Rauda reputedly discovered it.* They also show that Iceland was a Christian country long before the Norse arrived there.

Although these documents were first brought to light by Peter De Root in his *History of North America Before Columbus,* published in Philadelphia in 1900, they have been consistently and, I would suppose, necessarily overlooked by northern historians wedded to the view that the Norse led the way across the Atlantic. I have dealt with these documents at some length, and with the apparent mystery of their neglect, in *Westviking.*[5]

Whatever else may remain in doubt about the early history of Greenland, we can be certain people were living there in the ninth century; were being ministered to by Christian clerics; and were in touch with the old world…as well as with the new.

One July day three-quarters of a century after Farfarer's final departure from Tilli, her current namesake was preparing to put to sea from Sandhaven, which had become the clan's home port in Crona.

Shaggy cattle and long-limbed sheep ranged hungrily over greening slopes behind the sod-roofed houses of the two valuta clans that shared the harbour. The entire population was gathered in front of a small stone-and-turf-walled chapel, all wearing traditional white for the occasion. Even crewmen from the Bristol ship Saint Stephan, *anchored in the harbour, had covered their shoulders with white cloths. For this was the day ships were blessed in the name of St. Alban, founder of the foremost monastery on Tilli and patron saint of Alban seafarers.*

To the casual eye Farfarer *and her sister vessel,* Narwhal, *resting their bows together on the pebble beach, would have seemed virtually indistinguishable from ancestral vessels many hundreds of years older. Around fifty feet overall, they were nearly as long on the waterline as the oak-planked* Saint Stephan, *but of much lighter build and shallower draft.*

Saint Stephan *had come out late the previous summer and wintered in Sandhaven. Now she was about to sail for the Northfiords, after which she would cross Davis Strait on a venture to the western grounds.*

The crowd at the chapel formed itself into a white-clad procession and began moving towards the beach, led by an untonsured priest with black hair hanging raggedly over his shoulders. Several young men and women surrounded him, waving decorated woollen banners hung from long staves, and chanting prayers for the well-being of the ships and of the people who would be departing on the morrow.

It was a cheerful crowd, and would become even more so at the feast to follow: roast caribou; boiled seal and salmon; hot barley bread; and, best of all, several kegs of ale brewed from bere grain provided by Saint Stephan's skipper. This was an occasion for celebration. The people of Crona were enjoying peace and prosperity. Although none was wealthy, everyone had enough of what was needed and most of what was wanted. Part of their sustenance came from the land and waters of Crona, but the largest part came from the hunting grounds beyond the Labrador Sea, and all were sensible of this.

By the year 930 the western grounds had been known for a century. Valuta men had worked their way well to the north of Cape Dyer on the east Baffin coast; they had ventured a considerable distance southward along the Atlantic coast of Labrador; and they had investigated much of Hudson Bay and Foxe Basin.

They knew the places where walrus beached; where narwhals swam and eiders nested; where gyrfalcons built their eyries and white bears denned. They knew, in short, where the creatures upon whom their way of life had anciently depended were to be found.

CHAPTER TWENTY-ONE

UNGAVA

Saint Stephan's captain had taken extra precautions to ensure the safety of vessel, crew, and cargo on the voyage ahead. Not only had he shipped a valuta man familiar with the western grounds as pilot, he had arranged to sail in company with Farfarer and Narwhal.

The three vessels kept station for a day and a half after departing Sandhaven until they reached Cape Desolation. Narwhal and Saint Stephan then continued northward up the coast of Crona while Farfarer veered westward into the open sea.

The weather held fair for five days as Narwhal and the Bristol trader sailed along a deeply fiord-riven coast whose mountains, rugged as they were, seemed almost insignificant against the brooding backdrop of the Inland Ice.

On the sixth day Narwhal led the way into the island-studded bight masking the entrance to the Northfiords. The harbour here was cluttered with craft awaiting the arrival of the first trader of the season.

Saint Stephan's captain could have exchanged most of his cargo for country goods, but he had his eye on richer prospects. After two days he was ready to depart. Narwhal's people were no less eager to be on their way.

A stiff sou'wester gave the two vessels a rough crossing of Davis Strait. They encountered innumerable bergs, both large and small, and Narwhal had to pick a circuitous path through pans of pack ice which Saint Stephan could safely thrust aside with her strong oaken bows. They sailed continuously, for there was no real darkness, and on the third day made landfall at Cape Dyer on Baffin Island.

Here they parted company. Narwhal turned north, bound for Merchants Bay, where her crew would slaughter tuskers from amongst the multitudes that thronged the beaches there in early summer. When the surviving walrus departed for the far reaches of the Arctic, Narwhal *would turn south and make her way to her clan's station on the Ungava coast.*

Under the Alban pilot's guidance Saint Stephan *coasted southward from Cape Dyer across the wide mouths of Cumberland Sound and Frobisher Bay to Resolution Island and so into Hudson Strait. The pilot was at pains to point out distinctive sea and land marks along the way, and the master made careful note of these in his ruttier, his personal set of sailing directions. Charts and pilot books were not available in those times. Each master mariner prepared and jealously guarded his own record of how he sailed from one place to the other: what to watch for; what to avoid; time taken; weather encountered; and the nature of the seas he sailed through.*

The ship was swept into the tremendous tidal stream surging through Hudson Strait. During ebb tide the pilot kept her so close to the north shore that her people shuddered to see rocks and reefs directly under her forefoot as she crawled along. When the tide changed the pilot took her out into the flood, and then the land seemed to flash past.

This was fine so long as her people could see where they were going. However, for much of the time the ship was entombed in fog so thick her masthead and even her steeply up-tilted bowsprit could not be seen from deck level. The Foggy Strait, as mariners called it, was, and remains, one of the world's great fog machines.

Keeping the lead going and relying on his knowledge of the currents and of the bottom, the pilot at last brought the big ship safely around the prominent headland of Cape Hope's Advance and into Diana Bay. Poised strategically at the western junction of Ungava Bay and Hudson Strait, Diana Bay was easy to recognize and to approach. It also offered one of the best deep-water anchorages in the eastern Arctic, making it a natural entrepôt.

Saint Stephan's *arrival was a momentous event. Only a few European ships had previously ventured so far west, most preferring to meet and trade with returned valuta men in Crona. But mariners bold enough to voyage to Diana Bay reaped the benefits of first choice of valuta, and* Saint Stephan's *owner/master was bold enough to go anywhere if sufficient profit offered.*

Saint Stephan *had barely dropped anchor in the roadstead under the lee of a trio of great tower beacons on Diana Island before boats from the clan stations in the bay were away to carry the news west and south. These six- and eight-oared skin boats were light but hardy craft, and swift travellers. Within a week they had carried word of* Saint Stephan's *arrival to most clan stations and to many Tunit camps as well.*

Heavily laden Alban boats, together with smaller Tunit craft, were soon converging on Diana Bay. Before another week was out Diana Island had become the scene of a tumultuous and festive trade fair attended by Tunit bands, parties of Alban valuta men from the clan stations, and a number of livyers *of mixed Alban and Tunit ancestry.*[1]

Farfarer meanwhile had made heavy weather through a stormy day and night after leaving the coast of Crona. Then the wind had swung southerly, allowing her to reach across the Labrador Sea for Foggy Strait with a bone in her teeth.

When, on the eighth day out from Crona, the lookout raised the northern tip of Labrador, the southern entrance to the Strait, none of the twelve men and five women aboard was more delighted than the skipper's Tunit wife. This young woman was wildly excited at the prospect of returning to her own kind and land after a year spent with her husband's kin in Crona. She had been made welcome there—but home was in the west.

Farfarer met only streamers of mist as she entered Foggy Strait. Taking advantage of this rare good luck, her skipper shaped a direct course across the mouth of Ungava Bay to Pamiok Island in the estuary of the Payne River, some seventy miles south of Diana Bay.

Small, barren, but advantageously placed, Pamiok was a valuta station originally shared by four clans. Two of these had combined their efforts and built a double-length foundation almost ninety feet in length designed to support two vessels overturned end-to-end. The other clans, one of them Farfarer's, had built independent structures.

Over the intervening decades, three of the clans had become livyers in the western grounds. In consequence, they had largely abandoned Pamiok, spending their summer seasons on the far coasts of Hudson Bay and their winters in company with Tunit by the shores of a great lake in the interior of the Ungava peninsula.

EARLY IN THE SUMMER OF 1948 JACQUES ROUSSEAU, CHIEF archaeologist of Canada's National Museum, accompanied by a young French anthropologist named Jean Michéa, set out to cross the Ungava peninsula from west to east.

The four-hundred-mile canoe journey would take them up the Kogaluk River from Povungnituk Bay to Payne Lake, then down the Payne River to Ungava Bay. The route was unmapped and, according to Father

Steinman, the priest in charge when I visited the Oblate Mission at Povungnituk in the 1960s, had not previously been travelled by white men.

"Not in our time, anyway," he told me, "though the Inuit say it's a well-marked road. Many cairns along the way. *Big* ones; not *inuksuak*. The old people say they were built by *kablunait*—white men—before the Inuit came into the country. I can show you a picture of one on the coast not far from here. It used to have a twin, but a couple of years ago prospectors pulled it down to see if there was a message in it."

The remaining twin stood (and I hope still does) on Cape Anderson, the northern point of Povungnituk Bay. A massive cylinder about ten feet tall and more than four in diameter, it is artfully laid up of flat stones, some of which must weigh three or four hundred pounds. Steinman told me there were more like it in the island labyrinth at the mouth of the Kogaluk River.

Accompanied by an Inuk guide, Rousseau's party set off from Povungnituk in a twenty-two-foot freight canoe. They noted the beacons in the mouth of the Kogaluk, and thereafter, at almost every point along the way where they might have gone astray, encountered what Rousseau described as "symmetrical and well-made cairns."

At the height of land separating the two watersheds, they entered a maze of lakes and streams in which they could have wandered for days had not the vital connecting portage been marked by a stone pillar visible several miles away. Four days later the travellers were in Payne Lake.

The eastern end of this eighty-mile-long body of water constricts to form a narrows a few hundred feet wide and a mile long. Here the guide nosed the big canoe to the north shore. This, he told the white men, was the great crossing place of *tuktu*—the caribou. Indeed, the foreshore and the slope leading down to it had been so trampled by uncountable hooves as to have become almost as level as a highway.

Beginning in late summer, the Ungava caribou herds come drifting south, only to be deflected eastward by the barrier of water. By the time they reach the Payne Lake narrows, innumerable small herds will have coalesced into an aggregation so vast that, after the animals have swum across, the shores for miles downstream will be whitened with a yard-wide fringe of shed hair. Biologists estimate that as many as 100,000 caribou funnel through this defile annually.

The guide's ancestors, so he said, had always wintered here in order to take advantage of the caribou bounty. Rousseau and Michéa found the stony tundra along the north shore so heavily pocked with tent circles and house pits it had a lunar look. Moss-filled depressions were all that remained visible of semi-subterranean houses made of turf and stones. Michéa counted twenty-two of these, and later surveys have added at least thirty more. Even if all were never occupied at the same time, the land overlooking the narrows must, from time to time, have been the site of a virtual metropolis in what was otherwise a sparsely populated tundra world.

Exploratory excavations by Michéa and Rousseau uncovered masses of caribou bones, and revealed that some of the people who had lived here during a succession of occupations had belonged to the Dorset cultures. This was, in fact, the first Dorset site ever to be found any distance inland from a salt-water coast.

A few days later the little party continued on its way. They slipped swiftly down the Payne past two more tower beacons, then, near the river's mouth, came upon one of the most extraordinary monuments in the Canadian North. It is a stela, or standing stone, almost nine feet tall, weighing in the neighbourhood of two tons. Upon the top is balanced a stone cross-bar more than four feet long. The bar in turn is surmounted by a granite block roughly fourteen inches square, set slightly off centre.

The visual impact of this misshapen cross is stunning—if massively enigmatic. Standing on the floor of the valley, it cannot be seen from any great distance; but if one happened to be ascending the river in search of a Christian community supposed to be somewhere in the vicinity, it would unequivocally direct the searcher upriver and to the first of the beacons pointing the way to Payne Lake.

Rousseau never forgot the cross, or the Deer's Way. He was convinced that something of great historical significance was waiting to be uncovered hereabouts—something that did not fit into the seamless sequence of pre-Dorset, Dorset, Thule, and Inuit occupations of the Canadian Arctic that most professional archaeologists then espoused and, in fact, still do.

In 1957, shortly after becoming director of the human history branch of the National Museum, Rousseau sent a new employee, William Taylor, north to investigate the sites.

Taylor flew to Payne Lake, where he spent a month digging up Dorset, Thule, and Inuit artefacts. He also made some findings that, he would later tell me, "smelled of a European presence."

Although usually meticulous about reporting on his field work, Taylor never did publish a full account of the Payne Lake "dig." When, many years later, I asked him why, he replied in forthright style that any suggestion of a European component in a pre-Columbian Arctic site would have "given the high priests of the profession conniptions....I was a new boy in the field, so who was I to rock the boat? Besides which, I didn't have any hard evidence."

At the urging of the Hudson's Bay Company manager at Payne River Post, Taylor also visited Pamiok Island at the mouth of the Payne estuary. There he was shown what he described as an immense, stone-built foundation unlike anything previously reported from the North American Arctic. Taylor turned a few sods but left the island the same day. He never did return to excavate this extraordinary anomaly. But the ambivalence of his attitude towards it showed in the Inuit name he gave the site: *Imaha*—which translates as "maybe."

"Maybe what?" I asked him when we discussed the find.

He smiled. "A good scientist slams no doors. Maybe some day somebody will come up with proof there was a bona fide Norseman on Pamiok in days of yore. If so, I won't be struck all of a heap, as the Limeys say."

I reminded him that archaeologist Tom Lee had found human skulls associated with the longhouse structures on Pamiok; one of them, according to physical anthropologist Dr. Carleton S. Coon of Harvard University, "probably European" and another "predominantly, if not fully European." Lee had also found a corroded iron axe head typical of the kind used in tenth-century northern Europe. Metallurgic analysis by Canada's Department of Energy, Mines, and Resources established that its composition and mode of manufacture were consistent with that period and place.

There was also the presence in the vicinity of Pamiok (and of most other subsequently discovered Ungava Bay longhouses) of stone-built shelters designed to provide nesting places for eider ducks and so facilitate the collection of their down. Such shelters have been employed

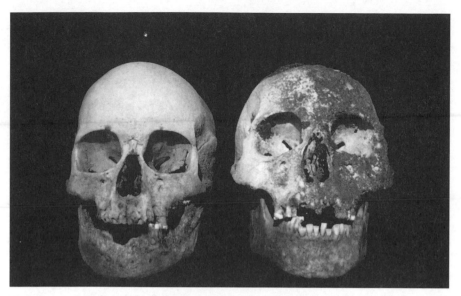

Two ancient skulls from graves on Pamiok Island. One (on the right) is typical Eskimoan in character; the other (on the left) predominately north European.

since ancient times in Europe's northern islands, and are still in use in Iceland. There is, however, no evidence to show that North American native peoples ever constructed such devices. They are considered to be strictly a European artefact.

Taylor nodded as I went through the list. "It's evidence, certainly, but it ain't *proof*, Farley. *Imaha!* But don't expect me to come out with a Norse helmet on my head."

In 1967 Dr. William Taylor became director of Canada's National Museum of Man, a post he held (as director, then as director emeritus) until 1994, when he died, full of honours and distinctions.

Thomas E. Lee's story is somewhat different. Lee was born in a fishing village in southwestern Ontario, where he also spent his youth. During the Second World War he served overseas with the Canadian Forces, returning to Canada in 1945 after surviving action in India and in Burma. He came home determined to realize a youthful ambition to become an archaeologist.

In 1950 he went to work at the National Museum, where he soon acquired the reputation of being a maverick for whom doctrinaire conclusions posed an irresistible challenge. Some of his associates con-

sidered him politically naive. As he himself told me, he was contemp-
tuous of "lickspittle scholarship." Nevertheless, his work was of high
calibre, and he remained with the museum until his chief and mentor,
Jacques Rousseau, was ousted by a cabal of graduates from U.S. univer-
sities who established de facto control over the Canadian archaeological establishment.

Lee's sense of loyalty was matched only by his fierce Canadianism. He
resigned from the National Museum and soon found himself effectively
blacklisted in his own profession. For seven years thereafter he was
unable to obtain a full-time archaeological job. Not until after Rousseau
became director of Laval University's Centre for Northern Studies did
the tide turn. In 1964 Rousseau was able to hire Lee part-time to investigate the Payne Lake site and two years later took him on staff.

Between 1964 and 1975 Lee made eight expeditions to Payne Lake,
Payne River, and the Ungava coast. Always underfunded, understaffed,
and under the guns of the archaeological establishment, he soldiered on.

He spent most of the summer of 1964 and part of 1965 painstakingly
excavating house pits at the Payne Lake narrows. Some of the pits had
previously been sampled by Michéa, then dug by Taylor. Lee took his
own excavations down through permafrost to the earliest occupation
levels. His work revealed that some houses had been established by early
Dorset, then occupied by late Dorset, Thule, and eventually Inuit of
both the pre-trade era and modern times.

Lee found that the final Dorset occupation layer exhibited a number
of non-Dorset characteristics. These included peculiarities in the shape
and manufacture of stone artefacts. But what most impressed him were
the quantities of bone and antler which *had been worked with metal tools*—
saws, drills, axes, and, evidently, knives.[2] Three carbon-14 tests from the
"metal tool-use" layers gave dates between 1200 and 1300.

Lee believed Taylor had found similar material but, since Taylor did
not publish a report on this aspect of his work at Payne Lake, we shall
probably never know.

Publication of Lee's meticulously detailed report of his 1964 dig loosed
the cat amongst the pigeons. After listing the anomalies found at the narrows site, he concluded: "These argue for Norse or other European influence, most easily explained by racial and cultural mixing."[3]

Thomas Lee atop a beacon tower in the Payne River estuary. This beacon is ten feet tall and six feet in diameter.

"The European element would not have been composed of new-comers," he wrote to me in 1978, "but in all likelihood consisted of people who had been in the country many generations and were well adapted to living as the natives did. At the Michéa (narrows) site they lived together in the same houses with Dorsets, bringing with them their own metal tool kits. They may have lived as one people, and perhaps that is the way we ought to think of them."[4]

With the summer of 1964 almost over, Lee happened on a canoe abandoned by airborne prospectors. A bear had ripped its canvas covering, but Lee repaired the damage as best he could with surgical tape then launched himself on a perilous reconnaissance of the south shore of the lake.

There he discovered what he believed might be the earliest European settlement in North America. He named it the Cartier Site.

In 1967, after visiting Pamiok Island, I flew in with Lee to see the

Cartier Site. We waded ashore from the Otter, and Lee trotted me around, making sure I caught every nuance of the place.

He told me that, when he first came to it, there had been little to see except some shallow depressions along a six-hundred-foot strip of foreshore. These had been vaguely outlined by grassy ridges from which occasional large stones protruded.

"They reminded me," Lee later wrote, "of filled-in cellar pits along a vanished village street...so regularly laid out I could hardly credit their presence here in the middle of the Ungava tundra. I sensed they did not belong to any native culture."

Three additional seasons spent excavating the site only strengthened his first impression.[5] Removal of turf and a thin layer of stony soil revealed long and relatively narrow house floors paved with size-selected stone cobbles from the beach. Rock-ballasted turf walls had long since collapsed, spilling their heavy stones across the floors. No post holes or remnants of rafters remained to suggest how these houses might have been roofed.

Although even during the palmy days of the Little Climatic Optimum, Payne Lake was a long way north of the timberline, Arctic willows lived there. Unable to hold up their heads against winter gales, they spread out almost at ground level. Lee found some of these flattened little "forests" adjacent to his village site. Individual trees were only an inch or two in diameter at the butt, but their ground-hugging branches fanned outward as much as fifteen feet. Lee thought such willows might somehow have been used as roof framing, but was unable to determine how a structure strong enough to withstand winter winds and snows could have been contrived from such slender, curving branches. At that time neither of us had even heard of boat-roofed houses.[6]

The floors of the Cartier houses were unlike any Lee had previously excavated in that they were almost totally free of artefacts, debris from tool making, or even kitchen and domestic garbage.

"It was as if," he marvelled, "they had been swept clean by a very fussy Dutch *hausfrau*. No bones. Only the merest traces of charcoal. Not even the kind of litter left by casual Thule or Dorset visitors, though both had camped on the site later on, tearing stones out of the house walls and other structures to make meat caches and to anchor their tents."

The cobblestone flooring of the westernmost house at the Cartier site at Payne House.

Among the structures damaged or destroyed by later comers were three massive constructs, one at the east end and two at the west end of the site. All had been reduced to mere piles of stones. Although Lee did not fully excavate them, he concluded they had been large beacons torn down by Thule or Inuit hunters and converted into meat caches.

How large did he think the beacons might have been? From the quantity of stones, he estimated each to have been of the order of four feet in diameter and perhaps three times that in height.

Dating the houses by carbon-14 testing proved impossible because there was insufficient organic matter in association with the original structures. However, latter-day visitors had made use of the wall stones from one house to build a tent ring. Lee found a fireplace inside the ring containing enough charcoal for testing. The sample dated to circa

1390, thereby establishing that the longhouse from which the stones came must have been in existence before that date. Lee thought the village might have been built as early as 1000, and concluded that its builders had been Europeans or, at least, people with European cultural affiliations.

Lee's deductions and tentative conclusions carried no weight with the archaeological establishment. Conventional wisdom continued to maintain that only native peoples were to be looked for in the Canadian Arctic of pre-Columbian times. As the years went by, Lee found himself more and more marginalized within his own profession. He did not endear himself to his orthodox peers with a comment to the effect that, if one of them unearthed the Holy Grail in an Arctic dig, it would be ascribed to Dorset culture.

Lee stubbornly continued to follow his own nose. Then Jacques Rousseau retired and his successor at the Centre for Northern Studies eased Lee out. Thereafter, Tom's requests for modest grants with which to continue his investigations were rejected by all official funding agencies, including the Canada Council.

Lee still refused to knuckle under. In the summer of 1982 he returned to one of his earlier, and most controversial, sites—Sheguianadah, on Manitoulin Island. Here, in the 1950s, he had unearthed convincing evidence that human beings had been living in the Americas *before* the last Ice Age. Such an early date was then unacceptable to the establishment, which rejected Lee's findings. Today many archaeologists accept the probability that human beings were present in North America as long ago as thirty thousand years. Tom had hoped to confirm his earlier work with one last dig.

A week later he was dead of a massive heart attack.

Through many centuries, Tunit families living along the coasts of the Ungava peninsula relied on the vast herds of caribou funnelling past the eastern end of Payne Lake to guarantee their winter survival. In early September the people travelled up river from the sea coasts to the narrows, there to refurbish caribou guide fences and hunting blinds before the main herds arrived from the north. The autumnal kill would have been made partially on land, using bows and arrows, but principally in the waters of the narrows where large numbers of swimming animals could be speared from boats. Once enough caribou had been slaughtered and cached to ensure a winter of plenty, the Tunit settled into their semi-subterranean houses to enjoy a prolonged social season.

We southerners tend to envisage winter in the Arctic as a dread and miserable time of cold and famine. Those who have experienced the Inuit way of life know this to be a misconception. For the Tunit at Payne Lake, winter would normally have been a relaxed and enjoyable season largely spent visiting, feasting, singing, making tools and clothing, making love, and sleeping as long as one chose. If people felt cramped in their small houses they could go out on the lake and fish through the ice. Or, when the moon was out, range the white countryside for hares and foxes. So long as the caches had been well-filled in the autumn, there would be meat, fat, and fuel enough to keep them well and happy until the caribou herds returned in spring.

When the ice finally roared out of the rivers, the Tunit would launch their boats and return to the coasts, there to spend the sunlit summer months living on the bounty of the sea.

I surmise that, after establishing themselves on the Ungava coast and getting to know the native people, some venturesome valuta men took a leaf from the Tunit book and went up the Payne to winter with the natives there. This would have been a more convivial way of putting in the long months than remaining in poorly heated longhouses set far apart along the frozen coast.

Over the course of several decades, more and more valuta seekers doubtless recognized the wisdom of wintering in the interior where there was an unlimited supply of the best possible food (caribou meat and fat, supplemented with fresh-caught fishes) together with a much better supply of fuel than could be found near the coast.

However, perhaps not all Albans would have been content to live cheek by jowl with Tunit in their cramped winter houses. I think many may have preferred a way of life closer to their own traditions, and these would have been the people who built the village at the Cartier Site. Significantly, it was located several miles distant from the teeming Tunit settlement and on the opposite side of the lake, as if its occupants deliberately wished to maintain a degree of separation.

Coastal valuta stations such as Pamiok were probably not totally deserted during the winter. Caretakers would have been required to protect vessels and their gear. These guardians could have been relieved at intervals, for men could travel quickly and easily along the frozen rivers between Payne Lake and the coasts.

In its heyday the Cartier Site had five houses that, together, were capable of sheltering three or four score people. As melding between Tunit and Albans continued, many or all the "village" folk may finally have drifted across the water to winter with Tunit relatives and associates at the narrows. As these *livyers* increasingly adopted Tunit ways, the village may eventually have been abandoned.

Farfarer arrived at Pamiok to find the Ungava-based clans only recently returned to the island from their winter quarters at Payne Lake. There was much news to exchange, but what most excited the residents was the imminent prospect of Saint Stephan's *arrival at Diana Bay. This brought the local people, Tunit and Alban alike, to fever pitch in their haste to load the year's collection of valuta into boats and be away north.*

The resident clans no longer possessed large ocean-going ships such as Farfarer, *relying on somewhat smaller craft with which they could navigate inland rivers, while still being able to engage in coastwise voyaging. These boats were large enough to roof the houses at Payne Lake, but too small to cover the old foundations on Pamiok Island. So, during summer occupations of that island, inlanders, livyers, and Tunit alike pitched their tents within the old foundation walls, taking advantage of previously levelled ground.*

Farfarer *was soon unladen. In a normal season she would then have been hauled to her foundation and overturned to become her people's home away from home until it was time to return to Crona. This year things would be different. While some of her folk remained at Pamiok to hunt and gather valuta in the vicinity, the ship, manned by a small working crew, was destined for a new farfaring.*

CHAPTER TWENTY-TWO

OKAK

THE PEREGRINATIONS OF THE WALRUS TRIBES MUST always have been of absorbing interest to valuta seekers. At an early date, hunters in the west would have noted how the approach of winter triggered an eastward exodus of tuskers out of Hudson and Ungava bays through Hudson Strait. Many then swam north towards Davis Strait to winter in company with their fellows from the high Arctic; but others turned south instead of north. Inevitably valuta hunters would have investigated this southbound movement.

Having rounded the northern tip of Labrador, scouts coasted south under the shadow of the mighty Torngat Mountains, which rise out of the sea at Cape Chidley and gain height and majesty until, after some three hundred miles, the awesome peaks plunge back into the sea again.

Labrador south of the Torngats subsides into a densely forested plateau. At the junction of the two regions, walrus prospectors from the north would have come upon a remarkable coastal enclave centred on Okak Basin.

Although this basin lay within the fringes of the Torngats, it was not one with them. Its extensive lowlands nurtured grassy bogs and pastures dotted with stands of spruce, larch, and birch.

It possessed other attractions. Thousands of caribou wintered on the extensive lowlands bordering the basin's many long inlets. Clouds of ptarmigan gabbled in willow swales and berry bogs. Snowshoe rabbits were everywhere. Wooded valleys harboured black bear, muskrat, beaver, mink, otter, and lynx. Sheltered on three sides by a semi-circle of guardian mountains, Okak offered a cornucopia of opportunities to people who were both pastoralists and hunters.

The first southern venturers returning from Okak undoubtedly brought back glowing accounts of the place—accounts reinforced by other visitors during ensuing decades. Descriptions of its natural pastures, groves of tall trees, wonderful fishing rivers, and exotic animals would have resonated strongly amongst crofters in Tilli made uneasy by the appearance of Norse marauders there. Indeed, when the time came to abandon Tilli, some crofters may have chosen to bypass Crona entirely and sail all the way west to Labrador, there to settle in the security and plenty offered by the Okak oasis.

I conclude that tenth-century Albans were familiar with the Labrador coast south to Okak, and that at least a few valuta men and some crofters may have already settled alongside the Tunit there.

All through the preceding winter, a move to the West had loomed large in the talk of Farfarer's clan. Other clans had already shifted their homes to the western grounds where permanent residence offered a considerable advantage over migrant competitors who came and went with the seasons. Furthermore, European merchants were showing increasing interest in doing business in the new land.

The elders at Sandhaven agreed that the time had come for their clan to shift west too. But where were they to go? Valuta folk who had made the move to Ungava had gained much thereby—but had paid a price. Domestic animals could not be husbanded, nor crops grown on the tundra of the western grounds. Immigrants to that region had therefore to forgo crofting, something which had been a cherished and intrinsic part of their lives since dim antiquity.

Farfarer's people did not want to follow suit. There was talk about the possibilities of Okak. However, although furs, falcons, and other valuables were to be had in the Okak region, tuskers—the sustaining core of the valuta trade—were to be found there only during migration and even then were wary and hard to hunt. Certainly Okak offered good crofting possibilities, but the region seemed less than ideal for valuta people.

There had, however, long been a belief that somewhere to the south of Okak was a place where tuskers might be found in numbers sufficient to gladden a valuta seeker's heart. In fact, it was the search for this mysterious wintering ground that had led to the discovery of Okak. The search had not been pursued because

Labrador south of Okak was darkly cloaked in forests which were the bailiwick of Innu, mysterious woodland dwellers whom Tunit took care to avoid.[1]

Avoidance between the two peoples was mutual. Although not overtly hostile, neither felt at ease with the other. They lived in different worlds. Innu restricted themselves to forest-covered country while Tunit (and their Alban friends and associates) generally kept to open ground.

In the middle of the summer previous to the decision of Farfarer's clan to abandon Crona, two unknown Tunit men had come paddling into Okak Bight from the southward. Their arrival caused something of a sensation. Their double-paddled sealskin boat was of unusual design, their skin clothing of slightly unfamiliar cut, and their dialect a little different from that of the Okak Tunit. They explained that they had come from a country far to the south bordering on an inland sea. They knew from tales told by the elders of their tribe that other Tunit lived to the north. So, being young and venturesome, they had set out to find these kinsfolk.

They had much to tell about their homeland and its denizens, human and otherwise. Of special interest to the Okak Albans was the news that walrus bred in astronomical numbers on the endless sandy beaches of the strangers' country.

An account of this visit had reached Crona in the autumn of that same year. It had been much discussed at Sandhaven and the clansfolk had tentatively concluded Okak might be the place for them. The decision was made that, come spring, Farfarer would sail to Pamiok as usual, but then, having left most of her people there, the skipper and a skeleton crew would undertake a reconnaissance to Okak and, if possible, beyond.

It was mid-July before Farfarer departed from Pamiok. In addition to her working crew, she had shipped several Tunit men and women, most of them kin to the skipper's wife. At least in its earlier stages the southern voyage promised to be something of a festive cruise offering the Tunit the opportunity to visit camps of distant compatriots and to see places known to them only through stories told during long winter nights.

Farfarer made a fast passage across Ungava Bay to a glacier-sculpted canal on the Labrador side, between whose walls tidal currents flowed with the velocity of mountain rivers. She shot through this short cut between the bay and the Atlantic on a rising tide.

Twin tower beacons at the canal's eastern mouth marked a cove where valuta men camped in spring while gathering down from the plethora of eiders nesting on nearby islands. The station was empty this late in the season, so Farfarer did not pause but steered southward through a maze of coastal reefs and islands alive with porpoises and small whales. The Torngats marched to starboard, rearing their crenellated ridges ever higher.

Crossing the mouth of Nachvak Fiord (a gigantic canyon flanked by mile-high peaks), Farfarer bore into Ramah Bay. Here she dropped anchor and her crew rowed ashore in the longboat. Tunit living in tents pitched along the beach greeted them warmly. They had recently killed a number of fat caribou so there was heavy feasting that night. But in the morning, heavy work.

People did not come to Ramah Bay just for the caribou. They came, and had been coming for thousands of years, for a smokily translucent stone, a form of quartz called Ramah chert, which lent itself admirably to the fashioning of points, knives, scrapers, and a host of other tools. Farfarer's people took aboard a cargo of chert "blanks" to be used in trade, as gifts, and to make tools for their own use.[2]

Continuing south across the mouth of Saglek Fjord, the vessel passed close to Nuliak Island where Tunit from all along the coast gathered in spring to take migrating harp seals.

When the ship was a few miles south of Nuliak the lookout spotted a pair of beacon towers at the tip of Cape Nuvotannak, which guards the entrance to Hebron Fiord. Within the fiord a third and singularly massive tower, over twelve feet high, looked down upon a summer settlement of valuta men from Okak.[3]

After receiving a rousing welcome, Farfarer's people were proudly shown ten newly fledged peregrines and gyrfalcons huddled on perches and squalling for strips of caribou meat. These had been taken from cliff nests in the mountains to the north and from the Kaumajet Mountains to the south. They represented a king's ransom. The pity was that only a few would survive the long and arduous passage to distant Europe.

Next morning Farfarer, piloted now by an Okak man, coasted beneath the mammoth wall of the Bishop's Mitre, which plunges nearly four thousand feet into the sea at the end of the out-thrusting Kaumajet peninsula. Instead of rounding the southern tip of this towering massif, Farfarer slipped through a narrow cleft between soaring cliffs to enter the broad bay which is the outer portal of Okak Fiord. The fiord's mouth lay concealed behind a massive island at whose northern end was Okak's principal harbour, its entrance presided over by twin beacon towers.[4]

Ghosting before an easterly zephyr, Farfarer entered the harbour to find it

ringed with tents. She had arrived at an opportune time, most of the region's
inhabitants, both Alban and Tunit, being foregathered here to mingle and to trade.

In the false dawn of July 23, 1995, the MV *Alla Tarasova* rounded the
southern extremity of the out-thrust Kaumajets and steamed into Okak
Bight. The helmsman eased the ship into Okak Island's harbour. The
sun came blasting over the peaks of the Kaumajets as the anchor chain
ran out with a roar. Within an hour the passengers had boarded a fleet
of Zodiac inflatables and were on their way towards the only level
stretch of shore in sight.

Claire and I were in the lead boat. We scrambled ashore behind the
expedition's archaeological mentor, a rangy Scots-Canadian who, during
the preceding week, had guided us over several Tunit sites he had previously excavated along the north Labrador coast.

Now Callum Thomson led the way up a ten-foot-high cut-bank onto
an ancient raised beach thickly overgrown with dwarf birch scrub, out
of which twenty or thirty decayed wooden crosses protruded at odd
angles. This, we deduced, must have been the cemetery for an eigh-
teenth-century Moravian mission to the Inuit, abandoned in 1919 after
the population had all but been wiped out by influenza.

It was clear that the Moravians had not been the first to make use of
this rare stretch of level ground along the harbour shore, a stretch that
included the only place for miles about with enough soil to permit the
digging of a decent grave. The whole of the raised beach was pocked
with tent circles, depressions betokening house pits, and symmetrical
arrangements of boulders. Intermingled with the habitation sites were
sturdy growths of angelica.5 Clearly, this had been a favoured place to
live since ancient times.

We had gone only a few steps when Callum stopped and beckoned
me to him. He pointed to the ground at his feet.

"Maybe this is one of those longhouse foundations you've been going
on about."

It was hard to tell if he was being jocular or not. I had been holding
forth for days on the subject of boat-roofed houses and at one point had
brashly said it would not surprise me if traces of such were to be discovered in Okak Bay.

Now I found myself on the verge of a depression whose size and shape were a good match for most of the boat-roofed house foundations scattered across the eastern Canadian Arctic. Roughly fifty feet long (nobody had a tape measure, so we had to pace it) it was perhaps eighteen wide. The walls, which had apparently been made of sod rather than stones and turf, had long since rotted down to mounds only a few inches high.

Callum gave me a sardonic look as if to say, "This is *your* baby," then turned and loped off to search for the ruins of the mission.

There was nothing much I could do except look. I had no shovel, and anyway it is against the law to dig archaeological sites without a permit. The most I could make of this enigmatic hole in the ground was that it seemed to be about what I had so off-handedly said we might expect to find.

Though the raised beach beyond this first depression was thigh deep in an almost impenetrable tangle of dwarf birch, I searched it anyway—and stumbled into a *second* depression. The vegetation was so dense here that I had to investigate mostly with my feet but was able to determine that it was of similar proportions to the first.

Clumping around for an hour in a thin, chill rain, I tried to make sense of this double discovery. I noted that the sites were no more than twelve feet above high-tide level and less than forty feet inland. It seemed to me that an approach had been cleared through the jumble of big boulders which littered the foreshore, leaving a relatively smooth place to land or to launch a good-sized boat directly below the putative longhouses.

Search as I might, I could find nothing else which might further illuminate the discovery. Then *Alla Tarasova*'s siren blew the recall signal and we hastened back to the Zodiacs. Shortly thereafter the anchor came up and we sailed away.

That evening I cornered Callum.

"So tell me…who do *you* think could have made those depressions, and what are they?"

He took his time replying, weighing his words carefully.

"They don't look like something the Moravians might have done. One would wonder why anyone would dig anything like that in a cemetery. At first glance they don't look like Dorset, Thule, Inuit, or Maritime Archaic work either. I think, Farley, there are lots of questions, but no answers. Not until you get an excavation permit. Then I'd be happy to have a go at finding who the culprits were."[6]

The wind fell out as Farfarer *entered Okak harbour, leaving her becalmed. She was soon surrounded by small boats filled with excited paddlers who eagerly took her lines and pulled her to the shore, where she was gently beached beside a well-built, but smaller, local vessel.*

The landing was directly in front of a pair of longhouses from whose low, turf-covered roofs blue tendrils of smoke curled. Farfarer's *people wrinkled their noses to catch its fragrance, for spruce smoke was something which, in their treeless land, they seldom had the pleasure of savouring.*

The voyagers were made much of by the residents, since ships that plied between Crona and the western grounds seldom visited Okak. Farfarer's *skipper was asked why he and his people had come so far south.*

"We've heard the talk about an inland sea full of tuskers. Maybe 'tis only a Tunit tale, but we thought we'd come along and look, so it please you."

Not all his listeners were pleased since, unexplored as it might be, they considered the southern territory their own preserve. However, the valuta *men who owned the local ship lying alongside* Farfarer *reacted with enthusiasm. They explained that they themselves were anxious to make a voyage of southern exploration but were hesitant about venturing into a part of the world dominated by forest people.*

"Our ship is small," their skipper explained. "Too small to carry men enough to deal with the forest folk if they come against us." He paused and glanced at Farfarer. *"But your ship now...she could easily carry another dozen or so able-bodied men alongside your own. With two well-manned vessels we'd be all right. What say we go south together?"*

It was a sensible offer.

The two young Tunit who had come from the south the previous summer willingly agreed to serve as guides. Farfarer's *skipper questioned them closely about their country. They told him they lived on the western shores of an island so vast few people had ever travelled right around it. It was separated from the mainland to the north, they said, by a strait of swift water running out of the inland sea. They added that they shared this great island with forest-dwelling people, but were quick* to assure the *valuta* men that these were peaceable folk with whom one could get along.

When asked why Tunit chose to live so far south of their compatriots, and in a country so alien to their ancestral tundra world, they replied it was because the inland sea was filled with uncountable numbers of seals and other sea mammals, including walrus, and, as the questioners surely ought to know, Tunit were pre-eminently People of the Seal.

So it was that preparations went forward for a joint endeavour; and in a few days both vessels were fully stored and manned for a southern voyage.

PART THREE

ALBA-
IN-THE-
WEST

CHAPTER TWENTY-THREE

THE GREAT

ISLAND

NEWFOUNDLAND IS LIKE A MIGHTY GRANITE STOPPER stuffed into the mouth of the Gulf of St. Lawrence. Four times the size of Iceland, twice that of Scotland and England combined, equal to that of California, it turns its back on North America. Jutting six hundred miles farther into the Atlantic than Halifax, and nearly twelve hundred miles farther than New York, it is the most easterly part of the continent.

During the last glaciation this great island was overmastered by a tyranny of ice that stripped away its vegetation and soil, scarifying its face with titanic furrows. When the ice eventually melted down to a glitter of lakes and rivers, life crept back over the bare bones slowly and with difficulty. Although the glacier itself was gone, something of its frigid presence remained. Out of the arctic sea flowed (and still flows) an oceanic river chilling the shores of Labrador and eastern Newfoundland and, in winter and early spring, investing them with enormous ice fields sprinkled with bergs.

For the most part the island is inhospitable to human beings beholden to the plough. Much of the interior became and remains a thickly thatched tangle of spruce and tamarack. What the forest did not claim was largely given over to rock or muskeg barrens. Pockets of soil capable of nurturing deep-rooted plants existed, but only in a few places.

However, what the land would not readily give, the surrounding seas could and did. After the passing of the glacier, life exploded in the off-shore waters. Fed by nutrient-rich cold currents, plankton bloomed, pro-

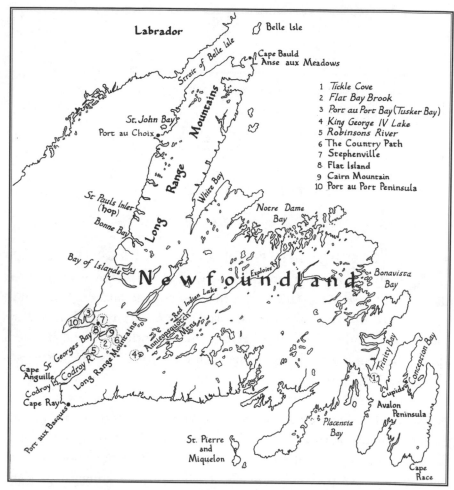

Map of Newfoundland.

ducing a living soup in which untold multitudes of fishes spawned. Horizon-filling flocks of sea fowl fed on small fry, and whitened islands and sea cliffs with their guano. Every autumn millions of pelagic seals came out of the Arctic to winter and, in the spring, to bear their pups on pack ice off the northern bays and in the Gulf. Pods of whales both great and small in numbers unsurpassed by those of any other place on earth lazed along the high sweep of rocky coasts. Hordes of walrus invaded bays and fiords and sported in sandy lagoons. Grey seals and harbour seals, together with vast shoals of porpoises, thronged the island's inshore waters. Lobsters, mussels, clams, winkles, and crabs encrusted its reefs, tidal flats, and shore rocks. Salt-water otter, the now-extinct sea mink, and both black and white bears laid claim to the landwash. Salmon, sea trout, eels, shad, and other fishes came crowding into streams and rivers in such multitudes their turmoil made the waters seem to boil.

The infinite variety of life within and upon the seas surrounding the Great Island flourished with such profligacy as to make the Gulf of St. Lawrence of those times the marine equivalent of Africa's Serengeti Plain.

It was life in the sea that enabled human beings to thrive on the island. The sea continued to sustain them until almost the end of the twentieth century, by which time modern man's genius for destruction had so wasted the surrounding oceanic life that it finally failed its human dependants.

People may have reached the island as early as eight thousand years ago. These first-footers, called palaeo-Indians, were followed by, or evolved into, what is known as the Maritime Archaic culture. Although the earliest Maritime Archaic sites so far discovered in Newfoundland only date back about 5,000 years, sites occupied some 7,500 years ago have been found on the Labrador shore of Belle Isle Strait at a point distant only about a dozen miles from Newfoundland.

The first comers prospered in their insularity. Their descendants eventually became the people European *arrivistes* would name Red Indians—because of their lavish use of red ochre. We remember them as Beothuks.

About three thousand years ago ancestors of the Beothuk began sharing their island universe with forebears of the Tunit. No evidence has so far come to light of conflict between these two very distinct peoples and cultures. But then, live and let live seems to have been the norm in tribal and communal relationships the world over, so long as human populations were small, and natural resources remained in sufficient supply so that people were not forced, or lured, into fatal competition with one another.

In the tenth century A.D. Newfoundland was sufficiently well peopled, and the bounty of land and sea was more than enough to provide for all.

Both Okak Albans and Tunit were apprehensive about encountering Innu on the voyage ahead. The outflung Kiglapait massif which forms the southern lip of Okak

Bight constituted a *cordon sanitaire* between the peoples of northern and southern Labrador. It seemed no light matter to venture beyond it.

The two southern Tunit were much less perturbed, partly because they had always lived amicably with forest dwellers of their own country and partly because Innu had given them no trouble on their northern voyage.

July was ending as the two vessels sailed out of Okak, passed under Cape Kiglapait, and entered the unknown. Fog enveloped them as they nosed cautiously into the island-studded labyrinth of Nain Bight.

Though the fog concealed them from hostile eyes, it made for painfully slow progress. Nevertheless, the Tunit pilots took the ship unerringly from island to unseen island, apparently by a sense of smell—or so it seemed to the Albans. No Innu were encountered or even glimpsed. Indeed, the outer islands seemed home only to birds and beasts of the sea.

Six days out of Okak the southeastward-trending and increasingly heavily forested coast began running almost due south, and two days later swung southwest. The two vessels had reached the mouth of what is now Belle Isle Strait.

Their pilots guided them along the north shore of this strait of swift water towards its narrowing throat until less than a dozen miles separated Labrador from Newfoundland. They kept a good offing, for spirals of smoke rising from the sombre mainland forests spoke ominously of the presence of Innu. Reaching Point Amour they turned away from Labrador to make a crossing of the strait.

The inflowing tidal current ran so powerfully it threatened to sweep them west into the Inland Sea. But it was not the untrammelled power of the tidal stream that most impressed the Albans during the crossing—they were awed by the truly prodigious numbers and variety of animal life filling the strait. They encountered pod after pod of great whales—greys, rights, blues, humpbacks, and finbacks; feeding, frolicking, or simply making a passage. The day would come when this concentration would bring down upon the whales such an enormity of slaughter as to virtually eliminate their kind from the inland sea; but that bloody time was still several centuries in the future.

Gaining the Newfoundland shore not far from Flower's Cove, the voyagers coasted south-southwest, continuing to give the land a good berth, not now for fear of Innu but because the low shore was so hedged with shoals and reefs as to be almost unapproachable.

A day or so later they crossed the island-filled Bay of Birds, now St. John Bay. They were not alone upon it. In the opalescent pre-dawn, a cluster of men whose hair and clothing were streaked with red ochre had gathered beside two twenty-foot birch-bark canoes drawn up on a stony mainland beach. At a signal from their leader, a tall tawny man, they had waded into the surf, carefully holding their fragile craft clear of kelp-slimed rocks. As the sun exploded over the rim of hills behind them, they had paddled towards offshore islands already haloed by a glitter of wings.

Phalanx after phalanx of arrow-swift murres and puffins filled the air with the sibilant rush and rustle of flight. Massed echelons of snowy gannets rowed steadily overhead on black-tipped wings. Terns, kittiwakes, and larger gulls flew arabesques. The sky everywhere seemed alive.

The sea also was visibly alive. Flying through water instead of air, virtually endless flotillas of great auks streamed past. As one such company came porpoising between the canoes, the men ceased paddling and their leader touched an amulet made from a great auk's mandible hung from his neck.

The morning was half spent before the paddlers reached the island of their choice. At their close approach, a myriad of birds began rising from it. Soon they were taking wing in such numbers the sky was obscured as if by a blizzard. The sun's light seemed dimmed. The surface of the sea hissed with the rain of droppings falling into it. Winged masses descended upon the human intruders like tornado funnels. The rush of air through stiffened pinions and the harsh clangour of bird voices made it hard for the men to hear one another's shouts as they leapt overside to carry their canoes through the surf of a low-lying island.

They moved with shoulders hunched as if against the weight of life above them. Not twenty feet from the landwash they were met by serried ranks of great auks so closely packed as to stand almost shoulder to shoulder. This was an army of occupation a hundred thousand strong.

The nearest auks faced the invaders with bodies erect and fearsome beaks thrust forward. The men moved warily, each holding a long, pointed paddle before him like a lance. The leader fingered his amulet once again and, in a voice inaudible above the cacophony, apologized for what was to follow.

The paddles became flails. The big birds began falling back, stumbling into those behind. Confused by the crush, those in the rear struck angrily at their neighbours until chaos rippled through the massed battalions.

The intruders continued flailing, crushing skulls and breaking necks. It was all done in a furious hurry, as if the raiders feared a counter-attack. Not half an hour had elapsed before they began retreating to the canoes, dragging tows of slain birds behind them.

Loading and launching was accomplished with the urgency of thieves. Half choked by the almost palpable stench of guano, the hunters were hurriedly paddling away from the island when they saw Farfarer *and her consort on the seaward horizon. The Beothuks were appalled by the size of these intruders. Turning their backs, they exerted all their strength to drive the heavily laden canoes towards the safe refuge of the mainland shore.*

The crews of the two vessels never noticed the distant Beothuk canoes. Their attention was concentrated on the out-thrust peninsula which forms the lower lip of St. John Bay; for this was the home of the two Tunit pilots.

One summer day in 1963, my wife and I arrived at that same peninsula, now called Port au Choix. We came by land in an old Vauxhall to visit Elmer Harp, an archaeologist from Dartmouth College who had been investigating the prehistory of Port au Choix since 1949.

Having established ourselves in a pink-painted room in Billard's Tourist Home—the only accommodation available in the little fishing community—we followed a guide over the bald pate of Point Riche to the site where Elmer and his students were excavating the remains of a large Tunit settlement.

It was sited on a crescent of sloping beach facing the Gulf, at a spot locally known as Phillips Garden, not because someone had once planted potatoes there, but because from early spring until late autumn the place is ablaze with wild flowers. Protected on three sides by a fringe of wind-swept spruce, it is a *natural* garden whose splendours of wild iris, buttercups, daisies, asters, and a score of others such are due to a remarkable layer of rich, black soil.

This fertile ground is mostly composed of organic detritus laid down by generations of Tunit who lived here for a thousand years or more.

Within the rather small compass of the garden (it is barely two hundred yards long by one hundred broad), Elmer's crew had located the remains of some forty Tunit houses. Most were semi-subterranean winter homes, now visible only as shallow pits about fifteen feet square. Once they had been turf walled, and roofed with poles covered by seal or caribou skins. This had been no transient habitation of nomads but the more-or-less permanent settlement of a goodly number of people.

How many? Rather reluctantly Elmer hazarded a guess: "Maybe fifty, maybe more; though at any given time some would have been away catching salmon, or hunting caribou in the mountains. Not a big crowd by our standards, but a lot to find in any one place in those times."

Unlike the post-Columbian Europeans who eventually settled at Port au Choix and made their livelihoods mainly from fish, the Tunit for the most part had been dependent on pelagic seals—harps and hoods— multitudes of which still gather in the Gulf every spring to bear their young on the shifting pack. Prevailing winds and currents tend to drive the floes south and east, bringing floating seal nurseries close to out-thrusting points of land, of which Point Riche is a salient example. Two thousand years ago, Tunit hunters ventured out from Point Riche upon the moving floes, returning to the land towing sleds laden with the fat and meat of young and adult seals.

The success and duration of these ancient hunts can be gauged by Elmer's calculation that he could fill a freight car with the seal bones his crew had already unearthed. However, it must be remembered that these bones represented the accumulation from animals killed over the span of a thousand years. The number taken in any given year would have been minuscule compared with the more than a million harp and hood seals butchered in the Gulf in 1997 and 1998, many of them shot at sea and never recovered, in an ongoing holocaust orchestrated and sub-sidized by the governments of Canada and Newfoundland.

Seal products, whether fresh meat, rendered oil, or sun- or fire-dried flesh, provided the Tunits' staple food. They also caught salmon and other fishes; took seabirds and their eggs (more than two hundred great auk mandibles were found in one Port au Choix grave); and lob-sters that, as late as 1906, were still so abundant in St. John Bay they kept ten canning factories busy. Shellfish and berries were collected in quantity, and Tunit hunted caribou, which formerly came down in great numbers from the Long Range Mountains to winter along the coastal plains.

Tunit were not the only people to take advantage of the fecundity of the region. Beothuks shared it on what appear to have been amicable terms. It is more than likely that Beothuks and Tunit borrowed from each other's technologies and cultures. They may also have exchanged genes.

Having spent time as volunteer diggers in Phillips Garden immersing ourselves in a now vanished way of life, Claire and I concluded it might have been no bad thing to have lived in this place a thousand years earlier, either as Tunit or as Beothuks.

The approach of the two ships to Point Riche was observed while they were still afar. By the time they poked their heads into the little cove just to the east of Phillips Garden, a crowd of men, women, and children had gathered near the shore. Any apprehension they may have felt at the appearance of these huge craft evaporated as the Tunit pilots shouted greetings and assurances.

While the Tunit from Ungava and Okak mingled with local people, the Albans sought information about what lay ahead and, in particular, about tuskers. They learned that walrus were abundant in local waters and on some of the islands, but it was in Tusker Bay, seven days' travel to the south, that they truly teemed. During certain seasons, so the visitors were told, walrus thronged there in such abundance that neither Tunit nor Beothuk cared to risk boats or canoes amongst them.

Talk like this whetted the valuta seekers' desire to press on, but they had to contain their impatience. Nearly a week passed before their pilots were willing to proceed, and then they insisted on bringing along a throng of Port au Choix compatriots.

Crowded to the gunwales, accompanied by, and sometimes towing, several Tunit boats, Farfarer and her consort made slow progress. Through the better part of four days they coasted the edge of a low and boggy plain beyond which the Long Range Mountains angled ever closer to reach the sea at Bonne Bay.

The voyagers did not explore Bonne Bay's awesome complex of fiords but, after spending a day and a night stormbound in a haven near its mouth, sailed on under the shadow of towering sea cliffs.

A day later they opened the green vista of a broad, island-filled bay extending deep into a heavily forested interior. This was Beothuk country. The pilots spotted a wisp of smoke on one of the islands and, steering towards it, entered a cove upon whose sandy shore stood several Beothuk tents.

Despite what they had been told about the amiability of the island's forest dwellers, the Albans remained somewhat apprehensive. The Okak and Ungava Tunit, too, were content to stay aboard until three Beothuks paddled out in one of their oddly shaped canoes which, seen from the side, looked like two birch-bark half moons joined together. Only after formal greetings had been exchanged did the mainland visitors go ashore.

Beothuks, men, women, and children, crowded around the newcomers, and the Albans found themselves the centre of insistent, if friendly, curiosity. They prudently elected to spend the night on board ship, although the Island Tunit slept ashore where they were entertained with food and dancing in and about the bark-clad teepees of their hosts.

Continuing the voyage next day, Farfarer led the way close under the hulking mass of Bear Head. By dusk she was abeam of Shag Island, whose shores were encrusted by walrus plunging into the sea in cascades of foam and spray as the ships approached. No one aboard needed to be told they had arrived at Tusker Bay.

The town of Stephenville sprawls on the northeastern shore of St. George's Bay. Five miles west of town the road splits. One branch continues on to the westward across a sea-swept gravel isthmus connecting the mainland with the almost-island peninsula of Port au Port. The other branch turns north along the mainland coast, skirting Table Mountain, whose 1,200-foot crest is crowned (or desecrated, depending on one's bias) by a huge white dome vaguely reminiscent of a mosque minus its minaret.

This is a radar dome—a relic of the 1950s when East and West were at nuclear daggers drawn. Intended to give warning of the approach of Russian bombers bound for the eastern seaboard of the United States, it has long since been abandoned. But if one cares to climb to it up a washed-out road that will no longer suffer cars, it affords a stunning panoramic view for thirty or forty miles around.

The vista is dominated by the Port au Port Peninsula itself, a mass of limestone shaped like a titanic spearhead whose tip, Cape St. George, thrusts twenty-five miles westward into the pallid waters of the Gulf. Between the peninsula and the mainland lies Tusker Bay, now Port au Port Bay. Twenty miles long and twelve broad, it was until quite recently one of the richest repositories of marine life on the eastern seaboard of North America.

On a September day in 1996, Claire and I stopped at the eerily silent fishing village of Boswarlos on the south shore of Tusker Bay to chat with the only person we could find—an elderly fisherman brooding over his gear. He told us the bay was now virtually abandoned.

"Not enough fish left out there to keep the gulls from starvin.' I hauled seven nets this mornin' and got four little mackerel, no more'n would feed me cat! 'Tis all fished out! Hard to believe, maybe, but they was even walrus here once—found their teeth and bones meself out on Shoal Point. And whales a-plenty. Even in my time porpoises was still thick as berries. And *fish*…cod used to drive in here chasin' the capelin and herring like a spring tide! Fill your nets so full they'd sink to the bottom! And lobsters! When I were a lad they was two, three hundred lobster men in the bay, all makin' a livin'. Nowadays they's no more'n a dozen, and every one of them hard put to land the price of a case of beer!"

Port au Port Bay, St. George's Bay, and adjacent waters were once alive with fish—and with fishermen. Fifteenth-century Basque and Portuguese barks and whalers were followed here by fleets of French then English smacks and then by flocks of white-winged American, Canadian, and Newfoundland schooners. These were succeeded in their turn by motor seiners, long liners, trawlers, and, finally, by the ultimate fish killer of all—the stern dragger.

They are all gone now. During our visit Claire and I saw *not one fishing vessel at work* on all the vast sweep of salt water bordering southwestern Newfoundland. Those once astoundingly fecund waters have been so drained of life that there is no longer any profit to be made from them.

Which is not the way it was a thousand years ago.

CHAPTER TWENTY-FOUR

A NEW
JERUSALEM

THE CLIMATE CONTINUED TO IMPROVE DURING the first half of the tenth century and so, I believe, did the fortunes of the Albans.

Here is how I envision those times.

The Viking threat posed no imminent threat to Crona. The "happy warriors" in Iceland were preoccupied hunting down "cavemen" and other such vermin, or with splitting the skulls and burning the houses of troublesome neighbours of their own kind. The more entrepreneurial among them sailed east to the Continent to hire on as mercenaries.

Occasional Norse hunters crossed Denmark Strait to the long-abandoned Alban hunting grounds in northeastern Greenland, but these visits would have been peripheral to Alban concerns.

Traffic between Crona and Britain prospered. Vessels carrying churchmen and other travellers as well as goods came and went with little interference from the Norse because ships kept well south of Icelandic coastal waters. Trade had never been better, and prospects for the future looked even brighter as the seemingly limitless resources of the Great Island were unveiled.

Word of its momentous discovery spread quickly through the maritime network to most countries bordering on the North Atlantic. It was soon common knowledge amongst European seafarers that a new land had been found far to the westward, one that harboured a mother lode of riches.

Soon after the first Alban scouting vessel returned from Tusker Bay, valuta seekers began exploiting these southern grounds. Within a few decades, the only valuta men remaining in the northwest were those whose lives were inextricably blended with Tunit there. Ungava and Hudson bays became backwaters. Fewer and fewer merchant ships visited Diana Bay. After some thousands of years, the dominance of the north in Alban affairs was slipping away.

Once Iceland fell into Norse hands, Cape Farewell at the southern tip of Greenland became the preferred western landfall for European merchant seamen. Ongoing skippers took departures from it, steering a direct course west to raise the mountains of Labrador. They then coasted south to Okak, the new trade entrepôt in the west.

Most valuta clans had by now abandoned Crona, establishing themselves especially at Hebron Fiord and Okak Bight, where they were at once close to a mercantile port and within relatively easy reach of the new southern grounds. Valuta clans were joined at Okak by a scattering of crofting families who, either prescient or paranoid about the proximity of the Norse in Iceland, were drifting west.

As of old, valuta clans tended to establish themselves along the outer coasts. Crofters preferred to homestead along the extensive river valleys running between the main fiords and the southern outliers of the Torngats. Here they built turf-and-log homes and outbuildings and husbanded their small herds of domestic animals.

Although Okak valuta hunters spent their summers on the Newfoundland coast of the Gulf of St. Lawrence, neither they nor Okak's crofters were tied to the steadings during the winter months. Some undertook prolonged hunting journeys westward into the mountains seeking moose, caribou, and black and grizzly bears.[1] Others worked woodlands closer to home, using deadfalls and snares to catch furbearers. Some preferred to hunt the outer coasts in company with Tunit friends or relatives, taking chiefly seals, small whales, white bears, and white foxes.

Women, children, and old or incapacitated men remaining at the homesteads had enough to do. Although most of the stock foraged for itself, watch had to be kept for bears and wolves. People fished through the ice of freshwater ponds and lakes. They gathered wood. They made and repaired clothing and gear against the demands of the new year.

When there was time and the weather was opportune, they visited neighbours, either on foot or on sleds drawn by shaggy little horses or, sometimes, by dogs.

They lived in much the same way as did Europeans who settled Labrador in modern times. There was one notable difference. Because of adverse climatic conditions, Labrador livyers of the historic period have rarely been able to keep domestic animals, other than dogs.[2]

During the summer Alban settlers looked after their animals; made what hay they could; caught and smoked or dried salmon, char, and trout; picked berries; and cultivated a few plants such as angelica.

Round about midsummer, most people foregathered at the harbour on Okak Island to await the arrival of trading ships. This was a time for both mundane and religious celebrations. The Albans were practising Christians though they rarely saw a priest or other guardian of their faith. The summer gatherings also attracted distant visitors, including families of mixed race from the northern grounds who were finding themselves isolated from the mainstream of Alban life. These festivals marked the high point of the year but, as the century passed the halfway mark, news from Crona began casting a shadow over them.

While Crona's population had been growing at a normal rate, Iceland's had exploded. In addition to the original in-pouring of land takers from Norway, thousands of Norse settlers arrived from the British Isles. These, facing fierce native uprisings together with invasions by Danes and others, had found it hard to hang on either to property or to life itself. In consequence, many decamped to Iceland. The combined exodus from Norway and Britain was so large that by 950 Iceland's population is supposed to have been nearing thirty thousand.

Useable land and opportunities to make a living in Iceland both grew scarce. More and more men found themselves compelled to seek a future off-island, and this at a time when the traditional Viking enterprises of piracy and brigandage in an aroused and vengeful Europe were becoming increasingly risky and unproductive.

For more than half a century, Icelandic Norsemen had been used to voyaging east in pursuit of fame and fortune. Now some went westviking.

The first black *knorr* to appear on Crona's coast perhaps produced an effect out of proportion to the cause, for the Albans remaining there were no longer a contented lot. Because most valuta traffic was now bypassing Crona, fewer and fewer merchant ships were entering her ports to take on local goods and discharge European products. A mounting dissatisfaction with a way of life growing ever more constrained was being fuelled by glowing reports of the new world across the water to the south and west.

The arrival of Norse pirates settled the matter for most Cronian Albans. They would have been grimly aware of what such raids presaged for the future. They had not forgotten what the Norse had done to their forebears in the Northern Isles and then in Tilli. The first raids on Crona triggered a wave of departures for the west.

By around 960 the last valuta clans had exchanged homes in Greenland for new ones in the west. During the ensuing two decades most crofter families followed suit.

Although Okak Bight was able to absorb many of the valuta clans, together with some few crofters, it could not accommodate the entire population of Crona.

Fortunately there was no need for it to do so.

By the middle of the tenth century, Albans had investigated the southwestern portion of the Great Island. Their descriptions of its fruitfulness, both on land and in the sea, had for long been the talk of everyone living in Crona. In small groups at first, then in ever-increasing numbers as migrant fever enveloped them, crofters abandoned Crona for a new Jerusalem in the west.

CHAPTER TWENTY-FIVE

ERIK RAUDA

BLOOD FEUDING WAS A WAY OF LIFE FOR TENTH-CENTURY Scandinavians, and Icelanders were no exception. Manslaughter—frequently a mere euphemism for murder—was commonplace. Every individual had a monetary value commensurate with his rank and connections. The lives of men or livestock could be paid for with almost equal ease. However, if blood money or other compensation was not forthcoming, a killer could face sentence of outlawry.

An outlawed man had to leave the district or even the country itself, depending on whether his banishment was local or national. If he refused to go, anyone with sufficient will and might was at liberty to kill him, with legal impunity.

Around 960 a man named Thorvald Asvaldsson was outlawed from Norway's Jaedar district for multiple "manslaughters." As many in his situation had done before him, he and his family, which included a red-headed son aged about fourteen, took refuge in Iceland.

The Thorvalders were latecomers. By the time they arrived, all the good land had been taken, leaving little except the lava deserts of the interior, and the forbidding mountains and fiords of the northwestern peninsula, which had perhaps been the final refuge of now vanished Albans. Thorvald ended up in the latter, settling under the chill shadow of Dranga glacier.

The sagas have little to say about what life in the north must have been like for the Thorvalders, but we can make an informed guess. A typical steading of those times consisted of a single room with low, turf

walls. It possessed one doorway and no windows. Rows of posts supported a heavy sod roof and divided the interior into three narrow aisles.
The centre aisle held an open fireplace; the outer two, raised earthen
platforms upon which the family sat, worked, and slept.

The economy of such a steading turned on meat and dairy products.
Usually fermented to make a sour curd called *skyr*, milk provided the
staple food. Butter, cheese, and *skyr* were hoarded against the winter
months when half-starved cattle, stabled in terribly crowded, lightless
burrows, went dry. In the impoverished north, dried fish, rancid seabirds
and their sometimes putrid eggs, and seal meat varied the diet.

When Thorvald's boy, Erik Rauda (Erik the Red), came of age, he
escaped from Dranga's poverty by marrying into a prosperous family from
the Haukadale district to the south. Here he acquired a holding—it was
probably his wife's dowry—and quickly demonstrated he really was his
father's son. Erik settled a disagreement with a neighbour named Valthjof
by sending some of his slaves to unleash a landslide on Valthjof's steading.

Thereupon Eyjolf the Foul, one of Valthjof's relatives, retaliated by
killing the slaves. So, naturally, Erik killed Eyjolf, together with a companion called Duel-fighting Hrafn. This exploit enhanced Erik's reputation, but got him into real trouble. Eyjolf's kinsmen cited him for
manslaughter and he was banished from the Haukadale district. He
decamped in such a hurry he had to leave his precious high-seat posts to
the care of Thorgest, another neighbour.

That winter Erik and his family shifted from island to island in
Breidafjord, living like the outlaws they were. When spring came Erik
made a surreptitious foray back to Haukadale to get his high-seat posts.
Thorgest declined to part with these, so Erik and his companions hid in
a neighbouring woods and kept watch until Thorgest set off on a journey. Thereupon they raided the farm, seized the posts, and headed home.

Nothing could ever be resolved that easily in Iceland. Thorgest
chased and caught the raiders and in the ensuing mêlée Erik's party
killed two of Thorgest's sons and several others of his supporters. These
new "manslaughters" brought both the Breidafjord and Haukadale districts into the fray. In the spring of 981, Thorgest's party forced an action
against Erik, who again found himself outlawed. This time from all of
Iceland—and for three years.

Like his father, Erik chose the westward path. Unlike his father, he was not seeking a new homeland—not yet, at any rate. He went west as a Viking, determined to make his time of exile as profitable as possible. He had a specific target in mind: Alba in Greenland.[1]

The assertion that Erik was the discoverer of Greenland is at the core of one of the most enduring myths contrived in his memory. In truth, he was not even among the earliest Norsemen to reach Greenland.

Landnámabók, that cornerstone of Icelandic history, describes how Gunnbjorn Ulf Kragesson, one of the first generation of Norwegian land takers in Iceland, was storm-driven to Greenland's east coast as early as 890. Thereafter, and for generations before Erik was born, eastern Greenland was known to Icelanders as Gunnbjorn's Land.

Landnámabók provides a vivid account of another early expedition to Greenland, one that took place forty years before Erik went into exile. It offers a revealing glimpse of how life was lived in Iceland in those times.

A man named Hallbjorn married Tongue-Odd's daughter Hallgerd. The young couple spent the first winter of their marriage at Tongue-Odd's house and there was little love lost between them. Snaebjorn Hog, who was a first cousin of Tongue-Odd, also lived there that winter.

In late May, which was moving time in Iceland, Hallbjorn got ready to move out of his father-in-law's house....

When Hallbjorn had saddled the horses he went to fetch Hallgerd from where she was sitting in her bower. When he called upon her to get up and come with him, she neither said anything nor did she move. Hallbjorn called her three times without result, then he sang a snatch of pleading song, but this did not move her either. At last he twisted her long hair in his hand and tried to drag her out of her chair, but still she would not budge. Thereupon he drew his sword and cut off her head.

When he heard about this, Odd asked Snaebjorn Hog to ride in pursuit of Hallbjorn. Snaebjorn did so, accompanied by twelve men. They caught up with Hallbjorn, and in the ensuing battle three of Snaebjorn's men and both of Hallbjorn's companions were killed. Finally someone sliced off Hallbjorn's foot and he too died.

To escape blood vengeance from Hallbjorn's kin, Snaebjorn set sail in a ship of which he was half-owner. Rolf the Redsander owned the other half. They each took twelve shipmates. Snaebjorn's companions included his foster-father Thorodd. Rolf's main companion was Styrbjorn....

They sailed away to Gunnbjorn's Land but when they reached it Snaebjorn would not let them go ashore by night. However Styrbjorn left the ship and found valuables hidden in a grave mound. Snaebjorn hit him with an axe, and knocked them out of his hand.

They made a stone hut for themselves and were soon snowed in. In the spring they dug themselves out.

One day while Snaebjorn was working on the ship, and his foster-father Thorodd was in the hut, Styrbjorn and Rolf killed Thorodd. Then the two of them slew Snaebjorn.

They sailed away after that and reached Halgoland [in Norway], from whence they returned to Iceland, where Rolf and Styrbjorn were killed by Sveinung, who in turn was slain by Thorbjorn....

Snaebjorn and Rolf sailed west to spend a season hunting in east Greenland while things at home cooled off. That they found a grave worth robbing makes it apparent *they* were not the first arrivals on that coast.

Although the sources recount Erik's life in Iceland and, later on in Greenland, in some detail, they have surprisingly little to say about the epochal "voyage of discovery" itself. We are left with no more than bare bones, and all too few of those. What follows is an abstract of my reconstruction of events, as given in *Westviking*.[2]

We begin with the actual saga account:

Erik told his friends he planned to go to the land Gunnbjorn Ulf Kragesson had encountered when he was driven westward across the sea. He put to sea from Snaefells Jokul and approached land at the glacier called Blaserk. Then he sailed south along the coast on the lookout for habitable [or inhabited] country.

He spent the first winter on Eriksey [Erik's Isle] near the middle of the Eastern Settlement [the southern fiords]. The following spring he went into Eriksfjord where he selected a site for a homestead. That summer he sailed to the western wilderness where he stayed for a long time, giving names to many places.

He spent the second winter at [another] Erik's Isle beyond Hvarfsgnipa; but in the third summer went north to Snaefells and into Hrafnsfjord. Believing he had reached the end of Eriksfjord, he then turned back and spent the third winter on [that] Erik's Isle near the mouth of Eriksfjord. The following summer he sailed back to Iceland.

Erik's ship departed from the Snaefells Peninsula crewed by twenty or thirty supporters and slaves. The supporters would have been drawn from among his close friends and relatives and, as we suspect, may have included a man named Ari Marson, whose wife was Erik's first cousin. The freemen aboard were armed with swords, spears, and battleaxes. Kegs of skyr and butter, and bundles of dried fish were stowed in the holds under sealskin tarpaulins. For the rest, the crew would be dependent on "country food."

Having rounded Cape Farewell, Erik soon reached "habitable country," but the surviving sources have nothing to say about that. All we are told is that he wintered on an islet off what would later become the Eastern Settlements of Norse Greenland. A passage in *Islendingabók* written two or three hundred years after the event does, however, provide us with a little additional information.

> The land which was called Gronland was discovered and settled from Iceland. Erik Rauda was the name of a man from Breidafiord who went there and took possession of it....Both east and west in the country they found human habitations; parts of skin boats, and tools made of stone, from which we understand that the same kind of people had been there as inhabited Vinland, whom the [latter-day Norse] Greenlanders called Skraelings.

To understand this account we must remember that tenth-century Norse did not think of Greenland as the discrete entity we know it to be. They thought of it as a ribbon of land which began far to the north and east of Iceland; ran south as far as Cape Farewell; then turned north to the head of Baffin Bay, which it rounded; to run south down the east coasts of Ellesmere, Devon, and Baffin islands.[3]

Islendingabók says Erik found "human habitations" and artefacts "both east and west in the country." Archaeology tells us that, at the time of Erik's visit, Dorset-culture natives (the Skraelings of the Icelandic scribes) did indeed inhabit the west side of Baffin Bay; but *no natives lived on the Greenland side of it*, nor had any done so for several hundred years. Who, then, could the builders of the habitations Erik found in the east of the country have been? I submit that they were Albans.

There is no way of knowing whether any of the dwellings were still occupied when Erik arrived in Greenland, but it would seem that he found only abandoned houses.

The Norse were brave men—none braver—but as Erik's Vikings worked their way up the west Greenland coast, I imagine they would have felt oppressed, even intimidated, by an apparently uninhabited landscape. What could it mean? Had trolls spirited the inhabitants away? Had they been destroyed by the gods, or by some mysterious human enemy? Or had they perhaps withdrawn to some secret place from which they were even then readying an attack upon the would-be raiders?

I expect Erik's ship gingerly poked her nose into one eerily empty fiord after another, the tension steadily mounting, until something untoward occurred.

One grey day the raiders found themselves far down a particularly extensive fiord. Erik dispatched his long boat to reconnoitre its narrow, inner reaches. Near the head of one convoluted arm, the boat's steersman spotted what looked like a drift of smoke.

Nosing the boat up on a gravel beach, the crew stepped warily ashore. They had gone only a few paces when a dozen howling men leapt out of the concealment of a patch of birch, showering them with arrows and sling stones.

The attack came so unexpectedly that the landing party panicked, broke for the shore, leapt into the boat, and rowed furiously for the safety of the open fiord. Perhaps they did not realize until too late that one of their number had been wounded and left behind.

That something akin to this imagined incident did take place seems indicated by the subsequent behaviour of Erik's band.

As autumnal squalls began sweeping down from the inland glacier, the Icelanders holed up on a small island at the mouth of one of the southern fiords. In this exposed place they prepared to spend what would have had to have been a most uncomfortable winter.

In rejecting the relative comfort and shelter available in any one of a multitude of places within the southern fiord complex, *they were behaving as Vikings characteristically did when forced to winter in hostile territory.* Rather than seeking out a comfortable winter haven, they *chose* a remote, outer island where they could not easily be surprised and from which they could make a swift departure to the open sea if things got desperate.

The Norse were not masochists. Surely Erik would not have selected this sort of a refuge (*which is what he did in each of the three winters he spent in Greenland*) unless he had reason to fear attack—not by wild animals, trolls, or spirits, but by human beings.

As the long night drew down and frigid gales screamed out of the north, we can imagine the Icelanders huddled together in their crowded, freezing hut on barren Eriksey with little physical comfort, and not much peace of mind. Regardless of whether they had as yet encountered any living Albans, the mystery of a mostly abandoned land would have haunted them.

The prospects for a profitable Viking voyage must now have seemed as bleak as the winter weather. There could, however, have been some solace in thinking and talking about the fine green country revealed to them in the inner fiords. It may even have been here, on this wind-scoured isle, that Erik envisioned a world inhabited by him and his kind over which he could be liege lord—virtually king of his own country.

The saga tells us:

The following spring he went into Eriksfjord where he selected a site for a homestead. That summer he sailed to the western wilderness where he stayed for a long time, giving names to many places.

When spring liberated him, Erik scouted to the foot of the greatest of the southern fiords where, we are told, he selected a site for the homestead that would be called Brattahlid. I have no doubt that he took careful note of the silent bulk of at least one, and probably several abandoned croft houses standing upon the chosen ground.

He did not linger in the fiord which would come to bear his name. It might be a fine place to settle—but the time was not yet. He had not embarked on this voyage as a settler but to enrich himself and his companions at other people's expense. This he could not do until he found appropriate victims.

He looked for them to the northwestward. By the time he had travelled some distance beyond Godthaab Bight he must have realized that all, or most, of the inhabitants had abandoned Crona.

Where could they have gone? Where else but to that country which the Norse knew as Hvítramannaland or Albania?[4]

Erik took up the search, but evidently had not much more than a general idea of Albania's whereabouts. Crossing Davis Strait, he seems to have roamed the Baffin coast for some undetermined distance "giving names to many places" but not accomplishing much else.

Mystified and frustrated, Erik returned to the east side of Baffin Bay.

He spent the second winter at Erik's Island beyond Hvarfsgnipa. But in the third summer went north to Snaefells and Hrafnsfjord.

The second winter was also endured on an island called Eriksey, this one somewhere to the north of Hvarfsgnipa, now known as Cape Desolation.

It would have been another dreary winter. Women slaves would have had a particularly thin time of it. The men may have found emotional release in quarrelling. Recalling the bloody winter Rolf and Snaebjorn spent on Greenland's east coast, we can believe that only Erik's ready hand with sword and dagger kept mayhem in check.

The following summer Erik sailed north along the west Greenland coast. He may still have nurtured hopes of at least finding Alban hunting camps in that direction. Or he may have relinquished the possibility of finding anyone to rob and have concluded that if his men were to acquire wealth they would have to hunt it for themselves.

They sailed well into the old northern hunting grounds of Alban Crona. Hrafnsfjord was either Disko Bay or Umanak Fiord (perhaps both), beyond which lay an enormous bay filled with bergs. Sailing in continuous daylight, Erik went far enough to see the northeastern horizon transformed into a towering wall of ice—the greatest glacier face in the northern hemisphere.

This was Snaefells; and here he turned back.

Erik's people survived their third and final winter of exile on the same isle where they had spent the first one; and this seems *most* peculiar. If Erik had been convinced by now that local people offered no serious threat to his safety, he would surely have chosen to spend this last winter in a place which promised some creature comforts, such as the site at the end of Eriksfjord where he had already hallowed land and intended some day to settle. That he did not do this suggests that a perceived threat must have existed, whether real or imagined, and one of sufficient magnitude to keep Erik's war band barricaded on a grim little island through the final winter.

Although this reconstruction of Erik's exile in the west fits the existing evidence, there are other possibilities.

It may be that the Alban evacuation of Greenland had barely begun, or had been only partly completed, when Erik appeared upon the scene. Instead of coming to a country effectively devoid of inhabitants, he may have found one still partially occupied, and that by an exceedingly hostile population. It may have happened to Erik in Crona, as had happened to Ingólf in Tilli, that he was unable to establish a proper foothold in a new land, and so was *forced* to roost on its fringes. It may be that, again like Ingólf, he had to return to his homeland and there assemble an invasion force before he could take possession. All that the sagas have to say is this:

> Next spring Erik sailed back to Iceland, landing at Breidafjord.... The following spring he fought a battle with Thorgest and his men and Erik's side got the worst of it. Later, peace was arranged between them.

That summer Erik set out to colonize the land, which he called Greenland because, he said, people would be more easily persuaded to go there if the land had a good name.

Wise men say that when Erik went out to settle Greenland, twenty-five ships sailed from Breidafiord, and fourteen of them reached Greenland. Some were driven back and some were lost. This was fifteen years before Christianity was established in Iceland.

There were many dissatisfied men in Iceland in those times. Some had arrived too late to find good land. Some felt it irksome to be beholden to overbearing chieftains. Others, involved in blood feuds, were feeling their necks. Still others were simply hungering for some good, old-fashioned rapine. Such men would have responded with alacrity to a proposal that they band together and take the "green land" in the west for their own.

As the spring of 985 advanced, ships began congregating in the havens of Breidafjord and Borgarfjord. Each carried about thirty people, including women, children, and slaves. There would have been room for only a few cattle on this initial voyage. The bulk of the livestock would have remained behind, to be ferried over later.

On a June day judged to be propitious according to the omens, the fleet set sail; but either the omens lied, or they had been badly misinterpreted. The ships were struck by a terrible calamity. Almost half were sunk or sent limping back to Iceland.[5]

The disaster, which was perhaps the consequence of an undersea volcanic eruption, certainly caused heavy casualties. Nevertheless, the surviving vessels made good the passage, with the result that for the succeeding four and a half centuries, Greenland (or at least the southern portion of it) would belong to the Norse.

If any Albans *had* remained in Crona until Erik's invasion fleet arrived, they would have lingered no longer. Hurriedly freighting their vessels, they would have slipped away to the west leaving Crona to new owners and a new fate.

CHAPTER TWENTY-SIX

ARI GOES TO

ALBANIA

LANDNAMABOK, THE FOUNDATION STONE OF
Iceland's Norse history, tells us that some time during the
tenth century an Icelander by the name of Ari Marson

sailed on the ocean to Hvítramannaland [the land of White Men], which
some call Irland Mikla [Greater Ireland], lying away west in the ocean near
Vinland the Good, which is said to be VI days sail due west from Ireland.[1]
Ari could not get back from that country, and was baptized there.

Hrafn the Limerick Trader, who had spent a long time at Limerick in
Irland, was the first to tell this story. Thorkel Gellirson said that Icelanders
who had heard Earl Thorfinn of Orkney tell the tale, claimed Ari had been
recognized in Hvítramannaland, and could not get away but was held in
much honour there.

To which the *Annals of Greenland*, an eleventh-century Norse chronicle, adds:

There is, as stated, south of the part of Greenland which has settlements,
wastelands, unsettled regions and glaciers; Skraelings, then Markland, then
Vinland the Good. Next to it and a little beyond lies Albania,[2] which is
Hvítramannaland. Thither formerly were sailings from Irland. Irishmen
and Icelanders there recognized Ari, son of Mar and Thorkatla from
Reykjaness, of whom no tidings had been received for a long time and
who had become a chieftain in that land.

Who was Ari Marson? The answer entails what may seem to be a somewhat tedious excursion into Norse genealogy, but one that is required in order to securely establish the authenticity of Ari's extraordinary adventure in the west.

Landnámabók tells us Ari Marson was descended from Ulf the Squinter, one of the founding fathers of Norse Iceland.

> Ulf…took the whole of Reykness between Godfjord and Goatfell. He had
> for wife Bjorg, daughter of Eyvind Eastman and sister to Helgi the Lean.
> Their son was Atli the Red, who had for wife Thorbjorg, sister of Steinolf
> the Low. Their son was Mar of Reyknolls, whose wife was Thorkatla,
> daughter of Hergils Hnappraz. Their son was Ari [this is followed by the
> account of Ari's western venture which we have already read]….Ari had
> for wife Thorgerd, daughter of Alf of the Dales; and their sons were
> Thorgils, Gudleif and Illugi. This was the race of the Reyknessings.

Ari's ancestry is as weighty as any in Iceland and as well attested. It links him with some of the most notable people in the island's history, including Eyvind Eastman and Aud the Deep Minded, the *grande dame* of Iceland's founders.

It also links him to future generations. Thorkel Gellirson (mentioned in the *Landnámabók* account) was Ari's grandson. Thorkel was the uncle of Ari Thorgilson, author of *Íslendingabók* and probably of *Landnámabók* which together form the very cornerstone of Icelandic history.

Thorkel Gellirson lived in the first part of the eleventh century and was widely travelled and well informed. He is known to have provided his nephew, Ari Thorgilson, with much of the information contained in the histories, including, we can be sure, the remarkable story of how his grandfather, Ari Marson, ended up in Albania, which, by the way, is simply the Latinized name of Alba.

Ari Marson's bona fides are impeccable and his story as unassailable as any from that period. Yet most historians have chosen to ignore or to reject it. One can understand why. If one accepts Ari's story, one must concede that the Norse were not, after all, the first Europeans to "discover" North America.

❧ ❧ ❧

Erik Rauda and Ari Marson were both born around the middle of the tenth century. Both grew to maturity in the western reaches of Iceland. They were related by marriage through Ari's wife, Thorgerd, who was Erik's first cousin. They must surely have known one another. They may well have been comrades, even though (or perhaps because) Ari belonged to a long-established and wealthy family and Erik was a latecomer with few resources other than his own skills and ruthless ambition.

During the winter of 980–81, while Erik was enmeshed in his blood feud with Thorgest, a Christian missionary arrived in Iceland from Norway. He was styled Bishop Frederik, and was accompanied by a soldier of fortune named Thorvald Kodranson, who served as the cleric's bodyguard.

Thorvald seems to have had his work cut out for him. Those who proselytized for White Christ in pagan Iceland were seldom greeted warmly. Not only were most doors shut to them, but arms (in both senses of the word) were often raised against them. Nevertheless, Ari Marson, who had by now become a leader of the important Reyknessing clan, befriended the missionary.

Although Ari himself was apparently not yet ready to embrace Christianity, his son Gudleif did so and became the sword-swinging champion of yet another missionary, who played a catalytic role in the eventual conversion of Iceland to the new religion.

Along with other principal men of the district, Ari would have attended the Thing of 981 which dealt with the feud between Erik and Thorgest. Almost certainly Ari would have been on Erik's side, if only because he was a relative. When Erik was banished abroad, he chose to go to Greenland and Ari could have accompanied him on what promised to be a profitable Viking venture.

Although we are not given a date for Ari's arrival in Albania, we can construct a time frame within which it must have occurred. We know that Thorfinn Skull-splitter, Earl of Orkney, knew of Ari's capture and that the earl himself died in 988. We also know Ari was still in Iceland in the winter of 980–81. Since news of Ari's capture could hardly have reached Earl Thorfinn in less than two years from the time of the event, I conclude that Ari became a prisoner in Albania between 981 and 986, which embraces the period of Erik's Greenland exile.

One wonders why Ari was treated so leniently by his Alban captors. Why, instead of cutting his throat, did they let him become a prominent man in their society? Perhaps it was because he was pro-Christian. It is stated that he *was* baptized in Albania.

For whatever reasons (love of an Alban woman? rejection of the bloody mores of Norse culture?), Ari became a *de facto* Alban.

The sagas dealing with Ari also help locate Albania/Hvítramannaland which, the sources make clear, is one and the same. The *Annals* relate that several lands lay south of Greenland. These included the western shores of Baffin Bay and Hudson Strait.[3]

We are told that, to the south of Skraeling country, which was Baffin Island and northern Labrador, lay Markland (Woodland), the forested portion of Labrador. South of Markland was Vinland (Grassland) which, most authorities now agree, must have been eastern or northeastern Newfoundland.[4]

Next to [Vinland] and a little beyond [behind?] lies Albania, which is Hvitramannaland.

Note that Alba/Albania is *next* to Vinland, not south of it. Translators disagree as to the precise meaning of the qualifier. Some say "a little back from"; others opt for "a little behind"; and still others, "somewhat behind." Regardless of which one accepts, it is clear that Alba, like Vinland, was in Newfoundland.

This is confirmed on a map drawn early in the seventeenth century by Icelander Jon Gudmonson, working from earlier maps which are now lost. Immediately south of the Strait of Belle Isle, Gudmonson depicts a land mass which can only be Newfoundland. It bears the single legend: ALBANIA. Not only does Gudmonson's map show us where Alba was then believed to lie, it dates his original source to sometime before the twelfth century, after which Albania is generally replaced on Scandinavian maps by Vinland in honour of Leif Erikson's famous voyage.

If Norse scribes then and later were less than precise as to Alba's exact location, European merchant mariners certainly knew where it was. *Landnámabók* tells us that Hrafn, a Norse seafarer living in Ireland, was the first to get wind of Ari's whereabouts, and the context makes it clear he had heard the news from traders who had seen Ari in Albania. The *Annals* entry is even more specific. It states categorically that Irishmen and Icelanders recognized Ari in Albania. "Irish men" could have meant merchants from English ports who took their westward departures from Ireland. The Icelanders referred to may have been the crew of a ship skippered by Gudleif Gudlaugson, of whom we will hear more in due course.

In the spring of 1997, Robert Rutherford, an artist friend, sent me a reproduction of a painting he had made of the eastern Newfoundland outport of Cupids. Rutherford had depicted the magnificent view from the crest of Spectacle Head, which dominates Cupids and its environs. In the foreground were some structures that looked uncommonly like tower beacons.

"Thought you'd twig the cairns," he said when I phoned him. "They caught my eye first thing when I visited Cupids. I've seen nothing like them in Newfie, or anywhere else in Canada for that matter. They remind me of neolithic stuff in Orkney and Shetland."

According to Ginevra Wells of the Cupids's Historical Society, the three towers—grouped within a hundred yards of one another—have suffered more from the ravages of man than of nature. Visitors have been in the habit of removing stones from the structures and carrying small ones away as souvenirs.

The largest tower rises, as a slightly tapering cylinder nearly five feet in diameter, to four feet in height before constricting to a diameter of four feet for the balance of its height. The total height is now about seven feet but was originally somewhat higher, perhaps eight feet in all. The double-cylinder outline is of a piece with the odd outlines of several Arctic beacons, and may have been a factor in conveying a specific message to the beholder.

The second-largest tower has a base diameter of approximately four feet. It also is cylindrical for about half its height, then tapers steeply to two feet in diameter at just under seven feet tall.

The third and smallest is barely six feet high and three in diameter. Narrowly conical, it gives the impression either of being an afterthought or of having been demolished, then partially reconstructed.

Ancient beacons of unknown origin overlook the village of Cupids on Conception Bay, Newfoundland.

The stones must have been carried up to the crest from a consider-able distance away. The nearest source, a talus slope, lies nearly three hundred feet below the site and can only be reached by a circuitous and difficult route. The beacon stones themselves are thickly lichen-covered and convey an impression of extreme age.

Nothing seems to be known about the "cairns'" origins, antiquity, or purpose. Local residents say they "have always been there." "Always" is a long time in Cupids, which is one of, if not *the* earliest of, the post-Columbian European settlements in North America, having been offi-cially founded in 1610 by John Guy on behalf of the London and Bristol Society of Merchant Venturers. However, there is a persistent belief that a family by the name of Dawes homesteaded the cove as early as 1550.

Unlike most such enterprises undertaken by the seventeenth-century English in Newfoundland, Seaforest Plantation (as Guy mel-lifluously named his settlement) was not primarily intended as a shore station for the exploitation of marine wealth. It was designed to be a pas-toral endeavour demonstrating that the New Founde Land could nur-ture agrarian enterprises.

Guy surveyed much of the eastern part of the island in search of the best site for such a project. He found what he wanted at Cuper's Cove in Conception Bay, so called because coopers (barrel makers) for the fish-ing trade were accustomed to set up summer shop there in order to take advantage of the cove's remarkably fine stands of hardwoods.

Cupids, as it would eventually become, also offered exceptional farm-ing opportunities, including a stretch of highland meadow unique in eastern Newfoundland. This natural commons, stretching almost four miles to the south, is called The Grasses, and still pastures cattle. And Cupids's gardens remain unmatched in eastern Newfoundland for their productivity. Cupids was the logical choice for a pastoral settlement.

Although Cupids has probably been continuously inhabited for the last four hundred years, nowhere in the historic record have I been able to find any mention of its distinctive beacons. And distinctive they surely are. A modern mariner with knowledge of them, but without charts or other means of locating the place, would experience little dif-ficulty finding it. A mariner in search of Cupids Cove a thousand years ago would have been able to find it just as readily, if the beacons had been standing then.

They may well have been.

The Alban crofters into whose hands Ari Marson fell during the brief skirmish in southern Crona had long been preparing to emigrate. They wasted no further time. Almost before the longboat filled with Erik Rauda's Vikings was out of sight, they were loading two little ships that had been lying hidden in the recesses of the fiord.

There were those amongst them who were for leaving Ari behind—with his throat slit. He was saved by the discovery that he was wearing a small silver crucifix around his neck. Limping from an arrow wound in his thigh, he was hustled aboard and bound to a thwart.

Laden to their marks, the little vessels sailed at midnight. Three score people crowded aboard scarcely left room for five cows, a favoured bull, three ponies, a dozen sheep, and the dogs—barely enough livestock to provide a new start in a new land.

Luck was with the emigrants at first. The voyage across the Labrador Sea was uneventful. Having raised the peaks of the Torngats, they coasted southward to the beacons marking the location of Okak harbour.

When they entered the port they found it vibrant with activity. Dozens of small craft streaked the surface like so many water-striders, circling a bulky English merchantman riding at anchor in midstream. Five valuta vessels were crowded alongside her, their crews vigorously engaged in trading while the merchant skipper entertained the principal local men in the after cabin, bargaining with them for a pilot to the new Alba in the south.

A crowd of Tunit and Albans gathered as the two ships from Crona nosed onto one of the prepared landing beaches. At the sight of a Norseman being led ashore bound and haltered, some of the onlookers were for stoning him to death, but the majority were willing to let the priest decide his fate. The difficulty was that Alba in the West possessed only one cleric and he was then far away to the south on the Great Island, where he might remain for months.

Ari's captors shrugged. They were themselves headed for the Great Island and the Norseman had given no trouble so far. In fact, one of the women, a widow with four children, was beginning to look upon him with considerable interest.

Early in August a small fleet of southbound vessels departed Okak Bight. It included the English merchantman, three local valuta ships (one of which was carrying immigrants), and the two recently arrived Cronian vessels.

Two days out of Okak a westerly gale caught the flotilla as it was about to round the out-thrust northern lip of Hamilton Inlet. The valuta vessels and the merchantman were able to find shelter among the off-lying islands, but the two Cronian ships, whose masters were unfamiliar with the coast, were swept offshore.

They never did rejoin the convoy. They spent the next several days and nights driving east under bare poles, while strong currents carried them south. It was a hard passage. Overburdened with people, cattle, and chattels, the little ships were often awash with spray and solid water. When finally the wind fell out, they found themselves drifting in a death-cold pall of fog.

Every living thing aboard was wet and chilled. The stench from the slopping bilges was almost palpable. There was no fodder for the cattle, and precious little food for people. Moreover, the skippers had no idea of their whereabouts. Nor would they have until the sun broke through the murk long enough to let them calculate the latitude. Meanwhile, there was nothing to be done but wait for the fog to part and a favouring wind to rise.

On the fifteenth day at sea, the sun at last burned through. Slack sails filled with a gentle nor'east breeze. The skippers took sun sights and found they had reached the latitude in which, so they had been told, the new Alban settlement lay. They laid a westerly course.

Dawn of the following day revealed a massive headland jutting out of the sea to the south, and a land horizon rippling distantly to the westward beyond a glittering expanse of open water.

The ships drew together while the skippers conferred. It seemed possible that the headland might mark the eastern cape of the Strait of Swift Waters, which, they knew, led to the Inland Sea. There was little choice but to investigate. It was urgently necessary that cattle and people should be put ashore to refresh themselves.

So the vessels bore southwesterly and that same evening made a landing on the west coast of the headland. After a few days' rest, they continued south and west until it became apparent that this was no strait, but an enormous bay. Disconcerted, they coasted around its foot and headed northward up its western shore.

One day they opened the mouth of a cove that seemed to offer everything they might have wished in a new home. Here was vibrant forest rich in maples, birches, and other exotic trees. They went ashore at the head of the cove, landing on an estuarine meadow of alluvial soil the like of which few Albans had ever seen before. To the south were broad expanses of open highlands given over to grass.

There was abundant natural food here for men and beasts. Berries, even wild grapes, abounded.5 The bottom of the cove was alive with fishes, lobsters, mussels, and scallops. Salmon thronged the river that ran into the head of the cove from a nearby lake filled with trout. Within yards of the landing place, the cattle found themselves knee deep in strand wheat and succulent beach peas.

The immigrants had been disheartened by the discovery that the "strait" was a dead-end bay, and by the realization that they might have to retrace their course to Okak. The temptation to spend what remained of the summer in this seductive cove was strong. After all, what could the new Alba to the west offer that might surpass this place?

So they lingered from day to day, roaming a luxuriant countryside, revelling in fragrant forests and fruit-laden slopes. Even when the high flight of geese told them summer was over, they still procrastinated. In the end they determined to spend the winter where they were. Search for the new Alba could be renewed next summer.

While children herded the cattle to the highland plateau, there to lay on fat against the coming winter, men and women worked together to build homes at cove head. Although for the most part these were of traditional design, posts were used instead of stones to give vertical strength to sod walls supporting wood-raftered, sod-covered roofs.

During the winter, which was mild enough that cattle could survive and even thrive in the open, men explored the surrounding countryside. They found many deep inlets along the northwestern coast of the bay, but none which offered amenities comparable to those of their own cove.

One party, venturing a long way to the west, came to the shores of what at first they thought might be the elusive strait, but which, on further investigation, revealed itself to be yet another dead-end bay.

Of singular significance was the failure of the scouts to find signs of human occupation, old or new, Alban or native. It seemed to the fifty-odd people from Crona that they had stumbled on a portion of paradise as yet unclaimed by humankind.

When spring came, crops were planted in the deep soil at cove head. What had been implicit was now established. These people would search no further for a home. Their new Jerusalem was here.

Early that summer one of the ships, manned by a bare-needs crew, was sent off to make contact with other *Albans*, if she could. She returned just before autumn having found and crossed the mouth of the Strait of Swift Water and reached Okak. There her people had exchanged furs for more cattle.

One task remained before the little community snugged itself in for the second winter. Every available pair of hands was set to the gathering, sorting, and carrying of flat stones up to the high crest of the ridge protecting the settlement from the north. Here a crew, supervised by one of the elder men, raised three tower beacons. Visible to any vessel approaching from the northward, they proclaimed the message.

"WE ARE HERE!"

CHAPTER TWENTY-SEVEN

ALBA-IN-THE-WEST

After losing the two Cronian emigrant vessels off Hamilton Inlet, the remainder of the little fleet continued on its way. Ten days after leaving Okak, the three valuta vessels and the English merchantman reached the entrance to Tusker Bay. Here they parted company. One valuta vessel turned into the bay, heading for its clan croft on the shores of Two Gut Pond. The remainder bore west across the mouth of the broad inlet, turned south along the outer coast of Port au Port peninsula, and entered the great sweep of St. George's Bay. They came to anchor behind Flat Island at the bottom of the bay.

The island was a scimitar of sand some seven miles long, covered with natural meadows upon which many shaggy little cattle and ponies grazed. The anchorage, as the master of the merchantman was glad to know, provided the best shelter to be had along the entire southwestern coast of the Great Island.

The emigrants aboard the valuta ship were delighted to hear that a strip of arable land extended for thirty-five miles around the foot of the bay, and to be assured that its quality exceeded that of anything they had ever known.

Good land was but one of many gifts the region had to offer. The summers were long, hot, and sunny, yet with enough rainfall to green all growing things. The winters were nothing like as severe as in Crona, and there was a limitless supply of wood and even outcroppings of coal.

Timber had always been a singularly precious commodity to the northern islanders. In the vicinity of St. George's Bay hardwoods and softwoods were to be found of a size and an abundance previously undreamed of.

Country food abounded. At the appropriate seasons the numerous brooks and rivers draining into the bay ran riot with shad, gaspereau, eels, trout, and salmon.

Capelin spawned on the beaches in such profusion that breaking waves could pile the glistening roe as high as a man's knees. Spawning runs of herring and squid made the bay waters seethe right to the edge of the landwash; and huge cod that followed the bait fish could be speared from shore rocks without getting one's feet wet.

The uplands were equally fruitful. Caribou abounded, as did rabbits, ptarmigan, and other small fry. Black bears roamed the woods while occasional white bears hunted the shores. Lynx, otter, mink, marten, beaver, fox, and wolf were not only abundant but relatively unwary, having not yet learned who their greatest enemy really was.

And then there was the sea....

The twin inlets of St. George's Bay and Tusker Bay were home to a concourse of walrus, great whales, lesser whales, porpoises, and fishes. Valuta hunters working these waters were able to take full cargoes in only a few weeks. The necessity of having to make voyages that had once taken them a thousand miles and a year or more from home was now a thing of the past.

The benefits of the new Alba-in-the-West seemed manifold. Not the least of them was freedom from the fear of human depredations. Albans and Tunit had long ago learned to get along. Now Albans learned to do the same with Beothuks who, more withdrawn than Tunit, were somewhat more difficult to approach. Inevitably there were fallings-out between the three peoples and, occasionally, bloodshed; but, in the main, they lived together on the same island in peaceable fashion.

The Norse threat was now distant. And if, in future, the black ships did come seeking, they would not easily find their way to the new Alba-in-the-West. Supposing that they did, they would have to deal with three peoples in arms against them instead of only one.

For three centuries Albans had been driven westward across the grey waters of Ocean. Now, at last, it appeared that they had found their promised land.

MY FIRST VISIT TO ST. GEORGE'S BAY WAS IN 1965, travelling with Newfoundland author Harold Horwood. We lived rough, pitching a tent, boiling our tea over an open fire, and catching brook trout for breakfast. We spent much of our time with a category of people whose social status might be compared to that of gypsies. They were called Jakatars.

Generally rather small and wiry folk, dark-haired and dark-complexioned, they spoke a mixture of French and English laced with a little M'ikmaw.[1] Some fished lobster, eels, cod, and herring. Others were "countrymen" spending the bulk of their time in the interior, trapping; guiding "sports" through the mountains and the barrens in pursuit of caribou; or leading fly-fishermen to the best salmon pools in the brooks, as rivers in the region are often called, regardless of size.

In addition, most kept one or two cows, a few sheep, a couple of tough little horses, and a brace of black water dogs. The places where they lived were crofts in all but name.

They were an enduring people. Peter Barfit, also known as Pierre Beaupatrie, was ninety-four when we met him. He talked at length of his childhood and dwelt on the extraordinary trips Jakatar hunters and "furriers" had been used to making into the country, sometimes being gone from home for several months.

"I suppose furs accounted for most of your income?" I enquired.

Peter gave me a wizened grin. "You supposes wrong then. We got something for the furs, certain, but the most of what we got come from selling beef and mutton to Americee and Frenchie schooner men as used to come fishin' onto the coast by the hunnerts, spring and fall. They was some starvin' for fresh meat."

I knew that until a generation previously almost every Newfoundland family had kept a cow and some sheep, but I had never considered the Rock capable of producing beef and mutton on what amounted to a commercial scale. I concluded Peter was stretching things.

On a later visit I enquired more deeply into what he had told us, and learned he had understated the matter. After the completion of the trans-island railway in 1898, people from around St. George's Bay produced the bulk of all fresh beef sold in the distant capital city of St. John's and in most communities in between. I was told that as many as three hundred cattle had sometimes been assembled in St. George's shipping pens. And I learned that until as late as 1940 the vast estuarine plain at the foot of St. George's Bay, degraded into a gravel and concrete desert during the war by a USAF Strategic Air Base, had embraced several farms, on some of which as many as a hundred head of cattle had grazed.

In the gentler climate of the tenth century, pastoralists would have found this region even more rewarding. They would not even have had to clear forests in order to free the soil for their use. Broad expanses of

natural grasslands exceeding twelve thousand acres in total still sur-
round the many coastal lagoons, spread across river deltas, or undulate
over sand spits and sandy islands.

As Claire and I discovered when we explored the district in the summer of 1996, it and the nearby Codroy valley remain the most productive
agricultural areas in Newfoundland, and amongst the best on the entire
Atlantic seaboard of Canada. We found laden apple, pear, plum, and
cherry trees; gardens producing a remarkable diversity and abundance
of vegetables; pig and poultry farming; and, along the so-called Highland
(southern) shore of the bay, not only cattle ranches but fields of corn and
grain as well.

But Flat Island, for so long the hub of human activity in southwestern Newfoundland, was such no longer. As late as 1900 Sandy Point, as
the community upon the island was called, numbered more than three
hundred inhabitants, making it by far the largest settlement on the west
coast. By the time Claire and I came on the scene, Sandy Point had been
abandoned for thirty years. It perished, so we were told by a grizzled
man walking his dog on the mainland shore, because of the wheel.

"Once the railroad and then the high road come by, there was less and
less call for vessels to bring the freight, or to carry off salt fish or people
to St. John's, to Canada, or to the Boston States. When I were a lad there'd
sometimes be vessels enough anchored out there you could almost have
skipped across Flat Bay from deck to deck.

"My people always belonged to Sandy Point. When we come out of it
in '62 we was near the last to leave. Then the houses was beat down or
floated off to the mainland. At the end of it only the headstones in the
graveyard was left standing.

"When did Sandy Point begin? Now that I can't tell ye, sir. There's
some as says people was living there before the flood.

"What odds? It's been a right long time."

CHAPTER TWENTY-EIGHT

SEARCHING
FOR ALBA

WHEN I WAS WRITING *WESTVIKING*, I WAS MORE concerned with where the Norse had gone than with their reasons for going. I accepted more or less at face value the orthodox explanation that they had been impelled by exploratory zeal combined with a desire to settle new and distant lands.

Working on the present book disabused me. It early became apparent that the primary and abiding motivation of Norse westfarers was the lust for loot. Land taking *did* follow in Britain, Iceland, and Greenland, but in all cases the path had been blazed by marauders bent on pillage.

Greenland Norse proved to be no exceptions. Those who are on record as sailing west across the Labrador Sea did so not as explorers or settlers, but as sea rovers seeking plunder.

This chapter and the next, both of which include synoptic accounts of known Viking voyages to mainland North America, are partly based on my reconstructions in *Westviking*, but this time around I have emphasized purpose and behaviour.

Bjarni, son of Herjolf, was a well-to-do merchant mariner from southwestern Iceland. Having spent the winter of 984 in Norway, he returned home in the summer of 985 to find his father gone to Greenland with Erik Rauda's land-taking expedition.

Bjarni decided to follow, even though, as he frankly admitted to his crew, "people may think us foolhardy, since none of us have been in the Greenland Sea before."

They departed from Iceland with their cargo of Norwegian trade goods still in the hold, and were struck by a fierce northerly which swept them far to the south and west of their intended course. After a long, hard time at sea, they sighted land. Closing with it, they came to a country of well-wooded hills behind a bold coast pierced by many fiord-like inlets.

They had reached the eastern coast of Newfoundland.[1]

From dead reckoning and his relative latitude, Bjarni knew he was far to the south and west of his intended port. He would also have known that, a few years earlier, Erik had crossed a sea to the west of Greenland and had found an extensive coast. It would have been reasonable for Bjarni to conclude that Erik's land was contiguous with the one he now saw before him. He decided to sail north along it until he had regained his lost latitude.

In a few days he was abeam the forested regions of Labrador. The crew wanted to go ashore here but Bjarni forbade it. He pressed on under the formidable shadow of the Torngats until he reached the northern tip of Labrador, which, it so happens, lies in the same latitude as Erik Rauda's Greenland settlement. It now remained only for Bjarni to turn his *knorr*'s head east and run down his latitude. Four days later the lookout raised mountains and glaciers ahead, and soon thereafter Bjarni brought his vessel into Sandfiord, where his father, Herjolf, had taken land.

The sagas say nothing about Bjarni having landed in the west but, considering that his *knorr* had been storm-buffeted all the way from Iceland, he must surely have sought a haven near his landfall, where he could make things shipshape and replenish his firewood and fresh water. That he did do this seems implicit in his refusal to let his men go ashore in Labrador. There was then no need, he said, since "of neither [wood nor water] are we unprovided."

Where might a Newfoundland landing have taken place? Conception Bay, the first protected body of water Bjarni's people would have been likely to encounter on an approach to Newfoundland from the northeast, is the best candidate.

And what might they have found there? Wood and water, certainly; fish and meat probably; but they might also have found people, or at least traces of them.

I am persuaded by Bjarni's behaviour during the remainder of this voyage, and by his subsequent history, that he found either Albans or strong indications that they were or had been in the vicinity.[2]

Because Bjarni was a far-ranging merchant who regularly visited European ports, he could hardly have failed to hear about Alba-in-the-West and to have acquired some knowledge of its whereabouts. He would, of course, have been fully aware that Albans hated Norsemen in general, and Icelanders in particular.

Bjarni was no Viking warrior. He was a merchant skipper backed by only a handful of men. Finding himself on an alien coast inhabited by potentially hostile people, he would have done the sensible thing and taken himself and his vessel out of there as fast as possible.

The sagas tell us that when Bjarni reached Erik's new settlement he was accused of timidity, if not cowardice, for his failure to investigate the far western land more closely. Whether there was justification for these accusations, the fact remained that he had pioneered a Norse route into that part of the world where western Alba lay.

This contribution to Norse knowledge did not fire any immediate reaction. The loss of almost half of the first wave of settlers sailing to Erik's new fiefdom seems to have chilled desire for further westward adventures, and the usual hard scrabble of getting established in a new land preoccupied Erik's people for some time. In fact, it was not until about 995 that the Norse Greenlanders looked beyond Crona's refurbished crofts to what lay over the western horizon.

The Alban shift from northerly to southerly hunting grounds in the new world brought about major changes in the valuta trade. Although tusker ivory remained a mainstay, seal tar was no longer worth commercial preparation and the European demand for sea mammal oil was largely being met by Basques who were killing Right whales on a massive scale in home waters.

Fortunately for Alba-in-the-West, the slack was more than taken up by a commerce destined to shape the future of the new world.

The North American fur trade was coming into being.

White fox and white bear skins had always been prime valuta. Now they were joined by a wide variety of New World peltries, including lynx, sea mink, otter, marten, black and grizzly bear, and beaver. The trade may even have included moose (called elk in Europe) and buffalo (bison), the hides of which were so sought-after for leather clothing, shields, and body armour that, before the end of the ninth century, both species had been virtually exterminated in Europe. Moose were, however, abundant in the Gulf of St. Lawrence basin, and wood buffalo still ranged the eastern forests almost, if not quite, to the shores of the Atlantic.[3]

As the demand for peltry grew, Tunit and Beothuks must inevitably have become involved in its collection. Such were the small beginnings of a commerce which would grow and spread until it encompassed an entire continent.

The flow of wealth from Alba-in-the-West must inevitably have stirred the rapacity of Norse Greenlanders, not least among them Erik Rauda. Something certainly impelled Erik to go westviking once again. Loot was the most likely motive, but he may also have hoped to "rescue" his kinsman Ari Marson, supposedly held captive in Alba.

In the winter of 996 Erik and his elder son, Leif, determined to go roving in the west. To this end they refitted Bjarni's *knorr*. When summer brought good sailing weather, Erik rode down to join the vessel lying in the fiord below Brattahlid. But Thor failed him. Erik fell from his horse, injuring himself so severely he had to give up the venture. So Leif sailed without him, accompanied by Bjarni as pilot and sailing master.[4]

The real nature of this expedition is revealed by the saga statement that, on this occasion, Bjarni's *knorr* carried thirty-five men! Clearly this was a Viking war band and, I believe, one with a specific target in mind.

The relative latitude of the new Alba-in-the-West would have been a more or less open secret amongst the North Atlantic merchant mariner community. As a farfaring merchant himself, Bjarni would have had access to such information. He would also have known the latitude of his own first landfall in the New World.

These two latitudes almost mirror one another. The mouths of Trinity and Conception bays, which bracket the stretch of eastern coast where Bjarni made his first landfall, open between 47° 50' north and 48° 40' north. The mouth of St. George's Bay in southwestern Newfoundland opens between 48° 0' north and 48° 30' north. From a comparison of these, Bjarni could have concluded that if he sailed west between the

Norse equivalents of 48° and 49° he would find Alba. If, on his first visit to Newfoundland, he had found indications of an Alban presence emanating from Cupids Cove, it would have reinforced this conclusion. He was not to know that the whole of Newfoundland lay between Conception Bay and Alba-in-the-West.

In the event, he made his second landfall at the northern extremity of the hundred-mile-long peninsula separating Conception and Trinity bays, probably on Baccalieu Island in latitude 48° 10' north.[5]

Leif and Bjarni were then faced with the choice of descending into Conception Bay or into Trinity Bay. They chose the latter.

Here is what I believe happened thereafter.

By the time the *knorr* sniffed her way into the many harbours and inlets along Trinity's eastern shore, summer was getting on. The Norse had been a long time at sea, so they made a halt at Tickle Cove Pond, from which secure and comfortable base reconnaissance parties using longboats investigated the west coast of Trinity Bay. They found nothing to feed their expectations.

Winter was now approaching so they hauled the *knorr* out on Tickle Cove Sands, built turf-and-log cabins for themselves, and settled in. The saga tells us they spent some of their time reconnoitring on foot, and some cutting timber and gathering grapevines. In the event of failing to make a real strike they would at least not have to come home empty-handed.

Nothing is said about encounters with other human beings but the sagas make it clear the Norse were on tenterhooks. We are not told who, or what, they feared. The region where they wintered has apparently never been favoured by native peoples. Wolves and bears would not have given Vikings pause. But the possibility of being surprised by Albans would have served to keep them on the *qui vive*.

At the coming of spring, they launched their *knorr* and set sail for home, with nothing to show for their venture but baulks of wood, grapevines, and perhaps some furs. Unless something untoward had happened, their venture would hardly have been deemed a success.

Something untoward did happen during the voyage home. The *knorr* arrived at Brattahlid carrying a cargo so valuable it made Leif's fortune.

Some sources say he found an Icelandic or Norwegian ship wrecked on an islet off the Greenland coast. He is supposed to have rescued crew and cargo. Thereafter the crew fortuitously died of some unspecified ailment.

According to the saga,

Leif was afterwards known as Leif the Fortunate because he was now so well off both in riches and renown.

The saga story was composed by a Greenlander, but the existing recension is the work of Christian Icelandic clerics of a considerably later era who were not much inclined to celebrate the piratical aspects of their pagan forebears' exploits. I suspect that behind the story may have been an encounter between Leif's *knorr* and either a European merchantman bound to or from Alba or an Alban valuta ship.

Farfarer's people were amongst the first valuta folk to move from Crona to Okak. Many clans that followed went on to settle at Alba-in-the-West. Farfarer's people chose not to shift again. Although they hunted the Inland Sea as diligently as other valuta men, and sometimes wintered over, they maintained their crofts in Okak.

Time was lost travelling between the two places, but there were compensations. West-bound European merchant ships generally made their landfalls on the Torngat coast, then visited Okak, after which they might or might not continue south. Okak valuta folk therefore had the first opportunity to trade, and could command premium prices for their goods.

Early in June of 997, Farfarer, with a crew of eight men, six women, and three youngsters, prepared to return to Okak from a cove in Tusker Bay where she had wintered. Walrus had been plentiful and the previous summer's slaughter on the beaches had yielded several casks of ivory.

During the winter Beothuks had guided some of Farfarer's men deep into the interior. That journey had produced a bonanza of fur, some of it trapped or snared by the Albans themselves, some traded for red-dyed woollen cloth, of which the Beothuks were especially fond. Amongst the furs were a number of prime marten pelts, of almost inestimable value in European markets.

Farfarer bore a rich, varied, and heavy cargo when she departed for her home port. In addition to her own lading she carried, on consignment, the cargo of another Okak valuta clan whose hunters intended to spend a second summer at Tusker Bay.

The ship was overladen but her people were not worried. She was a good sea boat and they intended to coast-crawl northward, taking shelter at the threat of bad weather.

They had an easy time of it until they reached the Strait of Swift Waters, which was choked with Arctic pack. The ice posed such a danger to an overloaded skin vessel that there was no question of trying to proceed. They went ashore at what is now Flowers Cove to wait out the ice.

June was almost over before the ice withdrew. By then all hands had become impatient. Once clear of the strait, Farfarer bore northward along the Labrador coast under a full press of sail. Then the southerly wind hauled into the nor'east. The skipper nevertheless elected to hold his course even though this meant beating into a rising wind and sea.

Farfarer's first tack took her several miles offshore and by the time she had come about and was heading in, wind and sea had risen markedly. She was soon taking water over her lee rail.

At this juncture someone spotted a sail between them and the land. It took a while to ascertain that the stranger was heading towards them and a little longer to realize she was not Alban. Nor was she a merchant vessel! By the time Farfarer's crew realized who and what she was, the knorr *was bearing down upon them.*

They turned and ran. Overburdened and plunging heavily down the slopes of rising seas, Farfarer nevertheless made better weather of it than the pursuing knorr. *All might have gone well for her and her people had not the tiller snapped off in the steersman's hands.*

Farfarer sheered wildly and fell into the trough. There she lay, wallowing helplessly as the knorr *bore down upon her. Then the Norse were alongside and grappling irons were flying through the spray.*

The Albans fought desperately. Women wielded walrus lances while their men leapt to the weather rail with hand axes and skinning knives. But they could not stem an assault by some thirty screaming warriors armed with swords and battleaxes.

The Norse swarmed aboard in a welter of blood, some part of which was their own. The Alban men were driven into the stern sheets, where they were cut down. The last of them, with an arm shorn off at the elbow, managed to stay on his feet until a Norse axe split his head into two red hemispheres.

The surviving women and youngsters were thrown aboard the knorr. *Before the hour was out, Farfarer had been emptied of her cargo and stripped of everything of value, including her walrus-hide rigging and her sail.*

Then the Vikings cut her adrift. High in the water, manned only by her dead, Farfarer bore away on her final voyage. Wind and current set her shoreward and a few days later drove her onto the surf-swept beaches of Labrador's Porcupine Strand.

As it happened, a party of Tunit bound from the Great Island to Okak chanced upon her there. Wary of encountering Innu, they had been sailing their boat a safe distance offshore when they spotted the wreck. They downed sail, paddled cautiously in to investigate, and found what remained of Farfarer serving as a coffin for her crew.

Assuming that Innu had been the killers, the Tunit wasted little time pushing off from that desolate beach, but they took with them the mutilated bodies of the dead Albans.

The Tunit brought the corpses to Okak where it was soon realized the killings had not been the work of Innu. Deep cleavages of flesh and bone testified to the use of iron battle weapons. The dead men carried the unmistakable stigmata of Viking slaughter.

It was not long before word that the Sons of Death had found their way to the waters of the new world spread up and down the coast.

The news chilled all who heard it. Although the Okak people were shielded by the barrier of islands masking Okak Bay, they nevertheless stationed watchmen on the heights, and everyone travelling along the Labrador coast maintained a sharp and apprehensive lookout.

In Alba-in-the-West there was less immediate concern, for it was believed unlikely that sea rovers would go so far afield or find so well-hidden a place.

The greatest fear was of attacks upon merchant ships, for this was something which could disrupt, or even sever, the vital transatlantic trade.

In or about the year 999 Erik Rauda made one more attempt upon the new world. The brief surviving saga account of this venture tells us more about Erik in his later years than about Alba.

[Returning from a trip to Norway] Leif landed at Eriksfiord and went home to Brattahlid....He soon proclaimed Christianity and the Catholic faith throughout the land....Erik was slow in deciding whether or not to forsake his old beliefs. But [his wife] Thiodhild promptly embraced the new faith and had a chapel built at some distance from the house.... Thiodhild would not let Erik make love to her after she received the faith, which infuriated him.

From this there arose the suggestion that he should investigate the country Leif had found. Thorstein Eriksson, a good and intelligent man blessed with many friends, was to be leader but Erik was invited along because everyone believed his luck and foresight would be a great help. They outfitted the ship in which Thorbjorn Vifilson had come out to Greenland. Twenty men were selected for the expedition. They took little with them except their weapons and provisions....

In high spirits over their plan, they sailed cheerily out of Eriksfiord. Then they were storm tossed on the ocean for a long time and could not maintain their desired course. They came in sight of Iceland and even saw birds from Irish waters. In truth their ship was driven hither and thither all over the ocean.

In the autumn they turned back, worn out by hardship and exposure and exhausted by their labours. They arrived at Eriksfiord at the very beginning of winter.

Then Erik said, *"We were more cheerful when we put out of this fjord in the summer, but at least we are still alive. It could have been worse."*

Erik would have been about sixty when this voyage took place—old by the standards of his time, but not too old to want to bed his wife or to go a-Viking.

That this *was* a Viking cruise can hardly be doubted. The Erikers shipped a picked crew of twenty men who "took with them little except their weapons and provisions." No trade goods, and no settlers' gear. This was another war band.

We do not know the details of what followed. Although the ship was battered by bad weather, it is hard to credit that she could have blown around the North Atlantic for three months or more without ever coming to land. Her people would long since have run out of food, water, and fuel, if not of patience and endurance.

I conclude that they must have made the land on one or more occasions. But either they never found an Alban settlement or they did and were repelled by the inhabitants.

One thing is certain. This time the raiders came home empty-handed. And the saga man made what excuses he could for their failure.

Although Leif's western voyage had been rewarding, his failure (and that of his father and brother) to find Alba seems to have put a temporary damper on enthusiasm for Norse ventures to the west.

CHAPTER TWENTY-NINE

KARLSEFNI AND COMPANY

FOR A TIME ERIK AND THORSTEIN'S UNREWARDING western venture cooled the Greenlanders' interest in Alba. Then, in 1003, it was fired up again by a remarkable Icelander named Thorfinn Karlsefni.

What follows is a condensation of the saga tellings of his story, together with my observations about motives.[1]

> Thorfinn Karlsefni was a successful Icelandic trader.[2] One summer he out-
> fitted his vessel for a voyage to Greenland. Snorri Thorbrandsson shipped
> with him, along with forty other men. Bjarni Grimolfsson and Thorhall
> Gamlason also outfitted a vessel to go to Greenland with Karlsefni. They
> too shipped forty men.

Because the saga identifies Karlsefni as a trader, historians have generally assumed he went to Greenland on a trading voyage. But consider:
each of the two vessels involved in the venture carried forty people, of
whom (as we shall later learn) thirty were fighting men. This many bodies together with the necessary provisions and equipment would have
left scant space for trade goods.

Normally a *knorr* required a working crew of only five or six. If she was
trading to potentially hostile shores, she might carry a few additional men.
But the only time a *knorr* would have been likely to carry *thirty fighting men*
in addition to her working crew was when she was going off to war—or
setting out on a Viking voyage, which amounted to much the same thing.

Each of the two Icelandic vessels undoubtedly carried *some* trade goods, if only to ensure a good reception from the Greenlanders, but trade was not the primary purpose of this venture.

Some historians have concluded that the size of the ships' complements points to a colonizing expedition. But colonists normally consist of family groups of men, women, and children. A band of sixty warriors does not qualify.

The same caveat obtains against settlement as against trading. The ships would have had insufficient room for even a modicum of settlers' equipment and supplies, let alone enough livestock to establish viable herds.[3]

Karlsefni normally traded to European ports, where, I conclude, he heard about the valuables coming from Alba-in-the-West and decided to try his luck in that direction, not as a trader but as a raider. The saga says, "The agreement was made between Karlsefni and his crew that they should share evenly in all the good things that came their way."

The voyage was uneventful as far as Greenland, where the two Icelandic crews spent the winter as Erik's guests at Brattahlid. During the long, dark months, Karlsefni wooed and married the beautiful Gudrid, widow of unlucky Thorstein Eriksson.

Enthusiastic discussion of Karlsefni's plans now resulted in two more ships joining the proposed expedition. One was a Greenland vessel commanded by Erik's third son, Thorvald, the other an Icelandic trading ship chartered by Freydis, Erik's bastard daughter.

> The same summer when Karlsefni arrived in Greenland there also came a
> ship from Norway skippered by two Icelandic brothers, Helgi and
> Finnbogi....Freydis journeyed from her home in Gardar to see these broth-
> ers. She asked them to take their ship to Vinland [with the expedition] and
> go halves with her of all the profits they might get....It was agreed
> between Freydis and Karlsefni that each ship in the expedition should
> carry thirty fighting men, and some women also. But Freydis immediately
> broke the agreement and secreted five additional men aboard the brothers'
> ship....The expedition had 160 men when they sailed.

Four ships carrying 160 people, most of them fighting men, represented a truly formidable force for that time and place.

They sailed to the Western Settlement and then to the Bear Isles.⁴ Then they bore away to the southward for two days and, coming to land, went ashore and explored. They found lots of great flat rocks…and many white foxes. They called the place Helluland [Flatrockland].⁵

From there they bore to the south and southeast for two days and reached a wooded country.…They sailed on southward and after two days came to a cape beyond which was a long sandy beach. They rowed ashore and found the keel of a ship on a headland, from which they named the headland Kialarness.

A little farther south they put two Irish slaves ashore to scout the land. These found nothing notable except strand wheat and berries. Then:

> They stood into a fjord with an island in its mouth around which strong currents flowed.…They sailed into the fjord and called it Straumfjord [Streamfiord]. Here they unloaded their vessels and established themselves ashore.

I assume that Karlsefni possessed more accurate information about the location of Alba-in-the-West, and of how to reach it, than did the Greenlanders. In addition to its relative latitude, he seems to have known that those travelling to it made their landfalls on the northern part of Labrador, then coasted south until they came to a strait famous for its strong currents. Thereupon they bore west through that strait into another sea, on the *eastern* shore of which Alba was located.

As the squadron coasted south, the lookouts would have kept their eyes skinned, as seamen say. However, if they maintained even a minimal safe offing from the innumerable shoals, reefs, and "sunkers" of the Labrador shore, they might well have failed to see any signs of human inhabitants, native or otherwise.⁶

Considering the seven-hundred-mile extent and the intricately indented nature of Labrador's island-shrouded coast, and that the raiders took only about a week to traverse its entire length, the chances of spotting an Alban lodgement would have been remote. In the event, the only indication of a human presence the Norse found on the Labrador coast was the keel of a ship discovered on Porcupine Strand. Of a *ship*, be it noted. Not of a boat.7

I judge that Karlsefni had been concentrating his time and effort on finding the strait which gave access to the Inland Sea and the new Alba. He appears to have glanced into both Groswater Bay and Sandwich Bay but, realizing they were not what he sought, sailed on until the expedition arrived at Belle Isle Strait.

Now something peculiar happened. Instead of pushing south and west through Straumfjord, the Norse went ashore only a few miles from its easternmost headland, Cape Bauld. And here, at one of the bleakest, most weather-blasted, and inhospitable places to be found in Newfoundland, they prepared to spend a winter that was still some months distant.

Such behaviour by colonists would be inexplicable. It would be equally bizarre by would-be traders. But it is precisely what one might expect of Vikings preparing to lair on the coast of a foreign land whose inhabitants had (or soon might have) good reason to be seriously hostile.

Epaves (Wreck) Bay, as the place is ominously called, is so storm-lashed that its shores seem never to have attracted human residents, other than Karlsefni's people. Having myself experienced a gale, albeit a summer one, at Wreck Bay, I can see why people in general, and mariners in particular, avoided it. My companion and I were so savaged by wind and sea from a nor'easter that we had to run our powered dory ashore through a thundering surf, nearly losing her in the process. When we tried to make our way across the barren, rocky landscape, we found ourselves scarcely able to stand against a wind roaring unobstructed all the way from Greenland. I have seldom been so severely buffeted by the storm gods; and this was in summer! I can scarcely imagine what life would be like at Wreck Bay in wintertime.

Devoid of sheltering cove or harbour, approachable from seaward only through a *chevaux de frise* of rocks and reefs breaking white most of the time, this place could only have appealed to people desirous of remaining unvisited. But it was admirably situated to command the southern approaches to, and departure from, the strait. Distant vessels could be spotted from nearby heights, and *knorrs* or longboats, or both, could have sallied out unexpectedly from behind shielding islands to surprise unwary shipping.

Wreck Bay was, in fact, an ideal sea-robbers' roost. It was here that Karlsefni's people built several wood-and-turf structures, excavated during the 1960s by the Norwegian explorer Helge Ingstad. These now constitute the main attractions of L'Anse aux Meadows National Historic Site.

> Now they explored the country thereabouts....They did nothing but reconnoitre....They spent the winter there but had a hard winter and one for which they had not prepared. Fishing fell off and they grew short of food....
>
> In the spring they took counsel regarding their expedition. Thorhall the Hunter wished to go north around Furdurstrandir [Porcupine Strand] and Kialarness [Keel Point] and look for Vinland there.[8] Karlsefni wished to go southward, believing that the farther to the southward he went, the better the chances would be.

Although the Norse evidently believed themselves to be in the general vicinity of Alba, reconnaisance failed either to locate it or even to indicate in which direction it should be sought. Disagreement between Karlsefni's Icelanders and the Greenland contingent about what to do next seems to have been intense. There was even conflict within Thorvald Eriksson's own crew, trouble which culminated in the defection of Thorvald's right-hand man, Thorhall the Hunter, soon after the strait became free of ice.

Setting out in a longboat with nine fellow Greenlanders, Thorhall, who was by all accounts a singularly thorny fellow, headed north along the Labrador, perhaps homeward bound. His luck ran out and he and his party were caught in a westerly gale. Their boat eventually drifted ashore in Ireland, where her crew met with even worse luck. "They were savagely treated and thrown into slavery; and there Thorhall was killed, according to what traders say."

Back at Wreck Bay the expedition really began to fall apart. Thorvald Eriksson determined to sail west through the strait with what remained of his party and see what he could find along the northern coast of the inland sea. He and his men spent the summer reconnoitring the north shore where, to their obvious disappointment,

> they discovered no dwellings of men or beasts. In one of the western islands they found a wooden storage shed, though no other works of man. They came back to the houses [at Epaves Bay] at harvest time...having achieved nothing of value.

The sagas are silent about how Freydis Eriksdottir, with her Icelandic ship and Greenland warriors, spent the summer. Some historians believe she and her people accompanied Karlsefni to the southward, but this is almost certainly a misapprehension arising from a scribal confusion of Freydis with Karlsefni's wife, Gudrid, during an incident at Hop.

I conclude Freydis decided not to join in an extended search for the place which had eluded her father and her brothers, choosing instead to stay at Wreck Bay, where she was well placed to intercept any ship that might pass through the strait. Instead of searching for prey, she would let it come to her.

Karlsefni seems to have been the only leader with a sense of where Alba really was. He may have had private knowledge or perhaps was simply more perceptive than the others. In any event, he was convinced the search had to be to the southward.

One spring day c. 1004 he and his fellow Icelanders in their two ships sailed through the strait.

> Now is to be told how Karlsefni cruised southward along the [west] coast [of Newfoundland] with Snorri and Bjarni and their people. They sailed for a long time until they came to a river flowing down from a lake into a lagoon and so into the sea. Great sandbars obstructed the outlet so it could only be entered at high tide. Karlsefni and his people sailed in here and called the place Hop.

Hop is an old Norse name for a body of water cut off from the sea by sand or gravel bars behind which vessels may shelter. This Hop was probably the great lagoon at the mouth of St. Paul's Inlet.9

A few days after the Icelanders arrived at Hop, nine skin boats filled with "natives," presumably Tunit, appeared from the south.[10] The sagas tell us that they landed, inspected the Icelanders, then got back into their boats and returned south, the way they had come. We are not told what took place between the two peoples.

Karlsefni's party had now travelled some two hundred miles from their base at Wreck Bay, yet Alba still eluded the Norse. They had finally found living beings (or been found by them), but these were armed and accomplished boatmen able to pose a serious threat even to Norse sea-farers. I conclude that this encounter with *Skraelings* (synonymous with natives), who are described as "swarthy and nasty looking, with ugly hair," decided Karlsefni against proceeding any farther southward, at least for the time being.

Blessed as it was with a fine harbour, ample resources of fish and game, and abundant natural pasturage, St. Paul's Inlet was an excellent place to pause and regroup while deciding what to do next. It was also well situated to serve as a sally port from which vessels bound up or down the coast could be ambushed.

Karlsefni and his people remained at Hop through the ensuing winter.

> When spring arrived they discovered, early one morning, a great number of skin boats rowing up from the south....

Peaceable signals having been exchanged, the natives landed. They brought with them packs stuffed with "peltries and skins." They had come to trade and, moreover, were familiar with what Europeans wanted.

There is some confusion in the saga accounts about what ensued, but it is clear the natives wanted metal goods and coloured cloth in exchange for furs. Karlsefni, who was not outfitted as a trader, improvised.

> Karlsefni considered the matter then ordered the women to bring milk [or skyr] to the Skraelings who, as soon as they saw it, wanted it alone. So this is the way it went: they carried off their bargains in their stomachs.

At this juncture, so we are told, the expedition's bull "happened" to run out of the woods bellowing loudly.

This so terrified the Skraelings that they ran to their boats and rowed away... leaving behind them their packs and goods.

Could it be that the Icelanders deliberately stampeded their bull in order to panic their visitors and so obtain "their packs and goods" without payment?

There seems little doubt that the Norse had a guilty conscience about the affair. When, a few days later, the natives returned a third time, they were met by Norse warriors wielding weapons. The Skraelings responded with a shower of arrows and sling stones. According to the saga, they also deployed a supernatural weapon so horrendous that "a great fear seized upon Karlsefni and his men so all they could think about was flight."

The Icelanders certainly fled. The saga says Freydis came out of the house and tried to follow, but the name is probably a clerical error and should be Gudrid, who "could not keep up for she was pregnant." Gudrid did, in fact, give birth to a son, Snorri, that same autumn.

Then, says the saga,

She seized a sword and, when some Skraelings approached, let fall her shift and slapped her breast with the naked blade. Whereat the Skraelings were terrified and fled to their boats and rowed away.... Two of Karlsefni's men had fallen and a great number of Skraelings.

Two Icelanders perished, but so did "a great number of Skraelings," which sounds like something approaching slaughter. Whatever the natives had hoped for as a result of this third visit had been drowned in blood.

It now seemed to Karlsefni and his people that though this was an attractive country their lives here would be filled with turmoil because of the inhabitants, so they prepared to leave.

A not unreasonable conclusion, considering what had happened. The idea of proceeding on to the south could have had little appeal now that the inhabitants were thoroughly aroused. So the Icelanders packed up their gear, and the pelts stolen or traded from the Skraelings, and headed back for Straumfiord.

> They sailed north along the coast and found five Skraelings asleep by the sea....Karlsefni decided they must have been outlawed from their own country, so he put them to death.

By Icelandic law the possessions of outlaws were forfeit to their executioners. Opportunities for raiding on this coast were not great and such as existed could not to be ignored. Murder could be easily justified.

The Icelandic contingent arrived back at Straumfiord in late spring or early summer. We are told nothing of what had happened during their absence, but pickings must have been lean there because both Karlsefni and Thorvald soon sailed off on summer cruises.

Thorvald sailed north, passed Kialarness, and entered Hamilton Inlet, where he spotted some skin boats upturned on a beach, with people sleeping under them. The Greenlanders rowed ashore, surrounded the boats and captured the people, all save one man who managed to escape. Thorvald's men then murdered the eight they had captured and, presumably, helped themselves to the contents of the camp.

Who were the victims in this attack? The sources do not call them Skraelings. Furthermore, the saga specifies that their boats were skin-covered. This seems to rule out Innu, who normally used bark-covered boats. They might have been Tunit. On the other hand, they could have been a group of Albans caught sleeping in boat-roofed houses at a hunting station. Whoever they were, their friends were not about to let them die unavenged.

Next morning the ship was attacked by a flotilla of boats filled with angry people who showered the murderers with arrows. The Greenlanders made sail and fled, but not before Thorvald got an arrow in his guts, from which he shortly died. His men brought the ship back to Straumfiord.

Karlsefni had better luck. A born entrepreneur, he decided to have another go at fur trading, Viking style. Realizing it would not be wise to attempt a reprise on the west coast, he gathered up whatever goods suitable for trade could be scraped together at Wreck Bay, then sailed south along the east coast of the northern peninsula of Newfoundland. At the bottom of White Bay he again encountered natives. This time they were almost certainly Beothuks and, like the natives at Hop, accustomed to trading with Europeans.

> A great troop of them came out of the woods...their packs full of grey furs and sable. They were especially desirous of obtaining red cloth....In exchange for perfect pelts the Skraelings would accept a span's length of red cloth which they would bind about their heads....Karlsefni's people began running short of cloth so they divided it into narrow strips of not more than a finger's width. But still the Skraelings gave [were required to give?] just as much, or more for it....[Then] one of Karlsefni's house slaves killed a Skraeling....Now there was a battle and many of the native host were slain. One man among them was tall and fair, and Karlsefni thought he might have been their leader. Then the Skraelings ran away into the woods, each man for himself...[but] left their goods behind....Then Karlsefni and his people sailed away towards the north...being unwilling to risk men's lives any longer.

The Icelanders had made another haul, but this form of "trading" could not become an established way of doing business. It was strictly a one-shot deal.

It is uncertain whether Karlsefni remained at Epaves Bay through another winter. Most likely he sailed for home that same autumn.

His return journey to Greenland was marked by only one incident thought worthy of record by the saga men.

> When they sailed away from Vinland they had a southerly wind which took them to Markland. Here they found five Skraelings, one bearded man, two women, and two children. Karlsefni's people captured the two boys [the adults are supposed to have escaped by "sinking into the earth"]....They bore the lads away with them and taught them to speak, and they were baptized....They stated that there was a land on the other side over against their country inhabited by people who wore white garments and shouted loudly, and carried poles before them to which cloths were attached. People believe this must be Hvítramannaland....[11]

Although this paragraph unequivocally establishes that Alba/ Hvítramannaland lay somewhere to the west of Greenland, and that Norse Greenlanders were aware of its existence and general location, it has been consistently ignored by most orthodox historians of the Norse westward voyages. One can see why.

Expressed in a language foreign to them, the childhood memories of the two young captives convey an impression of religious celebrations in keeping with what is known about Christian rituals in northern Britain at the time of the Norse invasions. Celebrants and participants alike clothed themselves in white. It is notable that no instances of ceremonial practices similar to those described in the saga have been described from pre-Columbian native cultures of northeastern North America.

Karlsefni did not return home empty-handed. Apart from the first native slaves to be brought from North America, he carried with him "many goods, including wood, vines, berries, and *skin-wares* [my emphasis]." When he and Gudrid left Greenland for Iceland, the saga teller noted rather enviously, "Many said that no richer ship ever sailed from Greenland than the one he steered."

Freydis Eriksdottir also made a killing—quite literally. We do not know whether she succeeded in capturing any Alban or European vessels, but she did succeed in laying hands on a big merchant ship.

It belonged to the brothers Helgi and Finnbogi and was the one in which Freydis had come out from Greenland. One winter night at Epaves Bay, Freydis led her contingent of Greenlanders to the hut where the Icelandic crew lived.

They walked in and took them sleeping; and bound them and led them out, one by one, and Freydis killed every one that came out. Now were all the men killed, but the women were left, and nobody would kill them. Then said Freydis, "Put an axe in my hand." It was done and she slew the five women who were there, and left them dead....After that they put to sea and had a happy voyage and came to Eriksfirth.

There is a vellum manuscript in the Arna-Magnean Library in Copenhagen written in Latin and Icelandic. It is a compendium of fragments of history, one of which is believed to be derived from a long-lost manuscript penned by Abbot Nicholas of Thingeyre in Iceland, sometime between 1125 and his death in 1159.[12]

> Southward from Greenland is Helluland, then comes Markland. Thence it
> is not far to Vinland the Good....It is said that Thorfinn Karlsefni made a
> husanotra [a navigational device] then went searching for Vinland. He
> came to [the region] where this land was believed to be, but did not suc-
> ceed in discovering it.

CHAPTER THIRTY

THE BEST
OF TIMES

THE CLASHES BETWEEN KARLSEFNI'S VIKINGS AND the natives must have filled western Albans with dire foreboding. Was the bloody pattern woven by Northmen through three centuries to be repeated yet again?

I envisage watch stations being manned along the coasts, vessels mounting extra lookouts and, when possible, sailing in company, hugging the protection of the coasts. Foreign merchants may have reduced their western sailings or temporarily withdrawn from what was threatening to become altogether too risky a business.

For a time the always tenuous transatlantic ties may have seemed ready to dissolve. However, not all merchant mariners lost hope—or nerve. And, in the event, the dangers conjured up by the Karlsefni expedition turned out to be more apparent than real. The Norse had learned the hard way that Skraelings were likely to be as much as, or more than, the crew of any raiding vessel could handle and that the costs of mounting raids in the west were formidable. In practical terms (and the Norse were a practical people), the risks entailed in undertaking further west-viking ventures evidently outweighed the prospects of gain.

As the first decade of the new millennium ended, the Norse threat to Alba-in-the-West receded. Transatlantic merchant shipping returned to normal, which, admittedly, may never have amounted to more than a handful of vessels a year. Valuta men went about their business as of old while new crofts spread over the good pastoral lands in southwestern Newfoundland. Life in the west was peaceful;

although the hostility Albans felt towards Norsemen doubtless remained unabated.

Around 1025 an Icelandic merchant named Gudleif Gudlaugson, who had wintered in Norway, departed from Dublin bound for Iceland or Greenland. He failed to reach either destination. When he eventually got home he had a remarkable story to tell. It has been preserved for us by the anonymous skald who composed the *Eyrbyggja Saga*.

Gudleif was a great seafaring trader who owned a large merchant ship.... Towards the end of St. Olaf's reign[1] Gudleif set out from Dublin on a trading voyage.... West of Ireland he encountered easterly, then northeasterly, gales and the ship was driven far from sight of land first to the west and then to the southwest.

This happened late in summer and the crew made all sorts of vows if only they might reach land. At last land came into view. It was a big country, but they had no idea what place it was. Weary with the struggle with the sea, Gudleif and his crew put in to shore.

They found a secure harbour but soon people came towards them. They did not know who these people were, but thought they might be speaking Irish. A great crowd of what seemed like several hundred gathered, took them prisoners, bound them and marched them some distance inland where they were brought before a meeting to have their fate determined.

Gudleif understood that some of the people wanted them put to death, while others proposed they be shared out as slaves.

The inhabitants were still arguing about this when Gudleif and his men saw a group of horsemen riding up with a banner carried ahead of them. It seemed as if one of these must be a chieftain. As they came closer, the Icelanders saw that the one riding behind the banner was an old man with a head of white hair, but tall and courageous-looking.

Everyone bowed to him and greeted him as their leader, and the Icelanders saw that every decision was left to him. After a while he summoned Gudleif and his crew. When they stood before him he spoke to them in Icelandic, asking where they belonged. They replied that most were from Iceland. He asked which were Icelanders and Gudleif stepped forward, greeted the old man, got a friendly reply [and they engaged in conversation about people in Iceland]....

The inhabitants started to demand that something be done about Gudleif and his crew so the tall man moved away from the Icelanders and, calling twelve of his people to him, held a long consultation. Eventually they all came back to the meeting and the tall man addressed Gudleif:

"My fellow countrymen and I have taken time to consider your case," he said, "and they have left it to me to decide what should be done with you. You now have my leave to go wherever you want. Although you may consider it late in the season to put to sea, I strongly advise you to get well away from here. These people are tricky and hard to deal with, and they think you've broken their laws."

"What shall we tell people if we make it back to our homeland?" asked Gudleif. "Who shall we say we owe our freedom to?"

"That's one thing I'm not going to tell you," said the old man. "I'm too fond of my kinsmen and blood brothers to encourage them to come here and get into the same kind of trouble you'd be in if I hadn't been here to help you. I've lived so many years I expect old age will get the better of me any moment now, but even if I survive there are still people in this country more powerful than I am, and they'd show no mercy to strangers like you. It just so happens they aren't here right now."

The old man had their ship made ready and stayed with them until there came a favourable wind to take them out to sea.

During this interlude he continued issuing dire warnings:

"I forbid anyone to come and look for me because no one could find this place unless he had your luck. It would be a most desperate undertaking. Harbours are few and far between and strangers can expect plenty of trouble here."

The skald ends his account with this statement:

Some people believe this man may have been Bjorn the Breidavik-Champion [a swashbuckling philanderer who was chased out of Iceland c. 1000] but their only justification for this is the story we have just told.

I believe it much more likely that the old man who wished to be left in peace in his adopted homeland was Ari Marson. Ari would then have been about seventy. We know he became influential among the Albans. We can believe that, having spent some thirty or forty years in Alba during which time he had doubtless acquired a family, he wanted neither to return to Iceland nor to have to deal with bellicose kinsmen bent on repatriating him by force if necessary.

Where did Gudleif land?

It is most improbable that he could have been storm-drifted to the back side of Newfoundland, and so to Alba-in-the-West. Okak or even Hebron are better possibilities. But most likely he ended up in the catcher's glove formed by the great bays and fiords of eastern Newfoundland, even as did that other Icelandic merchant, Bjarni Herjolfsson, when he was blown off course into the western North Atlantic.[2]

Who were the people Gudleif encountered?

If they had been indigenes, the skald would surely have said so since, by then, Icelanders certainly knew enough about Skraelings to be able identify them as such.

But they could *not* have been Skraelings—*because they had horses!*

The reference to horses has been used by a number of historians to discredit the whole story on the grounds that, as everyone knows, there *were* no horses in the New World prior to their introduction from Spain in the sixteenth century.

But Albans had horses, and undoubtedly took them along on their westward migrations. Offspring of ancient equine stock are still to be found in the Northern Islands, Iceland, and Greenland. It should not surprise us if the hardy, hairy, native ponies which still persist (if barely) in Newfoundland carry genes from ponies Gudleif saw there almost a thousand years ago.

If not indigenes—and nothing we are told about these people indicates this is what they were—who could they have been? I submit that they were Albans or, at least, people of mixed Alban and native stock.

Thanks to the old Icelander, Gudleif and his people escaped with their lives. Perhaps they did even better than that. The saga's failure to identify Gudleif's landfall, or to locate its position even in general terms, is distinctly odd. Having sailed both *to* it, and *from* it, Gudleif must have known where it was. I suspect that the *knorr*'s cargo of European trade goods remained behind when Gudleif departed—having been exchanged for a lading of Alban valuta.

It is surely significant that Gudleif did not proceed directly home to Iceland. Instead, he made a second transatlantic passage—all the way back to Dublin! This could hardly have been happenstance. But if he had disposed of his trade goods in Alba, Gudleif would have had nothing to sell in Iceland. He would, however, have had a cargo of valuta for disposal in Europe.

I think anticipation of future business in Alba explains the reticence of the saga's source about the whereabouts and identity of Gudleif's land. These were trade secrets. The saga's emphasis on the dangers and difficulties involved in trying to find the place, or in surviving there if one did find it, was probably intended to preserve the secrets.

Albans had been Christians since at least as early as the seventh century. At the turn of the millennium Iceland and Greenland finally embraced Christianity. Thereafter all three peoples were brought together under the aegis of a single arm of the Roman church: the diocese of Hamburg and Bremen. The prelates of that see had powerful reasons to maintain close contacts with its distant western adherents, one of them being to ensure a steady flow of "pence for Peter's purse"—and for their own.

According to Icelandic annals, a Saxon or Celtic priest called Jon travelled west to "Vinland" in circa 1059. Scholars have suggested he was sent to convert the Skraelings, but the Church was not then interested in proselytizing "savages," who, according to many ecclesiasts, did not possess human souls. It makes more sense to suppose Jon was sent to Alba-in-the-West to deal with affairs of the Hamburg and Bremen see.

He was not the only churchman to go west. A legend on the Yale Vinland map informs us that

> Eric, legate of the Apostolic See and bishop of Greenland and the neighbouring regions, arrived in this truly vast and very rich land [Vinland], in the name of Almighty God, in the last year of our most blessed father Pascal [1118], remained a long time in both summer and winter, and later returned northeastward towards Greenland and then proceeded in most humble obedience to the will of his superiors.

This was Bishop Eric Gnupsson, who may have come out to Greenland as early as 1112. He was not *just* Bishop of Greenland, but of the "neighbouring regions" (except Iceland, which had its own bishop). Presumably the "neighbouring regions" meant Vinland/Alba.

The awkward-looking Flemish cog was the third merchantman to reach Alba in the summer of 1118, but her arrival prompted the most excitement for she carried clerics as passengers, and one of them was a bishop!

Never before had a high-ranking prelate visited the New World. In fact, during much of their existence, Alban congregations had had to manage with no priest at all, or with one harried father shared amongst them. Now, so it seemed to the faithful, the distant princes of the church were making amends for long neglect.

As the cog opened St. George's Bay, Bishop Eric beheld a vast amphitheatre of darkly forested hills rising to heights of a thousand feet. Conspicuous upon the crest of an isolated hill a few miles inland from the only secure anchorage in the bay, two tall stone pillars thrust upward like the blunt fingers of a buried giant.3

The ship sailed deeper into the bay, and the bishop saw that in many places the forests were fronted by grassland, most extensive near the mouths of the many streams and rivers. Embedded in this verdant strip stood unobtrusive clusters of croft houses and outbuildings.

In due course the cog rounded Flat Island's Sandy Point and came ponderously to anchor in the well-protected haven behind the island. Her approach had been reported hours earlier and a considerable crowd had assembled around a scattering of log cabins on Sandy Point, the nearest thing to a village in Alba.

The bishop and his clerics could detect few overt indications of the prosperity Alba was reputedly enjoying, except in the festive clothing and ornaments worn by some of the welcomers. This was an unostentatious people whose affluence was mainly determined by the number of cattle on the pasture lands, and the quantity of food preserved in snug cellars and storerooms. If the bishop had not previously examined the manifests of cargoes delivered to Baltic ports by ships trading to Alba, he might have been deceived.

Those cargoes had included some of the largest shipments of walrus ivory in memory. Port officials and merchants alike were realizing princely profits from these imports, whereas the Church was not receiving anything like what she deemed to be her proper share. It was one of Bishop Eric's tasks to rectify this situation.

When valuta men first entered Tusker Bay, they doubtless believed they had found the mother lode of walrus ivory. It could not, however, have been many years before they discovered the *true* mother lode barely a hundred miles to the westward. This was the Magdalen Island archipelago, anciently called Ramea, now renamed by the province of Quebec, Îles de la Madeleine.

As late as the eighteenth century, the Magdalens were still hosting the greatest concentration of walrus ever reported in any one place. In earlier times these herds alone would have been able to provide enough ivory and other walrus products to satisfy most of Europe's requirements. This was something about which Bishop Eric would have been well informed.4

During his stay, which lasted at least a year, the bishop probably visited most of Alba-in-the-West. On his return to Europe, we can be sure he reported to his superiors what he had seen and heard. That report may still lie buried in the labyrinth of the Vatican archives, but verbal accounts of Eric's travels in the New World would have circulated through ecclesiastical, maritime, and commercial circles in western Europe. If the existence and location of Alba had once been something of a secret, it would no longer have remained so.

Since about 900 climatic conditions in the western Atlantic had been steadily improving, bringing longer, warmer summers; milder winters; and a decrease in stormy weather. By 1100 this trend had wrought great changes in the region, most of them advantageous to the Albans.

Not so for the Tunit. Newfoundland Tunit were sea-mammal hunters first and foremost. Their principal prey was ice seals (harps and hoods), which every spring congregated by the millions on the pack ice of the Gulf to whelp and to nurse their pups. As the changing climate brought warmer weather, the thickness and duration of ice cover in the Gulf waned, until it could no longer provide secure seal nurseries. In consequence, most pelagic seals abandoned the Inner Sea to whelp instead on the Arctic pack along the coast of Labrador.5

As the ice seals withdrew, some Tunit followed them north. The remainder underwent a metamorphosis, becoming so closely associated with Albans as to become virtually indistinguishable from them.

Alban ways of life themselves underwent momentous changes. A warm climate disastrously shortens the life of skin-covered boats and this, together with the presence of good timber in abundance, encouraged a switch to wooden ship construction. But wooden vessels require much more time and labour to build and, since the Albans were no longer faced with the necessity of making extensive ocean voyages, they built smaller vessels.

There were no more oceanic Farfarers. New World Albans had become coastwise sailors.

Something similar took place in Greenland during the same period. Although timber could be fetched from Markland, Greenlanders lost the knack, or the need, to build big vessels. In consequence, they, like the Albans, became ever more dependent on foreign bottoms to maintain their connection with Europe.

Traders from England, Ireland, Flanders, and Baltic ports were now making transatlantic voyages and reaping satisfying profits. Walrus ivory was in ever-increasing demand. New World furs continued (and would continue into modern times) to be avidly sought in European markets. Other valuta, such as falcons, maintained or increased their worth. Good weather, good markets, and good supplies of valuta worked to everyone's advantage.

While valuta men killed tuskers on the beaches of Tusker Bay and Ramea, and trapped fur in the interior of Labrador and Newfoundland, Alban crofters prospered along the southwestern coasts of the Great Island. Clement weather enabled them to extend their pastures and enlarge their herds. They were able to grow ample supplies of grain, including precursors to modern oats and barley.

Crofting conditions were at their best in southern Alba, although they would have been good at Cupids too. They were less satisfactory at Okak, with the result that emigrants from there, together with a spillover from the St. George's district, homesteaded the Codroy district and perhaps elsewhere as well.

The Norse in Greenland were also doing well, both as crofters and hunters. They could obtain valuta (if not all they desired) from their own northern regions. By 1150 Greenland's twin settlements were prospering as never before, and supporting a population numbering as many as three thousand people.

As the twelfth century waned, the western regions of the North Atlantic were enjoying the best of times.

CHAPTER THIRTY-ONE

DROGIO AND ESTOTILAND

T HE NORTHWESTERN REACHES OF THE ATLANTIC were the scene of considerable maritime activity in the thirteenth century. During this time, a merchant vessel, which may have been, but was not necessarily, Norse, found her way into Kane Basin at the head of Baffin Bay. Here she came to grief, perhaps at the hands of aggressive indigenes, now called Thule culture, who had recently arrived from the west.[1]

Archaeologists Peter Schledermann and Karen McCullough have unearthed bits and pieces of the ship and her cargo (including iron rivets and even some chain mail armour) from Thule ruins on the western shore of Kane Basin. Another Canadian archaeologist, Patricia Sutherland, found the bronze balance arm of a merchant's scale belonging to the same period, on Ellesmere Island at a Thule site not far distant from Kane Basin.

Around 1266 the ecclesiastical powers of the southern Greenland Norse colony sent an expedition into northwestern Baffin Bay, ostensibly to determine how far south Thule had penetrated, but quite possibly also to determine what had happened to the missing merchant ship.

Vessels were sailing west as well as north into Arctic Canada. Icelandic annals for 1285 report the finding of a previously unknown land to the west of Iceland. Originally called the Down (Eiderdown) Islands, it was renamed Newland. Eight annal entries make ongoing mention of Newland and, in 1289, King Eric of Norway was sufficiently intrigued to send an emissary named Rolph to investigate it.

We are told Rolph was in Iceland the next year "soliciting men for a Newland voyage." The annals have nothing to tell about what success he had, but other sources provide some tantalizing glimpses of Norse west-faring during this era.

These include five sagas, all partly fictitious, but based on traditional sources. I have reported on them in *Westviking*.[2] They confirm Norse knowledge of Hudson Strait, which they called Skuggifjord, knowledge evidently acquired during several voyages to that region, any or all of which could have been concerned with the Newland discovery.

Where was Newland? It could not have been in Greenland proper; nor could it have been in Helluland, Markland, or Vinland, all of which were then relatively well known. The annals specify that it was *west* of Iceland, which, in the parlance of the day, meant that it was to be looked for in the same latitudes as Iceland.

Overleaping Greenland westward from Iceland takes us to that section of the north shore of Hudson Strait lying between Markham Bay and Cape Dorset. The coast here forms a bight about 160 miles long and 30 deep, packed with islands that even yet have not been fully explored, but which host the largest populations of breeding eider ducks in the Canadian Arctic. These islands lie between 63° 30' and 64° 30', latitudes that embrace the southern third of Iceland.

In 1978 archaeologists excavating a thirteenth-century Thule house ruin at Lake Harbour, which is on Hudson Strait just east of Markham Bay, uncovered a wooden figurine dressed in European style, including a hooded cloak. The little figure has a cross carved on its chest.

Nothing indicates that Greenlanders sailed south during this period, from which I conclude that Albans and their native allies continued to make Norse ventures in that direction unproductive.

By this time Alban valuta seekers would have found their way around most of the coasts of the Gulf of St. Lawrence. They would, however, have had little reason to settle there. Apart from Prince Edward Island, the Gulf had nothing to offer crofters comparable to southwestern Newfoundland, which was distant enough from Europe to strain the sea links between the two continents.

Walrus products, and especially ivory, continued to be a mainstay of New World trade. *The King's Mirror*, a Norwegian compendium dating to about 1250, tells us that in Greenland,

This robed and hooded figure bearing a cross carved on its chest was found in a 12th century Thule Inuit ruin at Lake Harbour on Hudson Strait.

everything that is needed to improve the land must be purchased abroad, both iron and all that they use in building houses. In return for these wares the merchants bring back [to Europe] the following products: reindeer skins, hides, sealskin, and rope of the kind which is called "leather rope" and is cut from the fish called walrus, and also the teeth of walrus.

Also the teeth! In 1262 Bishop Olaf left Greenland carrying so much ivory aboard his vessel that, after she was wrecked on the coast of Iceland, tusks continued to wash ashore for three hundred years.

In 1323 the papal legate for Norway and Sweden received tithes from the diocese of Gardar in Greenland amounting to about 1,400 pounds of walrus ivory. This was sold in Flanders, which had by this time become a major marketplace for New World valuta.

The enduring importance of walrus is highlighted by these words about the Magdalen Islands, written in the late 1500s by that indefatigable chronicler of English voyaging, Richard Hakluyt.

> The Island...is flat and shoal: and the fish cometh on the shores to do their kind in April, May and June by numbers thousands; which fish is very big and hath two great teeth...and they will not go away from their yonge ones....These beasts are as big as Oxen...the hides big as any Oxe hide....The leather dressers take them to be excellent good to make light targets [shields]....The teeth have been solde in England to the comb and knife makers at 8 groats and 3 shillings the pound, whereas the best [elephant] Ivory is sold for halfe of that. A skilful Phisition showed me one of these beast's teeth and assured me that he had made a tryall of it in ministering medicine to his patients and found it as sovereigne [a remedy] against poison as any Unicorne's horne.

If the thirteenth and fourteenth centuries dealt kindly with Albans in Newfoundland, they were less benevolent towards the livyers of Hudson Bay and Hudson Strait.

Sometime around 1000 a formidable new people from Alaska began moving across Arctic Canada. They were bearers of the Thule culture, the ancestors of modern Eskimos.

According to archaeologist Moreau Maxwell, they had experienced a long history of warfare with encroaching tribes from Siberia, and of internecine strife resulting from overcrowding in Alaska. They knew how to fight, and when they moved east, they carried wickedly effective, sinew-backed bows of Asiatic pattern.

The Tunit were unable to withstand this alien tide. They had no knowledge of, or experience with, warfare; nor did they possess weapons designed for use against their own species. The Thule invasion rolled eastward, overwhelming the Tunit.

Thule's progress was as swift as it was deadly. By about 1200 the new-comers had reached Kane Basin and were in sight of Greenland. Less than a century later, they were at Disko Bay, halfway down the west coast of Greenland, and close enough to Norse settlements in the Godthaab fiords.

Their penetration of the southerly part of Canada's eastern Arctic was not so rapid. Although by about 1250 they had established a foothold on the northern tip of Labrador, for another century they got no farther south. They also failed to occupy the western coast of Ungava Bay.

I believe this was because people of mixed Tunit and Alban ancestry were able to hold the intruders to a stand-off. After Thule belligerence had been blunted by time, perhaps the livyers melded with the newcomers to become the forebears of the modern Inuit of Hudson Strait, Ungava, and northern Labrador, a people who earned a reputation for stubborn and effective resistance to the incursions of latter-day Europeans.

Conditions in south central Labrador during these two centuries evi-dently remained peaceable, but by about 1350 a marked deterioration in the weather (the onset of the so-called Little Ice Age) would have begun making life difficult for crofters. As the climate grew colder and stormier, it would have become increasingly difficult to carry livestock through the winters. And then, to make matters worse, Greenland Norse reappeared on the Labrador coast.

In 1347, according to Icelandic annals, a Greenland vessel carrying eighteen men "that had been to Markland" arrived in Iceland. After spending the winter there, ship and crew sailed on to Norway.

Most scholars have viewed this as a peaceful visit to Markland by Greenlanders in need of timber. But Greenland vessels of the period were small and could scarcely have had room for eighteen men together with their gear *and* a worthwhile cargo of lumber. And why would so many men have been needed for a tree-felling expedition? We must also ask why, instead of returning to her homeland, the ship sailed first to Iceland then on to Norway. Carrying wood to Norway would have been as pointless as carrying coals to Newcastle!

I think it likely that these eighteen men made up a band of latter-day

Vikings who had sailed to Labrador to raid Alban settlements, Tunit camps, or coastal shipping.

The effects of increasingly adverse climatic conditions, together with piratical attacks, may eventually have led to the abandonment of Alban lodgements on the Labrador; but, before that happened, Okak hosted some unintentional European visitors, to one of whom we owe our most informative account of Alba-in-the-West.

In 1558 a book dealing with a New World voyage was published in Venice. Translated into English, it was included by Richard Hakluyt in his *The Principall Navigations, Voiages and Discoveries of the English Nation*, as "The Discovery of the Isles of Frisland, Iseland, Engroenland, Estotiland, Drogeo and Icaria: made by two brethren, namely M. Nicholas Zeno and M. Antonio, his brother."

Nicolo Zeno, great-great-grandson of the aforementioned Nicholas, was the nominal author, having assembled the text from letters and other documents written by the brothers, which he found in the Zeno family archives.

Although the accent was accepted in its own time, recent historians have generally rejected it because a number of names in the text and on the accompanying map do not correlate with modern names. What the critics fail to realize is that many names were intentionally invented to hide real identities.

Merchant adventurers (which is what the original Nicholas and his brother were) of those times routinely tried to conceal the whereabouts of their sources of wealth. In consequence, Nicolo the younger, separated from his sources by nearly two hundred years, had to work with code names intended to mislead fourteenth-century competitors. And he did not have the code.

The bulk of the book deals with a series of piratical voyages to Norway, Orkney, Shetland, and Iceland mainly conducted by the Zeno brothers serving as mercenaries in the employ of a chieftain whom they referred to as Zichmni. The chieftain's real identity remains unknown, but he seems to have been a sea lord from Scotland's western isles.

The book includes the account of a transatlantic buccaneering expedition launched between 1386 and 1396 that appears to have been aimed at Alba-in-the-West.

The text establishes that a raiding fleet led by Zichmni and Antonio Zeno crossed the Atlantic to what was almost certainly the eastern shore of Nova Scotia. Sailing northward, the fleet then either rounded Cape Breton Island or passed through Canso Strait into the Gulf of St. Lawrence to reach the vicinity of Pictou, Nova Scotia. Here Zichmni succeeded in provoking the natives to the point where they almost wrote *finis* to the entire expedition. The Indians may, in fact, have disposed of Zichmni himself after Antonio Zeno fled home with most of the fleet.

The genesis of Zichmni's foray was an accidental visit to the New World made some years earlier by a number of Hebridean or Icelandic fishermen. It is with their story that we are chiefly concerned.

> Zichmni, being a man of great courage and valour, had determined to make himself Lord of the sea. Wherefore, using always the counsel and service of M. Antonio, he determined to send him with certain barks to the Westward, for that towards those parts, some of his fishermen had discovered certain Islands [the words *Islands* and *Lands* were then interchangeable] very rich and populous: which discovery [Antonio, who heard it firsthand from the fisherman] in a letter recounts from point to point in this manner....
>
> Six and twenty years ago [c. 1360] there departed four fisher boats, the which, a mighty tempest arising, were tossed for the space of many days very desperately upon the Sea, when at length, the tempest ceasing, and the weather waxing fair, they discovered an Island called Estotiland, lying to the Westward more than 1000 miles from Frisland [Iceland], upon which one of the boats was cast away, and six men that were in it were taken by the inhabitants and brought into a fair and populous city, where the king of the place sent for many interpreters, but there was none could be found that understood the language of the fishermen, except one that spoke Latin, who was also cast by chance upon the same Island, who in the behalf of the King asked them what countrymen they were: and so understanding their case, rehearsed it unto the king, who willed that they should tarry in the country; wherefore they obeyed his commandment for that they could not do otherwise.

The distance travelled gives us our first clue to the whereabouts of the fishermen's landfall. A voyage of one thousand nautical miles westward from the Hebrides would place a vessel only about three-quarters of the way across the Atlantic; whereas the same distance from Iceland would bring a ship to within a hundred miles of southeastern Labrador, the nearest part of North America. Either Labrador or Newfoundland could have been the landfall but, as we shall see, Newfoundland was the *second* "Island" to be visited by the fishermen.

The six castaways found themselves in Estotiland, represented on the map put together by Nicolo the younger as part of Labrador. This agrees with the position given to it in the *Theatrum Orbis Terrarum* of cartographer Abraham Ortelius published in 1570. Petri, in his seventeenth-century map of the New World, is even more specific, plotting Estotiland on that part of Labrador north of Hamilton Inlet.

The reference to another castaway, who spoke Latin, suggests a cleric, for in those times few secular folk knew Latin. He is not identified as a priest, but something of a Christian connection seems to be indicated by a later reference to certain old Latin books that were still held in high, if not sacred, regard.

> [The castaways] dwelt five years in the Island, and learned the language, and one of them was in divers parts of the Island, and reports that it is a very rich country, abounding with all the commodities of the world, and that it is little less [in size] than Island [Iceland], but far more fruitful, having in the middle thereof a very high mountain.

Reference to a high mountain may help localize Estotiland as the region around Okak/Nain, for this is where the Torngat Mountains rise abruptly before beginning their northward march.

> The inhabitants are very witty [wise] people, and have all the arts and faculties as we have: and it is credible that in time past they have had traffic with our men, for he said that he saw Latin books in the king's Library, which they at this present do not understand: they have a peculiar language, and letters or characters [known only] to themselves.

"All the arts and faculties we have" is hardly the way fourteenth-century Europeans would have described wilderness inhabitants. Evidently the fisherman did not find the residents of Estotiland singularly different from himself, except in language. His description of them is in sharp contrast to the way he delineates other people he encountered later, whom he forthrightly calls "savages."

"It is credible [believed] that in time past they [the Estotilanders] have had traffic with our men [which is to say, with Europeans]" is a singularly significant statement.

The comment on Latin books seems to echo references which occur in *Islendingabók* and *Landnámabók* relating to the pre-Norse occupation of Iceland by Christians. Use of the phrase "the king's Library" may be stretching things, but makes the point that the Latin books (which would presumably have been holy books) were still venerated.

> They have trade in Engroenland, from whence they bring furs, brimstone and pitch: and he says that to the Southwards, there is a great populous country very rich of gold. [There] they sow corn, and make beer and ale, which is a kind of drink that North people do use as we do wine. They have mighty great woods, they make their buildings with walls, and there are many cities and castles.

Much of what Antonio describes in this passage is generalized information about the entire territory to the south of Estotiland, but the comment about trade with Engroenland (Greenland) has particular significance. Furs and pitch produced from the coniferous forests of the New World could have gone to Greenland for trans-shipment to Europe; and brimstone (sulphur) from Iceland could have reached Estotiland via Greenland.[3]

> They build small barks and have sailing, but they have not the lodestone, nor know not the use of the compass. Wherefore these fishers were held in great estimation, insomuch that the king sent them with twelve barks Southward to a country which they call Drogio: but in their voyage they had such contrary weather, that they thought to have perished in the seas: but escaping that cruel death, they fell into another more cruel: for they were taken [captive] in the country and most of them were eaten by the Savage people.

The six were presumably sent south to Drogio because it was the chief settlement. The reference to a squadron of twelve vessels suggests that a shift from Okak to the south may already have been under way.

The fishermen's tribulations were not yet over. They were wrecked again, this time on a coast inhabited by "savages." It appears from what followed that their ill-fated vessel was driven westward through Belle Isle Strait and the fishermen fell into the hands of Indians living on the north shore of the Gulf.

But that fisher, with his fellows showing them [the savages] the manner of taking fish with nets, saved their lives: and [they] would go every day a fishing to the sea and in fresh rivers, and take great abundance of fish and give it to the chief men of the country, whereby he got himself so great favour, that he was very well beloved and honoured of everyone.

The fame of this man being spread abroad in the country there was a Lord there by, that was very desirous to have him with him, and to see how he used his miraculous art of catching fish, insomuch that he made war with the other Lord with whom he was before, and in the end prevailing, for that he was more mighty and a better warrior, the fisherman was sent to him with the rest of his company. And for the space of thirteen years that he dwelt in those parts, he says, he was sent in this order to more than 25 Lords, for they had continual war among themselves, this Lord with that Lord, and he with another, only to have him to dwell with them: so that wandering up and down the country without any certain abode in one place, he knew almost all those parts. He says that it is a very great country and as it were a new world: the people are very rude and void of all goodness,...they have no kind of metal, they live by hunting, they carry certain lances of wood made sharpe at the point, they have bows, the strings whereof are made of beasts skins: they are very fierce people, they make cruel wars with one another, and eat one another.

The Indians living along the north shore of the Gulf at this time would have been Algonkians, forebears of the Montagnais and Naskapi tribes who call themselves Innu.

The most revealing aspect of this part of the story is the characterization of the natives, who are specifically called *savages*. They are described in the same general terms employed by almost every other early European observer. *But this description is in clear contradistinction to what we are told about the inhabitants of Estotiland.* That the two peoples were *not* one and the same is surely beyond question.

The narrator and his companions spent several years amongst Indians, moving from tribe to tribe for some considerable distance westward along the north shore of the Gulf. The fishermen seem to have been adopted into the native population and treated well, as is implied by the phrase "well beloved and honoured by everyone."

> Now this fisherman, having dwelt so many years in those countries, purposed, if it were possible, to return home into his [own] country, but his companions, despairing ever to see it again, let him go in God's name, and they kept themselves where they were. Wherefore he bidding them farewell, fled through the woods towards Drogio, and was very well received of the Lord that dwelt next to that place; who knew him and was a great enemy of the other Lord; and so running from one Lord to another, being those by whom he had passed before, after a long time and many travels he came at length to Drogio, where he dwelt three years.

This is a reasonably straightforward description of how he found his way back eastward until he came to the territory of a tribe on the northwestern shores of Belle Isle Strait, which he presumably crossed with Indian assistance. He then made his way south to Drogio, which I take to be Alba-in-the-West.

Significantly, there is no description of the Drogians. Presumably the fisherman was now back amongst people with whom he felt familiar, and so did not repeat what he had already said about the Estotilanders. If the people of Drogio had been of another and markedly different culture, the narrator would surely have described them in at least as much detail as he employed in describing the Savages.

> When as by good fortune he heard by the inhabitants, that there were certain boats arrived upon the coast; wherefore, entering into good hope to accomplish his intent, he went to the seaside and asking them of what country they were; they answered, of *Estotiland,* whereat he was

exceedingly glad, and requested that they would take him in to them, which they did very willingly, and for that he had the language of the [Indian] country, and there was none [in the ships] that could speak it, they used him for their interpreter.

And afterwards he frequented that trade with them in such sort, that he became very rich, and so furnishing out a bark of his own, he returned into *Frisland* where he made report to this Lord [Zichmni] of that wealthy country.[4]

Here we have a straightforward account of the narrator trading with Indian tribes, of how he prospered and eventually was able to sail back to Frisland.

In sum, this is what was, for those times, a relatively unadorned record made by a European, cast away on the coast of Labrador, of how he was succoured by the inhabitants; travelled with some of them on a voyage bound south for Newfoundland; was again cast away, this time on the northern coast of the Gulf; lived for a time with coastal Indians; eventually found his way to Drogio; and sailed from there as a trader until he became rich enough to get his own ship or buy his passage back to Europe.

The narrator clearly distinguishes between a native population and another people, who were of European cast. I conclude these were Albans and that, c. 1370, they still constituted a society recognizable to a European as being cut from much the same cloth as his own.

It was this fisherman's account which induced Zichmni to sail to the New World, but, as Antonio tells us,

our great preparations for the voyage to Estotiland was begun in an unlucky hour: for three days before our departure that fisherman died who should have been our guide: notwithstanding this the Lord [Zichmni] would not give over the enterprise.

So Zichmni sailed west without a pilot, and in consequence failed to find either Estotiland or Drogio.

The fisherman had unwittingly repaid his New World benefactors by dying when he did.

CHAPTER THIRTY-TWO

GREENLANDERS

OUR SHIP HAD STEAMED ALL NIGHT, THOUGH, STRICTLY speaking, there was no night for the sun sank below the horizon only to rise again within the hour. We had made an extraordinary passage across Baffin Bay, dreaded by mariners for its great gales and ice-filled seas; we crossed without hindrance in dead-calm weather. The waters had been so stilled that only our vessel's wake disturbed a glassine surface in which were reflected images of hundreds of towering icebergs drifting majestically southward from Melville Bay—nursery of Titans.

When I went on deck at 6:00 A.M., land had just been sighted. Only it wasn't land. It was a horizon-filled glitter of ice and snow that dazzled the mind as well as the eye.

The Norwegian second mate came and stood beside me on the wing of the bridge.

"See those black specks to starboard?" he asked, pointing with the stem of his pipe. "They're islands along about Upernavik. Nothing but rocks. Nothing behind them but snow and ice. Nothing in front but a sea full of ice." He paused to puff.

"My grandfather used to seal in east Greenland in about this latitude. He had a name for the country. The mill-tail of hell! The frozen other end of the hot place, you could say. Yet he kept going back to it for fifty and more years. No need to tell a Norwegian to go to hell. He'll get there on his own."

Kingiktorsuak is one of the pimples of black rock making up the fringe of coastal islands squeezed between the inland ice and the sea. It lies only fifteen miles north of the small town of Upernavik. As we steamed towards that port we came close enough to Kingiktorsuak so I could see its naked summit.

At one time some small cairns had stood upon its crest. By 1824 all had collapsed or, what is more likely, been pulled apart by Eskimos hoping to find something of value within. In the summer of that year a man named Pelimut *did* find something lying beside one of the ruined cairns. The object was a small stone rudely inscribed with Scandinavian runes:[1]

Erling Sigvatsson, Bjarni Tordsson and Einride Oddson made these cairns on the Saturday before Rogation Day, and runed well.

Scholars argue about the year when this record was scratched on stone, but agree it would have been after 1135 and before 1333. So sometime between these dates Norsemen must have wintered near Upernavik, a thousand miles to the northward of Cape Farewell. The former valuta grounds of the departed Albans had come under new management.

This was not the only aspect of Greenland to change management around this time. In 1152 jurisdiction of the Greenland bishopric was transferred from the See of Hamburg to the See of Nidaros (Trondheim) in Norway.

The Church had exerted powerful influence over the Greenland Norse since shortly after Leif Erikson brought the first priest to them c. 988. Around 1075, Adam of Bremen wrote that "bishops ruled Iceland and Greenland as if they were kings." In succeeding centuries the Church lost power in Iceland, but the Norse settlements in Greenland continued to live in a theocracy made almost absolute by the archbishops of Nidaros, for whom the remote island was an invaluable source of wealth.

By the middle of the thirteenth century Greenland's southern settlement (officially the Eastern Settlement) had become a Church-run state. The bishopric, based at Gardar, owned more than a third of all useable land outright—and this by far the best and most productive third. Many of the nominal owners of what was left were indebted to the Church and seem to have been little better off than serfs. Although the population of the Eastern Settlement amounted to not much more than two thousand, it had to support a cathedral, eleven other churches, an Augustine monastery, a Benedictine nunnery, and a bishop's "palace" with an associated farm that could stable 120 cows.[2] At least four of the churches were massively built of cut stone. Considering the resources available, their construction must have represented a per-capita expenditure of time, energy, and wealth comparable to that consumed in rearing some of the great medieval European cathedrals.

Although by c. 1200 the Church was exercising almost total control over south Greenlanders, this was not so in the north. During the two centuries following upon the founding of the two settlements, each had evolved along different lines.

The northerners (the so-called Western Settlement) had become Greenland's valuta folk. Although pastoralism remained an ingredient in their lives, it was not paramount. By the turn of the thirteenth century they were spending much of their time, and getting most of their income from, hunting, fishing, and trapping. They were a free-ranging people and, like all such, resistant to absolute authority in whatever guise.

What follows is my assessment of them and of their history.

The northerners built only four churches, and it appears that, by the thirteenth century, just one of these was still functioning—if it *was* functioning as anything more than a forlorn ecclesiastical outpost in a settlement that was becoming, or had already become, apostate.

The northerners not only rejected theocratic rule very early in their history, they did the same for the rule of kings. In 1261 the southern settlers abandoned their independence and swore allegiance to the king of Norway. Thereafter they paid tribute to, and accepted the strictures imposed upon them from, Norway. It appears that the people of the northern settlement did neither.

A development in the latter part of the thirteenth century widened the split and increased antagonisms between the two groups.

By as early as 1250 Thule people had drifted south as far as Upernavik. Although only faint echoes of the first meetings between Norse and Thule remain, they suggest that the Greenland Norse initially treated Thule Skraelings in the same manner Karlsefni's people had treated Tunit and Indians in Newfoundland and Labrador.

Historia Norwegiae, written in the thirteenth century, tells us:

> To the north of where the Greenlanders dwell, hunters have found some
> pygmy people called Skraelings. They are such that when they are struck
> with weapons, but not mortally, their wounds whiten without bleeding;
> but when they are wounded to death their blood will scarcely cease to flow.

The information in the *Historia Norwegiae* probably came from southern settlers. If it also reflected the attitudes of the northerners then, as
we shall shortly see, they changed their tune.

The arrival of these "trolls" (as Thule people were regarded by Norse
Christians) seems to have evoked the same sort of reaction in south
Greenland evidenced by cattle ranchers of our times if wolves approach
the neighbourhood. When Thule reached Disko Bight, it was time to
bring on the exterminators.

In 1266 theocrats at Gardar, the bishop's seat, sent an expedition north
to see what could be done about halting this invasion by creatures the
Church regarded as the devil's spawn. More than one ship was involved
and, presumably, a considerable force of well-armed men. The record is
vague as to where they went and what was accomplished, but they
reached Melville Bay where

> they beheld some Skraeling dwellings, but could not land because of the
> bears....Upon going ashore on certain islands south of Snaefells [the
> Upernavik region] they found Skraeling dwelling places...then they
> returned home to Gardar.

While we are not told of any actual encounters with Skraelings, it is
hard to believe that—bears or no bears—none occurred. If they did, we
can confidently conclude they involved the use of swords and battleaxes wielded in a manner which would confirm the *Historia Norwegiae*
report that mortally wounded Skraelings bled profusely.

Devout Christians of the southern settlement reacted to the
Skraelings with hatred and loathing, but apparently people in the northern settlement did not. Although there is no written confirmation from
the period of early contact, everything indicates that the Norse of the

Godthaab district accommodated themselves to a Thule presence.3 Although there may have been initial conflict, relationships evolved into a mutually advantageous arrangement. As Albans and Tunit had earlier discovered, it was the sensible way to go.4

Renowned northern traveller Vilhjalmur Stefansson, who knew as much as anyone about relationships between Eskimos and Europeans, concluded that:

> The less numerous Norsemen in the more northerly colony, less in touch with Europe, less successful with their cattle and sheep, and more dependent on hunting would for these reasons, and because they met the Eskimos more frequently, come much more readily to a feeling of tolerance and later of equality....Hunters would have increasing reason to adopt Eskimo views and ways, until in great probability, a majority had Eskimo wives, just as the majority of northerly Canadian and Alaskan white trappers have Eskimo wives....Eskimoization of the ways of life progressed, in all likelihood peaceably, to a stage where the Western Settlement was no longer an outpost either of European culture or the Christian religion.5

The currency most commonly used by Greenlanders in their dealings with the outer world was walrus ivory and hides. These were mostly produced by the Western Settlement. Both materials remained in good supply until around the middle of the thirteenth century when a scarcity developed.

By 1260 this "currency shortfall" had become so serious that the Gardar theocrats found themselves unable to pay the tithes demanded by Nidaros. The cause of the shortage is no mystery. The northerners had stopped paying tithes to Gardar; and the inhabitants of the Eastern Settlement could by no means make up the deficit through their own efforts.

The bishop at Gardar was not the only one upset by this. Around 1275 the archbishop of Nidaros found himself having to apologize to Pope John XXI for his failure to meet the Vatican's levy. The archbishop pleaded that Greenland tithes were no longer flowing into his coffers.

The Pope replied with a lecture on the duties of subordinates and imposed a ban of excommunication upon the Greenlanders until they paid up.

In 1279 the somewhat more lenient Pope Nicholas III lifted the ban, but Greenland valuta remained in short supply. In 1282 the tithe was paid mostly in cattle hides and seal skins, produce of the Eastern Settlement that, alas, was of comparatively little worth in European markets.

According to Stefansson, the power of the Greenland theocracy peaked prior to 1300 and went downhill from then on. I believe this to have been a direct result of a schism between the two settlements. The annals for 1342 kept by Bishop Oddson in Iceland get to the crux of the matter.

> The inhabitants of Greenland voluntarily abandoned the true faith and the Christian religion, and amalgamated themselves with the people of America [*ad Americae populos se converterunt*].

As Stefansson has pointed out, the use of "people of America," instead of Skraelings, must be a latter-day attempt at clarification by the Icelandic Latinist who, about 1637, made the existing transcript of the bishop's annals. There is another failure in transcription. The original entry must surely have read, "The inhabitants of *northern* or *western* Greenland." Why so? Well, because we know with absolute certainty that Christianity maintained itself in the Eastern Settlement for another century. Bishop Oddson could not have failed to be aware that southern Greenland was still Christian in his time.

Archaeological evidence shows that Thule people were at Godthaab by c. 1330 and that amalgamation between them and Norse settlers was apparently well under way by then.[6]

Those northerners who wished to practise pastoralism were still doing so, but the bulk of the population of the Western Settlement was being sustained chiefly by hunting, a way of life at which the Skraelings were past masters.

The Church undoubtedly did everything it could to halt what the clerics must have reviled as a descent into heresy and paganism, but without effect. A full-scale rupture between the two settlements had become inevitable.

Such a rift would not have worked serious hardship on the northerners. They would have continued hunting valuta, and trading it to English, Flemish, and other merchant ships which bypassed the Eastern Settlement and came direct to the western one. This they did of necessity because Greenland was now officially closed to all foreign merchants by order of the king of Norway, who was determined to make the trade a royal monopoly. His problem was that the apostate northern settlers rejected the overlordship of Norway as resolutely as they did that of the Vatican.

It was the Eastern Settlement that suffered. Not only was it starved of valuta produced by the northerners, its people were cut off from access to the northern grounds. In consequence they had little to offer traders. When a king's *knorr* arrived in Greenland (and they sometimes failed to appear for years on end) the people had little to exchange for European goods other than cattle hides, seal skins, and rough woollen cloth, none of which was of sufficient value to much more than defray the freighting costs to Bergen. It was little wonder that visits of the king's vessels became more and more infrequent.

The resulting deprivations must have hurt the southern laity (already an impoverished lot), for they retained a considerable dependence on European supplies. The effect upon the theocrats would have been catastrophic. Not only was the Greenland church deprived of the largest part of its revenue, it also had to endure a severe loss of the prestige upon which its power depended. The situation was intolerable. The Western Settlement had to be brought to heel.

The death of Bishop Arni in 1348 left the Gardar see vacant for twenty years. During most of that time a priest named Ivar Bardarson was in charge. Shortly before or after 1350 Bardarson went with an expedition to the Western Settlement. Although historians have assumed this was a rescue mission designed to save the northerners from the Skraeling threat, the truth appears otherwise.

Around 1364 Bardarson returned to Norway where he dictated a report on his Greenland experiences.

Up there in the Western Settlement stands a big church which is called Stensness church....At present the Skraelings possess the entire Western Settlement. There are indeed horses, goats, cattle, and sheep, but all wild, and no people [natives were not considered "people"], either Christian or heathen.

All this that is recorded above was told us by Ivar Bardarson, a Greenlander who for many years was steward of the bishop's household at Gardar in Greenland; how he had seen all this, and was one of those who was chosen by the Laugmader [lawmaker] to go to the Western Settlement against the Skraelings, in order to expel them from the settlement. But when they arrived there they found nobody, either Christian or heathen, merely some wild cattle and sheep. They made use of these cattle and sheep for provisions, and killed as many as the ships could carry, and with this sailed back, and the aforesaid Ivar was one of their party.

This affair smacks not of a rescue attempt but of a raid. Without human care horses, cattle, goats, and sheep could not have survived long enough in the Godthaab region to become "wild." The animals found by the Bardarson party must have belonged to someone. Ivar would hardly have admitted that they belonged to people of Norse descent for then his actions would have been tantamount to robbing his own kind. However, if the inhabitants were stigmatized as sub-human (or non-human) Skraelings "who possess the entire Western Settlement," he would be off the hook.

I conclude that racial integration had by this time proceeded so far that the theocrats in the south were prepared to write off all the inhabitants of the Western Settlement as renegades who had gone native. Having mingled their proud Aesir blood with that of Skraelings, the northerners deserved no better treatment than was meted out to savages and should, in fact, be categorized *as* Skraelings themselves.

The squadron of vessels from the south probably entered Lysefiord (southernmost of the Western Settlement fiords) and sailed up it as far as Sandness, site of the principal church and of estates owned by the church. Finding the country in the hands of "Skraelings," the southerners filled their ships with loot, then fled back to the Eastern Settlement.

Apostasy in the west now became a matter of royal concern. In 1355 King Magnus Eriksson ordered a functionary named Powel Knudsson to take a force to Greenland because, the king said,

for the sake of Our soul and Our parents, who have also supported Christianity in Greenland as We have, We will not let Christianity be destroyed in Greenland in Our time.

Since there was no threat to Christianity in the Eastern Settlement, the king could only have been referring to the Western one. Nothing in the existing record indicates that Knudsson ever went to Greenland. *If* he did, he failed to bring the Western Settlement back into the fold.

In 1379, according to Icelandic chronicles, "The Skraelings attacked the Greenlanders, killed eighteen men and captured two youths and a slave woman."

Historians have generally assumed this was an Eskimo attack on the Eastern Settlement. Indeed, the incident *could* have been a retaliatory raid by "Skraelings," but it could equally well describe the fate suffered by the crew of an Eastern Settlement vessel (the numbers and genders of the victims sound right) killed and captured during a raid on the northerners.

Stories collected from native Greenlanders by the first modern Europeans to visit the country certainly speak of troubled times in earlier centuries. The majority of historians have concluded that these accounts are based on memories of raids by European pirates on southern Greenland. I submit that most probably originated in clashes between the two Norse settlements.

Early in the fifteenth century there was a major escalation in the conflict. In 1448 Pope Nicholas V wrote to the bishops of Skalhölt and Hólar in Iceland, directing them to send priests to Greenland. The situation there, he told the bishops, had become desperate.

Thirty years ago [that is, in 1418], the barbarians came from the nearby coast of the heathens and attacked the inhabitants of [southern] Greenland most cruelly, and so devastated the mother-country and the holy buildings with fire and sword that there remained on that island no more than nine parish churches.... The pitiable inhabitants of both sexes...they carried

away as prisoners to their own country. But, as is added in the same com-
plaint [from which the Pope was quoting] because the greater number
have since returned from captivity to their own homes and have here and
there repaired the ruins of their dwellings, they most earnestly desire to
restore and extend divine service.

Scholars have long been at odds about the interpretation of this letter. Some think it refers to an attack on the Eastern Settlement by
Greenland Eskimos. Some, to a raid by natives from Labrador. Some
believe the villains were European pirates, Britons by preference. Some
question the authenticity of the letter, on the grounds that what it says
does not make sense.

But it would make sense—and very good sense, too, if in 1418
"Skraelings" from the Western Settlement had mounted a devastating
raid on the Eastern Settlement—an attack whose primary target was the
theocracy and all its works.

The systematic burning of holy places in "the mother country" suggests that this was the work of men who harboured a powerful hostility
towards the Church. This animosity apparently did not extend to ordinary folk. Although people were taken prisoner and carried off (as
hostages?), they were brought, or permitted to come, home again and
resume their freedom. Credulity boggles at the idea of European slavers
behaving in such a manner. One thing is established beyond question: the
raiders came from a "nearby coast"—from relatively close by. I am persuaded that their home was no farther away than the Godthaab fiords.

The Greenland theocracy never recovered from the raid of 1418, during which most of the clerics seem either to have been killed or to have
fled the country. No priest is known to have again set foot in Greenland
until 1721 when a Lutheran pastor named Hans Egede found his way there.

During the intervening centuries Greenland was not only out of
touch with the Church, but with Norway too. However, all contact with
Europe was not lost. By early in the fifteenth century Basque whalers
were working Greenland waters, and during the first half of that century
increasing numbers of English and other European ships were fishing
cod on Iceland's banks, and trading with the Icelanders.

Some of these venturers must have come into contact with

Greenlanders. Excavations of an old cemetery at Herjólfsnes have produced clothing cut in fifteenth-century continental styles, though made of local materials.

Egede reported that when he arrived in Greenland the only inhabitants were Eskimos. The Norse had seemingly vanished, leaving nothing of themselves but long-abandoned ruins.

Since Egede's day countless scholars have busied themselves trying to account for the disappearance of the Greenland Norse. It has been variously, and often vehemently, maintained that they were exterminated by the Black Death; that they were massacred by incoming Eskimos; that they starved after plagues of insects defoliated the pastures; that they were destroyed by a deteriorating climate; that they were carried into slavery by British pirates; that they emigrated to North America.

Scores of books and hundreds of learned papers have been devoted to finding a solution to the mystery, but only a few authors, Fridtjof Nansen and Vilhjalmur Stefansson among them, seem to have got close to the truth. Which is that the Greenland Norse *never did disappear*—they just changed shape.

Shape changers are a recurring theme in the mythology of all native peoples. The Greenland Norse changed shape by intermingling with the natives.

Almost every observation of Greenland natives back to 1500, which is about as far as the modern record goes, indicates that they were, and are, of mixed race, exhibiting significant differences from pure Thule-Eskimo culture in appearance, activities, possessions, and behaviour. Furthermore, most of the traditional accounts of interaction between Norse and natives preserved in folklore point to a prolonged and comprehensive process of intermingling.

The present-day inhabitants of Greenland do not, as is sometimes claimed, display European characteristics simply because of their association with Danes and other Europeans who followed Hans Egede to Greenland. They do so primarily because they are the descendants of Eskimoan and Norse people who came to Greenland a thousand years ago.

And who remain there still.

CHAPTER THIRTY-THREE

JAKATAR

LTHOUGH MY ALBAN QUEST SEEMED TO BE NEARING
an end, I lacked substantive evidence that they had reached St.
George's Bay.

One day I opened a book of sailing directions called the *Newfoundland Pilot*. This seamen's bible is based on the work of Captain James Cook, who surveyed and charted the island's coasts in the 1760s before going on to find fame and death in the Pacific. Since the *Pilot* contains all the information a mariner needs to sail anywhere in Newfoundland waters, I wondered if it might have something useful to tell me about St. George's Bay. I came upon this entry:

> *Head of St. George's Bay*...St. George's Harbour is protected...by *Flat Island*...the settlement of *Sandy Point* is situated at the eastern end of that island and had, in 1945, a population of 250...3 ¹/₂ miles southwestward... are *Muddy Hole* and *Flat Bay Brook. Cairn (Steel) Mountain* lies 7 miles east-southeastward of Muddy Hole. It is a remarkable mass of ironstone, 1005 feet high. There are two stone cairns on the mountain, reputed to have been erected by Captain Cook.[1]

Because Cook was the first person to describe and chart Newfoundland's west coast I had already examined his journals, maps, and meticulously detailed notes. They had told me that in 1766 when he surveyed the coast it had no permanent European inhabitants. Fishing vessels—mostly French—worked the grounds seasonally, but seldom overwintered. Apart from such occasionals the only people Cook encountered were "a tribe of Indians" in St. George's Bay.

Cook made no mention of having erected any cairns. If he had indeed gone to the considerable trouble of building two beacons big enough to be visible well to seaward, on top of a mountain seven airline miles from shore (ten miles overland), surely he would have mentioned the fact. Although the first modern Europeans to settle at St. George's Bay, c. 1830, may have attributed the beacons to Cook, I could find no grounds for sharing that assumption.

But if Cook did not build them, who did? And when?

An investigation on the ground seemed called for. I would have preferred to sail my own little Newfoundland schooner into St. George's Bay to view Cairn Mountain from the sea but, alas, she had (as seamen say) taken the ground for the last time.

So Claire and I settled for a half-ton truck which we took to Newfoundland in the bowels of the ugly box of a car ferry that plies between North Sydney and Port aux Basques.

A fine September morning in 1996 found us belting north out of Port aux Basques on the Trans-Canada Highway between the massive granite paps that mark the southern terminus of the Long Range Mountains. Late in the afternoon we came to a bridge over a rapid-filled river. A sign told us this was Flat Bay Brook. We pulled off the highway for our first and much-anticipated view of Cairn Mountain and the twin beacons crowning its crest.

There was a mountain before us, certainly; a prominent spur outthrust from the flanks of the Long Range. But its bald dome was unblemished by cairns or by any other visible constructs.

Were we in the wrong place? The topographical maps assured me we were not. Was the *Pilot* in error? Impossible! The *Pilot* is as nearly infallible as human authority can be. Baffled, we drove to a nearby forestry station and asked the middle-aged man in charge if he knew of any structures on Cairn Mountain, or Steel Mountain as it was now called.

"That I do, surely. You'd be wanting to know about Bowaters' fire tower. Well, sir, they tore it down some years past."

Of stone cairns he knew nothing at all, although he had been born and reared within sight of Cairn Mountain.

"Not to worry," he added with a Newfoundlander's eagerness to please, "Len Muise might know a thing or two. His old dad used to be a ranger on the tower. I'll give him a ring."

Which is how I came to meet Leonard Muise; a handsome, ruggedly built man in his mid-forties; dark-complected, dark-haired, and vibrant. Born near Cape St. George, he is a Jakatar.

A prospector for many years, Len is now a mining instructor at the local community college in Stephenville. But he has always been, and remains, he told me, a countryman. "Far back as you can go my folk were countrymen. Fished and farmed on the shore in summertime, then, come winter, 'twas off into the country, to the woods, the mountains, and the barrens to hunt and trap 'til spring. That was my people's life. The finest kind!"

Len told me that, as a boy, he had often climbed Cairn Mountain with his father and a cousin of his own age. While the elder Muise kept watch for forest fires from a tiny cabin atop a flimsy tower, Len and his cousin played war games in make-believe forts centred on two piles of stones on the crest of the mountain. These were the closest things to "cairns" he could remember seeing there.

Len undertook to investigate the mystery of the missing cairns on my behalf. He discovered that both had still been standing as late as the early 1940s, but sometime during the war years Bowaters Pulp and Paper Company had ordered a fire-watch-tower built on Cairn Mountain. When the contractors found they needed heavy stones with which to ballast the tower, they tore down one of the two beacons.

Ellis Parsons, eighty years of age, remembered working on the tower in 1953. He recalled that the remaining beacon stood eight or nine feet tall and had a circumference of at least ten feet. However, during the next few years it too was dismantled to provide additional ballast. By the late 1950s both beacons had been reduced to the rubble heaps Len and his cousin had used as forts.

Not many St. George's people are old enough to remember the "cairns" as they once were, but Len tracked down some who could. They agreed in describing the structures as cylindrical, or nearly cylindrical, towers eight to ten feet high, about four feet in diameter, and carefully laid up without the use of mortar.

Neither Len nor I could find anyone who knew of a basis for crediting Cook with their erection, nor could anyone explain their purpose. Their location so far inland made it most unlikely they were intended to serve as navigation aids. It is at any rate certain they were not sited as range markers to guide ships into any of the Bay ports. Considering the time and effort which would have been required to raise them (each must have been composed of at least 120 cubic feet of rock), there can be no doubt that they were built for some compelling reason. I conclude it was the same reason—and the same builders—that produced the tower beacons of Labrador, Ungava, and the high eastern Arctic.

September is often the most splendid month in Newfoundland. So it was in 1996. The sun blazed upon us, warming the steady westerly breeze until it felt almost like a Caribbean zephyr. The nights were cool and brilliant. Day after day Claire and I explored the coasts; picnicked on sounding beaches; scrambled up hoary old hills through swathes of ripe blueberries; or drove into "the country" on rutted logging roads that snaked alongside rattling brooks at the bottom of darkly forested valleys.

We spent much time listening to local people while sampling such examples of Newfoundland's fabled hospitality as plum pie made from fruit grown in the maker's garden; smoked eels; bottled moose; clam chowder; and bakeapple (cloud berry) conserve. Everywhere we encountered a robust optimism. Despite the failure of the sustaining fishery, and the several other desperate economic woes which plagued the island, these people were not bowed down. They remained calmly confident in and of themselves.

"'Tis true enough they's not many dollars on the go," admitted an older man in one of the small Jakatar communities. "But what odds? We've plenty of garden truck, country meat, a cow and a pig, wood to burn and to build whatever we needs. We've neighbours and kinsfolk, and good times for all hands. We'll weather hard times like we've always done. We'll not come to any great harm, because 'tis a bit of heaven we're in."

Here is how I envision that "bit of heaven" on a September day six hundred years earlier.

Alba-in-the-West was preparing for winter. From Port aux Basques to the Codroy Valley, and along the green coasts of Port au Port and St. George's Bay, crofters were out on their scattered little fields sickling the last of the season's bere and oats. In the blueberry patches, boys and girls competed with fat black bears.

Far out on the glittering waters of the Gulf, valuta men were homeward bound from a summer spent killing tuskers on the teeming beaches of the Magdalen, Prince Edward, and Miscou islands. Some had traded for peltries with natives of these islands and of the mainland, offering in exchange homespun cloth together with a few copper and iron wares. When metal goods were not to be had, valuta men traded blanks of Ramah chert.[2]

Trade with Europe had always been subject to ups and downs. Even in the best of times only the most intrepid European merchant skippers dared the Atlantic crossing, and it was an exceptional year when more than one or two succeeded in reaching Alba-in-the-West. In some years none appeared and, due to baleful events then beclouding Europe, such lapses were becoming increasingly frequent. However, periodic shortages of European goods wrought no great hardships on the western settlers. Except for metals, they were essentially self-sufficient.[3]

Centuries in the New World had altered many aspects of their lives. But not all. Although they had grown closer in blood and habits to the aboriginal inhabitants, they retained an allegiance to their ancient crofting heritage and to their Christian tradition. Although they lived in common with native races, and blended blood and culture with them, they nonetheless remained a people in their own right.

And by the standards of the time—perhaps of any times—early fifteenth-century inhabitants of southwestern Newfoundland lived a good life.

Their compatriots to the northward were not so fortunate. These faced the implacable encroachment of the Thule tide. Alban and Tunit resistance had combined to slow this invasion, but had not halted it. By 1300 Thule, which had succeeded in occupying the northern tip of Labrador, was posing an imminent threat to coastal peoples to the south.

Those inhabitants who lived native fashion and were able to maintain mobility found the situation tense but not impossible. Those whose crofting dependencies kept them tied to one place found it unendurable. Eventually they abandoned Labrador.

Thule oozed south with glacial certainty until, by mid-century, even a mixed Alban presence would no longer have been detectable as such in Labrador or in the old hunting grounds to the north and west. Tunit culture, whether of pure or mixed ancestry, itself vanished not long thereafter. Archaeologists believe the Tunit may have made their last stand in eastern Ungava and north-central Labrador, lingering there in recognizable form until around the end of the fifteenth century.

By the beginning of the fifteenth century, the Norse were effectively out of the Alban story. In Greenland, as we have seen, internecine strife, the collapse of Norwegian hegemony, and the arrival of Thule were eroding Norse dominance and influence.

Iceland, too, was out of the western saga, having undergone a series of horrendous disasters. Four major volcanic eruptions took place during the fourteenth century and a succession of epidemics culminated, in 1402–3, in a devastating outbreak of the Black Death that killed two-thirds of the remaining population. Nor was this the sum of the island's afflictions. Thereafter, her coasts and coastal waters increasingly became a battleground for hordes of rapaciously competing European fishermen, many of them no better than pirates. Instead of going raiding in distant waters, Norse Icelanders found themselves fully engaged trying to repel foreign despoilers of their own shores. Alban Icelanders had once tried to do the same. The wheel had come full circle.

By the latter part of the fourteenth century, most of Europe was in a state of turmoil bordering on chaos. Wars and rumours of war were everywhere. The so-called Hundred Years War (1339–1453) between France and England was but symptomatic of a general state of political, religious, social, and commercial tumult and unbridled lawlessness. Piracy at sea and brigandage on land had become the norms of human behaviour.

These disruptions seem to have been intensified by three factors. First was the appearance of firearms and their rapid evolution until, by 1400, they had become deadly weaponry. The second was the fifteenth-century evolution of the lodestone into an effective mariner's compass.

The third was a combination of population expansion and the beginning of long-term climatic deterioration which ruined crops and led to widespread famine and social disruption.

The consequent ferment began bursting out of Europe in the latter part of the 1400s. It was borne abroad by a new breed of mariners in new kinds of ships who, with the aid of the perfected compass and the baleful power of firearms, were eventually able to carry the virus of manic greed to the uttermost parts of the earth.

Zichmni's little freebooting venture seems to have been a first flick of the lash destined to scourge the new world in the west. Other entrepreneurs soon followed his sea-track or made their own. History has recorded the names and exploits of only a very few of what, by the end of the fifteenth century, had become a burgeoning flood of European marauders ferociously competing for the avails of a virgin world.

Not all were cut from the same sable cloth. Spaniards and Portuguese seem to have excelled in ferocity and brutality, especially in their chosen role as slavers. In 1501 Gaspar Corte-Real and his brother Miguel sailed from Lisbon on their second western voyage. They cruised the coasts of Newfoundland and Labrador until autumn, when their two caravels turned eastward. Only Miguel's ship reached home. Amongst other trophies, she brought seven captured natives: "men, women and children, and in the other caravel, which is expected from hour to hour, are coming fifty more." Contemporary observer Pietro Pasqualigo added, "These resemble gypsies in colour, features, stature and aspect...are very shy and gentle but well formed...[the sailors] have brought from there a piece of broken gilt sword....One of the boys was wearing in his ears 2 silver rings....They will be excellent for labour and the best slaves that have hitherto been obtained."

How they were obtained is not described.

Nothing is known of what happened to Gaspar's vessel. It is not impossible that the fifty captives he had aboard proved to be something less than "gentle" slaves—revolted, took the vessel, and may even have managed to make their way back to a friendly coast.

The earliest English venturers, mostly from Bristol, went west via the Icelandic fishery, nominally to exploit the astronomically abundant cod on the Grand Banks and in the waters of eastern Newfoundland. But

they had no compunction about seizing anything else of value that came
their way. Including people. If slaving was not their main enterprise, they
nevertheless indulged in it. They decimated the natives, especially the
Beothuks, killing them as vermin who interfered with the legitimate
pursuits of honest working men by their occasional thefts of metal
implements, sail cloth, and nets.

The French were perhaps a little less savage, although the atrocities
they are known to have committed were terrible enough.

A point to bear in mind: at almost every first contact with Europeans
the indigenes are described as having been welcoming and friendly.
However, during subsequent encounters arrows were wont to fly in one
direction while blunderbusses bellowed in the other. In short order the
natives had been brutally disillusioned as to the intentions of, and the
behaviour to be expected from, Europeans.

Basques appear to have been something of an exception. Although
their destruction of non-human life in the New World, especially of
great whales, was horrendous, they seem to have committed few crimes
against native humanity. They may have felt empathy with the indigenes
because they themselves were treated as primitives by Europeans con-
temptuous of their ancient language and culture. Envy of the Basques'
remarkable seafaring abilities, and of their success as providers of most
of Europe's whale oil (a vital staple of the times), also helped place them
beyond the pale.

The pursuit of whales for oil and baleen led Basque ships into the
Gulf of St. Lawrence. Big, seaworthy vessels followed the great whales
through Belle Isle Strait to become the forerunners of what would, during the sixteenth century, become a vast fleet of whalers. Many worked
the western coast of Newfoundland, which became as familiar to the
Basques as their own Bay of Biscay.

A goodly number of the names they bestowed are still in use, if in
somewhat corrupt form. Thus Port au Choix (*Portuchoa*), Port au Port
(*Oporportu*), and Cape Ray (*Cadarrayco*).

The Basques also gave names to inhabitants of the coasts where whaling stations were established.

One such name may have been *Jakatar*.

Jakatar (spelled in a multitude of ways, including Jack-a-tar, Jakotar,

Jackitar, Jockataw, and Jacqueetar) makes its first appearance in the historic record as an entry in a mid-nineteenth-century journal kept by the Anglican minister at Sandy Point, St. George's Bay. On May 23, 1857, the Reverend Henry Lind wrote:

> Went to see a poor man....He and all his family belong to a much despised and neglected race called Jack a Tars, they speak an impure dialect of French and Indian, [are] R.C.s and of almost lawless habits.

Although Britain did not take formal possession of western Newfoundland until 1904, a few Jersey merchants had established themselves in St. George's Bay as early as the 1840s. They noted that the indigenes consisted of nomadic Micmac Indians from Nova Scotia; some Acadian French; and dark-skinned, dark-eyed, dark-haired "natives" called Jakatars.

Leonard Muise has this to say about Jakatars:

"We have always adapted to the ways of the times. Inter-marriage was never a problem and we have a history of sharing as well as getting along with other people. We were always taught we were a mix of M'ikmaw, possibly Beothuk, French and other European peoples, but we look different and act different than others. Frank Speck in his book about early cultures tells of the old people here talking (c. 1922) about 'the ancients'—not Beothuks—who lived in St. George's Bay before the M'ikmaw came here. Maybe we Jakatars are descended from them too."[4]

Some philologists assert the name is derived from Jack-tar, a nickname given to Royal Navy seamen in the days of sail. However, westcoast Newfoundlanders had only the most peripheral and transient contact with the British navy prior to 1840 (and not much more thereafter). The similarity of names must surely be coincidental.

Could *Jakatar* be of French derivation? There is no evidence that it is. How about *M'ikmaw*? The answer is the same. Could it be Beothuk? All that we know of the Beothuk language consists of a vocabulary derived from two of the last known survivors of this race; and it contains nothing which throws light on the origins of *Jakatar*.

One prospect remains.

During the Middle Ages a Basque name for God was *Jakue*, evidently a variant on *Jainko.*5 *Tar* was, and remains, a Basque suffix signifying (amongst other things) a connection with, or a relation to. Basque linguists tell me that in fifteenth-century usage *Jakutar* could have been an acceptable way to describe a follower or adherent of (the Christian) God.

The first Basques arriving on Newfoundland's west coast might have felt this to be an appropriate name for indigenes who showed an awareness of, perhaps even a recognizable allegiance to, their God. Such attributes would certainly have set them apart from any other aboriginal peoples the Basques might have encountered, and would have warranted a nominal distinction.

Certainly, elements of religious belief and practice do remain deeply embedded in human cultures even after these have endured momentous changes and dislocations over long periods of time. In 1585, when the English navigator John Davis landed on the southwest coast of Greenland, he met no living people. He did, however, find a burial ground (probably of stone crypts) containing the bodies of several natives dressed in seal skins. Nothing about the dead indicated any previous European contact...except that crosses stood over the graves.

Whatever their origins, and the origin of their name, Jakatars *still* consider themselves a people in their own right, and declare southwestern Newfoundland, especially St. George's and Port au Port bays, to be their native and ancestral land.

CHAPTER THIRTY-FOUR

THE COUNTRY PATH

The day was young; but he was old, and the climb up the mountain had wearied him. Gratefully, he sat himself down in the long shadow of one of the twin beacons. From this high vantage point he could look far out across the broad bay along whose green shores most of the people lived.

He had poled his canoe up Flat Bay Brook to the mountain path, and had then begun his climb, impelled to do so by a dream. No European vessel had entered the Bay for almost a generation, but last night he had dreamed one was coming—was almost here.

Only the middle-aged and elderly remembered the last merchantman to visit the Bay. She had brought a wealth of goods, but also a burden of ill news. Her supercargo, who spoke the local tongue, described seaborne freebooters swarming so thickly in European waters that only men-of-war had any security, and even they were at risk. Merchant ships were being pillaged, burned and sunk, or driven from the seas. The supercargo, a burly Bristol man, had made his decision: "If our old hulk lives to feel Severn water under her keel again, I'll swallow the anchor and go ashore for good."

The merchantman's departure had been a gloomy event; those who watched her grow small on the horizon being all too well aware that they might not see her like for a long time.

Now, as the old man shaded his eyes against the glare of sun on sea he thought he saw the flicker of a distant sail. Aged he might be, but his sight was still keen. He watched, transfixed, as his dream of the night became a reality in the morning—a kind of reality—for he had never imagined a vessel the like of the one bearing towards him now.

She sat cliff-high in the water, her size exaggerated by bulky fore- and aftercastles. Instead of the traditional single mast and square sail, she carried three masts, a large one stepped amidships and smaller ones at bow and stern. And on these she bore so many sails they made her look more like a fleet than a single vessel.

Astounded by her appearance, the old man watched until it was clear her course would bring her to Flat Island Haven, whereupon he hurried down from the lookout to spread the amazing news.

As the stranger rounded-to under the head of Flat Island, she unfurled from her stern a great flag of a design unknown to the people hurriedly gathering along the beach. Then a smaller pennant was streamed from her mainmast top. This one had a more familiar look: a white cross set against a crimson background. Whoever she might be, and wherever she came from, the alien vessel was flying a Christian flag.

She was in fact a Basque carrack, one of the first to sail deep into the Gulf. Her lookouts had spotted the twin towers on Cairn Mountain while still well to seaward and her master had determined to see what they portended.

More than idle curiosity impelled him. His big vessel (she displaced more than two hundred tons) was a whaler. Since entering Belle Isle Strait she had been sailing through an abundance of whales. Now her people were impatient to find a suitable haven where trypots could be set up on shore and from which boats could sally out to harpoon the giants whose rendered oil was almost as good as gold.

The bold coast to the north had rebuffed them, but they found what they were seeking in St. George's Bay. They also found a welcome here from a people who, so it seemed, were not altogether different from their own kind.

WHAT FOLLOWS CONTAINS MUCH SUPPOSITION, BUT I am sufficiently confident of its validity to dispense with the usual continuous barrage of qualifications.

Alba-in-the-West welcomed the fifteenth-century arrival of the Basques. For many decades thereafter natives and newcomers maintained friendly and mutually useful relationships. Arriving in early summer and usually departing late in autumn or, occasionally, wintering over, the whalers brought European goods that they traded for furs, food, and labour. Local men assisted Basques on the cutting ramps and at the trypots, and some became adept at pulling oars and at wielding harpoons from the slim, swift whale boats.

Crofters supplied the whalers with farm produce and with relaxation from the gory, greasy butchery that filled long days of labour. Valuta men, who had all but abandoned their age-old trade for want of markets, now found reason to return to it. They revisited the fabulous walrus haul-outs on the Gulf islands and were soon doing a brisk business with the whalers in hides and ivory.

From year to year more and more Basques arrived until their try-works were belching black, oily smoke along Newfoundland's west coast from Cabot Strait to the Strait of Belle Isle, and along much of the south coast of Labrador. By the end of the fifteenth century scores, if not hundreds, of Basque whaling ships were working the waters of the Gulf.

The crews were a rough-and-ready lot, but they seem to have adhered to a code governing not only how they treated one another but how they treated indigenes. Scanty as it is, the record indicates that they consistently behaved more humanely towards the natives than did other Europeans of their time.

By the beginning of the sixteenth century, west-faring Basques were bringing great riches in oil, baleen, ivory, and fur into Biscayan ports. Basques were secretive; nevertheless, it was inevitable that Frenchmen to the north, and Portuguese and Spaniards to the south, would catch the smell of money on the west wind. Even before the new century got under way adventurers from all three nations were following the Basques into the Gulf.

Some of the newcomers were fishermen chiefly concerned with catching massive quantities of cod. But many were, in effect, the Vikings of their age. If they adhered to any code of conduct, it was one based on the prescript: every man for himself and devil take the hindmost.

These adventurers were of the same breed as the marauders who had been wreaking havoc in European waters for more than a century. And just as their peers had visited chaos and destruction on the coastal inhabitants of many European countries, so these men ravaged the coastal regions of the western Atlantic.

They had never shown much compunction towards their European countrymen. They showed little or none towards the natives of the New World, treating them with a degree of savagery that only civilized man seems fully capable of mastering.

Indigenes and their belongings were regarded as objects to be turned to account. For as long as natives proved to be of use helping the new-comers siphon off gold, furs, and other valuables, they *might* be suffered to survive—preferably as slaves. However, if they resisted or were unco-operative, they were all too often given over to slaughter and rapine. Some of the "adventurers" arriving on the New World coasts seem to have taken as much pleasure from discharging culverins loaded with grape-shot into crowds of natives as Norse berserkers had once taken from tossing babies on spear points.

Freebooters on the south and western coasts of Newfoundland were at first few in number and so constrained to be somewhat circumspect. Initially they may even have paid the crofters for meat and grain, and traded with them for furs and ivory. But that way of doing business did not last. As the newcomers grew more numerous, many abandoned the pretence of being traders and turned to outright robbery.

The natives of the southwest coast of Newfoundland, whose Tunit, Beothuk, and Alban ancestors had been able to see off Karlsefni's Norsemen, could not withstand these new marauders who came armed with crossbows and canon. Crofts or encampments within a day's march of the coasts were subject to sudden descents bringing death to those who resisted the seizure of goods, cattle—or of people. Valuta men hardly dared raise a sail offshore for fear they might draw a corsair down upon them. The islands and beaches where they had long been used to gathering walrus ivory and hides were now possessed by rapacious new-comers who shed the blood of competitors and walrus with almost equal profligacy.

Beothuks were early victims. Traditionally they had been used to wintering deep in the interior where caribou were most abundant and accessible. In spring they had gone out to the coasts to take advantage of fish, seabirds, and sea mammals. They remained safe in the interior, but disastrous meetings with Europeans forced them to largely abandon the coasts and the natural resources which had once sustained them there.

Alba-in-the-West would have offered almost irresistible targets to transatlantic mariners recently arrived in New World waters and des-perate for fresh food after barely surviving weeks at sea on a diet of salt-junk and weevily biscuits.

Crofters would have found themselves under mounting pressure to abandon their coastal holdings during the raiding season, which extended from early summer to late autumn—the very time when crops had to be grown and harvested. Many were already in the habit of wintering some distance inland, where they could shelter from the worst of the weather in what Newfoundland outporters to this day call "winter houses." But now the people of Alba-in-the-West found themselves becoming *summer* exiles, forced to seek places in the interior where crops could be grown and natural hay harvested.

Few such existed. One of the few was the upper reaches of the Codroy Valley, which extended far enough inland to offer reasonable security and was broad and fertile enough to provide sustenance for a considerable number of homesteaders and their animals.

There is no way of knowing when the people of the Codroy coast (between Cape Anguille and Port aux Basques) withdrew inland, but history has preserved one record that may bear upon the matter.

In 1497 a Venetian adventurer with the Anglicized name of John Cabot set sail from Bristol for certain lands in the west which Bristol seamen had already visited. Cabot commanded an English ship and crew, and was almost certainly piloted by a man with knowledge of the New World.

After some thirty-five days at sea, a lookout raised the highlands of northwestern Cape Breton Island. Cabot then bore away towards a second and adjacent land, which would have been southwestern Newfoundland. Here in the final days of June he made his one reported landing.

Only fragmentary accounts of his voyage have been preserved, mostly in letters written by Cabot's contemporaries. The best of these is an account by John Day (who may have been a Spanish agent), addressed to the Lord Grand Admiral of Spain.

...they disembarked with a crucifix and raised banners with the arms of the Holy Father and those of the King of England...and they found tall trees of the kind masts are made of...and the country [hereabouts] is very rich in pasture....They found a trail that went inland, they saw a fireplace, they saw the manure of animals which they thought to be farm animals.... He [Cabot] did not dare advance inland beyond the shooting distance of a crossbow, and after taking in fresh water he returned to his ship,...[They then sailed east] following the shore [and]...it seemed to them that there were fields where they thought might also be settlements.

Cabot sailed east along the south coast until he reached Cape Race where he took his departure for England without ever meeting a native. He and the Newfoundland indigenes evidently avoided one another. Doubtless they had their reasons.

Short as it is, Day's account contains matters of signal interest.

Pastures, for instance. The Spanish word used by Day specifically identifies land used for grazing *domestic* animals.

Mention of a *trail* (which can be translated as *lane*) suggests something more than the often-almost-invisible paths used by Indians.

Manure meant the dung of *domesticated* animals. I think it safe to assume that Cabot's west-of-England crew would have recognized the dung of farm animals when they saw it, and would have called it by its proper name. They would scarcely have been deceived by the dung of bears or caribou, then the only large wild animals to be found in the region.

A fourth point has to do with Cabot's obvious nervousness about encountering indigenes. Why would he have been so apprehensive unless he knew full well that the hive had already been thoroughly stirred up and the bees could be expected to be angry and dangerous?

A final point to consider is the reference to possible *fields* and *settlements*. The Spanish word used by Day for settlement translates equally well as habitations. Why would Cabot's people have thought they might be seeing fields and habitations in what was otherwise a wilderness? Perhaps because they had found convincing evidence that a pastoral people lived along this coast.

Although we may never know precisely where Cabot landed or what he found, Day's account provides a convincing, if second-hand, description of what could have been a crofting site on the Codroy coast.

The people of Port au Port Bay and St. George's Bay had no such convenient retreat available to them. Although many small rivers empty into those two bays, most are so hemmed in by mountains as to be useless to homesteaders.

There is one notable exception—Robinson's River, emptying into St. George's Bay some twenty miles southwest of Flat Island. Cutting west through the Long Range Mountains, Robinson's turbulent waters are still some nine hundred feet above sea level at a point only twenty-five miles east of its mouth. Here, for a distance of two miles, the river inexplicably runs straight, slow, and level between steeply wooded walls towering six hundred feet above it. The result is a small but marvellously protected hidden valley with a microclimate all its own nourishing an extraordinary assemblage of grassy meadows.

This remarkable oasis amongst the mountains has recently come to the attention of scientists and, because of its uniqueness, has been designated an ecological reserve. But it has long been familiar to local people, who call it The Grass.

During the early part of this century, several families still lived on The Grass and took a livelihood in sheep and cattle from it. Ruins remain of their occupancy, including those of a small grist mill. It used to take these people as much as two days to journey between the coast and The Grass across terrain so difficult it is today barely navigable by four-wheel-drive vehicles. Here was a sanctuary whose nearly five hundred acres of pasture and arable land could have supported a dozen or more crofting families in almost unassailable security.

The Grass could not, however, have sufficed for *all* the people of Alba-in-the-West.

While living in Newfoundland during the 1960s, I spent a good deal of my time investigating the disappearance of the Beothuks.

Their heartland was the Exploits watershed. Exploits River rises in the headwaters of a remote body of water grandiloquently named King George IV Lake, in the southwestern corner of the island. Lloyds River carries the flow northeastward into Red Indian Lake. The waters leave this lake as the Exploits River and eventually debouch into the sea in Notre Dame Bay, almost two hundred miles from their source.

Michael John, who was chief of the Conne River M'ikmaw band in Bay d'Espoir in my time, told me his people believed King George Lake had been the last refuge of the Beothuks. Unable to find anyone who could tell me about the place first-hand, I decided to visit it myself. No roads led to it, but a pilot friend volunteered to take me in by float plane.

We flew first to Red Indian Lake, landing at several coves where large winter settlements of Beothuks had once stood. Not a trace of them now remained. Reaching the southwest end of the forty-mile-long lake, we flew up Lloyds River over white-water rapids bordered by tall spruce forests. To either side grey hills rose higher and higher until we found ourselves shoulder to shoulder with the Annieopsquotch Mountains.

Abruptly the valley released us into a vast amphitheatre cradling King George Lake, whose several long arms were flung wide across a plateau guarded by encircling mountains of barren and forbidding countenance. However, the land around the lake rippled with luxuriant forests veined by countless streams and ponds fringed with grassy swales. Nowhere was there any sign of man.

The plane banked gently in a circuit of the plateau, then swept in low over a broad delta at the lake's southwestern edge. The waters below us seemed to explode as thousands and tens of thousands of ducks and geese rose in protest against our intrusion. We swung hastily away, but not before I had glimpsed a herd of perhaps fifty caribou stampeding across one of many grassy islands.

We flew another circuit, staying high enough to avoid avian collisions, and saw that the southern portion of the lake, its islands, and the shores of several streams running into it, were embroidered by hundreds of acres of pasture so vividly green as to seem cultivated.

I was looking for words to express my astonishment when my pilot friend forestalled me.

"What a hell of a hideout! Nobody'd ever believe this place! It's like some kind of Indian Shangri-La!"

By now it was late afternoon and because of the risks involved in making a night landing at the seaplane base, we reluctantly turned back. I had seen enough to understand why the last Beothuks might well have sought refuge in this extraordinary place.

Thirty years later, while pondering the problem of where west-coast Alban crofters might likewise have found sanctuary from a plague of European marauders, I recalled my all-too-brief glimpse of King George Lake. Could it have served the Albans as it had reputedly served the Beothuks? It seemed unlikely, for how could west-coast pastoralists have moved themselves, their chattels, and animals across the intervening barrier of the Long Range Mountains? And how, if they had somehow managed what appeared to me to be a most difficult trek, could pastoralists have survived in the heart of what was effectively an island of virgin forest embedded in a sub-alpine wilderness?

I posed these questions to Len Muise.

"Nothing to that. They could have easy walked in and out of there whenever they wanted, along the Country Path."

"You mean there's a road in from St. George's Bay?" I asked, incredulously.

"Not a road, old son. The Country Path. You start at Flat Bay Brook near Cairn Mountain, climb a ridge alongside Three Brooks till you get up on top of the country. After that it's just a saunter across the high barrens till you come down again to King George Lake—Chris's Pond, our old people used to call it. It's no more'n thirty-forty miles; two days' walk, and easy going. Melvin White, he's a Jacko like me, been into King George a dozen times."

We left it at that until one November evening Len telephoned me.

"Old man, I got news for you. Melvin White says you can easy take cattle, ponies, sheep to Chris's Pond along the Country Path, so long as you takes your time. Mel says there's a big stone cairn, taller'n a man, on top of a high hill about halfway in. You head for that, he says. The hill's called Dolly's Lookout, after an old M'ikmaw lady used to trap back there.

"And I almost forgot. Looking east from Cairn Mountain you can see the cairn on Dolly's Lookout. And from Dolly's you look straight ahead to Blue Hill on Lloyds River, right near where it runs into King George Lake. Some says there's the ruins of a cairn on top of Blue Hill too."

Len explained that he and Melvin White intended to drive their Skidoos in to Dolly's Lookout as soon as there was enough snow. "Bring you a picture of it. So's you won't think we're story telling."

Early in 1997 he sent me a letter, together with a number of photographs.

"I am happy to inform you, myself and Melvin travelled on Skidoos to the cairn. The first try the weather turned so stormy when we got on top of the country we had to retreat.

"Sunday we tried again. It was bitter cold, -25°C plus the wind chill. The cairn stands at 1,800 feet and is a very unusual sight, approximately

*This tower beacon marks the midway point on the Country Path connecting St. George's Bay
and King George IV Lake, in western Newfoundland.*

seven feet high and more than three wide. It was too cold to do any real measuring. If we took off our gloves for long our hands would start to freeze. This cairn is at the half-way mark along the country path that leads to and from all parts of the Newfoundland interior."

Melvin White and his wife rode back to Dolly's Lookout during the winter of 1997–98, on a day when there was no risk of being turned into ice statues. This time they also photographed a pile of large, sharp-angled stones twenty feet south of the standing pillar.

"There was plenty stones enough," Melvin reported, "to make another cairn. I'm sure there *was* two there once. One must have been tore down. Couldn't have fallen down by itself. They were too well built. The crest of Dolly's Lookout is smooth as a bald man's head. No loose stones on it. All swept off by the old glaciers. The stones for the cairns had to come from the bottom of a gully half a mile away and three or four hundred feet below the crest."

Len Muise summed it up.

"Somebody went to a devil of a lot of work putting the towers on Cairn Mountain and Dolly's Lookout. In pairs, too, like a kind of code pointing the way to King George Lake. I don't believe old Captain Cook ever did that. M'ikmaw nor Beothuks didn't do things like that either. I've asked woodsmen and countrymen from all around and they tell me there's nothing like those cairns anywhere else in the interior of Newfoundland."

The Country Path answered the question of how coastal crofters could have travelled between the sea and King George Lake. But could they and their livestock have survived deep in the interior?

During the 1980s King George Lake was discovered by the outer world when a highway was built across the mountains to link a number of isolated outports on the south coast with the provincial highway system. The Annieopsquotch country, which had previously been almost inaccessible, now came under assault from four-wheel-drive trucks, all-terrain vehicles, and snowmobiles. Almost overnight King George Lake became a mecca for hunters, fishermen, even tourists. Scientists came too. And they were so impressed that they recommended the lake be protected. In 1996 the provincial government proclaimed the southern arm and adjacent shores an ecological reserve.[1]

This was belated recognition of what had long been known as a unique place to Beothuks, M'ikmaws, Jakatars, and, as I believe, the people of Alba-in-the-West.

Natural meadows, or "grasses," on the deltas and lower reaches of the two streams (Second Exploits and Lloyds rivers) flowing into the southern arm amount to more than 1,600 acres. Melvin White, who has extensively explored the area, estimates that the King George Lake grasses could currently meet the forage and hay requirements of forty to fifty smallholders, such as his own people had been in the past and, to some extent, still are. Furthermore, there is plenty of good alluvial soil upon which to grow cereals, vegetables, and possibly even fruits.

"There's no a better place to farm in Newfoundland," Melvin told me. Recent studies would seem to bear him out. Not only does the King George Lake enclave possess the richest ecosystem in Newfoundland, it is blessed with the longest growing season. It has always supported a plethora of wildlife ranging from arctic hares to caribou, from ptarmigan to Canada geese, from trout to land-locked salmon, from pine martens to black bears. There is no doubt but that it *could* have supported a sizeable crofter settlement.

But *was* it a sanctuary for the people of Alba-in-the-West?

"If the old people had to go somewhere away from the coast to live that's where a good many would likely have gone," Len says. "Somebody surely did go in there a long time ago, and took the trouble to build up those big old cairns along the Country Path so others would know how to find them.

"One of these times something will turn up around Chris's Pond. Maybe a cow's skull. Maybe a hole in the ground where there was a house. Melvin and me will be going in next summer for a look around. It's Jakatar country, you know; and whoever was in there was our people too."

POSTSCRIPT

MOST OF THE NATIVE COMMUNITIES ALONG THE Atlantic seaboard of the New World withdrew from the coasts during the sixteenth century in order to avoid frequently fatal assaults by European fishermen, oilers, slavers, and other rapacious seekers after wealth.

Because pastoralists were particularly vulnerable, they would have been amongst the first to retreat. I believe something of a pastoral tradition was maintained at The Grass and around King George IV Lake, but Albans most likely turned increasingly to the Beothuk way of life in order to maintain themselves.

During the seventeenth century the unbridled lawlessness of European marauders declined somewhat as France and England established *de facto* control over more and more of the New World's coastal regions. Indigenes who had taken refuge "in the country" began to emerge, if cautiously, to trade, to fish and hunt on salt water, and perhaps to re-establish themselves as crofters.

Return to the coasts was not everywhere possible. On Newfoundland's eastern and northeastern seaboards, English "planters" and seasonal fishermen alike continued to treat Beothuks with a hostility amounting to genocide—a persecution that would eventually lead to the extermination of the Red Indians in the eastern and central parts of the Island.

French fishermen frequenting Newfoundland's southwestern and western shores dealt with the natives more humanely, possibly because the French lacked the means with which to overwhelm *les sauvages*.

So it happened that the ancient peoples in the southwest corner of the Island were able to endure and even to prosper. During the early decades of the eighteenth century, they were joined by parties of M'ikmaw from Cape Breton Island. These came initially as itinerant trappers, but some stayed to become an integral part of the southwest coast community.

The latter part of the eighteenth century brought a few score Acadians, farmers of French descent fleeing English seizure of their Nova Scotian lands. Having long since established blood relationships with mainland M'ikmaw, the Acadians found no difficulty in melding with the existing cultures of southwestern Newfoundland. They brought with them a new impetus towards pastoralism, so that human life in the region became even more of a mix of small-scale crofting and native country pursuits.

While nineteenth-century M'ikmaw trappers established a transient presence in much of southern and northern Newfoundland, the native Beothuks ceased to exist, or so the Europeans, who by then dominated the entire Island, maintained. But they were wrong. Men and women still lived around St. George's Bay and in the Codroy Valley who thought of themselves as, and called themselves, Beothuks. Not until the turn of the next century did they nominally disappear.

Which brings us to our own times—and to the apparent end of our story.

However, according to Leonard Muise, the end is not yet.

"All those early people—Dorsets, Red Indians, the ones you call Albans, Farley—they didn't just dry up and blow away, you know.

"Don't you believe it! Truth is they're all of them still round about. In St. George's, Port au Port, and Codroy too. One of these times, scientists will likely show up here looking to test our DNA to see whereabouts we come from. I don't doubt they'll be some surprised by what they find.

"But us Jakos, now…we won't be the smallest little bit surprised because, you see, we know just who we are."

NOTES

FOREWORD
WHY AND WHEREFORE

1. Farley Mowat, *Westviking: The Ancient Norse in Greenland and North America* (Toronto: McClelland and Stewart, 1965; and Boston: Little, Brown and Company, 1965).

CHAPTER ONE
BEGINNINGS

1. Farley Mowat, *Canada North*, published in the Canadian Illustrated Library series (Toronto: McClelland and Stewart, 1967).
2. Payne River, Payne Lake, and many other topographical features in Ungava have arbitrarily been given new, French names by the provincial government of Quebec. I have generally retained the time-honoured originals.

CHAPTER TWO
FARFARER

1. Her remains must long since have perished, but vessels belonging to *Farfarer*'s lineage remained in service in Ireland at least as late as the 1970s, although tarred canvas and even sheet plastic had by then replaced animal skin as the sheathing material.

   "Curraghs," as the Irish Celts called them, evolved from the boats used by the indigenes of northern Britain long before the Celtic invasions and were part of the circumpolar tradition of skin-clad vessels. Irish records tell us that, by the sixth century, curraghs were being sheathed with ox hides. Presumably this was because walrus hides were no longer available.

   In 1976 a thirty-six-foot curragh replica sheathed in leather carried a crew of five and nearly a ton of supplies from Ireland to Newfoundland via Iceland. Siberian and Alaskan *umiaks*, sheathed in walrus or bearded seal hides, are known to have reached lengths of sixty feet and more, and to have been capable of carrying as many as forty passengers and their gear in voyages across the Bering Sea. We can assume that the skin-clad craft of aboriginal north Europeans would have been at least as effective.

Ireland's National Museum has a tiny model of a curragh equipped with rowing and steering oars, a mast, and a spar, all hammered out of gold. Found in County Derry, the model is thought to date from the first century A.D. It represents a beamy, undecked, bluff-bowed, double-ended, soft-chinned vessel primarily intended to be wind-driven, but fitted with auxiliary power in the form of eighteen oarsman, whose presence still left half of the vessel's capacity free for carrying passengers or cargo. Such a vessel would necessarily have had to been close to fifty feet in length.

No model of a Northern Islands (Alban) boat has come to light, but thirty-foot sealskin fishing boats persisted in northern Shetland until the twentieth century. In 1810 the isolated island of St. Kilda was maintaining contact with the mainland by means of a *churaich*, a lightly framed vessel sheathed with the hides of grey seals, capable of carrying twenty passengers, several cattle, or a considerable quantity of freight.

The foundations of North American boat-roofed houses provide us with a series of deck outlines of their covering vessels. These fall into two groups. Twenty-five that are sufficiently well preserved to permit an accurate measuring give an overall vessel length of from forty to fifty-five feet. Six others fall into the seventy- to eighty-foot range. The former seem to represent the general run of sea-going vessels. The latter were perhaps especially constructed as transatlantic traders.

Ships of both classes have a length-to-beam ratio from 3.1:1 to 3.5:1. All were beamy vessels, well rounded fore and aft, presumably of relatively shoal draft, with only slight to moderate sheer. Although tenth- or eleventh-century Norse *knorrin* were sheathed in wood instead of skins, their lines and scantlings were probably derived from Alban models and may not have differed materially in outward appearance from those Northern Islands vessels.

CHAPTER THREE
TUSKERS

1. Siberians use the word *valuta* to designate goods of small bulk but great value, including precious metals, gems, furs, and ivory. This is the sense in which I use the term in this book.

2. I have dealt in detail with the catastrophic destruction of the walrus in *Sea of Slaughter* (Toronto: McClelland and Stewart, 1984), Part V, Finfeet.

3. See Chapter 4, endnote 2.

4. Most early maritime records, including Egyptian, Greek, and Carthaginian, traditionally noted marine distances in multiples of the "sailing day"—the distance a vessel could be expected to cover in one day under optimum conditions. Sailing days as marine units of distance remained in use in northern Europe until after the fourteenth century A.D. Although the unit varied in value according to the kind of vessels involved, it was roughly equivalent to one hundred of our statute miles.

C H A P T E R   F O U R
PYTHEAS

1. One classical source refers to a great promontory northwest of Gaul called Calbion. This is almost certainly a corruption of Cape Albion (C. Albion) and most probably refers to Land's End, the southwestern extremity of Cornwall.

2. The entrance of *orca* into Greek, and later Latin, may have been one of Pytheas's achievements. I suggest that the natives of Britain's Northern Islands called the walrus *orc*, which was why Pytheas called the archipelago the Orc Islands—later, Orcadies. Eventually orca acquired the more generalized meaning of "sea monster," which is how it was used in the Middle Ages. In the nineteenth century, it was again particularized by its inclusion in the Linnaean system of animal classification as *Orcaella*, a generic name for grampuses and killer whales. So, with regard to word usage, the walrus has now become the killer whale.

3. Pliny (the Elder) tells us in his *Historia Naturalis* (written about A.D. 77) that a much earlier historian, Timaeus, whose work is no longer extant, made reference to an island called Mictis, "lying inward in the sea; [i.e., to seaward] six days from Britain where tin is found, and to which Britons cross in boats of osier covered with stitched hides." Whether Mictis and Tilli are one and the same may be argued, but this reference establishes the fact that natives of Britain were capable of making oceanic voyages six days long, in skin-covered boats.

C H A P T E R   F I V E
ALBANS AND CELTS

1. Modern historians have generally assumed the *alb* root to be of Latin origin. However, Vittorio Bertoldi, in *Problems of Etymology, Zeitschrift für Romanische Philologie*, vol. 56, 1936, pp. 179–88, demonstrates that *alb* is pre-Indo-European. It probably entered Latin as a loan word with a connotation of "white," acquired by association with snow-capped mountains. "Alban" and "Albania" are Latinized forms of Alb and Alba.

2. Dr. Ian Grimble has admirably summed up this catastrophic but seldom-told episode in European history in *Highland Man* (Inverness, Scotland: Highlands and Islands Development Board, 1980). The following quotation is from p. 47.

    "At the time when the Celtic invaders swept through Europe, it was inhabited by non–Indo-European peoples who were defeated, enslaved, or pushed into inaccessible regions. Amongst these were the Ligurians, who became concentrated in the Ligurian Alps and in Corsica, where Seneca remarked in A.D. 41 that they still spoke their Ligurian tongue. Others were the Basques, who speak their own non–Indo-European tongue in the Pyrénées to this day. In Caesar's time they occupied a significant part of Gaul with their own laws and customs, despite the double menace of the Celts and the Romans. But by then a great number of these dark, aboriginal inhabitants had lost their language and traditions; those who had not were the ones who had settled in remote places.

Today, so long do genetic characteristics persist, there is still a marked similarity between the blood groups of the Ligurian lands, the Basque country, Wales, Ireland, and the Scottish Highlands, which cannot be explained as accidental."

CHAPTER SIX
ARMORICA

1. The Gaelic-speaking Celts known as the Scotti then lived in northeastern Ireland. They did not cross over into the part of north Britain that now bears their name until the third or fourth century A.D.

2. Bede was not the only early historian to view the Picts as immigrant invaders from the Continent. Nennius, an eighth-century Welsh chronicler, believed they came from overseas to "the islands called Orcades then laid waste many regions in the north and [in Nennius's time] occupied about one third of Britain." Gildas, a sixth-century ecclesiastic, also believed they came from overseas and "settled in the most remote part of Britain and with the Scots seized the whole land as far south as the wall [Hadrian's Wall]."

CHAPTER SEVEN
WAR IN THE NORTH

1. It is by no means certain that the Armoricans were, in fact, welcomed to northern Alba as refugees. Possibly they were refused sanctuary, and so came ashore as invaders. Whichever it was, the consequences and outcome remained essentially the same.

2. Broch is a Norse word, bestowed on the towers by Viking raiders in the eighth century. It, too, means "fort."

3. Some historians have suggested these forts were deliberately fired by their builders in order to produce a vitrified effect, but there is no convincing evidence to support this theory.

4. Another excellent example of an interdependent complex is on the Orkney island of Rousay, where three brochs stand within five hundred yards of one another. Such propinquity has puzzled historians, as the official guide book makes clear: "This concentration is, indeed, a quite extraordinary and, as yet, inexplicable phenomenon."

CHAPTER EIGHT
PICTLANDIA

1. We do not know how the Picts gained nominal preeminence amongst their fellow Armoricans. It may be that, having suffered least at Caesar's hands, they emerged in exile as the strongest surviving tribe. Whatever the reasons, Picts and Pictland became names that would endure in the north through nearly eight centuries.

2. History has long believed that no Roman invasion of Ireland was ever attempted. However, the recent discovery of a Roman military camp in eastern Ireland demonstrates that the legions must have at least made a beachhead there.

3. Roman naval auxiliaries carried siege weapons for use on land, including ballistae and catapults, either of which would have been able to destroy or reduce a broch.

CHAPTER NINE
FETLAR

1. Plutarch (c. A.D. 75) tells us of a Greek by the name of Demitrius who was employed in Britain by the Romans in the first century A.D. and who reported having heard from the natives of a large island a long way west of Britain, which bore a name that sounded to the Greek like Cronus. This island seems to have been Greenland. It is, at any rate, certain that the waters between Iceland and Greenland were known to geographers of the early Christian era as the Cronian Sea. Cf. *Westviking*, pp. 5 6.

CHAPTER TEN
ALBA REBORN

1. Chroniclers of those times were well aware that Scotland was inhabited by two peoples. They distinguished between the two by calling them the Northern and the Southern Picts. "Pict" had by then become a generic name. The Northern Picts were, in fact, Albans.

CHAPTER ELEVEN
SONS OF DEATH

1. F.T. Wainwright, *The Northern Isles* (Edinburgh: Th. Nelson and Sons Ltd., 1962).
2. John Marsden, *The Fury of the Northmen* (New York: St. Martin's Press, 1993).

CHAPTER TWELVE
FURY OF THE NORTHMEN

1. A.W. Brøgger, *Ancient Emigrants* (Oxford, 1929).
2. *Originally it was the "Peti" and the "Papae" who inhabited these islands. The first of these people, I mean the Peti, were scarcely taller than pygmies.*

   Peti is a corruption of Picti, the Latinized generic name by which Norse scribes referred to all the non-Irish inhabitants of Scotland. *Papae* may refer specifically to Christian priests, but more probably also carried a generic meaning: Christians as opposed to heathens. It is to be noted that the *Historia* does not state that the Picti were pygmies; the intended connotation is that they were physically inferior to the Norse.

   ...they busied themselves to an amazing degree with the building and fitting out of their towns. There were then no towns, or even villages, in the twin archipelagos. There were,

however, over a hundred brochs in various states of repair to which people could rally in times of duress. Archaeology has revealed that Gurness (one of eight brochs on the shores of Eynhallow Sound in Orkney) was extensively repaired during the seventh century. New external walls and ditches were added, and houses were built close under its protective walls.

But at midday, thoroughly drained of their strength, they lay low in their little underground houses under the pressure of their fears.

The standard contempt of victors for vanquished is evident here, but we are nevertheless given a poignant glimpse of a people harassed, exhausted, and so in fear of their lives that they felt obliged to hide in their thick-walled, semi-subterranean dwellings during daylight hours.

As to where these people [the Picti] came from to that region we have no idea. Now as for the Papae, they have got their name on account of white garments in which they dress themselves, like clergy. It's because of this that in the Teutonic language all clergy are called "papae."

Scholars generally interpret *papa* (plural *papae*), as found in Norse Latin sources, in the narrowest sense as meaning "Father," or priest. It probably had a much broader meaning, as in "papist," a follower of the religion headed by the Pope. This may seem like a trivial point but it has important overtones. Using only the narrow interpretation, many historians have been led to conclude that the *papae* of the Norse Atlantic sagas were priestly hermits, few in number, and widely scattered in the wilderness. The alternative explanation, that *papae* referred to sizeable communities of men, women, and children who were members or followers of the Church of Rome, can then be conveniently disregarded. We shall see the importance of the interpretation when we deal with the pre-Norse settlement of Iceland.

The *Historia* further notes that the people known as *papae* wore white clothing similar to, but not necessarily identical with, that worn by Christian clergy. This also becomes a matter of importance when we come to consider the identity of the inhabitants of *Hvitramannaland* (Whiteman's Land), which is also called Albania by Norse scribes.

...But in the days of Harold the Hairy—I mean the King of Norway, of course—some pirates kin to the very powerful pirate Rognvald advanced with a large fleet across the Solundic Sea. They threw these people out of their long-standing habitations and utterly destroyed them; they made the islands subject to themselves.

As used by scribal clerics of the time, "pirates" was a synonym for Vikings. Whatever interpretive uncertainties there may be in the body of the *Historia* text, there can be none about the fate which overtook the Northern Islanders.

3. Archibald R. Lewis, *The Northern Seas* (Princeton: Princeton University Press, 1958).
4. Many historians have identified the Lochlannach with the Vikings. This is almost certainly incorrect. The name is Gaelic, meaning Men of Loch Lann (variants: Lainn, Loinn, Linnhe, Lyn, Lorne, Larne).

Originally the Lochlannach were Celtic sea raiders from Ireland's Loch Larne coast. They first appear in history in connection with a raid on Ulster in the first century B.C. They were one of the Dalriad tribes that raided, then invaded, western Scotland, there to establish themselves in the contiguous fiords of Loch Linnhe and Loch Loin. From this well-situated base they raided north and south as opportunity arose. According to the *Annals of Innisfallen*: "The Hebrides and Ulster were plundered by the Lochlann" as late as the year 798.

Although the Lochlannach probably collaborated with the Norse, as many of the Scotti seem to have done, they themselves were sea rovers and pirates of unassailably Irish Celtic ancestry.

CHAPTER THIRTEEN
TILLI

1. As late as the 1880s, congregations of fin whales numbering above a thousand individuals were still being encountered in these waters. This was just before Norwegians began exterminating them with the steam whaler and the harpoon canon. In 1884 a Captain Milne, commanding a transatlantic Cunarder, sailed through such an assemblage southeast of Iceland. He likened it to "a space of about half-a-county filled with railroad engines, all puffing steam as if their lives depended on it."

2. Cf. Farley Mowat, *Sea of Slaughter* (Toronto: McClelland and Stewart, 1984), Chapter 6, White Ghost.

3. Grey whales were exterminated in the western Atlantic during the nineteenth century.

4. Cf. *Sea of Slaughter*, Part V, Chapter 15, Sea Tuskers.

5. All-round foundations may not have been needed when a vessel was required to provide only short-term shelter. Sites in northwestern Greenland and Labrador suggest that ships were sometimes overturned, then propped up on *one* side only to provide what was in effect a lean-to type shelter. In places where suitable stones for support were not available, the ships could have been propped up on one side with wooden supports. Greenland and Alaskan umiaks often carried shaped pieces of wood intended for just this purpose. I have myself sheltered through very bad weather, including a blizzard, under a freight canoe that had been propped up on one side. We kept the wind and snow out by means of a curtain wall of caribou skins pegged along the high side.

CHAPTER FOURTEEN
SANCTUARY

1. Conventional wisdom has it that the Irish were the first British Islanders (if not the first Europeans) to explore the western reaches of the North Atlantic. Irish claims loom large because most of the few surviving accounts of pre-Norse activity in the Western Ocean are preserved in ancient Irish documents called "immrama." Written

in Latin by clerics, the immrama purport to record the adventures (and misadventures) of sixth- and seventh-century Irish priests engaged on religious quests.

Anything the Albans may have possessed comparable to the immrama has long since vanished. So, indeed, has their language, taking with it an entire folk history. Unless, of course, fragments of that history have been preserved through absorption into the folk tales of other people. There is a good case to be made that the immrama do, in fact, include references to non-Irish western voyages that latter-day clerical scribes attributed to Irish mariner-saints.

2. As we have already seen (Chapter 12, note 2), *papar* was probably a generic Norse term meaning followers of White Christ in general.

3. The fact that Iceland was well known to continental Europeans for centuries before the Norse claim to have discovered it seems firmly established by the following:

c. 330 B.C.	Pytheas voyaged to Thule.
3 B.C.–A.D. 65	Seneca wrote: "The time shall come…when Thyle shall not be the last of the lands."
A.D. 23–79	Pliny referred to the island as Tylen.
84	Agricola's fleet rounded northern Britain and reported seeing Thule.
100–168	Ptolemaic maps, probably from the first century, showed Thule in approximately its correct geographical position.
363	The naval expedition of Theodosius attacked Picts in Thule.
c. 500	The (probably mythical) voyages of Arthur and Malgo to Thule at least recognized the existence of such a place.
500–600	The Gothic historian Jordanes located Thule far to the west of Europe.
c. 550	Brendan visited the Faeroes and Iceland.
600–700	Bishop Isidore of Seville described Thule as the most remote of islands and placed it northwest of Britain.
c. 620	A European-type homestead was built on the Westman Islands.
730–733	Bede wrote of Thule.
700–800	Selenius mentioned Thule in his *Book of Marvels*.
770–790	Dicuil recorded the visit of monks to Thule. Bishop Patrick of the Hebrides referred to Iceland as Thule.
865	The first recorded visit of the Norse to Iceland.

4. Margrét Hermanns-Audardóttir, *Islands Tidiga Bosattning* (Umea, Sweden: Umea Universitet, 1989).

It should be noted that, although the validity of Dr. Hermanns-Audardóttir's findings on Heimaey have not been seriously questioned outside of Iceland, the primacy of Norse claims to the discovery and settlement of that island are still generally defended by most historians there.

5. The exploration of such distant regions need not have taken as long as we might choose to think. During the summers of 992 and 993 Erik Rauda cruised the whole

west coast of Greenland north at least to Melville Bay, as well as apparently crossing Davis Strait to explore part of the coast of Baffin Island. Cf. my reconstruction of his travels in *Westviking* and in Chapter 25 of the present book.

CHAPTER FIFTEEN
ARCTIC ELDORADO

1. As we shall see, there were no indigenous people in Greenland when the Albans arrived there.
2. Cf. endnote 4, Chapter 16, Tunit.
3. Peter Schledermann has described his Arctic archaeological work in two books: a scientific report, *Crossroads to Greenland*, 1990, and *Voices in Stone*, 1966, a popular and personal account. Both are published in the Komatik Press Series by the Arctic Institute of North America, University of Calgary, Calgary, Alberta.

CHAPTER SIXTEEN
TUNIT

1. Although "Inuit" is currently the preferred name in the eastern Canadian Arctic, western Arctic, Alaskan, and Siberian peoples of the same ancestry use the name "Eskimo."

    "Tunit" is found in several variants, including "Tornait" and "Torneq." It comes to us through the Inuit and one of the meanings given to it by the Inuit is "unworldly one," as in alien being.
2. For a full account of the Tunit and their ancestors, I recommend Robert McGhee, *Ancient People of the Arctic* (UBC Press: Vancouver, 1996).
3. H.B. Collins in *Yearbook of Physical Anthropology*, vol. 7, pp. 75–123.
4. Heather Pringle, "New Respect for Metal's Role in Ancient Arctic Cultures," in *Science*, vol. 277, 8 August, 1997, touches on this problem. "Only recently have [archaeologists] come to realize how widely dispersed and relatively abundant metal objects were in the ancient arctic," writes Pringle. She goes on to point out that new techniques for identifying rust stains and other metallic oxides have led to the conclusion that "metal objects were common in sites hundreds of kilometres from the few northern sources of [natural] copper and iron, implying the existence of elaborate trade networks....Researchers have been slow to recognize this brisk commerce in metal... largely because metal objects were so precious that they were rarely left behind for archaeologists to find."

    She quotes University of Arkansas anthropologist Allen McCartney: "Metal is a material you can keep using until it is dust practically. So it's hard to find [in Arctic sites] because if it was big enough for someone to have seen it, they walked off with it."

    Pringle reports that a team from the University of Calgary, using metal detectors and other high-tech equipment, found evidence, some of it almost microscopic, of 288 pieces of copper and iron in two Dorset (Tunit) sites on Little Cornwallis Island. These sites are within a few miles of two boat-roofed foundations.

Much of the iron found in eastern Arctic sites is thought to have come from fragments of a massive nickel-iron meteorite that struck Cape York, the northwestern point on the Melville Bay coast, sometime between 2,000 and 10,000 years ago. According to Pringle, "Current research suggests that prehistoric Arctic dwellers began hammering the metal into tools about 1200 years ago," which would be in the latter part of the eighth century.

However, during the eighth century, as for several centuries previously and for at least two centuries thereafter, *no native peoples inhabited Greenland, Ellesmere Island, or the northern portion of the Baffin Bay basin.* The only people who seem to have been in that region at the right time would have been Alban valuta seekers. I find it reasonable to suppose they were the first to find and exploit the Cape York meteoric fragments; that they made meteoric iron available to Tunit in the northeastern Canadian Arctic as a trade item; and that they pointed the way to the source both for Tunit and for the successor, Thule-culture people.

CHAPTER SEVENTEEN
WESTERN GROUNDS

1. A period of cold and stormy weather returned to the north towards the end of the eighth century. It endured for about a hundred years and brought a renewal of heavy pack ice, which would have made navigation to Kane Basin and beyond difficult, if not impracticable.

2. Thomas E. Lee, "Archaeological Findings, Gyrfalcon to Eider Islands, Ungava, 1968," in *Travaux Divers*, no. 27 (Quebec: Centre d'Etudes Nordiques, Université Laval, 1969).

CHAPTER EIGHTEEN
WESTVIKING

1. The Icelandic sources are discussed at some length in Part 1, Appendix A, of *Westviking* (Toronto: McClelland and Stewart, 1965).

CHAPTER NINETEEN
LAND TAKING

1. A Norse chieftain presided over his household from a raised seat beside which stood two, often ornately carved, posts, which were symbolic of his authority. If he moved to a new home, he was careful to take his high-seat posts with him. Mention of the posts here is indicative of his intention of establishing himself in Iceland.

2. Presumably the brothers had reconnoitred, and may even have wintered at, one or both places during earlier visits. Some geographers conclude that both features may

actually have *been* islands in Ingolf's and Hjorleif's time.

3. *Vestmannaeyjar* is the name they still bear.

CHAPTER TWENTY
CRONA

1. Icelandic historians are generally in agreement that most of the island's existing topographical names were acquired during the Norse settlement period and have been retained more or less unchanged.

   The Norse name givers of that period were pagans (Iceland did not accept Christianity until A.D. 1000) yet a number of Icelandic place names include one of three words signifying a Christian presence or connection. The words are *kross, kirk,* and *papa. Kross* seems to have referred especially to standing crosses visible from some distance. *Kirk* now generally means "church," but in early Icelandic times frequently designated a small, but always Christian, chapel. Norse pagans referred to their places of worship as temples.

   The Norse were pragmatists. A land taker, seeing a cross standing on a point of land, would be apt to call the place Krossness (Cross Point), the name by which inhabitants probably already knew it. The name would remain. If he homesteaded land upon which a chapel or Christian shrine stood, he might very well have named it *Kirkjubol* (Chapel Place), even though he himself was a staunch follower of Thor.

   Chapels, shrines, and standing crosses were distinctive features in early Christian countries. I believe the Norse occupiers of Iceland accepted and continued to use an existing toponymy that included the names of many such places. New Norse-inspired names of similar origin were undoubtedly added after the Norse accepted Christianity, but the elder names endured.

   A cursory examination of the map of Iceland reveals fifty-nine *kirk, kross,* or *papa* names in the eastern region; thirty-three along the south coast; twenty-five in the western district; and twenty-nine in the northwestern peninsula. The names identify thirty-six places where crosses once stood; twenty-nine chapel sites; seven places distinguished by the *papa* component; and some thirty-four crofts or steadings whose names include one or other of the above trio. I conclude that many, if not the majority, of such names owe their existence to Alban habitation of the country.

2. When the Norse took over a country, one of several fates awaited the native inhabitants. They might flee. They might stay behind at the considerable risk of being slaughtered or enslaved. If enslaved they might be sold abroad, or put to work at home. Another choice was to withdraw into a remote and unwanted region where they might hope to survive until the Norse came to look upon them as predatory nuisances (like wolves) and hunted them down or captured them.

   One way or another, a genetic residue of the original inhabitants would nevertheless have been preserved in the ongoing population. Its size and influence would have varied according to local conditions.

In Shetland a distinctive physical residue seems to have survived for some time on Yell, Unst, and Fetlar.

Orkney appears not to have had a visible residue, probably because there was no place in that archipelago for outcasts to hide, except perhaps briefly on Hoy.

I believe an important refuge in Iceland was the Dranga peninsula on the gnarled northwestern fist Iceland shakes at Crona. It was one of the last districts to attract Norse settlers. Alban refugees may well have hung on in its grim valleys for a generation or two until, inevitably, they were overwhelmed even there.

3. When Brattahlid was excavated C-14 dating techniques had not yet been devised, so the site could not be accurately dated. Scandinavian historians have assumed it could not be earlier than the year of Erik's arrival in Greenland. Although the site has been considerably disturbed, it should still be possible to obtain usable C-14 samples from it and so determine its real age. However, neither Danish scholars nor any others have shown an interest in doing so.

Many Norse steadings in the Northern Islands, Iceland, and Greenland may well have been built on existing habitation sites. Since the sequential structures were often very similar, as were the tools and utensils used by many generations of inhabitants, it is not possible to accurately determine the identities of the first comers, or when they came, except through the use of modern dating techniques.

4. I have evaluated the nature and qualities of sea-going ships of those times, and discussed how they were navigated, in *Westviking*, appendices E and F (Toronto: McClelland and Stewart, 1965).

5. *Westviking*, Appendix J, The Old Church Documents.

CHAPTER TWENTY-ONE
UNGAVA

1. *Livyers* is a Labrador term for people of mixed race. It means "people who live here." I use it in preference to any of the other terms signifying people of mixed race.

2. Although it is sometimes difficult to distinguish between the marks made by steel knives and those of flint tools, metal saw and axe marks are readily identifiable. It is of particular importance to note that Dorset culture is not supposed to have possessed the drill, yet Lee found numerous artefacts from Late Dorset layers that had been neatly and cleanly drilled, almost certainly with metal bits.

3. Thomas E. Lee, "Payne Lake, Ungava Peninsula, Archaeology, 1964," in *Travaux Divers*, no. 12 (Quebec: Centre d'Etudes Nordiques, Université Laval, 1966); "Archaeological Discoveries, Payne Bay Region, Ungava, 1966," in *Travaux Divers*, no. 20 (Quebec: Centre d'Etudes Nordiques, Université Laval, 1968).

4. Some authorities reject the postulated presence of Europeans in North America in pre-Columbian times because few European artefacts of that period have been found in situ. This would be a valid objection if it related to the massive movements of trade goods in post-Columbian times. But the fact is that pre-Columbian trade between

Europe and North America (including Greenland) was on a relatively small scale. Trading ships were few, small, and often far between. Records confirm that it was unusual for more than two or three to reach Norse Greenland in any given year, and there were intervals of several years when no trading ship arrived there. Commercial congress with mainland North America would probably have been as scanty.

Furthermore, inbound cargoes were mostly consumed by settlers, leaving little to be traded to the indigenes. And "consume" is the right term. Hard goods, especially metal wares, were safeguarded through the generations until they virtually disintegrated from use. The scarcity of such goods on homestead sites in Greenland occupied by Norsemen for four centuries testifies to the care with which imported goods were husbanded. We can rest assured that pre-Columbian European settlers in Ungava, Labrador, and Newfoundland would have guarded imports in like manner and would have left just as little evidence of them.

Significant quantities of European hard goods probably did not even enter North American native cultures prior to the sixteenth century—not because Europeans were not present, but because they themselves would have engrossed most of what imports were available. In any case, trade between natives and early European immigrants may never have been predicated on durable goods. We know that Norse expeditions to Newfoundland mainly traded perishables such as coloured cloth and even dairy products. And this despite the fact that some of these expeditions were mounted by Icelandic merchants who ought to have been relatively well provided with hard goods.

5. Thomas E. Lee, "Payne Lake, Ungava Peninsula, Archaeology, 1964," in *Travaux Divers*, no. 12 (Quebec: Centre d'Etudes Nordiques, Université Laval, 166); "Fort Chimo and Payne Lake, Ungava, Archaeology, 1965," in *Travaux Divers*, no. 16 (Quebec: Centre d'Etudes Nordiques, Université Laval, 1967); "The Cartier Site, Payne Lake, Ungava," in *Anthropological Journal of Canada*, no. 1 and 2, vol. 17 (Ottawa, 1979).

6. The Cartier site houses may have been boat-roofed. Although three of the five have suffered so much damage that their lengths cannot now be accurately determined, in all cases the internal width was close to fourteen feet. The two whose original length can be reliably estimated were between thirty-five and forty feet long. Roofing such structures with boats (allowing for bow and stern overhang) would have required vessels forty to forty-five feet in length. Their length-to-width ratios would have been between 2.8:1 and 3.0:1—rather narrow for ocean-going vessels, but adequate and even advantageous for those intended for use mainly on rivers and inland waters.

Could such relatively large vessels have navigated between Payne Bay and the mouth of the Payne River? Probably yes. Twenty-six-foot Hudson Bay freight canoes manned by Inuit which, because of their narrow beam and heavy wood-and-canvas construction, doubtless drew just about as much water as a forty-foot skin boat, regularly made this journey into recent times.

CHAPTER TWENTY-TWO
OKAK

1. "Innu" (not to be confused with Inuit) is what the Indians of Labrador call themselves. The Innu are descendants of the Maritime Archaic tradition and include the tribes known to Europeans as Nascopie and Montagnais. They are primarily nomadic caribou hunters, who until recently moved seasonally over most of forested Labrador and northern Ungava.

2. Albans in the west would have made extensive use of Ramah chert, not only as an article of trade but also in the manufacture of their own artefacts. Thomas Lee concluded that a number of chert artefacts he excavated at the "longhouses" on Pamiok Island in Ungava Bay were not of Dorset, Thule, or Inuit origin, and might have been manufactured by Europeans. These are discussed and illustrated in *Travaux Divers*, no. 20 (1966) and no. 27 (1968), and in *Collections Nordicana*, no. 33 (1970), all from the Centre d'Etudes Nordiques, Université Laval, Quebec.

3. All three of these beacons are still extant, although the two smaller ones have sustained some damage.

4. Only the stub of one beacon remains. The other has been reduced to rubble.

5. *Angelica archangelica*, commonly called angelica, is a robust umbelliferous plant whose succulent stem somewhat resembles tough celery. Indigenous to northern Europe and parts of Asia, it was a staple in the diet of the first people to settle the northern regions after the withdrawal of the glaciers. Angelica may, in fact, have been the first plant "cultivated" by these early hunter-gatherers.

    Wherever the northerners went, angelica went with them. It is now to be found in many parts of Iceland, southern Greenland, and northeastern North America. It may even have been the first of the multitude of alien plants to be brought to the new continent by Europeans. I have found it growing in close proximity to most of the sites I believe were once inhabited by Albans.

6. In September 1997, I was again briefly able to visit the Okak site, accompanied by Callum Thomson and Keith Nicol, a geographer from Newfoundland's Memorial University. We had only time for another cursory look, but Nicol was at least able to conclude that the twin depressions were not attributable to natural causes. For his part, Callum pointed out that, *if* the depressions indeed represented habitations, the abundance and availability of timber locally would have made it likely that they had been timber roofed.

    I agree that, assuming the structures were in use for any significant length of time, they would eventually have been roofed with some combination of timber and turf. However, *initially*, they could have been boat-roofed.

CHAPTER TWENTY-FOUR
A NEW JERUSALEM

1. The Barrenland Grizzly was found in Ungava and eastward into the Torngat Mountains until historic times, when the species was extirpated in the region. Cf. *Sea of Slaughter* (Toronto: McClelland and Stewart, 1984).

2. During the eighteenth century, Newfoundland fishermen came to the Labrador in great numbers, and not a few remained to settle. Some brought girls from home, but many married Inuit women. Attempts were made by the livyers at keeping domestic animals. Missionaries at Okak kept a few cattle for a time, and an occasional family elsewhere had a pony, but in general few succeeded in pastoral enterprises. The failure of animal husbandry was primarily due to a severe deterioration of the climate that began in the fourteenth century and continued into the nineteenth. Conditions in the eighteenth were so severe that cattle and horses could not survive the winter unless fed and stabled. But local hay had by then become so scarce as to be almost non-existent, and the cost of shipping in feed from abroad was prohibitive.

CHAPTER TWENTY-FIVE
ERIK RAUDA

1. I have detailed the material supporting this statement in *Westviking*; however, new evidence has recently been brought to my attention.

   A chart dated c. 1598 in the collection of the Wm. Barentz Museum in Terschelling, Holland, traces the Arctic explorations of Willem Barentz. Although primarily concerned with Barentz's famous voyage to the European Arctic, the chart extends its coverage far to the west. Greenland is figured, and the name "Alba" appears on its coast. The source of the western material is unknown, but may well have been Norse.

2. *Westviking*, Chapters 2 to 5 inclusive.

3. *Westviking*, Appendix D, Norse Geographical Concepts.

4. By the latter part of the tenth century, when this account was committed to parchment, Hvitramannaland and Albania had become interchangeable names referring to a land lying to the west of Greenland.

   Clerical scribes rendering oral sagas into Latin may have assumed the word Albania was cognitive with the Latin *alba*, meaning white. From this misapprehension the word Hvitramannaland—White Man's Land—could have arisen.

   On the other hand, the Norse may have bestowed the name Hvitramannaland on Alba-in-the-West because of the white clothing that seems to have been a distinguishing characteristic of Alban clergy, if not of the entire population on ceremonial occasions. This is established in the account of the western Albanians given to

Karlsefni's party by Skraeling children captured on the coast of Labrador. Cf. Chapter 29, Karlsefni and Company.

There is also the possibility that the name White Man's Land was an example of racism, meaning white-skinned people as opposed to natives.

5. *Westviking*, Chapter 6, The Ocean Whirl, pp. 75–76.

CHAPTER TWENTY-SIX
ARI GOES TO ALBANIA

1. *"VI doegr"* in the surviving Latin texts. But six days would not have taken a vessel of those times even to mid-Atlantic. The original saga must have said *"XVI doegr,"* which is close to the actual sailing distance between Ireland and Newfoundland. Numerical errors of this sort are common in mediaeval documents.

2. Cf. endnote no. 4, Chapter 25, Erik Rauda.

3. *Westviking*, Appendix D, Norse Geographical Concepts.

4. *Vin* in ancient Norse meant grass or pasture. It was not until the arrival of Christianity and Latin in Norway and Iceland that *vin* became confused with the Mediterranean (Latin-based) word for wine and eventually acquired that meaning. Thereafter scribes mistakenly translated Vinland as Wineland, an error perpetuated by scholars into our time.

5. Wild grapes apparently grew in eastern and probably other parts of Newfoundland until the post-fourteenth-century climatic decline. Cf. *Westviking*, pp. 125–28.

CHAPTER TWENTY-SEVEN
ALBA-IN-THE-WEST

1. Micmac was the name used by Europeans for the natives of Nova Scotia and some adjacent regions of the Atlantic provinces. It is now being replaced by the native usage: M'ikmaw or M'iqmaw.

CHAPTER TWENTY-EIGHT
SEARCHING FOR ALBA

1. I arrived at this conclusion after an extensive reconstruction of the voyage, as detailed in *Westviking*, Chapter 9, America Discovered.

2. There is the possibility that Bjarni met natives, but the Avalon peninsula was one of the least attractive regions of the island from the native point of view until the post-Columbian period brought numbers of European fishermen to it. These attracted some (but never many) Beothuks seeking European goods. Current archaeological findings suggest that the Avalon may have been effectively devoid of indigenes in Bjarni's time.

3. Cf. *Sea of Slaughter*, Chapter 9, The Passing of the Buff (Toronto: McClelland and Stewart, 1984).

4. Bjarni's presence on the voyage is confirmed by the legend on the Vinland map. R.A. Skelton *et al., The Vinland Map and the Tartar Relation* (New Haven, Conn.: Yale University Press, 1965).

5. I have dealt with these matters in *Westviking*, Chapter 11, The Vinland Voyages; and in Appendix L, Leif Erikson's Vinland Discovery. Grape vines were in much demand as withies, used for sewing the lap planking of Viking vessels together.

CHAPTER TWENTY-NINE
KARLSEFNI AND COMPANY

1. My reconstruction of Karlsefni's voyage is to be found in *Westviking*, Part III, and in appendices M, N, and O.

2. It is worth repeating that, among the Norse, trading and raiding were traditionally interchangeable and complementary activities. The Norse raided when it suited them, and traded when it didn't. The masters/owners of three of the four ships on the Karlsefni expedition were nominally traders.

3. As previously noted, Norse ships engaged on long voyages frequently carried a couple of milch cows, and a bull to freshen the cows. But these would hardly have sufficed to establish a settlement herd.

4. The Western Settlement of that time was in Ivigtut Bight, just west of Cape Desolation. It became known as the Middle Settlement a good many years later when the Godthaab fiords usurped the name Western Settlement. Cf. *Westviking*, p. 152, footnote.

5. The name Helluland may have been descriptive of the enormous, near-vertical cliff faces that form portions of the walls of many north Labrador fiords and outer coasts.

6. In 1995 and again in 1997, I sailed the entire length of the Labrador and, although our vessel held as close to shore as safety permitted, we saw *no* indication that this vast land was, or ever had been, inhabited until we entered some of the deep fiords and inlets, and even then signs of human life were few and far between.

7. The saga specifies that this was a *ship's*, not a *boat's* keel, but gives no clue as to its origin. However, the keel of a wooden ship is an integral part of the vessel and does not usually separate from the hull of a wreck. On the other hand, the keel of a skin-covered vessel (by far the most enduring part of the structure) is readily detached and will survive long after the skin covering and light wooden framing have decayed or been washed away. The keel found on Porcupine Strand may well have come from an Alban ship.

8. Copyists who made the late recensions of the sagas (the ones we now possess) appear to have systematically substituted Vinland for Albania or Hvitramannaland, the original Norse names for the region.

9. See *Westviking*, Chapter 21, The Land of Hope.

10. The identity of the Skraelings encountered at Hop is uncertain. We can deduce from the given evidence that they were probably not Beothuk. In all likelihood they were Tunit, although archaeologists have so far not found evidence for a continuing Tunit presence in Newfoundland later than the ninth century.

A slight possibility exists that they might have been Albans but, if so, why were they not recognized as such by Karlsefni's people? My conclusion is that they were either Tunit or of mixed Alban-Tunit ancestry. There can be no question but that they were used to trading with, or that they were friendly towards, Europeans but could put up a good fight in their own defence when needs must.

11. These natives could have been Tunit, but might equally well have been Innu.

12. No. 194, 8vo, the Arna-Magnean Library.

CHAPTER THIRTY
THE BEST OF TIMES

1. King Olaf, who ruled Norway from 1015 to 1028.

2. It is apparent from the saga account that the place where Gudleif landed was not the only, or even the chief, settlement.

3. Two tower beacons were in existence when the first surveys of St. George's Bay were compiled in the nineteenth century and stood until near the mid-twentieth when both were destroyed by contractors erecting a fire observation tower on Cairn Mountain, whose name has since been changed to Steel mountain. Cf. Chapter 33, Jakatar.

4. Walrus were also abundant in other parts of the Gulf. Enormous concentrations were to be found on the beaches of Prince Edward Island and Miscou Island. These, too, were exterminated, mainly for their oil, by eighteenth- and nineteenth-century commercial exploiters. Cf. *Sea of Slaughter*, Chapter 16, Sea Tuskers.

5. In an attempt to avoid culpability for the decline and virtual disappearance of Canadian Atlantic ground fisheries, the governments of Canada and of Newfoundland blame depredation by the harp and hood seal populations and are waging relentless war on them. Since 1996 a government-supported pogrom has resulted in the slaughter of a million or more seals. Most of what little financial return has resulted from this butchery has been from the sale of seal penises to the Asian market, where they are used in aphrodisiacs.

   In the spring of 1998, unusually mild weather conditions resulted in a drastic reduction in the amount of ice suitable for seal nurseries. Some biologists estimate that seal pup losses from this cause may have amounted to as much as forty per cent. Despite this horrendous natural disaster, the governments concerned allowed, and encouraged, a further holocaust that is believed to have resulted in the deaths of at least half a million adults and sub-adults.

   The Canadian seal "hunt" currently entails the biggest ongoing destruction of large, wild mammals anywhere in the world. For a history of this cf. *Sea of Slaughter*, Chapter 18, Death on Ice (Old Style) and Chapter 19, Death on Ice (New Style).

CHAPTER THIRTY-ONE
DROGIO AND ESTOTILAND

1. This palaeo-Inuit culture is called Thule because some of the first artefacts attributed to it were found near a trading post in northwestern Greenland named "Thule" by its founders. The name has no connection with Tilee, or with Albans.

2. *Westviking*, Appendix P.

3. Around 1516 Erik Valkendorf, Archbishop of Nidaros, collected information about Greenland from merchants trading at Trondheim. He noted that Greenland's exports included black bear, lynx, beaver, otter, sable, stoat (weasel), and wolverine, none of which were to be found in Greenland. The pelts could only have reached Greenland from North America.

4. Prior to his transatlantic venture, Zichmini had led at least one major expedition against Iceland. It was probably here that he heard the fisherman's tale and took the man back with him to Scotland, intending to use him as a pilot in a venture to the new world.

CHAPTER THIRTY-TWO
GREENLANDERS

1. These were not tower beacons. Archaeologists who have examined the site report finding three accumulations of stones, none of which could have provided materials for a cairn more than three or four feet high. The runic inscription tells us that three men built the cairns in a single day, from which we can judge that they must have been small constructs.

2. Supposedly there were 190 farms in the Eastern Settlement and 90 in the Western, but surveys have located fewer than 170 in the former and 70 in the latter. Population estimates have run as high as 8,000. I believe such figures to be greatly inflated. High infant mortality combined with the low productivity of most of the farms would have severely limited the number of people each settlement could have supported at any given time. There may never have been more than eight hundred people in the Western, and two thousand in the Eastern, Settlement.

3. What remains of a written record of the Norse in Greenland is almost exclusively concerned with events in the southern (Eastern) settlement. No accounts of what took place in the northern one have survived. Since the keeping of written records was a function of the clergy, the absence of such from the northern settlement would seem to indicate a parallel absence of priests.

4. Icelandic Norse do not appear to have colonized the Western Settlement for some time, even decades, after Erik Rauda led the first land taking in the south. It is not impossible, therefore, that some Albans who, for one reason or another did not leave Crona at the time of the exodus may still have been living in the western fiords when the first Icelanders reached that region. If the two peoples had then been relatively

equal in numbers they may have made an accommodation, rather than waging war. An element of Alban blood and traditions in the Western Settlement might help explain the antipathy that developed between Eastern and Western Settlements.

5. Vilhjalmar Stefansson, *Greenland* (New York: Doubleday Doran and Co., 1942).
6. A study of skeletons from churchyards in the Western Settlement made in 1942 by K. Fischer-Møller indicates that there had already been considerable racial mixing between Norsemen and Eskimos, even before the Norse in the Western Settlement abandoned the church (K. Fischer-Møller, "Skeletons from Ancient Greenland Graves," *Med. Om. Gronl.*, vol. 89, no. 4 [Copenhagen, 1942]).

CHAPTER THIRTY-THREE
JAKATAR

1. *Newfoundland Pilot*, pp. 254–55, 1st ed. (Ottawa: Canadian Hydrographic Service, 1952).
2. Ramah chert flakes and artefacts have been found on the Magdalen Islands and several other localities around the Gulf of St. Lawrence.
3. Early settlers at St. George's Bay may have been able to provide themselves with a limited amount of iron by smelting nodules of ferrous oxides known as "bog iron," which are to be found in many bogs in Newfoundland. There is evidence that bog iron was smelted by the Norse occupants of the L'Anse Aux Meadows site c. A.D. 1000.
4. There can be no doubt but that both M'ikmaw and French contributed to the Jakatar inheritance. Both reached St. George's Bay in the eighteenth century: the French as refugees from Acadie and the M'ikmaw as emigrants from Cape Breton Island. Both peoples were Roman Catholic and had long been closely associated.

    Leonard's reference is to Frank G. Speck, *Beothuk and Micmacs*, Indian Notes and Monographs, Museum of the American Indian (Heye Foundation, 1922). "The Micmacs claim to have had some knowledge of Newfoundland from remote times. They speak of a people called 'ancients' who lived on the southern and western coasts before the 18th century."
5. Aymetic Picaud, a twelfth-century pilgrim to the Basque country, wrote that the Basque name for God was *Jakue*, which may have been a dialectic variant on the more usual *Jainko*.

CHAPTER THIRTY-FOUR
THE COUNTRY PATH

1. King George IV Ecological Reserve Management Plan (St. John's, Newfoundland: Parks and Natural Area Division, Department of Tourism, Culture and Recreation, Government of Newfoundland and Labrador, 1997).

INDEX

Page numbers appearing in italic type refer to pages containing illustrations, maps, and photographs. The notes are indexed as follows. If note material is taken out of context, the text page number may appear in parentheses; 343n1 (151) means page 343, note 1 (page 151 in text).

VOYAGES OF THE ALBANS

Kane Basin
Ellesmere
Island
Lancaster Sound
Baffin Basin
Baffin Island
Foxe Basin
Greenland (CRONX)
Davis Strait
Cape Dyer
NORTHERN FIORDS
SOUTHERN FIORDS
Cape
Hudson Strait
Hudson Bay
Ungava
Ungava Bay
Payne Lake
Cape Chidley
Okak
Labrador Current
Labrador
Belle Isle
Newfoundland
Gulf Stream

Spitsbergen

Arctic Ocean

Greenland
Sea

Scoresby Sound

Husavik

Strait

lik
Breidafjordur
Faxafloi
Vestmannaeyjar?
nger Current

Iceland
TILLI
Vatnajokull
Hofn

Norway

Sweden

Faeroe Islands

Shetland Islands

Orkney Islands

Hebrides

Scotland

Denmark

North
Sea

North
tlantic

Erris Head

Ireland

Irish
Sea

England

Belgium

St. George's Channel

Land's End
Isles of Scilly

Ushant

English Channel

Channel Is.

ARMORICA

Seine R.

Loire R.

Rhone R.

Marseille

LIGURIA

Bay
of
Biscay

Corsica

Basque
Provinces

Oporto

Spain

Sardinia

FARFARING
OF THE
MEN OF ALBA

Gibraltar

Mediterranean Sea